BECOMING ALLIES

BECOMING ALLIES...

With Your Partner, Yourself, and Others:

Addressing the Abuse and Control in Your Relationships

by

Dr. Chris Huffine

Allies Press

Becoming Allies: with your Partner, Yourself, and Others: Addressing the Abuse and Control in Your Relationships

Published by Allies Press
Allies in Change
1675 SW Marlow Ave., STE 110
Portland, OR. 97225
www.alliesinchange.org

Cover image by James Foss

Library of Congress Control Number: 2021939127

ISBN (paperback): 9781662914515
eISBN: 9781662914522

TABLE OF CONTENTS

DEDICATION

This book is dedicated to abused partners everywhere and their deep commitment to being loving, kind, caring, collaborative, and respectful, even in the face of significant and severe abusive and controlling behavior. You are an inspiration!

A Message to the Reader

If you are reading this book, you probably have a good reason. Perhaps someone who cares about you has shared concerns about ways you have behaved. You may have questions or concerns yourself. It might also be a requirement or a recommendation of a program that you are in. Perhaps someone who cares about you is concerned about you and encouraged you to read this. Regardless of why you are picking this book up, we encourage you to at least read this introduction before putting it back down. Stay open to the possibility that what is written here is of relevance to you and can help you in how you live your life.

No one behaves perfectly in their relationships with others. Everyone occasionally says or does the wrong thing. The best anyone can hope for is to learn from those moments of behaving badly and do their best to not repeat them. Sometimes, though, they repeat similar hurtful behaviors over and over again. These are not simply moments of being imperfect. They reflect ways of living and thinking in the world. They form patterns that cause greater problems in relationships, especially close relationships with partners and children. Those behaviors that are hurtful to others and happen over and over again can be described as abusive and/or controlling.

When most people hear the word "abuse," they think of awful physical violence. However, abuse covers a wide range of behaviors, most of which are not physical and do not seem as extreme. Some people who struggle with being abusive have never been physically abusive in any way. Just because you have rarely or never been physically violent does not mean that being abusive is not a problem for you. Abusive behavior can include words, facial expressions, the way decisions are made, how you express unhappiness, and how you deal with people you love acting in ways you do not like or agree with.

There are a number of other words people use so the abusive and controlling behavior doesn't sound so bad: "type A," "perfectionist," "problems with conflict," and "communication issues" are a few. But easily the most common euphemism people use instead of talking about someone having problems with abuse and control is to say they have "anger" issues. They say someone "needs anger management," has "anger problems," or that they "lose their temper" or have "temper" issues. Having issues with "anger" does not sound nearly as bad as having issues with being abusive. Besides, everyone gets angry at times, and occasionally "losing your temper" is common, even normal.

There are tons of books about anger issues, written by all kinds of people—therapists, clergy, executives, even Buddhist monks! Likewise, there are many professionals who help people with their anger. But the therapists and books that deal with anger rarely, if ever, even mention the words "abuse" or being "controlling" with others. They focus solely on managing the emotion of anger. They talk about "losing control" of anger, and learning how to "take control" or "manage" their anger. It's almost like there is a wild beast inside some people that needs to be tamed and managed and contained.

The problem with focusing on anger is that it completely ignores the real problem. It's true that some people need to process the emotion of anger and that some people have unresolved anger about certain issues. But that is different from someone we have identified as having an "anger management" issue or having "problems with anger."

Take a moment to make a mental list of people you think might have an "anger management" issue, a "temper," or problems with their anger. What leads you to think that about them? Usually it is because they have "lost their temper" with others. How have they "lost their temper"? Usually by yelling or cussing or hitting or throwing things. They have gotten into physical fights or said hurtful things or acted in ways that scared and alarmed others, right?

All of those indicators are types of abuse! Nineteen times out of twenty, if not more, the reason people think someone has an anger issue is because they have repeatedly acted in abusive ways. The point here is that the problem is not their "anger" or "temper." It's that they have been abusive! But even so, most of the books and professionals who deal with "anger" issues focus far more on the emotion of anger than on the abusive behavior that is the actual concern. They erroneously think the bad behavior is caused by anger, when, more typically, anger is actually a symptom of the person's underlying pro-abusive beliefs. (We will talk about this in more detail in Chapter 5: Abusive Thoughts and Beliefs.)

Even if you don't think you have issues with being abusive, do you think you have issues with being controlling? How about with anger? How about with being a perfectionist? How about with being type A? Or being intimidating? If you can answer yes to any of those, you should probably continue to read this book and see how much of it applies.

Another reason you may think abuse is not an issue for you is the images and stereotypes of what abusive people look like. People who are abusive are often portrayed as angry, mean, cruel, and sadistic. They are often portrayed as evil and vile, or have a lengthy criminal history, or come from poor homes. They often wear "wife-beaters," the sleeveless undershirts once common among working-class people. They come from messed-up homes where they were horribly abused, and now they're passing those behaviors on to their children.

While a small number of abusive partners do fit the stereotype, many do not. Abusive people are just as common in middle- and upper-class neighborhoods, but they are less likely to get arrested for domestic violence—in part because their abusive behavior may not be illegal. Although some abusive people did grow up in abusive homes, many did not, especially among those who have committed little or no physical abuse. The reality is that abusive partners are like everyone else—coming from every class, every occupation, every ethnic background, every sexual orientation, and so on. Furthermore, most only behave badly with their immediate family. With everyone else, they are perfectly well-behaved. Most do not truly have problems with anger or angry outbursts. They can be funny, charming, polite, respectful, cooperative, and engaged—or quiet, shy, withdrawn, and awkward, and everything in between. People who are abusive usually have many positive and likable qualities in many different areas. The point is that you cannot tell that someone is an abusive person just by meeting them. There is no single profile of someone who is struggling with being abusive. People with this issue are, in many ways, just like everyone else.

It can be difficult for people to admit that they have been abusive because of the shame that they have about what they have done. Clearly, being abusive is not okay. It is common to think that if you admit to being abusive, then you're admitting to not being okay, even to the point of being unlovable. When famous people are discovered to have been abusive, they are often harshly judged. They may lose their job and their status; their reputation may be permanently marred. They may be forever labeled as an abuser.

The part that is rarely given much attention, though, is that many of these abusive people are still loved by their partner, family, and friends, especially if they put an end to their abusive behavior, often with the help of a specialized program. In fact, making these changes often strengthens their relationships in the long run. An important part of stopping abusive behavior is moving past the shame you might have about it. We will look at shame in more detail in Chapter 9: Addressing Shame.

What all this is leading to is that one of the first challenges that many people have in dealing with being abusive and controlling is admitting that they are abusive and controlling. Whether it is because their abusive behavior does not seem extreme, or they don't fit the stereotype of an abusive partner, or they are too ashamed to admit to what they have done, many people who are abusive cannot and will not admit that they have been abusive. But change cannot happen if a person cannot admit that they have a problem. The reality is that everyone who has a pattern of abusive behavior has some denial about it being a problem, which is one big reason it continues to be a problem. On the other hand, when people successfully stop their abusive behavior for good, it usually starts when they get honest with themselves and admit that it is a problem in the first place. This is the first critical step in making real change: admitting that it is an issue. We will talk about this in more detail in Chapter 7: Denial.

Which brings us back to you. If you do not think you have a problem with being abusive and controlling, it could be that you do not. But it could also be that you are simply not being honest with yourself, perhaps for the reasons given above. Which is it?

To get to the bottom of that, keep your mind open to the possibility that you might have an issue with being abusive and controlling. Again, there was some reason you picked up this book and are reading it now. We understand that reading the words "abuse" and "control" may be difficult, and that it's even more difficult to describe yourself or your behavior. For now, that's okay. You do not have to admit or acknowledge that you have been abusive or controlling. Instead, focus on the fact that there is a clear reason you are reading this right now. Whether it is because someone required you to or encouraged you to or that you, yourself, were wondering whether it might be relevant, there was a reason you picked up this book. All we ask is that, for now, you keep reading!

Picking up this book does not mean you have to admit that you are an abusive person. It is not an admission of guilt. Maybe you are not an abusive or controlling person! Just because someone is worried that you are abusive does not mean for certain that you are. But certainly, there is a possibility they might be right, don't you think? All we ask is that you start reading this book with an open mind, that you stay open to the possibility that you might have patterns of abuse and control in your relationships. If you keep your mind open as you read the first few chapters, it will likely become clearer and clearer to you whether you are or you are not. If you are abusive, we hope that you will have the courage to admit this first to yourself and then to do the courageous and important work of changing the way you live in the world to stop your abusive behavior. If you truly do not have patterns of abuse and control, you will still probably learn a helpful thing or two along the way, especially in the second half of the book.

As you read this book, you will certainly find that parts of it do not apply to you. Perhaps certain kinds of abusive behavior are described that you have not done. Or certain ways people justify it do not apply to you. As you read, do your best to focus on what does apply rather than what does not. Ultimately, the goal is for this book to be of help and of use to you, to help you be a better person, a better partner, and a better parent. Try to focus on what is relevant and true for you, regardless of whether you think you are abusive or controlling.

Finally, if and when you do think you have issues with abuse and control, we strongly encourage you to consider joining a specialized group focused on helping people stop their abusive and controlling behaviors. Most of us learn new skills and concepts best in a group setting; that's why people take classes in groups, learn skills in groups, and undertake significant behavior change (like getting sober) in groups. However helpful you find this book, it is in no way a substitute for learning, developing, practicing, solidifying, and making permanent real changes by being part of a regular group. Most people who are serious and successful in stopping their patterns of abuse and control do so by getting involved in and successfully completing a specialized abuse-intervention group. For those of you who are not yet in such a group, we will talk more about them at the very end of the book, in the Afterword.

Think of joining a specialized abuse-intervention group as getting an advanced degree or developing a trade skill. Would you trust a mechanic who learned how to work on cars by reading a single book? Or let a doctor treat you who had only read one book? This book is intended to get you ready to join a program, support you while you are in one, and be a resource you can refer to after you complete your program. You get out of things what you put into them, and while reading a book is a good start to making changes, it's rarely enough, especially for making deep, enduring changes.

A MESSAGE TO WOMEN AND FEMALE-IDENTIFIED PEOPLE READING THIS BOOK

While the vast majority of violence in this world is committed by men, there are women who are also abusive. (We will address people who do not identify as male or female in just a few minutes.) In our many years of working with women who have been labeled abusive, we find that they fall into two separate and fairly different groups.

The first, larger group is of women who have been arrested on a domestic violence charge and mandated to engage in services by the criminal court. We find that many of these women turn out to have very limited histories of being abusive toward others, but very significant histories of being abused, particularly by their current partner who is often identified as the "victim" in the criminal case. This pattern has been noted all over the US by many programs working with women whose treatment has been mandated. What we have all observed is that most of these women do not have ongoing patterns of abuse and do not have pro-abuse belief systems. This is observed throughout their involvement, from beginning to end. Most court-mandated men admit to patterns of abuse over time, but most court-mandated women do not.

For most of these women, their biggest problem is having had the misfortune of ending up with an abusive partner. Typically, the abuse they were arrested for was either done in self-defense, was staged by their partner, or was an isolated moment of acting poorly, for which their partner had them arrested. Whatever the situation, these women turn out not to have a significant pattern of abuse and control and do not have a belief system that supports abusive behavior.

If you are in this group, reading this book may validate and affirm things you already practice and do. It may also give you greater clarity about your abusive partner's behavior. As you read this book, you need to remember that the only abusive and controlling behavior you are responsible for is your own, not your partner's.

The other, much smaller group of women who engage in abuse-intervention services are women who do have significant patterns of abuse and control. They have typically behaved that way with multiple partners, and if they are mothers, toward their children. These women and female-identified people present much the way that abusive men do: with plenty of denial, rationalizations and justifications, and a heavy external focus. These women are much less likely to reach programs through the criminal court system than to be referred by family court or child welfare services, or to engage voluntarily, at times to appease the concerns of their partner, children, or employer. We find that this group of women is very similar to the abusive men in our program, with many of the same beliefs and behaviors that need changing. One of the most striking differences is that nearly all of these women have been the victims of childhood abuse and domestic violence, whereas around half of our men have been victims of childhood abuse and a much smaller percentage than that have been victims of domestic violence from a partner.

If you are one of those women, much of what is written in this book is relevant and applicable to you. There are some small differences, particularly when we are more directly speaking to our male readers, but most of what we cover is relevant.

TO OUR READERS WHO DO NOT IDENTIFY AS CISGENDER

For those of you not familiar with the terms, being cisgender means that the gender you were assigned at birth is the gender you relate to; you agree, deep within, that you are that gender. Being transgendered means that your gender identity differs from the sex assigned at birth, and you are seeking to shift the way you live to conform to the gender you relate to more strongly. People who resist being labeled male or female sometimes identify as gender queer or nonbinary. Regardless of your gender identity (or sexual orientation, for that matter), if you have patterns of abuse and control, most of the material in this book is still applicable and relevant for you. Abusive behavior is just as common in LGBTQ+ communities as in other communities, and we have tried to use gender-neutral language to be as inclusive as possible.

A MESSAGE FOR ABUSED PARTNERS

Although this book is written for people who have patterns of abuse and control, we expect that there will also be some interest in this book among people who have been abused and controlled. Part of their own process of growth, change, healing, and recovery is to make sense of what was done to them, to help understand and explain why their abusive partner did what they did. If you fall into this group, then you are likely reading this book to understand your abusive partner. You may find this book helpful because it clearly names and describes some of what you have experienced and observed. We hope this book validates and facilitates your understanding, increased awareness, and change. It may help you make sense of the otherwise senseless things that were done to you. It may help you understand why these things happened and realize how very little you had to do with any of this happening to you in the first place, even if your abusive partner repeatedly said otherwise. Keep in mind that this book is written for the ears of abusive partners, so there may be times when it is not as sensitively or thoughtfully written for you and your experience.

It is also vital that you not take on any responsibility for your loved one's abusive behavior. Like everyone, you are imperfect, but there is nothing that you did or said that caused your partner to be abusive toward you. Ultimately, they are 100% responsible for their abusive behavior. Likewise, there is nothing you could have done to have stopped their abuse, especially not in any enduring way. Abused people typically try a vast range of things to stop the abuse, but the abuse continues, regardless. You may learn from this book ways to improve your own behavior and manage yourself, but do not expect them to have a significant impact on your partner's abusive behavior.

"HOW DO I GET HELP FOR MY ABUSIVE PARTNER?"

An entire book could easily be written on that subject, but there are a few things that typically do not help: couples counseling, short-term anger management, and individual therapy.

Couples counseling typically focuses on the "dance" of interactions between the two people in the relationship. It examines how each person contributes to the dynamics of the relationship, the interaction between them, and what each can do differently. But none of this applies when one of the people has patterns of abuse and control. The person who is abusive is 100% responsible for their abusive behavior, no matter what the other person does. Abuse and control is not a "couples" issue; it is an issue with the individual being abusive and controlling. This would be like using couples counseling to treat someone's addiction, as if the partner is to blame for the other's substance abuse. Ironically, though, abusive behavior is a common reason couples seek therapy, and most couples therapists do not adequately understand or screen for abusive behavior. To learn about other reasons that couples counseling is not an appropriate intervention, see Appendix A.

Anger management counseling, whether for individuals or groups, has been around for more than fifty years. It posits that what drives abusive behavior is the emotion of anger, and that addressing the emotion of anger will stop the abusive behavior. Typically, cognitive behavioral therapy techniques and a few interpersonal skills are taught to help a person change their thinking and physically calm their bodies. The first programs that focused on abusive behavior used anger management techniques, but also spent time listening to the abused partners of the people they were treating. What they heard over and over again was that traditional anger management did not work. It might stop some of the most severe abuse, but the less severe abuse continued or even got worse. This led to the development in the late 1970s of the new field of abuse intervention, which had a stronger focus on abusive behavior and the beliefs that supported it than on managing the emotion of anger. We have learned that anger is often a euphemism for abuse, but is more of a symptom than a primary cause of it. Based on feedback from abused partners, abuse-intervention groups have continued to evolve away from traditional anger management. Most programs, including ours, use anger management techniques, but they are just a small part of what we teach and do. Anger management alone is inadequate to help someone stop being abusive and controlling.

Individual therapy is problematic for two broad reasons. First, most mental health professionals offering individual therapy have little understanding of abusive behavior and its causes. They often believe abusive behavior is caused by substance abuse, low self-esteem, trauma, family of origin issues, and so on. They believe that by treating those other issues (about which they may know a great deal), the abusive behavior will disappear. While it may decrease, it rarely disappears. This is because although all of these issues (and many others) can trigger abusive behavior, none of them are the cause of it. What causes abusive behavior are belief systems that lead a person to give themself permission to be abusive. If those belief systems are not directly addressed and changed, then the patterns of abuse and control are unlikely to stop—although they may change. Mental health professionals used to mistakenly think that most substance abuse issues were caused by other mental health issues. That left it to people with substance abuse issues to create their own, more effective interventions, such as twelve-step programs like Alcoholics Anonymous and specialized substance abuse programs, to replace what had been largely ineffective individual therapy work. The same is true for abusive behavior. It needs specialized work.

Even if individual therapy is offered by someone knowledgeable about abusive behavior, it does not begin to compare to the impact of doing that work in a group setting. This is widely agreed upon within the field. There are many reasons why this is so, but most of all it is because group work is more intensive, immersive, confrontational, and supportive than individual work can be. Without question, the most effective modality to do this change work is in a specialized group that is focused on this behavior.

"IF MY ABUSIVE PARTNER GOES INTO SUCH A GROUP, WHAT ARE THE ODDS THAT THERE WILL BE TRUE CHANGE?"

First, it is important that a person stays with the group through completion. Most people who start a program drop out before completing it. Among those who stay, some will make some substantial sustained changes, others will change a little, and some will not change at all. If you are still in contact with them, you will know better than anyone if there has been true change.

"WHAT CAN I DO TO GET MY ABUSIVE PARTNER TO ENGAGE IN SERVICES?"

Many of the abusive partners who voluntarily engage with us are what we refer to as "partner-mandated"—they are there because their partner has insisted they attend. Sometimes that is enough to convince them to engage. Other times, they need their partner's mandate to be backed up by a therapist, an employer, minister, or family or friends. Usually, though, a partner mandate comes with a warning that if they do not engage in services, the partner will end the relationship. Sometimes the couple has already separated and the only chance for reconciliation is to engage in and complete a program.

If your abusive partner agrees to enroll in a program, make sure to keep in touch with the program to assure that your partner is actually attending. It is common for programs to obtain written permission from your partner to contact you. If they don't, or if your partner is not willing to give them permission, that alone should be a significant concern. Keep the program apprised of how you think things are going. Things going well in the program does not always mean better behavior at home. Bad behavior in the program, on the other hand (not attending, maintaining a lot of denial, not doing the homework), is often a negative sign in terms of potential for change.

If your abusive partner will not agree to enroll in a program, you might encourage them to read this book. Regardless, we strongly encourage you to get your own support from someone who is knowledgeable about abusive behavior to help you sort out how to best take care of yourself and your children.

A MESSAGE FOR PEOPLE READING THIS WHO ARE TRULY NOT ABUSIVE

The last group of people who might start reading this book are those who truly are not abusive. Some of you may be reading this to make sure that you are not an abusive and controlling person. If you keep an open mind as you read, it will become increasingly evident whether you have significant issues with patterns of abuse and control. If you do not, you still might find this book helpful. Even people who are not abusive and controlling struggle with gender stereotypes and the fallout from growing up in dysfunctional homes. This book, especially starting with Chapter 13: Moving from Disconnection to Connection, can provide clarity on what healthy relationships with yourself, your partner, and others truly look like.

Finally, it is our intent to continue to revise and improve this book. You are welcome to offer constructive input to us via email at allies@alliesinchange.org.

Thank you to whoever you are for taking the time to read this book. We hope you find value and growth and benefit in doing so.

PART ONE

WHAT ABUSIVE AND CONTROLLING BEHAVIOR LOOKS LIKE

CHAPTER 1

ABUSIVE BEHAVIORS

THE DIFFERENCE BETWEEN HURTFUL AND ABUSIVE BEHAVIORS

Anybody who is in a close relationship with another person is occasionally hurtful to the other. They say or do something that inadvertently hurts the other's feelings, perhaps by not taking their emotional reaction seriously (*"How could you be so upset over this?"*), minimizing their concern (*"Don't worry!"*), or not paying attention when they are sharing (getting distracted by their phone).

Usually, the person who did the hurtful behavior did not intend to be hurtful, but that does not matter, because the other person felt hurt by what was said or done to them. The person who was inadvertently hurtful will typically quickly acknowledge the behavior and do their best not to repeat it. But this can be complicated, because even some inadvertently hurtful behaviors are hard to stop. For example, one person's loud snoring may disrupt the other person's sleep. There is no intention to disrupt anyone's sleep, but it happens. Sorting out how both people can get a good night's sleep may require multiple discussions and interventions.

Many hurtful behaviors are not automatically or always hurtful. When a behavior that was not hurtful with one person or in one situation turns out to be hurtful in different circumstances, someone may not realize it until the other person lets them know. But once they know, they do their best to behave differently so as not to hurt the other again.

It is very important that the person who has behaved hurtfully acknowledges and responds to the other person's complaint, even though they had no intention of hurting them. The acknowledgment and validation of the legitimacy of the other person's experience, regardless of what the hurtful person's intent was, is vital. For example, when you step into a stranger's path, you typically say "excuse me." Although you certainly did not intend to step in their way, you acknowledge that you did and ask for forgiveness. You may do this common courtesy without even thinking about it, but the exact same courtesy applies when you inadvertently hurt someone you know. When you behave hurtfully, even if you did not intend to, you should acknowledge it and strive to the best of your ability not to do it again.

Abusive behavior, on the other hand, is not just being hurtful. There is on some level a willful disregard for the other person's rights and feelings or an intention to hurt. You either want to hurt or violate another's boundaries, or you do not care if you hurt or violate another's boundaries. This includes willfully continuing your hurtful behavior even after someone has made it clear that it is hurtful. The exceptions are behaviors you have no control over, like coughing, or blowing your nose, or things you need to do for your own well-being, like staying in touch with someone the other person does not want you to, or maintaining a particular religious practice the other finds objectionable. When that is the case, the two of you need to negotiate a mutual agreement. We will discuss this in Chapter 24: Practicing Conflict-Resolution Skills.

When people hear the words "violence" or "abuse," they usually think of physical aggression that causes pain and injury—like shooting or stabbing someone, breaking their nose, or giving them a black eye. However, physical aggression is only the most extreme type of abusive behavior. Abusive behavior describes any kind of willful hurting or violation of one person by another.

There are many different ways one can willfully hurt or violate another. Physical abuse is the most obvious and coarse, but other types of abuse include verbal, psychological, property, financial, sexual, and one we call "collateral." Each type of abuse is described in more detail below.

PHYSICAL ABUSE

Physical abuse describes any kind of unwanted physical contact or proximity. It includes getting into someone's physical comfort zone, even without touching them, and even if there is no injury or physical discomfort. Physical abuse can also describe being physically controlling. For example, you could pin your partner against the wall by their shoulders without causing physical harm or physical pain, but they could still be terrified and emotionally hurt. For those reasons, it would qualify as physical abuse. Note that this is much broader than the legal definition of physical abuse.

Examples of physical abuse
Choking
Hitting
Kicking
Pinching
Poking
Pulling hair
Punching
Slapping
Blocking someone (even without touching them)
Grabbing someone
Holding someone when they do not want to be held
Moving someone against their will
Restraining someone
Shaking someone
Throwing things at someone

VERBAL ABUSE

Verbal abuse involves hurtful or disrespectful words and tone of voice. This may be the easiest type of abusive behavior to identify. Most people understand it pretty well if they are being honest with themselves.

Some people underestimate the damage that hurtful words can cause. The schoolyard saying "Sticks and stones can break my bones, but words can never hurt me" is a common but misguided way of thinking. Many abused partners, including many who were seriously physically abused, report that verbal abuse can actually be more damaging. To put it another way, "Sticks and stones may break my bones, but words will break my heart."

Examples of verbal abuse

Demeaning comments

Name-calling

Put-downs

Yelling or screaming

Swearing at them (unless both have agreed that this is an acceptable way to communicate)

Tearing a person apart with words

PSYCHOLOGICAL ABUSE

Psychological abuse involves nonverbal and nonphysical ways of being hurtful toward another. This can be quite subtle and is often characterized by facial expressions, gestures, and other body language.

Examples of psychological abuse

Contempt

Facial expressions

Intense looks

Stares

Gestures such as flipping someone off or shaking a fist

Radiating intensity

The silent treatment

Radiating intensity and contempt are worth explaining in more detail. They are quite common in abusive relationships, but they can be hard to name and understand.

Radiating intensity is a phrase we coined to describe a state of emotional distress in which you're making it clear that you are not doing well, and that in some way the other person is to blame, or that they will "get it" if they don't act right around you.

People can radiate intensity by going about tasks or crossing a room, and through facial expressions, tone of voice, and other subtle nonverbal behaviors. These behaviors typically lead others to feel anxious and on edge, as if they are walking on eggshells so as not to set you off.

Radiating intensity is different from simply being grumpy or being in a bad mood, although you may think that is how you are feeling. Almost everyone is occasionally in a bad mood or a little grumpy, but others typically do not feel particularly anxious or concerned about you "losing it." Although they may be concerned about you, they feel emotionally safe and can be themselves. Radiating intensity, on the other hand, is a bad mood plus blame—it conveys that others are either to blame for your mood or responsible for not making it worse. Radiating intensity typically happens regularly—usually when you are feeling distressed—and can be quite toxic and wearing on family members. Because the behaviors are subtle, it can be hard to identify, akin to an odorless, colorless toxic gas that gradually poisons those exposed to it.

Another common form of psychological abuse that is often overlooked and unacknowledged is **contempt**. Contempt is an attitude of general disdain for the other person. It can be thought of as a negative valuation of someone's worth, and it sometimes involves putting your partner down to lift yourself up. Open and overt ways of expressing contempt include talking derogatively about your partner, telling people how messed up they are, and presenting them as basically unlovable, unworthy, and unintelligent. Most of the time, though, contempt is expressed in covert ways that are hard to identify but easy for your partner to feel.

John Gottman, a renowned researcher on couples, identified contempt as one of the "four horsemen" of a failing relationship (along with defensiveness, criticism, and stonewalling). Its presence does not bode well for the future of a relationship. The key to stopping contempt is not to stop any particular behavior, but to change your stance toward your partner, which requires changing your underlying thinking and beliefs. We will talk further about this in later chapters.

Some people have suggested that in some ways, *all* abusive behavior has a psychologically abusive component to it. It is often not just the behavior, but also the meaning of the behavior. This is why being shoved to the floor is experienced so differently than being stumbled into and accidentally knocked to the floor. In each case a person may end up on the floor against their will, but there is a huge difference in what it means when it was done accidentally rather than on purpose. While you are welcome to code all of your abusive behavior as psychologically abusive as well as some other category of abuse, this specific category refers to behaviors that do not fall into another category.

Examples of contemptuous behavior

Devaluing the other
Dismissiveness of the other
General irritability or frustration toward the other
Intolerance of the other's foibles
Limited consideration of the other's wants and needs
Limited warmth toward the other
Talking about the other in a disdainful tone
Tending to view the other as oppositional
Undervaluing the other's opinion
Using nonverbal cues like eye-rolling, head-shaking, or a sarcastic smile while talking about the other

PROPERTY ABUSE

Property abuse refers to mishandling property out of anger, regardless of whether it belongs to you or you do any damage to it. For example, if you throw a wrench you are using across the garage, that is considered property abuse even though it's your wrench and it is undamaged. Property abuse is typically psychologically abusive to anyone who witnesses it or sees the aftermath of it, like the hole that was punched in a wall or the remains of a destroyed item. It is often unsettling and stressful and can create fear. For these reasons, it is a significant concern.

Examples of property abuse

Banging on things
Breaking things
Hitting things
Kicking things
Punching walls
Slamming doors
Throwing things

FINANCIAL ABUSE

Financial abuse involves mishandling money, finances, or financial agreements. It is most common when there are shared finances or living arrangements. Financial abuse is quite common, but it is underreported because it is not well understood. We will examine it thoroughly in Chapter 4: Financial Abuse.

SEXUAL ABUSE

Sexual abuse is probably the most difficult type of abuse to understand and admit to. It is also particularly damaging to the victim, arguably more so than any other type. Because this category has so many examples and is easily misunderstood, we will focus extensively on this in Chapter 3: Sexual Abuse.

COLLATERAL ABUSE

We coined the term **collateral abuse** to describe what happens when people who are not the target of abusive behavior are nonetheless exposed to it and negatively affected by it. We include this category because it is easy to forget that simply witnessing abusive behavior can be damaging.

Children are the primary victims of collateral abuse, and the ones most seriously damaged by it. Neighbors, friends, bystanders, and passersby can also be negatively affected whether you are aware they were witnesses or not. Extensive research indicates that children can be as emotionally damaged by seeing or hearing abusive behavior as by being directly physically abused.

Examples of collateral abuse

Children and others who are physically present during the abuse

Children and others who overhear the abuse

Children and others who witness or overhear the effects of the abuse (like sobbing or physical injuries)

Children and other witnesses of abusive outbursts (like yelling at the television)

Children and others who see destroyed or damaged property

Children and others who are in the car during a road rage incident

ANIMAL ABUSE

Animal abuse refers to any sort of mistreatment of animals, whether it is physical abuse, willful neglect, or both. Appropriate physical discipline of an animal (usually a dog) is not included in this category—although there is debate about whether physical discipline with an animal is ever appropriate. Sometimes the abuse is intended to hurt the animal, usually because the person is angry and upset at the animal. Other times the animal abuse is more about causing pain and suffering to other people who love and care for the animal. It is a way of getting back at them through the animal.

Examples of animal abuse

Hitting an animal
Kicking an animal
Torturing an animal
Yelling at an animal
Provoking an animal to make it agitated
Intentionally depriving an animal of food, water, or shelter
Getting rid of a shared animal without mutual consent

SELF-ABUSE

Self-abuse refers to overtly abusive behavior toward yourself. It is no more acceptable to abuse yourself than anyone else. No one deserves to be abused, including you! Although negative self-talk can be self-abusive, it is typically not coded as self-abuse unless it is said out loud.

Examples of self-abuse

Hitting yourself
Trying to physically hurt yourself
Destroying your own property to punish yourself
Destroying property to cause physical injury (punching a wall and aiming for the stud)
Saying abusive and derogatory things out loud about yourself (*"I'm such a fucking idiot," "I'm a complete loser"*)

SPIRITUAL ABUSE

Spiritual abuse uses a person's spirituality against them. Although it can fall into other categories, including controlling behaviors (discussed in Chapter 2: Controlling Behaviors), this type of abuse is particularly damaging for people who are deeply spiritual.

Examples of spiritual abuse

Using or misusing religious passages or religious quotes to denigrate, dominate, or control someone

Preventing someone from practicing their spirituality as they want to

Using people within a spiritual community to reinforce an abusive or controlling perspective

Twisting religious concepts to promote an agenda

Making someone adhere to religious practices that are contrary to their beliefs

RELATIONSHIP NEGLECT

A category of abusive behavior that is often overlooked is neglect of the relationship itself. Relationships are living things that require regular energy, care, and attention. Without them, they tend to fade and wilt and struggle, just as other living things would. Neglect describes what you are *not* doing. It is not about the presence of hurtful behaviors, but the absence of loving ones. Neglect can be quite subtle.

Our evolving understanding of relationship neglect parallels the evolution of our thinking about the mistreatment of children. Child abuse used to be thought of primarily in terms of physical or sexual abuse. Then it was acknowledged that other forms of child abuse can be quite damaging as well, such as verbal abuse and psychological abuse. Finally, it was acknowledged that neglect can hurt a child, too. Child neglect is the failure to meet a child's basic needs for food, shelter, and physical safety, at the very least. Relationship neglect is the failure to meet the basic needs of a relationship. An adult is not necessarily responsible for meeting their partner's basic needs, but they *are* responsible for striving to support their partner's basic relationship needs.

Although relationship needs vary from couple to couple and culture to culture, every couple has needs that must be met in the relationship. Not meeting them is neglectful, which is disrespectful and hurtful behavior. Below is a very brief list of neglectful behaviors, but the ways of neglecting a relationship are virtually endless. If you attend an abuse-intervention program, it might be helpful to discuss in group the many ways of being neglectful in a relationship.

One rampant form of neglect in abusive relationships is the refusal to acknowledge abusive and controlling behaviors and the impact that they have on the other person. Accountable and timely acknowledgment of an abusive behavior can significantly decrease the damage it causes. Think of the abuse as a scraped knee: If it is quickly seen, cleaned, and cared for, it is much less likely to get infected. This is what accountable acknowledgment can do. On the other hand, if the scraped knee is ignored, it is much more likely to get infected and cause other problems. People who are abusive often deny, minimize, rationalize, justify, or ignore the abusive behavior. This makes the abuse significantly more destructive. It also significantly increases the likelihood that the abusive behavior will cause trauma in the other. We will talk about denial in much more detail in Chapter 7: Denial.

Examples of relationship neglect
Not acknowledging the other person
Not thinking about them
Not thinking about their needs
Not giving them your full attention
Not considering their input or preferences
Not thinking about how they are different from you
Not listening to and validating their emotional experiences
Not expressing gratitude and appreciation for who they are and what they do
Not acknowledging them when you come home or enter a room
Not providing them emotional support during difficult times
Not accompanying them to important medical appointments when you can
Presuming that everyone sees the world the same way you do, that your perspective is the only one, that your concerns and needs are the only ones that are important

CHILD ABUSE

Many abusive partners have been directly abusive toward their or their partner's children. Nearly every type of abuse that can be inflicted on a partner can be inflicted on a child.

Physical abuse toward a child can include hitting, kicking, and other physical aggression. Physical mishandling of a child includes grabbing, restraining, blocking their way, pushing, and dragging them. Undesired physical contact includes unwanted tickling, wrestling, tossing into the air, or "playfully" grabbing or punching them when they do not want to play like that. As with adults, any kind of unwanted physical contact qualifies as physical abuse, even if it does not cause injury or pain.

One frequent justification for physical abuse is that it was to "save their lives" or was "for their own good." The key question is this: Was it absolutely necessary to physically handle your child in that situation? Were there realistic nonphysical alternatives to what you did? If there were not—if they were running into the street without looking for cars—then it is justified physical control. Those situations are rare, though; far more rare than most people can admit.

Sometimes this behavior toward a child is justified as "punishment" or "physical discipline." We discourage physical discipline for a variety of reasons, including a large body of research that indicates it causes significant emotional damage and is not a particularly effective form of parenting. But for those who insist on using corporal punishment, several widely accepted guidelines must be followed. First, the child must have a clear understanding of the rule that was violated. Second, the physical punishment must be administered in a calm, controlled manner. Third, the physical punishment must be very brief, no more than a few swats to the butt. Fourth, the physical punishment must never cause any sort of injury, including bruising. Finally, physical punishment should never be used with teenagers. If you are not following these guidelines, then the "physical discipline" you have used qualifies as physical abuse, even among those who believe physical discipline is acceptable.

Verbal abuse toward a child includes yelling, name-calling, put-downs, and profanity. It also includes teasing and excessive criticizing or correction. The belief that children are inferior to adults and that it is the adult's responsibility to "guide" the child toward appropriate behavior is often used to justify this unnecessary and excessive harshness.

Psychological abuse of a child includes looks, stares, and gestures that create fear and intimidation or are openly disrespectful. It also includes behaviors that convey strong negative judgment or moral disapproval (that they are a bad kid, rather than a good kid who has done something you disapprove of). This form of abuse is more frequently inflicted on children than on others. The innate power differential and children's dependency on adults for survival, as well as the common belief that adults are superior to children because of that dependency, makes it easier to use a tone, gesture, or facial expression with them that you might not with others.

Sexual abuse of a child includes any kind of sexual contact or interaction with a child. A child cannot truly consent to sexual behavior with an adult, so any sexual interaction of any kind with a child is considered sexual abuse. This is different from nonsexual physical affection that a child is receptive to, such as hugs, kisses, and snuggling. Sometimes sexual abuse of a child is masked as nonsexual physical affection, but if the adult's intent is to create sexual arousal either in themselves or in the child, it is abusive.

Children consensually interacting sexually with other children may or may not be abusive, particularly if they are close in age. The greater the age difference between the children, the more likely that "consensual" sexual interaction is abusive or coercive toward the younger child. If a child is forced to do sexual things by another child of any age, whether younger or older, the interaction is sexually abusive.

Child neglect is a category specific to children that refers to a failure to meet a child's innate, basic needs for food, shelter, safety, nurturance, education, and health care. Depriving a child of a basic need as punishment qualifies as neglect; only privileges, not rights, can be taken away as punishment. For example, children, like all people, have a right and a need to eat, but having dessert is a privilege. It would not be okay to deprive a child of food in general as a consequence, but depriving them of dessert would be acceptable.

THE KEY CONCERN: PATTERNS OF ABUSE

Although abusive behavior is the easiest way to identify abuse, that alone is not enough to identify an abusive person. Theoretically, a person could have an isolated act or two of abusive behavior without being in an abusive relationship; it may just be an imperfect one. It is not the presence of any one abusive behavior that is the main problem, but an ongoing pattern of such behaviors. It's the difference between being drunk and being an alcoholic. Just because someone gets drunk, it does not mean they are an alcoholic. What makes a person an alcoholic is not any one moment of drunkenness, but an ongoing pattern of being drunk. While all alcoholics occasionally get drunk (if they drink), not everyone who gets drunk is an alcoholic. Likewise, it is the pattern of abuse that makes someone an abusive person, not just an isolated act or two of abuse.

Having a pattern of abusive or controlling behavior is what turns a relationship from imperfect to abusive. The exact nature of the pattern—which abusive behaviors are involved and how often they occur—can vary a great deal. It is important to keep in mind that certain specific abusive behaviors (including physical abuse) may rarely or never happen in an abusive relationship. However, if there is a pattern of other types of abusive behavior (verbal, psychological), then that person is an abusive partner, even if they almost never or never engage in physical abuse.

What causes this pattern of abuse is an underlying belief system. If the abusive behaviors are the flowers on a plant, the beliefs are the roots. You can cut the flowers off, but as long as it still has roots, the plant is still alive. Even if one type of abuse or specific abusive behavior stops, until the underlying beliefs are changed, the abusive behavior is likely to happen again, in some form or another. This is why the key work to be done is not just to stop your behaviors, but to change your beliefs. We will talk about these belief systems in Chapter 5: Abusive Thoughts and Beliefs.

Abusive behaviors are just one set of problematic behaviors that need to be addressed. An even larger set of behaviors that are of concern are those that are *controlling*. It would be rare for someone with patterns of abuse not to have patterns of control. The next chapter focuses on behaviors that are controlling: what they are and why they are problematic.

CHAPTER 2

CONTROLLING BEHAVIORS

Most people would agree that freedom is a core human right. But what do we mean by *freedom*? While it can be defined many different ways, one is being able to make your own choices, provided you are not hurting others in the process. This includes the freedom to have your own opinions, to have your own beliefs, and to have your own emotions. It means living the way you want to live, preferably in a way that honors who you truly are. This can include the freedom to love who you want to love, to pursue your own spiritual practices, and to live according to your own internal morals and values, as long as they do not hurt others.

Behaviors that are controlling interfere with someone's basic liberties by trying to make them think or act in ways they would not freely choose. Rather than using influence or persuasion to convince them to change their mind, controlling behaviors use power—physical, mental, financial, political, etc.—to dominate others.

While anyone can be the target of control, the most likely targets are the people closest to you—your romantic partner and children. This is true for a few reasons. First, you may feel more entitled to control people you think of as "belonging" to you. Second, it is easier to get away with controlling your family because of their dependence on you and your status in their lives. Third, it is easier for people outside your family to end your controlling behavior—by ending the friendship or quitting their job, for example.

There are many, many ways of being controlling. Take some time right now to look over the list presented in Appendix B at the end of this book. We will explain those behaviors later, but first, there are a number of general points we wish to make.

The first thing to note is that although it may seem like a long list to you, it is incomplete. The behaviors listed are only some of the most common ways of being controlling. Many other examples are not included, in part because there are so many of them. This will become clearer as we go on.

Second, you will undoubtedly recognize some of the behaviors on that list as your own. In truth, virtually everyone could circle at least a few of them. We will talk more about that in a little bit.

Nearly all controlling behaviors fall into one of two categories: they are either **intimidating** or **manipulative**. Intimidation involves pressuring or coercing someone to give in to your will. Badgering, nagging, and guilt trips fall into this category, as do abusive behaviors. Manipulation involves getting someone to do what you want by keeping them ignorant or misleading them so they cannot give informed consent. Lying, withholding information, and making empty promises are a few examples. You could think of controlling behavior as either pushing (via intimidation) or pulling (via manipulation) someone into doing your will without them freely choosing to do so.

It is difficult to fully grasp what this means. You are likely to have a lot of questions and confusion about what is and is not controlling. It can seem like everything is controlling! It can also seem like it is impossible to not be controlling. Typically, it takes multiple discussions and a lot of reflection to get really clear on what it means to be controlling. There are a number of reasons for this.

For one, while many abusive behaviors are intrinsically abusive (for instance, there is no nice way to slap someone or to say "fuck you"), many controlling behaviors are not intrinsically controlling. A particular behavior may or may not be controlling, depending on how it is used. For example, an apology becomes controlling when it is not genuine, as when someone apologizes only to manipulate another into doing something they want. (*I'm sorry I called you stupid. Can we go out to dinner now?*)

Genuine apologies are not typically controlling, because the other person does not have to do anything in return. Giving a gift is not inherently controlling, but it becomes controlling when something is expected in return. (*"Look at the expensive ring I gave you. The least you could do is have sex with me tonight!"*)

Virtually anything can be twisted into a controlling behavior. For example, the phrase "I love you" becomes controlling when the person is expected to say it back. If it's okay for the other person not to say "I love you" in response, saying it is not controlling.

Even the skills taught in this book can be twisted into controlling behaviors. In Chapter 14: Learning to Stop Your Abuse in the Moment, we teach that time-outs include returning to the situation. But we have found that people twist time-outs into a silencing tactic by walking away and never following up on the situation. That shifts the time-out from a helpful tool to a manipulative one. Many other program skills can be twisted in similar ways as well.

One way to determine whether a behavior is controlling is to see what happens if someone does not respond in the intended way. If "noncompliance" leads to more controlling behaviors, then the initial behavior was probably controlling. For example, if someone in the passenger seat suggests an alternate route to the driver, are they being controlling? It depends on whether the suggestion is actually an order or directive. This becomes clearer if the driver decides not to follow the suggestion. If the passenger is okay with the refusal, then it was a suggestion. If, on the other hand, the passenger follows up with criticism, sarcasm, badgering, or another controlling behavior, it was not a suggestion in the first place. It was a directive, and therefore controlling.

Another reason it can be so hard to understand what is and is not controlling is that there is sometimes a very fine line between the two. One determining factor is whether the focus is inward or outward. The actual wording of a threat and a warning could be exactly the same—"If you yell at me one more time, I am going to walk away"—but a warning has an inward focus and a threat has an outward focus. A warning announces what the speaker will do if the listener continues a behavior; the listener is free to choose, and the speaker typically follows through. A threat is intended to get the listener to comply; if they don't, the speaker often doesn't follow through, and tries other controlling behaviors to get the other person to comply. For another example, if someone refuses to be sexual with a sexual partner with the intent to punish their partner by withholding sex, the focus is outward; it is a controlling behavior. If their intent is to set a limit because they don't feel like being sexual, the focus is inward; it is an appropriate boundary. Warnings are respectful; threats are controlling.

If you are attending a group, you can gain clarity about this by asking the group whether a particular behavior is controlling and exploring alternatives if it is. If you are not in a group, you'll need to be careful about having these discussions with people. Many people do not have a good understanding of this subject and may either unwittingly justify your controlling behavior or mischaracterize it as not controlling when it actually is. This is one of many ways a specialized group is important and why it can be so difficult to make these changes on your own.

YOUR PATTERNS OF CONTROL MAKE YOU CONTROLLING

In the last chapter we made the point that being abusive once in a great while does not make someone an abusive person. To be an abusive person means demonstrating a pattern of abuse, even if the type of abuse varies over time. This demonstrated pattern is even more essential when it comes to identifying controlling behavior. Pretty much everyone is occasionally controlling. In part, this is because it is quite easy to be controlling; you can do it without even being aware of it. It is also quite tempting to be controlling, which can be quicker, easier, and more effective (at least, in the short run) than the alternative. It is a great example of the saying "There's the right way and there's the easy way." Almost anyone who reviews the list of controlling behaviors should be able to circle at least a few that they have done in the recent past.

Controlling behaviors occur with great frequency and regularity, even among people who do not demonstrate patterns of control. If they kept a close count, noncontrolling people might rack up dozens of controlling behaviors a week. However, those behaviors are scattered across many different situations with many different people. They may interrupt a coworker at work, get sarcastic with a friend at lunch, and withhold information from their partner at home, but the number of controlling behaviors exhibited with any one person is low. If you think of each controlling behavior as a single drop of rain, and you experience three moments of being controlled in a week, it's like getting hit by three raindrops. You're technically getting wet, but is it that big a deal? Being in a controlling relationship, on the other hand, is like being in a rainstorm: you are being hit by lots of drops of rain, and some are hitting you at the same time. Even though there's space between the raindrops, all you know is that you are getting soaked, and no matter where you turn, more rain is falling. The only way to avoid all those drops of rain is to seek shelter from the storm—by removing yourself from the controlling person. As with abuse, it's the patterns of control that are the problem, and the patterns are driven by underlying belief systems. We will explore this in Chapter 5: Abusive Thoughts and Beliefs.

It is common for people who are abusive and controlling to seriously underestimate how frequently they behave this way. They tend to consider only the most extreme situations, or when their emotions were intense or their partner complained, and they overlook all the control they exerted in a low-key, undramatic way. This is like only calling it a rainstorm if there's thunder and lightning and pouring-down rain, and ignoring the fact that it was raining lightly for a long time before and after the squall.

One reason it is hard to notice all of your controlling behaviors is that they often come in bunches—a dozen in just a few minutes. They can also show up in such a casual, undramatic way that you don't even notice them, the same way you usually don't notice that you are breathing. While it is certainly possible to go an extended period of time without being abusive, it is close to impossible to go for long without being controlling, unless you aren't interacting with anyone.

For this reason, the question to ask yourself is not whether you have been controlling at all, but how often and in what ways, in which situations, and with which people.

It is possible to stop virtually all of your abusive behavior. There are lots of people in the world who can honestly say that they have never been abusive toward others. But this is not possible when it comes to being controlling, because it is so easy to be controlling. Almost everyone occasionally does it. It is unrealistic to expect yourself to stop all of your controlling behavior all the time, but you can stop your *patterns* of controlling behavior. It is the patterns of control, especially over time, that are the most damaging. You may still have moments of being controlling, but if those moments are infrequent and do not become part of a larger pattern, they are not nearly as problematic or damaging as abusive behavior.

Going forward, to be succinct we may say things like "stopping your abuse" or "your abusive behavior." Although we may not always include the word "control" in the phrase, any reference to your abuse indicates your patterns of controlling behaviors as well. We understand that it's probably impossible to stop all of your controlling behaviors, but we know that doing so is not necessary to significantly improve your relationships. These shortcuts are solely for ease of expression.

CONSENT IS KEY

It may start to seem like everything you do with another person is controlling, but that's not the case. Remember that the goal of controlling is to get people to do things without their full, informed consent. If there is true consent, then the behavior is not controlling, even if it appears to be. For example, one person keeping track of all the expenses and setting a budget, including putting their partner on an allowance, is not controlling if the partner has fully agreed to the arrangement. The behavior would become even more apparent if the partner withdrew their consent and wanted to change the arrangement. If the behavior stops or changes (in this case, if the partner is granted their request for a changed arrangement), it is not controlling. On the other hand, if the behavior continues (if the person continues to manage the finances without their partner's input), controlling behavior is evident.

Some relationships that may appear to be controlling are not necessarily so, as in the two primary examples of supervisor-employee and parent-child. Consenting to work for an employer means that you will likely have one or more people who supervise and oversee your work. This is normal and expected, and may include giving orders, providing unsolicited advice, and giving directives on how to behave differently on the job. While this might be controlling from a peer, it is expected of a supervisor, and consent to it is a condition of employment.

Here is a true story that illustrates this point very clearly. A number of years ago, a new agency staff member was in training with a seasoned facilitator. He was expected to be an active participant so his skills could be evaluated, and had been in the group for several weeks, getting increasingly comfortable, when a group member he had not met before returned from a leave of absence. The group member quickly became irritated when he spoke up and offered his perspectives, and it was clear the member did not appreciate having the new facilitator present. The group took its regular break halfway through the session, and at the end of the break, the group member came up to the new facilitator and apologized for his reactivity. He had thought the new facilitator was a new member acting like a facilitator, since he had neglected to introduce himself. Viewing the new facilitator as a group member, some of his behaviors— interrupting, redirecting, and that sort of thing—seemed controlling, and the member was bothered. When he realized the man was a new facilitator, those same behaviors did not seem controlling at all.

At the same time, being a manager, supervisor, or facilitator does not give you a free ride to do anything you want. The others' consent only applies to areas within the supervisor's job description. For example, giving unsolicited advice on how to better do a work task is acceptable, but such advice about a new relationship is not. Consent is implicit for one, but not the other, which makes the latter controlling. Likewise, consent does not make it okay to be disrespectful or demeaning. While you may agree to your supervisor giving you criticism, you have not agreed to being put down or yelled at by them. Think about your own experience with supervisors over the years. Good supervisors typically fulfill their supervisory responsibilities without becoming abusive or controlling. Bad supervisors, on the other hand, typically either do not fulfill their responsibilities, or become abusive or controlling in the process. It all boils down to consent!

A related category of behaviors that only appear to be controlling are some of those demonstrated by people who need to manage the general public, like police officers, security guards, and bouncers. Good police officers carry out their job descriptions, which people have consented to on a social level by passing laws they expect to be enforced. So, for example, if you have done something wrong while driving, such as speeding, the police have the right to pull you over. They are not controlling you, because we have given consent as a society to this interaction. On the other hand, we have not given consent for law enforcement officers to beat us or shoot us if we are doing nothing to resist. Pulling someone over for speeding is not abusive or controlling, but beating someone is. Just as with supervisors, "good" cops fulfill their job responsibilities even if it means detaining or restraining someone. "Bad" cops, on the other hand, take advantage of their power and go beyond what they are supposed to just because they can.

If you are currently in a program, you can observe your group facilitator to see if they are being controlling. As long as they are fulfilling their role, an otherwise controlling behavior like interrupting would not be controlling. On the other hand, that same behavior might be controlling if there is not a clear and appropriate reason for it. For instance, interrupting to get a group member back on topic is not controlling, but interrupting because the facilitator wants to make their point right then is controlling. Most programs have new members sign an informed consent agreement that outlines the program's expectations and agrees to uphold them. If the person does not agree with those expectations, they can choose to leave.

The other supervisory role that many of us fill at some point is that of a parent. The guidelines described above apply here as well, but the complicating factor is that children cannot—and sometimes will not—consent in the same way. ("*I will not take a bath!*" and "*I'm not going to school!*") On the other hand, they may give consent without knowing or understanding that they don't have to, which makes their consent uninformed, as in the case of agreeing to do inappropriate things or thinking such things are normal or acceptable. The feedback children provide on consent is complicated and may or may not be justified, but it gets much clearer when as adults they reflect on the parenting they received. In the meantime, the goal is to manage your child in a consistently respectful way, following the "job description" of being a parent. There should always be a good, parental reason for what you are doing as you manage your child. If there isn't, you are probably being controlling. For example, telling a child to change their clothes because they are not appropriately dressed for the weather is generally not controlling. On the other hand, telling a child to change their clothes because you don't like that color on them is about satisfying your preference rather than fulfilling your parental role.

In truth, virtually every parent occasionally crosses the line and becomes controlling. Common reasons are impatience (since control is often faster) and fatigue (because it's easier and they can get away with it). Those imperfect parenting moments cause far less damage and are more easily forgiven when they are not part of an ongoing pattern of controlling behavior. What makes a person a controlling parent is not just a moment or two here or there, but an ongoing pattern of control that causes damage over time.

THERE'S NO SUCH THING AS "GOOD CONTROL"

Some people talk about "good control" and "bad control," but there is no such thing as good control. It is an oxymoron; controlling behaviors are bad because they violate the other person's freedom. What people usually mean by "good control" is controlling with consent—as in the role of a supervisor or parent. What they mean, though, is consensual control, which is not actually control, because both parties have consented to it. So "good control" does not exist. It's either not control because there is consent, or it's not good, because there's not consent.

For a variety of reasons, a person may not have a realistic alternative to being controlling in a particular moment, and as a result, they may feel justified. It is important to give serious thought to whether it was necessary to be controlling. If it was, we do not call it "good control," but rather "necessary control." Sometimes it is—like grabbing a young child before they chase a ball into a busy street—and sometimes it is not—like refusing to ever let them play outside again. You need to be very careful not to give yourself permission to be controlling too easily or too often. People who are prone to patterns of control often feel their controlling behaviors are necessary, but they rarely are.

KEEP THE FOCUS ON YOU—NOT YOUR PARTNER OR CHILD

If it's true that pretty much everyone is occasionally controlling, then that includes your partner and children. You can probably spot controlling behaviors on our list that you have seen from them, but it is vital that you stay focused on yourself and deal with your shortcomings FIRST, before starting in on your partner's. You also need to be honest with yourself about why you want to focus on your partner or children. Is it truly because you have serious concerns about them? Or is it to avoid looking at yourself? Control tends to beget control, and you may find that as you decrease your controlling behaviors, those of your loved ones naturally decline in response. If you continue to have significant concerns about your partner or child's controlling behaviors once you have made significant, sustained, positive changes in yourself, then you might want to share your concerns at that time—which is not now or in the immediate future. Chapter 24: Practicing Conflict-Resolution Skills will address how to advocate for yourself and share your concerns with your partner.

Listed below are brief explanations of many, but by no means all, controlling behaviors. (The list is also found in Appendix B.) What is not stated is how each behavior is used to control people, because each behavior is used in many different ways. This is like a list of tools with a description of each tool but not a description of what it can be used for or how it is used. There are a few main ways these behaviors are used. One is to exhibit unpleasant behaviors to get someone to do your will—by abusing or badgering them, for example. This is referred to as being "coercive." Another is to mislead someone—by lying or withholding information, perhaps—so they'll go along with something without realizing what they're doing. Another is to get someone to drop an issue— perhaps by apologizing or agreeing insincerely—so you don't have to resolve or acknowledge it. These are examples of being manipulative.

Examples of controlling behaviors
1. Abusing the other person
While this is an alphabetical list of examples of controlling behaviors, it is still quite appropriate that the very first example is abuse. Every act of abusive behavior is intrinsically controlling because it is by definition coercive, and often intimidating.

2. **Accessing their electronic devices**
   Looking at the other person's cellphone, computer, or other personal electronic devices without their permission.

3. **Acting forgetful**
   Pretending to forget or making yourself forget in order to avoid doing something.

4. **Agreeing insincerely**
   Saying you agree when you really do not.

5. **Apologizing**
   Apologizing when you do not really mean it or think you have done anything wrong.

6. **Arguing**
   Arguing just to argue, typically to wear the other person down.

7. **Asking leading questions**
   Asking questions intended to steer the other person in the direction you want to go without their agreement.

8. **Asking rhetorical questions**
   Making statements masked as questions.

9. **Backseat driving**
   Giving unwanted directions or advice to the driver.

10. **Badgering**
    Repeatedly making a point, asking a question, or raising an issue to wear the other person down.

11. **Being contrary**
    Automatically disagreeing with whatever the other person is saying.

12. **Being defensive**
    Shifting the focus from what the other person is saying in order to defend yourself.

13. **Being impatient**
    Pressuring someone to go faster than they want.

14. **Being overly sensitive**
    Overstating or overplaying your sensitivity and reactivity.

15. **Being overprotective**
    Making a choice for the other person without their approval "for their own good."

16. Being sarcastic

Using a sarcastic tone of voice and saying the opposite of what you actually think to get the other person to comply.

17. Being superficially polite or nice

Being polite and nice when you don't need to be and don't actually feel that way in order to get something from the other person.

18. Being willfully incompetent

Intentionally doing a poor job on a task.

19. Blackmailing

Threatening to disclose sensitive information if someone does not do what you want.

20. Blaming

Shifting the focus to the other person to avoid focusing on yourself.

21. Blowing up

Intentionally overreacting to intimidate the other person.

22. Bringing up the past

Using historical information to pressure or distract the other person.

23. Brown-nosing

Intentionally saying complimentary and positive things you may not fully mean.

24. Calling excessively

Repeatedly calling someone to make them answer the phone.

25. Changing the subject

Intentionally shifting the focus to avoid addressing the current issue.

26. Correcting them repeatedly

Exclusively focusing on things you think are done wrong; exclusively finding fault.

27. Criticizing

Making broad negative statements about the other person to get them to comply.

28. Doing their tasks

Doing something for the other person that is their responsibility that they do not want you to do.

29. Dominating the conversation
Not giving the other person the opportunity to speak or share what they want.

30. Eavesdropping
Listening in on a conversation without the other person's awareness or permission.

31. Exaggerating
Intentionally overstating something to get the other person to do what you want.

32. Flattering
Saying positive or affirming things you do not really or fully mean.

33. Gaslighting
Intentionally denying or disputing the other person's experience to leave them off balance, questioning reality, and more easily manipulated.

34. Gesturing dismissively
Making gestures intended to silence or undermine the other person.

35. Getting the last word
Making sure the conversation ends on your final point.

36. Giving gifts
Giving the other person a gift with a string attached, expecting something in return.

37. Giving the silent treatment
Openly and defiantly refusing to speak to the other person when you routinely would.

38. Giving the third degree
Repeated and relentless questioning focused on a situation that the other person doesn't wish to discuss in as much detail as you do.

39. Giving unsolicited advice
Offering input when it is not requested or wanted.

40. Going off the deep end
Overstating things and overreacting to get compliance.

41. Going over their head
Going to another person's supervisor before talking directly with them because you expect them to deny your request.

42. Gossiping

Talking to other people about the other person to pressure them to do what you want.

43. Handling their belongings

Handling the other person's belongings without asking or having permission first.

44. Hanging up on them

Abruptly ending a phone call without formally ending the conversation or giving someone a chance to close.

45. Having a short fuse

Intentionally becoming escalated and reactive.

46. Hiding their things

Intentionally putting the other person's item where they cannot find it.

47. Humiliating them in public

Intentionally embarrassing the other person in front of others.

48. Hurrying them

Getting the other person to go quicker than they want to accommodate your timeline.

49. Ignoring

Intentionally ignoring the other person when they are trying to communicate with you.

50. Ingratiating yourself

Intentionally using flattery and compliments to get the other person to go along with you.

51. Interrogating

Relentlessly questioning the other person about a situation and forcing them to share more than they wish about it.

52. Interrupting

Not allowing the other person to finish their statement before you start to talk.

53. Intimidating

Making the other person feel afraid and uncomfortable so they do what you want to stop the discomfort. Virtually all abusive behavior and many controlling behaviors fall into this category.

54. Invoking a higher authority

Invoking higher powers (someone the other looks up to, the Bible, a book) to get the other person to do what you want.

55. Invoking your experience or expertise

Pointing out your greater experience or knowledge to give it greater weight.

56. Isolating

Keeping the other person away from others. There are a variety of ways this can be done, including not allowing them to keep in touch with friends, limiting access to the phone or transportation, and alienating them from their friends.

57. Joking or kidding insincerely

Preventing the other person from feeling hurt or upset by something you said by falsely claiming you were not serious or were "just joking."

58. Keeping items exclusively in your name

Not including your partner's name on shared items like bank accounts or the title to the house or car.

59. Keeping them ignorant or uneducated

Intentionally not sharing relevant information so the other person will not fully understand what is going on.

60. Limiting access to shared items

Not allowing the other person access to items that they have the right to. This might include shared belongings or documents.

61. Limiting access to finances or financial information

This is one of many ways of being financially controlling. Refer to the longer list of financially controlling behaviors in Chapter 4: Financial Abuse.

62. Listening selectively

Only listening to or quoting the part that supports your perspective.

63. Looking at them intensely

Using intense stares to intimidate them and get them to comply.

64. Lying

Not being truthful in your statements to the other person, either by making false statements (commission) or failing to include all the relevant information (omission).

65. Making demands

Demanding things that fall outside of your basic human rights without acknowledging the other person's legitimate right to make their own choices.

66. Making dismissive sounds

Making sounds intended to silence or undermine the other person.

67. Making faces

Making facial expressions intended to control or intimidate the other person, such as rolling your eyes or giving an insincere smile.

68. Making fun

Teasing the other person to get them to behave differently out of shame and embarrassment.

69. Making promises you don't intend to keep

Making promises you have no intention to keep or without any idea of how you will keep them.

70. Making secret purchases

Not telling the other person about purchases they would expect to know about.

71. Making them feel sorry for you

Playing on the other person's sympathies by overstating or emphasizing your struggles.

72. Making unilateral decisions

Making a decision alone that both people should have a say in.

73. Making wild statements

Intentionally overstating or exaggerating things.

74. Managing impressions

Putting yourself in the best light possible; highlighting your positive qualities and status with others.

75. Manipulating

Misleading or misguiding the other person to get them to do what you want. Many controlling behaviors fall into this general category.

76. Micromanaging

Requiring the other person to do a task exactly the way you think they should, with no room for making their own decisions.

77. Mimicking
Imitating the other person in a derogatory manner.

78. Mischaracterizing what others say
Distorting or misrepresenting the words of others to get the other to behave a certain way.

79. Misusing material from this book or your group
Virtually every program concept and skill covered in this book can be twisted into a tool of control.

80. Monopolizing their time
Taking up significantly more than your fair share of the time so the other person does not have adequate time to express themselves.

81. Nagging
Repeatedly bringing up a request even after the other person clearly knows what they need to do.

82. Negating them repeatedly
Intentionally undermining what the other person is saying by disagreeing.

83. Not passing on messages
Intentionally failing to share information intended for the other person.

84. Offering unreasonable choices or alternatives
Making alternative choices so undesirable or unreasonable that the other person has to make the specific choice you want them to.

85. Ordering them around
Telling the other person what to do when they have not acknowledged your authority to do so.

86. Pausing extensively
Intentionally extending the space between sentences to hold the other person's attention in ways that make them uncomfortable.

87. Playing dumb
Pretending you do not know or understand what is going on.

88. Playing mind games
Saying and doing things to make the other person question their perceptions or beliefs.

89. Playing the expert
Presenting yourself as knowing more about something so your opinion is given greater weight.

90. Playing the victim
Misrepresenting yourself as more powerless than you actually are to get the other person to do what you want.

91. Pretending to listen
Hiding your disinterest by making it appear you are listening when you are not.

92. Psyching them out
Intentionally misleading the other person so they question their reality.

93. Pushing their buttons
Trying to provoke the other person to get them to react how you want.

94. Raising your voice
Using the intensity of your voice to instill compliance.

95. Rationalizing
Giving distorted explanations to convince the other person to do what you want.

96. Requiring your approval
Requiring the other person to get your okay on something that is not yours to approve.

97. Requiring your permission
Requiring the other person to ask permission before doing things they should be able to do freely.

98. Responding ambiguously
Intentionally being unclear in your responses.

99. Rewarding them
Giving the other things they desperately need so that they will do what you want even when they do not want to.

100. Sabotaging their belongings
Damaging the car or other items so the other person is not able to use them.

101. Scaring
Making the other person afraid so they will do what you want.

102. Shaming
Intentionally doing something to make the other person feel embarrassed and ashamed.

103. Showing up late on purpose
Intentionally showing up late to further your agenda without the other person's agreement.

104. Speaking for them
Speaking for the other person without their permission when they could speak for themselves.

105. Stalking or following them
Having contact with the other person when they do not want you to, usually at unexpected times and places.

106. Staring
Giving the other person intense looks and stares to make them do what you want.

107. Stonewalling
Repeatedly refusing to discuss a topic the other person wishes to discuss.

108. Taking things away
Confiscating items that you do not have a right to, such as their phone.

109. Taking things out of context
Mischaracterizing information to make the other person do what you want.

110. Talking down to them
Using a demeaning tone that implies the other person is not as intelligent or as knowledgeable as you.

111. Teasing
Making fun of the other person to get them to comply.

112. Telling them how to behave
Telling the other person what to do rather than asking.

113. Telling them what they are thinking or feeling
Imposing your interpretation of the other person's thoughts and feelings regardless of whether they agree.

114. Texting them excessively
Texting the person far more than they wish, typically to get them to respond.

115. Threatening
Stating what you intend to do if the other person behaves a certain way, without any serious or actual intent to respond that way.

116. Trivializing
Minimizing the other person's concerns or needs to avoid having to address or consider them.

117. Using children
This covers a wide range of behaviors that coerce or manipulate the other person through shared children. Examples include encouraging the children to side against the other person, concealing your agenda by saying something is for the children, limiting access to or contact with the children, or leveraging your behavior around the children to get the other to do what you want.

118. Using courts or the legal system
Using legal maneuvers to pressure the other person to do things unrelated to the legal proceedings. Examples include filing legal complaints, suing simply to harass, drawing out proceedings to hurt someone, and tying someone up in court issues to undermine them.

119. Using fear
Making the other person feel afraid in order to get them to comply. Most coercive behaviors do this in some way.

120. Using friends
Using or manipulating people who are friends with you or the other person to push your agenda. For example, mischaracterizing a situation to friends, getting friends to take your side without their full understanding, or mischaracterizing a friend's perspective to the other person.

121. Using guilt
Making the other person feel guilty and using that guilt to manipulate them.

122. Using illness or symptoms
Faking or overstating your physical illness or level of impairment.

123. Using inappropriate humor

This covers several different behaviors, including making jokes at the other person's expense to manipulate or hurt them and masking complaints or concerns as jokes.

124. Using intoxication

Intentionally giving the other person alcohol or other drugs to get them to be more compliant. This includes taking advantage of someone who is intoxicated.

125. Using money

Using money to manipulate or coerce the other person; this relates to financial abuse.

126. Using physical size

Using your physical size to intimidate the other person, such as standing over them.

127. Using privilege

Taking advantage of benefits you have as a member of a privileged group (male, white) to assert your agenda over someone. Any privilege that you have relative to your partner (being documented, being native-born rather than an immigrant, making substantially more money) can be used to control the other person.

128. Using quid pro quo

Doing something for the other person so they will feel obligated to do something in return.

129. Using silence

Refusing to speak, acknowledge, or respond to the other person's inquiry.

130. Walking away

Walking away from the other person in the middle of a conversation without first warning or informing them of this.

131. Whining

Intentionally using an annoying tone to convey your suffering.

132. Withholding belongings

Keeping things from the other person that belong to them to punish them.

133. Withholding information

Keeping information from the other person that they have the right to know.

134. Withholding sex or affection

Refusing to be sexual or affectionate in order to punish the other person or make them behave differently.

The above list is not intended to be complete, but rather to give you an idea of the most common ways of being controlling and just how broad and extensive controlling behaviors can be. Since virtually anything can be twisted into a controlling behavior, there is an almost infinite number of ways to be controlling. What they all have in common is using coercion or manipulation to make someone do something they don't really want to do.

If there are any behaviors on the list that you do not understand, ask your group if you are in one.

CHAPTER 3

SEXUAL ABUSE

When most people think of sexual abuse, they think of violent rape or child molestation, but sexual abuse covers a much larger category of sexually inappropriate behaviors. Although we typically think of strangers as the victims of sexual abuse, a person is in fact most likely to sexually abuse their sexual partner.

Sexual abuse is the category of abusive behavior that most abusive partners deny, even when they have actually demonstrated those behaviors. There are two main reasons for this. The first is the tendency to think of sexual abuse in a very narrow way, focusing on obvious criminal sexual behavior such as physically forceable rape or sex with a minor. In that narrow way, many abusive partners can honestly say they have not committed a sex crime, even though they might have committed other forms of sexual abuse. The second is the intense shame involved in talking about sex and sexual abuse, and the fear of being judged and labeled. Few abusive partners initially admit to sexual abuse, but most have committed it. Just as with every other category, it is important to identify and acknowledge these behaviors so they can be stopped. In its broadest definition, sexual abuse includes any kind of unwanted sexual contact, whether physical, verbal, or psychological.

Examples of sexual abuse
Physically forcing sexual contact
Verbal sexual abuse
Unwanted sexual comments

Sexual pressuring
Badgering someone for sex
Disrespecting sexual boundaries
Retribution for setting a sexual boundary
Sexual contact with an intoxicated person
Sexual contact with an unconscious person
Taking advantage of your power
Infidelity
Using sex to manipulate your partner

FORMS OF SEXUAL ABUSE

PHYSICALLY FORCING SEXUAL CONTACT
This is perhaps the most recognizable and easily understood form of sexual abuse with a sexual partner. The other person's resistance may be physical or verbal, but their boundary must be respected. There are a number of justifications for using physical force, including that your romantic partner "owes" you sex, that once they start the sexual contact they need to see it through to the end, or that "no means yes," but none of these ways of thinking make it okay. For couples that are roleplaying forceful sex (including using BDSM), it is vital to have a way to indicate that they truly want to stop. If that safe word or other indication is not respected, the interaction stops being consensual roleplay and becomes sexual abuse.

VERBAL SEXUAL ABUSE
Another easily recognizable form of sexual abuse is being verbally abusive about the other person's appearance or sexual ability. This kind of verbal abuse tends to hurt even more deeply because it targets someone's sexuality and sexual identity, which are very personal and intimate aspects of their life.

UNWANTED SEXUAL COMMENTS
Sexual behavior involves more than just physical contact or physical behaviors. It includes things you might say as well. Many of these behaviors may be appropriate with a sexual partner, but they are often inappropriate with a nonsexual partner. They are also inappropriate if a

person has previously indicated that they don't like being spoken to that way.

Examples of unwanted sexual comments
Being flirtatious
Commenting on a person's appearance in a sexual way
Making seductive comments or saying things intended to arouse them
Making sexual remarks
Offering sexual compliments
Speculating out loud about their sexual ability
Talking about ways you would like to be sexual with the person

When it comes to sexual comments and conversation, it is important to be as clear as possible about where the line is between acceptable and unacceptable talk. Determining this line is complicated because people can have very different boundaries.

A good place to start is to use your best judgment about what you think people in general would be comfortable with. For example, most people would be uncomfortable having sexual conversations in front of their parents, so you probably should not do that. Next, use your best judgment about what you think your partner in particular would be comfortable with. For example, if you have seen your partner make sexual jokes with some of their close friends, you might presume that it's okay for you to make sexual jokes with them in front of close friends. Inevitably, there will be moments when you think a remark was okay and discover that it was not. You may occasionally inadvertently cross your partner's boundary, but what is key here is that as your partner makes their boundaries clearer, you remember and respect them. Inadvertently hurtful behavior becomes abusive behavior when you keep doing it even after your partner lets you know that it hurts them.

SEXUAL PRESSURING
A wide variety of controlling behaviors can pressure a partner into being sexual when they don't really want to be. If the other person says yes but truly doesn't want to, they are simply giving in against their will. Some of the most common ways to pressure someone into sex don't involve physical force at all, such as guilt, threats, and intimidation. They are all

forms of coercion, which means when they are used to get someone to be sexual, they are all abusive.

BADGERING SOMEONE FOR SEX

There is certainly nothing wrong with being sexually assertive and asking for what you want, but it becomes a problem when you do not accept your partner's refusal or respect the sexual boundary they set. Badgering means continuing to request sexual connection after someone has made it clear that they are not interested. Once their answer is clear, repeated requests become a form of pressure and coercion.

DISRESPECTING SEXUAL BOUNDARIES

Just because someone agrees to be sexual does not mean they are, across the board, agreeing to do everything. Manipulating someone into or making them do specific sexual activities they don't want to do is sexually abusive. It is vital that even after you start having consensual sex with someone, you are mindful of whether they want and are truly willing to engage in the specific sexual interaction you want to pursue. It might be a certain sexual position, sex act, or other sexual behavior, but if they indicate that they do not want to do it, you need to respect that sexual boundary.

RETRIBUTION FOR SETTING A SEXUAL BOUNDARY

If your partner declines your invitation for sexual connection, it is understandable that you might have a variety of emotional responses, like feeling disappointed, sad, frustrated, or lonely. While having these feelings (and any others) is absolutely okay, taking them out on someone because they are not interested is problematic. You do not have to like their response, but you need to respect it. Whining, pouting, sulking, and complaining are all ways of punishing someone for setting a boundary. Doing this is unacceptable because it pressures them to compromise themselves and remove the boundary, which is a form of coercion.

SEXUAL CONTACT WITH AN INTOXICATED PERSON

It is widely known that a person under the influence of alcohol or other drugs has compromised judgment because they are not thinking as clearly as usual. Does that mean that if a person has been drinking or using drugs, they cannot give consent to sexual activity? The answer is complicated. First, it is clear that intentionally trying to get someone intoxicated so they will agree to be sexual is a form of sexual manipulation. The only exception is if a sexual partner freely chooses to drink or use drugs—and is fully aware of what and how much they are consuming—and then freely chooses to be sexual. If that is not their agenda, or if what they ingest is more than they planned or realized, then sexual contact with them is a form of sexual manipulation and qualifies as abuse.

A debatable point is how to know when someone is too intoxicated to freely give consent. That exact line may not always be clear, but if you have any reason to wonder, the respectful and thoughtful choice is to not engage in sexual contact. Any time you take advantage of an intoxicated person, you are being coercive.

SEXUAL CONTACT WITH AN UNCONSCIOUS PERSON

An unconscious person cannot give consent. Therefore, having sex with a sleeping or unconscious person is sexual abuse. The only exception to this is if a sexual partner has made it clear that they are fine with being awoken sexually.

TAKING ADVANTAGE OF YOUR POWER

If you have more power than your sexual partner, that power can be used to get them to be sexual when they don't actually want to be. Doing this on purpose is more obviously abusive than doing it inadvertently, but in both cases, it is abusive. Intentionally using Power Over status to get sex includes threatening to withhold money and threatening to divorce or leave them. While they may give in, their "yes" is not true consent. It is coerced, and comes from a place of fear and intimidation.

It is less obvious that using Power Over status is still abusive when you are not doing it on purpose. Say you are the primary wage earner and your partner isn't capable of self-support at this time. You have made it clear that you need to have sex regularly. Your partner might agree to that, even if they don't want to, out of fear that you could abruptly leave them, which would make them homeless. While you have not directly or intentionally threatened to abandon them, just the possibility that you could is enough to get them to agree to sex even when they don't want to do it.

How can that be addressed if you don't even know it is happening? The solution is simple: make it clear to your partner that you will never use the power you have to punish them for setting sexual boundaries with you. Make it clear that you only want them to be sexual with you if they freely choose to do so, without feeling pressured or coerced.

INFIDELITY

Infidelity, or having affairs, involves having another sexual partner without your current partner's knowledge and consent. This includes "emotional affairs," where there is no direct sexual or physical contact with the other person, but the relationship has a romantic rather than platonic feel to it. An affair is the clearest violation of a sexual agreement, which is discussed later in this chapter. It has been argued that if your partner does not learn of the affair, it's not abusive, because "what they don't know won't hurt them." However, keeping an affair a secret does not make it okay or any less disrespectful. It is still a transgression. If someone spits in your drink and you don't know about it, does that make it any more okay?

USING SEX TO MANIPULATE YOUR PARTNER

Using sex or affection to get what you want and willfully withholding sex or affection to punish someone are two ways of being manipulative and abusive. Rather than using what your partner wants to force them to agree to sex, in these cases you use their desire for sex to force them to do things for you they otherwise might not do. This includes withholding not only sex, but also other forms of affection like hugs, kisses, and touching—not because you are setting a boundary, but because you want to make them suffer or to make them do something.

Each of these can be easily confused with sexually appropriate behavior. Using sex to get what you want can look like simply choosing to be sexual and gaining additional benefits because of that. Likewise, willfully withholding sex can look exactly the same as setting a sexual boundary. So how do they differ? One key difference is whether the behavior has an outward or an inward focus. Outwardly focused behaviors typically try to get another person to behave the way you want them to, which means you are being controlling. Inwardly focused behaviors are typically focused on meeting your needs regardless of how the other person behaves. If you are being sexual simply because you want to be sexual, which is indicative of an inward focus, then you are not being sexually manipulative. On the other hand, if you are being sexual because you want the other person to do something else in return, which indicates an outward focus, then you are being sexually manipulative. Likewise, if you are refusing to be sexual because you do not want to be sexual (inward focus) then you are setting a boundary. If you are refusing to be sexual to make the other person suffer or to punish them (outward focus), then you are being sexually abusive.

VIOLATION OF A SEXUAL AGREEMENT

One of the more common forms of sexual abuse with a sexual partner is the violation of sexual agreements. A romantic relationship is built upon hundreds of agreements between partners—some explicit and others implicit. Some of these are sexual agreements. Examples of common sexual agreements are acceptable ways to initiate sex, acceptable locations and circumstances in which to be sexual, and acceptable ways to touch each other sexually. An agreement is violated when someone intentionally does something they have agreed not to do. One obvious example is having an affair, which violates a sexual agreement not to have other sexual partners.

There are four domains in particular where it is sometimes difficult and awkward to discuss and negotiate sexual agreements: masturbation, the use of pornography or erotica, sexual fantasies, and looking at or interacting with other people sexually. There are several reasons these four areas can be especially difficult to talk about honestly with a sexual partner. First, they all involve sexual behavior beyond the relationship. Two common misconceptions about human sexuality are that partners should meet all of each other's sexual needs and that people have no sexual identity outside of the relationship. Both are wrong. Your partner has no right to demand that you behave in a certain way. They may have opinions and preferences, but your own personal sexual behavior is ultimately yours to manage. The same goes for your partner, as well.

Second, these behaviors can invoke a sense of infidelity or jealousy because your sexual energy is not necessarily focused on your partner as you engage in them. In truth, we all have the freedom and the right to have whatever thoughts we want—including sexual thoughts—and to meet our own sexual needs in whatever way we see fit, provided we are not hurting anyone. Just because someone becomes your sexual partner does not give them the right to control your thinking or your behavior, even in sexual areas.

Third, there is a lot of shame around these behaviors, although that is slowly changing. People rarely acknowledge doing these things, which makes it that much harder to talk about them.

Finally, there is a wide variety of sexual behaviors and opinions about those behaviors. For each one, there are people who have never done them and people who do them routinely. Likewise, people vary in their judgment of each of these behaviors, from seeing them as sick and perverted to incredibly healthy and acceptable, and everything in between. There is a good chance that you and your partner will not be in perfect alignment, and will need to sort out some uncomfortable differences. People can become indignant, and even morally outraged, about what they think is acceptable; this makes it tougher for partners to disclose how they feel and what they do.

Because conversations about these issues can provoke anxiety, it is not unusual for people to avoid talking about them. In that case, the unspoken understanding is that no expectation has been set and no agreement has been made about how each partner is expected to behave.

Where people get into trouble is when they agree, either passively or overtly, to their partner's implied or stated expectation of their behavior even though they don't intend to comply with it. For example, say your partner declares that pornography is gross and unacceptable in a loving relationship, and that they should be enough for you, so there's no need to use porn. You nod your head in agreement, even though you occasionally look at porn and know you probably will in the future. Bringing it up would just lead to a big fight, hurt feelings, and probably no real resolution. Better just to sneak it on the side without them ever knowing, right? The problem is that you have conveyed agreement with your nodding and silence that you do not really feel. You have agreed to something that you do not intend to follow through on, which is deceptive. The moment you look at porn after that, you are in violation of the agreement you appeared to make with your partner, which is disrespectful of them. Instead, you need to be clear and honest with your partner about what you do and do not intend to do. If you do not agree with a sexual agreement they are suggesting, you need to speak up. This does not mean you have to share all of your personal sexual information. You do not even need to disclose whether you engage in that behavior. What you do need to share is whether you are willing to agree to and comply with the sexual agreement—especially if you aren't.

Another reason people make sexual agreements they don't intend to uphold is that they want to avoid talking about or admitting to certain behaviors that they are ashamed of. Shame around sexual behaviors is significant, but as difficult as it may be to talk about them, it is more important not to mislead your partner. You are not required to comply with their wishes or rules about what you do, but you do need to be honest, and not deceptive, with them. Honesty is a core aspect of respect.

You do not need to specifically tell them what you are doing, just that you can't promise to keep the agreement. For example, you are not obligated to tell the other person *who* you might have sexual thoughts about if you tell them you can't promise not to have sexual thoughts about other people. Likewise, even if you tell the other person that you can't promise never to use pornography, you are not obligated to tell them if, when, or what kind of pornography you use. Be aware that your refusal to comply with their wishes or share specifics could lead them to end the relationship. They need to respect your boundaries, but they don't need to like them, nor do they have to remain in the relationship. We will address these kinds of conflicts in more detail in Chapter 24: Practicing Conflict-Resolution Skills.

What if you have agreed to a sexual agreement that you no longer want to keep? It is vital that you inform your partner, preferably before you break the agreement. You do not need to share the particulars of your sexual behavior (e.g., how often you masturbate or what kind of porn you are viewing) if you don't want to, but you need to tell them you are no longer willing to comply with the existing agreement. You do not need your partner's approval or permission to make that change, but you do need to be honest. If you do not inform them of the change, then you are misleading them, which is disrespectful.

SEDUCTION VS. COERCION

In addition to the examples of sexual abuse above, there are other aspects of your sexual relationship that you need to consider to ensure that you are not being sexually abusive toward your partner. It is important to understand that being seductive (which is an acceptable behavior) is different from being coercive. Even if your partner has agreed to being sexual, and even if you're not doing anything inappropriate at the time, their "yes" might still be forced. Seduction typically refers to persuading someone to be sexual when they initially might not have wanted or planned on it. So is seduction a coercive or abusive behavior? It depends.

When done appropriately and respectfully, seduction is not coercive. Respectful seduction involves engaging in a series of behaviors that your partner agrees to at each step along the way. For example, say you ask your partner if they feel like having sex, and they say they're a little on the tired side and not really in the mood. You respect that, but then offer them a shoulder rub, which your partner happily agrees to. While doing that, you start nuzzling your partner's neck in a way you know they like. While doing that, you start breathing into their ear, which starts to arouse them. A few sweet and sexy words from you, and your partner finds themself very much in the mood and not so tired after all, and soon you are fully involved in a sexual encounter. This is the equivalent of sexual influence— you got your partner to freely agree to be sexual, but it required respectful persuasion.

A second example of this is very important to consider, though. Say things start the same way, with your partner not interested in sex, but agreeing to a shoulder rub. But when you start nuzzling your partner's neck, they say, "I told you, I'm not interested in being sexual tonight." With that prompt, you stop the neck nuzzling, but continue the shoulder rub, since that was a genuine gesture that was not solely intended to seduce. You may feel some disappointment, but you're respectful and understanding of your partner's clear boundaries.

In contrast to seduction, coercion would be doing those (or other) behaviors, despite your partner saying no and without them wanting them to. If your partner says no and you then give them a shoulder rub to "warm them up," which they do not really want anyway—in part because they know you expect it to "get them in the mood," and they truly do not want that tonight. They tell you to stop in a clearly annoyed voice and again say that they are not in the mood. Refusing to take no for an answer, you try to nuzzle their neck and say sexy words, and your partner pulls away, even more upset because you do not appear to care at all that they said no, and that you're solely focused on your own needs. This attempted "seduction" leaves your partner feeling even worse than when they first expressed their disinterest, because they have had to repeatedly set and defend their boundaries. It is exhausting, discouraging, and ultimately feels like a violation.

COULD "YES" MEAN "NO"?

In recent years, public awareness of date rape has increased in the US. Campaigns using phrases like "No means no" and "Respect the no" have replaced older ways of thinking, which held that "no" might mean "yes" if someone tried to set a sexual boundary, and that marital rape was not wrong or illegal. Laws and public opinion now reflect the firm belief that saying no and setting sexual boundaries should be respected without question.

Could the opposite be true—that sometimes when your partner says "yes," they might not actually want to, and it's your fault? Yes, that could certainly be true! While it is up to everyone to say what they mean and mean what they say, abused partners have often learned the hard way that if what they say is not what their abusive partner wants to hear, they are going to be abused. Once that becomes a clear and consistent pattern, they might start to avoid saying no, even when their partner isn't threatening them, because the consequences are worse when they do.

Here is a mild example (which is probably far more common than more extreme ones). A person is exhausted as they climb into bed next to their partner. The partner asks them if they can be sexual. The person is not the least bit interested; they are too tired, and they've been feeling distant from their partner anyway. But they imagine what is likely to follow if they say no, based on previous experiences: typically, if they say no, the partner will ask once or twice more, sometimes after a few minutes. After being told no again, the partner will try to nuzzle up and get them "in the mood." They then have to ask them to stop. Then the partner turns away and pouts, muttering to themselves, tossing and turning before resentfully falling asleep. This whole process typically keeps the person up for at least half an hour longer than they wanted and leaves them feeling bad. On the other hand, if they say yes right at the start, they can have sex briefly and quickly, solely focused on meeting their partner's sexual needs. Within ten minutes it is done and they can both go to sleep. It's not that the person hates their partner or never wants to be sexual with them, but they only said yes that night because it would allow them to get to sleep faster and with less hassle than if they said no.

If "no means no" and sometimes even "yes" means "no," how can you ever be sure your partner truly wants to be sexual? It's not as complicated as it might seem. First, you need to be willing to have honest conversations about what they are and are not okay with. It is important for them to be able to express what they think and feel without being made to suffer. Second, you need to respect the limits they set. They need to be able to say no, without invoking consequence or punishment—including the subtler sexually abusive behaviors described earlier in this chapter. Third, if they do say yes, pay attention not only to what they say but to how they say it. This means being honest with yourself about what you see in their facial expressions and body language, even if you do not like it. An engaged and respected sexual partner should enjoy sharing, and be happy to share it. They should be energized and uplifted by the connection. Even if the focus is mainly on you, they are happy and willing, and freely choosing to do that. All that should be evident not only in their words, but their tone of voice, facial expressions, and body language. If you are not sure, directly ask them.

THE CORE PRINCIPLE OF RESPECTFUL BEHAVIOR: ONGOING UNCOERCED
INFORMED CONSENT

In discussions about sexual abuse, group members often ask whether
sexual activities that involve pain, power, and control are automatically
sexually abusive. The key to answering that question is whether there is
ongoing uncoerced informed consent between the people involved. If
there is, even though the sexual behavior may involve or seem to involve
pain, power, and control, it is consensual, and therefore not abusive.

Four conditions need to be present for a behavior to not be abusive or
controlling.

1. **Consent** means that the other person has agreed to the behavior.
They have given their okay for it. They have signed off on it. Ideally, their
consent is explicitly expressed, but there are a number of ways it could be
implicit. It is important that, as far as you can tell, they are giving consent
not only with their words, but with their body language as well. Their facial
expressions and body language should be saying "yes." If you detect
ambiguity or mixed signals (e.g., they say yes, but their voice is subdued
and their face is unexpressive), check it out more directly. Make it clear to
them that it really is okay to say no or deny consent.

2. **Informed:** Consent alone is not enough. It needs to be informed
consent. The person needs to fully understand what they are saying yes to.
If they do not completely understand, then they cannot give true consent.
Many controlling and manipulative behaviors involve keeping someone
ignorant or less than fully informed in order to get their cooperation. The
person may be giving consent, but they do not fully comprehend what they
are consenting to. Uninformed consent is not true consent. For example,
say someone goes on a first date and conceals the fact that they are married.
They have a great date, and it ends in sex. While the other person may have
freely consented to sex, they were led to believe that their date was single.
If they had known they were married, they might never have agreed to
have sex, or even to go on a date. Although they gave consent, it was not
informed consent, so it does not qualify as true consent.

3. **Uncoerced:** Another key aspect of informed consent is that it
needs to be okay and safe to deny consent. What happens if the person says
no? Are they punished? Abused? Otherwise coerced into changing their

answer? A person cannot give consent if they feel like they don't have a choice, or that there will be substantial consequences if they say no. This can be the case even when no direct threat is made. When there is a significant power differential—as when bosses sexually abuse employees, clergy sexually abuse congregants, or celebrities sexually abuse their fans— it can be very difficult for the person being targeted to say no. A boss may get an employee to "agree" to be sexual, but if the employee could lose their job if they say no, they might say yes to avoid that consequence, not because they truly want to be sexual.

4.   **Ongoing:** Even if uncoerced informed consent is given, it can be withdrawn at any time. A person may say yes now, but they can change their mind whenever they want to. For example, your partner may agree to be sexual with you later in the evening, but change their mind after a while because they are feeling quite tired. That is absolutely okay. It is not about breaking a promise, it is about changing their mind, which they have a right to do at any time they want. You do not have to be happy with it, but you need to respect it and not punish them for it.

Ongoing uncoerced informed consent does not just apply to sexual relationships and sexual agreements, but to all relationships and agreements. It is the litmus test that determines whether an agreement is mutual or coerced. It is important to keep in mind not what the agreement is for, but how it was reached. While it may appear controlling on the surface, if it was reached via ongoing uncoerced informed consent, it is a fine agreement. For example, limiting someone's access to a shared bank account is generally considered financial abuse and control. However, if the person who has limited access has fully agreed to this because they can be impulsive with money and prefer not to have the responsibility, and if the agreement could be modified at their request at any time, then it is not financial abuse, because there is ongoing uncoerced informed consent.

SEXUAL ABUSE IN NONSEXUAL RELATIONSHIPS

Much of this chapter has focused on sexual abuse with sexual partners, which is far more common than sexual abuse with strangers or nonsexual partners. However, we want to briefly touch on the most common types of sexual abuse committed against nonsexual partners. This group includes friends, neighbors, coworkers, strangers in public places, passersby, and others with whom you interact. We will elaborate below on some of the most common ways of being sexually inappropriate with nonsexual partners.

CATCALLS AND UNWELCOME COMMENTS ABOUT APPEARANCE

Among the most common ways that people, primarily women, experience sexual abuse from others are unwelcome sexual remarks and comments about their appearance. While this may not seem like a particularly big deal, if it happens to a person repeatedly over time, it can feel increasingly oppressive and demoralizing, as if their only value and relevance is their physical appearance and sexuality. This can be especially discouraging in settings where the focus is supposed to be elsewhere, like in the workplace.

There are certainly times and places that people dress to be noticed and where comments about their appearance are generally welcome, like at a party or a club. But most of the time, in most settings, people are there for other reasons than to simply be looked at. This includes at work and in public, and while shopping or using public transportation, for example. While people's feeling about being complimented by strangers vary a great deal, many people, especially younger women, find it distressing, especially when it happens repeatedly in such situations.

There are several reasons this is so disturbing. One is that when it happens repeatedly, it leads people to feel like their only worth is in their physical appearance. How would you feel if the only thing strangers ever commented on was how much money it looked like you made? After a while you might start to feel that was all that mattered about you.

Second, those comments often have a sexual tinge to them. The same compliment that's welcome from a romantic partner can feel creepy from a stranger. A common defense against this suggestion is that "I was only trying to be nice" and "I was just giving a compliment." What's wrong with that? You need to ask yourself whether you make those comments to people you are not sexually attracted to, maybe a man, if you are a heterosexual man, or an elderly person. Typically, the answer is no.

One comment that may not seem sexual in nature but can be particularly bothersome to women is being told to "smile." While such a comment may seem well-meaning or encouraging, it is problematic for several reasons. First, there is an assumption that the person is unhappy, which may not be the case. Second, even if they are unhappy, telling them to smile is completely dismissive and invalidating of their actual feelings. Third, the request is far more about the observer's desire (*"You look so much prettier when you smile"*) than any genuine concern for the person's emotional state.

EXCESSIVE STARING

It is normal and natural to look at other people, and to find some people more interesting to look at than others. Looking at someone becomes disrespectful when it turns from a look to a stare, or worse, into leering or gawking. A stare is a steady look. If a stare is held long enough, others are likely to become aware of it, which draws more attention to the person being looked at. Gawking and leering are ways of staring that are intended to make someone aware that you're watching them and having some kind of reaction like desire or disgust. The boundary between respectful and disrespectful behavior is when the person being looked at becomes aware that you are looking at them.

UNWANTED FLIRTING

Flirting can be fun, playful, and affectionate, and it does not have to have a sexual element to it. For example, people flirt with babies by playing peekaboo with them. So when does flirting become disrespectful? When it is unwanted or unwelcome. How can you know? First, you need to ask yourself whether it is socially appropriate to flirt in this situation. For example, in a professional relationship, flirting is often inappropriate, and is therefore disrespectful. Second, you need to see to what extent the person is receptive to your flirting. They may indicate this in a variety of ways: with a look, a facial expression, body language, or with clear language asking you to stop. If that is conveyed and their boundary is not respected, flirting becomes abusive.

UNWELCOME SEXUAL JOKES AND COMMENTS

People vary greatly in their level of comfort with talking and joking about sex. While some people find sexual joking fun, others find it uncomfortable and inappropriate, so it's best to err on the side of caution.

You also need to ask yourself whether the situation is appropriate for sexual conversation and whether the people you are talking with are comfortable talking in such ways.

Men in particular have a longstanding history of feeling entitled to make sexual remarks to pretty much anyone they want to—female acquaintances, coworkers, strangers, neighbors, etc. Because sexual remarks are "just words" and are often portrayed as complimentary or playful, it is assumed that they are automatically welcome and okay. Often, however, women simply tolerate, rather than enjoy or welcome, these remarks. At worst, they are significantly traumatized by them.

Here are a few questions to ask yourself to determine whether sexual comments are appropriate for a situation. First, considering what you know about the other person, do you have clear reason to believe they would feel comfortable with a sexual remark? Your default presumption should be that they would not unless you are confident that they would. Second, does the relationship you have with this person allow for sexual banter and comments? In many roles—coworker, salesperson, customer—sexual conversation is not expected and would be inappropriate. Third, is the setting appropriate for sexual comments? Sometimes, even if it would be appropriate to make sexual comments with a particular person, such comments might not be appropriate given the particular setting you are in. The most appropriate time for such comments and conversations would be in social settings like a club or party. Another time would be during a personal conversation.

PROSTITUTES AND SEX WORKERS

Prostitutes are typically thought of as people who are paid to have sexual contact with someone. They are part of a larger group of people described as sex workers, who are paid for sexual interaction. Besides prostitutes, sex workers include strippers, phone sex workers, and people behaving sexually over the internet through paid broadcasts. Sex workers might be compensated with cash, drugs, or services, like lodging. The question of whether using prostitutes and sex workers is a form of sexual abuse is far more complicated than it appears to be. A quick yes or no response fails to consider all the factors that need to be examined.

First, is the person freely choosing to be a sex worker? Many sex workers, particularly those engaging in illegal activity, do not freely choose to engage in this behavior. They are often compelled to engage in sex work by other factors like an active addiction or a sex trafficker. If a person is being coerced into providing sexual services, your use of those services is a form of sexual abuse, even if you are not the one overtly coercing them. You are still taking advantage of that coercion. Likewise, if a person is willing to offer you sexual services in exchange for cash or some other commodity because they have no other means of getting that commodity, your use of those services would be abusive.

Second, people who freely choose to be sex workers still have clear boundaries about what they are willing to do. Any violation of those boundaries (e.g., touching someone's body when you were only supposed to look) is a form of sexual abuse.

Third, even if there is true consent between you and the sex worker and all boundaries are respected, does the contact violate a sexual agreement you have with your partner? If so, it is sexual abuse of your partner, like having an affair would be.

To summarize, if the sex worker is truly freely choosing to engage in that activity, and their boundaries are respected, and contact with them is not a violation of the sexual agreements you have with someone else, then using the services of that sex worker is not a form of sexual abuse. In the real world, rarely are all three of those boxes checked, particularly when the sex worker is doing illegal things. Most of the time, using a sex worker is a form of sexual abuse.

PORNOGRAPHY AND EROTICA

The use of pornography and erotica for sexual arousal is considerably widespread. While it has likely been around since almost the dawn of humanity, never before has it been as pervasive and easily accessible as it is now, thanks to the internet and smartphones. Opinions about it vary greatly, but regardless of your personal beliefs and values, there are several important factors to consider about its use.

The first challenge is to define pornography in the first place. Different people define it different ways. One US Supreme Court justice famously stated that he could not define it, but he knew it when he saw it. In this book we define pornography and erotica quite broadly: any media that is used for the purpose of sexual arousal. This covers photos, stories, movies, drawings, and sound recordings, but can also include material not originally intended for erotic use. For example, if a person has a foot fetish, shoe ads could be erotic to them. Photos of fully clothed women in nonsexual positions could be erotic to somebody for a variety of reasons. We include in this category not just hardcore porn, which features explicit depictions of sexual acts and genitals, but any material that is used in an erotic manner.

Erotica is another name for pornography that has a less negative connotation. Some people differentiate between pornography and erotica, arguing that pornography is somehow unacceptable and erotica is somehow healthier, but we use the terms interchangeably. One person's porn could be another person's erotica and vice versa.

Is the use of pornography or erotica harmful? Personal responses to that question vary greatly. Some people maintain that porn is an inherently negative force that undermines healthy sexuality and relationships. Because it is often associated with masturbation, people who disapprove of masturbation often disapprove of pornography. On the other hand, many others view porn as a positive thing that can even enhance sexual connection. Research into these issues does not offer easy answers. While it is clear that pornography use is harmful to some people, it has not caused problems for many others, and has been shown in some cases to enhance sexual relationships. Ultimately, the value of pornography and erotica is subjective and personal. It is important to honor your own values while respecting the values of those who may have a different perspective.

The big question, though, is what impact porn has on your own life. There are four things to consider here:

1. Whether you are making value-consistent choices
2. What role it plays in your life
3. Whether you are able to control your use
4. Whether you are honoring your sexual agreements

ARE YOUR CHOICES CONSISTENT WITH YOUR VALUES?

To what extent is your use of pornography or erotica consistent with your morals and values? This not only involves whether you feel it is appropriate to use such material at all, but also the types and content of the material as well the frequency and timing of the use of it. To determine this, you need to first consider what your sexual values and morals are.

If you are not sure about your values concerning pornography and erotica use, there are ways to gain greater clarity. One is to engage in conversation about it. This could be with your romantic partner, friends, a therapist, a member of the clergy, or your group. While it may initially be awkward, conversations with others can help you figure out where you stand on things, even if you disagree with what the other person is saying. Using words often makes things clearer.

A second way of gaining clarity is to notice how you feel as you use the material. Your feelings might vary depending on what you use, when you use it, and for what purpose. For example, you may feel comfortable masturbating to a movie scene of two people having loving sex, but feel guilty after masturbating to a scene in which a person is forced to have sex. As a result, you might decide not to masturbate to a scene like that again. Or you might feel content when you look at pornography to give yourself a break, but notice that you feel uneasy when you look at it angrily after your partner declines to be sexual with you. As a result, you might decide that you do not want to look at pornography when you are feeling resentful toward them.

If your behavior and values are in conflict, don't presume that it's the behavior that needs to change. With closer consideration, you may find that you've adopted other people's values, and they don't reflect what you actually believe. For example, there is still a great deal of shame about sex in our culture, and about masturbation in particular, so it might be tempting to presume that the only "right" and appropriate choice is to avoid pornography/erotica. However, if you realize and accept you do like and want to use it, you could find a way to do so appropriately, rather than trying to make yourself behave in a manner that is not right for you. The goal of determining your values is to act with integrity, by being true to your own values and morals in the ways you behave. When the two are in sync, you will find yourself feeling happier and in better alignment.

WHAT ROLE DOES PORNOGRAPHY PLAY IN YOUR LIFE?

If you use pornography or erotica, it is important to look at how you use it and what impact it has on your life. How does it fit into your day-to-day living? Do you see it as having any negative impact on your lifestyle? For example, do you think you spend too much time using it? Do you use it at inappropriate times, like at work, or when children are around? Does it compromise the quality of your sexual relationship with your partner? Just as alcohol can have a positive or negative impact on your life depending on how you are using it, so can pornography.

Another thing to consider is to what extent you are using pornography to artificially alter your mood. Pornography and erotica can change the way you are feeling, through sexual arousal and by distracting you from uncomfortable feelings. Do you ever use it to avoid your feelings? If so, you need to keep an eye on this. This is elaborated on further in Chapter 8: Mood-Altering Substances and Experiences.

IS YOUR USE OF PORN AN ADDICTION?

The concept of addiction is explored in Chapter 8 as well, but for now, the question is whether you are repeatedly unable to appropriately manage and control your pornography or erotica use to the point that it causes problems. If you repeatedly spend too much time on it, if it interferes with your responsibilities, or if it undermines your relationships, it's causing problems. If your pornography use has a compulsive feel to it and you are not able to reliably and appropriately manage and control it, you may have an addiction. If you have an addiction, you may need to stop using pornography or erotica altogether.

ARE YOU HONORING YOUR SEXUAL AGREEMENTS?

Pornography use is problematic if it violates sexual agreements you have with a partner. It is not unusual for someone to promise their romantic partner they won't look at porn and then do it anyway, but because this is a violation of a sexual agreement, it is considered sexual abuse. If you intend to look at porn, it is important that you are honest about it with your partner. You don't necessarily have to tell them whether you actually use it, or how often you use it, but you do need to indicate that you cannot promise not to use it. It is not okay to mislead or lie to your partner about your pornography use. The goal is to make and keep your sexual agreements with your sexual partner related to your pornography use. If you are not able to keep such agreements, then you either need to change the agreement or change the behavior.

CHAPTER 4

FINANCIAL ABUSE

Financial abuse involves mishandling money, finances, or financial agreements. It is most common in abusive relationships between people who share finances or live together. It is often not self-reported because the abusive person has not examined the behavior or considered how it might be abusive and disrespectful. Physical and verbal abuse are pretty obvious, but financial abuse is easier to overlook. For that reason, we want to examine it in detail.

One significant reason financial abuse is not understood very well by abusive partners is that they often wield significant economic power in the relationship. While financial abuse can be present regardless of how much either partner makes, it is typically easier to engage in (and tougher to stop) if you are the primary wage earner. Part of what drives this is a sense that the money you bring into the relationship continues to be "yours," even though you have made financial agreements that it is "ours."

FINANCIAL SELF-RELIANCE VS. FINANCIAL INTERDEPENDENCE

Throughout human history, the driving force for marriage and cohabitation has not been love or romance, but financial survival and well-being. Marriage and cohabitation allow people to pool their resources—financial, material, mental, social, and physical—to accomplish more together than they can apart. In many cultures, this has meant bringing together the resources of the couple's extended families or tribes, as well.

These alliances create webs of interdependence that allow for greater advances than self-reliance does.

When you first meet a romantic interest, the two of you are financially independent of each other. This means that you are each separately and independently responsible for your money: how you generate income, how you manage the money you have, and which financial values drive your decisions. You each get to decide, independent of the other, what to do with your money.

If the romantic involvement gets serious and committed, you become interdependent. This may include deciding to live together and pool your finances. Taking these steps can save money, time (since you don't need to commute between separate homes), energy (if you combine efforts on errands and chores), and more. People who end a committed relationship experience the opposite of this; they have to spend more money and do more work to manage their separate households than they did when they shared one. Breaking up is expensive.

The ways finances are managed and expenses are shared vary a great deal from couple to couple. Some couples use a single bank account for all income. Others maintain separate accounts and contribute to a joint account. Still others develop a mix of separate and shared finances and financial expectations. But in any arrangement, there is potential for abuse when differences are not respected or adequately acknowledged. Rather than doing what is right—having the discussions, disagreements, and negotiations necessary for a truly shared economic partnership—some people choose what is easy: to become economically abusive. There is also potential for abuse when people continue to manage their finances as if they were still single, rather than acknowledging that they are now in partnership and taking into consideration their partner's perspectives and priorities.

If you are not in a relationship where finances and expenses are in some way shared, most of the examples below will not apply to you. We encourage you, though, to consider how you want to behave in the future, as well as how you have behaved in the past.

Because there is limited understanding and awareness of financial abuse, we have provided an extensive list of examples. This category is labeled financial abuse, but many of the examples below include another form of controlling behavior, like micromanaging, or making unilateral decisions.

Examples of financial abuse

Being under-involved in financial decisions
Controlling your partner's use of the car
Denying money for basic needs
Destroying or damaging your partner's property
Dismissing your partner's math or financial-management skills
Dividing the financial responsibility unfairly
Failing to acknowledge the family's needs
Giving your partner an allowance
Imposing your financial values on your partner
Keeping hidden accounts or hiding money
Limiting access to finances
Lying about finances
Making secret purchases
Making unilateral economic decisions
Not honoring your financial obligations
Not paying child or spousal support
Not sharing domestic expenses
Referring to "my" money versus "our" money
Refusing to get a job
Registering assets in one name
Requiring your partner to get a job
Scrutinizing your partner's spending
Setting the financial agenda alone
Spending excessively
Throwing out or giving away your partner's property
Undermining your partner's financial decisions
Undervaluing domestic work
Using higher income as leverage
Whining, complaining, badgering
Withholding financial information

78

Examples of behaviors that interfere with your partner's ability to work outside the home

Being dismissive about your partner's abilities

Harassing your partner about being away from home

Isolating your partner from a support network that could enable them to work

Keeping your partner from getting a job

Restricting your partner's access to transportation

Restricting your partner's educational development

Sabotaging their job or doing things that could get your partner fired

Taking actions to prevent your partner from getting a job

Each of these will be discussed in further detail below.

FORMS OF FINANCIAL ABUSE

BEING UNDER-INVOLVED IN FINANCIAL DECISIONS

While involvement in financial decisions varies from person to person and couple to couple, everyone has equal responsibility. It is fine to let your partner take the lead, but only with their consent. If they want or need your involvement and you refuse, that is a form of being financially abusive. Examples include refusing to decide on a retirement plan and refusing to set or change a budget at your partner's request.

CONTROLLING YOUR PARTNER'S USE OF THE CAR

Except in the case of a clear, mutually agreed exception, each person has the right to access mutually owned items, including vehicles. It does not matter who makes the money or in whose name something is registered; your partner has as much right to use a vehicle as you do. Telling them whether and when they can use it is a violation of those rights.

DENYING MONEY FOR BASIC NEEDS

It is inappropriate to impose your financial values on your partner by defining what is and is not important to spend money on. At times you may disagree about what is and is not essential, especially about items that you yourself never use. You do not get to define someone else's basic needs. This is something that needs to be discussed and mutually agreed upon. Examples include money for beauty products, personal services like haircuts or massages, dietary needs or preferences, and needs for clothing.

DESTROYING OR DAMAGING YOUR PARTNER'S PROPERTY
Engaging in property abuse is also a form of financial abuse if it involves items that belong to your partner. Besides the negative psychological impact of having their belongings damaged or destroyed, there is also the financial hardship of replacing them, if they choose to do so.

DISMISSING YOUR PARTNER'S MATH OR FINANCIAL-MANAGEMENT SKILLS
Being dismissive of your partner's math or financial skills is another way of limiting their financial influence. Sometimes such an evaluation is inaccurate, and they actually have fine skills. But even if they are not as good at math or managing money as you are, their opinions are just as important as yours. Regardless of their skills, their questions, concerns, and opinions should be taken just as seriously and given just as much weight as your own.

DIVIDING THE FINANCIAL RESPONSIBILITY UNFAIRLY
It is not fair to put more financial burden on your partner than they can carry. A common way to share expenses equitably is to have each partner's contribution match the percentage of the household income they generate. Examples of inequitable division of financial responsibility are to evenly split expenses with a partner who only makes a third of the total household income, or expecting your partner to cover all of their and the children's expenses while you cover only your own.

FAILING TO ACKNOWLEDGE THE FAMILY'S NEEDS
This tends to happen when the family's financial need is not one you share. It may not be your need or priority, but that doesn't mean it is not important to other family members. Their financial needs should be given the same weight as yours. A common example of this form of financial abuse is not allowing enough money for clothing or school supplies for children at the start of the school year.

GIVING YOUR PARTNER AN ALLOWANCE

This involves you deciding, alone, how much money your partner can spend on their own. This is actually an example of a unilateral financial decision, but it is so common we list it as a distinct problem. All budgetary decisions need to be mutually agreed to, including how much personal spending money (allowance) each person receives.

IMPOSING YOUR FINANCIAL VALUES ON YOUR PARTNER

A common mistake is to presume that the way you think about things is the only way—or at least, the only right way—to think about things, including finances. In truth, there is no one right way of managing money. A method that might be right for one person could be quite problematic for another. The key point is that no matter how important and strong your views of money and its management are, they are not necessarily right for your partner. Imposing your financial values on your partner means failing to respect their financial values. It is vital that you seriously consider your partner's perspective and negotiate an outcome that is respectful of both partners' perspectives.

For example, people tend to be either spenders or savers. A spender is someone who prioritizes spending money over keeping substantial amounts in reserve. A saver tends to spend less to make sure there is a substantial cash reserve.

Traditionally, savers are considered to be more financially responsible; they choose to save money for retirement, investments, and cash reserves. But this perspective can lead to shortsightedness about long-term financial success. The cheapest brand may save money in the short run, but be of lower quality and at greater risk of breaking down or needing replacement. Spending more money on the front end may actually save money on the back end when it comes to investing in appliances or vehicles. In addition, savers may trade the benefits of higher-quality items or a nice vacation for savings they ultimately never use.

Spenders, on the other hand, may have to scramble to make a payment. They may end up borrowing money from a bank or by using a credit card, which means paying for the item as well as the interest on the loan. They may also have greater stress about unexpected expenses or how to retire with the lifestyle they prefer.

The point here is not which perspective is better, but how to be respectful of a partner who has different financial priorities than you without dismissing or devaluing them as irresponsible or careless or stupid. The core issue is that as right as your values are for you, they are not necessarily shared by your partner, nor are they necessarily right for your partner. The trick is to find a way to uphold your financial values while respecting your partner's. Working through these differences is covered in detail in Chapter 24: Practicing Conflict-Resolution Skills.

KEEPING HIDDEN ACCOUNTS OR HIDING MONEY
People have a right to know where their money is and how much they have. They should know about all the accounts that hold shared money, and know about any significant shuffling of money from one account to another. Opening a new account or using a new line of credit without informing your partner is a violation of this rule, and therefore financially abusive.

LIMITING ACCESS TO FINANCES
When a couple shares or pools their money, both people should be able to freely access it. Limiting your partner's access to the money—or information about it—is a violation of their rights. Examples include refusing to share login information for a shared credit card or bank account, refusing to share the PIN for an ATM card, and not allowing your partner to have a debit card.

LYING ABOUT FINANCES
Lying about finances refers to being intentionally deceitful with your partner about money. It includes lies of omission, in which you do not correct their mistaken understandings. Examples include saying you have paid a bill when you have not, lying about how much money is in a particular account, or not telling the truth about how much money you have been spending lately.

MAKING SECRET PURCHASES
Although it is not necessary to disclose to your partner every single thing you buy, like a pack of gum or cup of coffee, making secret purchases is

different. Secret purchases refer to items you have previously agreed not to buy, like cigarettes or lottery tickets, or expenditures above a certain amount without your partner's knowledge. The dollar amount varies from couple to couple; in one home, it might be $20, and in another, over $100. There might be exceptions to this rule for birthday or holiday presents, but even then, there is often an understanding about whether the partner needs to be consulted with, particularly if the purchase exceeds a certain amount.

MAKING UNILATERAL ECONOMIC DECISIONS

Sharing a household is not simply about sharing resources, but also sharing the decision-making. It is okay for one person to make a decision alone if the other person fully supports it. However, when a decision is made without the other person's approval and support, it is financially abusive. Examples include borrowing money, buying a car, using a line of credit, and making investment decisions without your partner's consent.

NOT HONORING YOUR FINANCIAL OBLIGATIONS

When a couple maintains separate checking accounts, it's common for them to each take care of certain bills or expenses. That agreement is honored when each person consistently fulfills those obligations. If financial problems prevent you from meeting those obligations, the respectful thing to do is inform your partner and do everything you reasonably can to meet those obligations, including adequately prioritizing them. This form of financial abuse tends to show up after a couple has separated but before they renegotiate a new financial agreement. While it can be tempting to stop fulfilling your financial obligations after you break up, you are still expected to do so until you have made a new agreement or have given adequate warning that you will stop. Examples include not paying spousal support or child support (or paying it late) and letting medical, dental, or car insurance lapse for your ex-partner or the children.

NOT PAYING CHILD OR SPOUSAL SUPPORT

Throughout world history, a driving force of marriage and romantic partnerships has been to enjoy the economic benefits of pooling resources—not only assets, but also labor. One common approach is for the person capable of generating the most income to work outside the home while the other spends more time and energy on childcare and domestic responsibilities like cooking, cleaning, laundry, and running errands. Because domestic work and childcare tend to be uncompensated and do not generate revenue, it is easy to undervalue and underappreciate them. But part of what allows one person to develop their career is having another person take care of aspects of day-to-day living like domestic work and childcare. Without a partner at home to do those things, they would have less time, energy, and money to pursue a career—and other things they enjoy doing.

Spousal support is intended to provide fair compensation to the person who opted to prioritize domestic responsibilities over professional advancement. Think of the person with the career as the goose that lays the golden eggs. Both partners have helped raise the goose, but when the partner with the career leaves, they get to keep the goose for themselves. It is only fair that if one gets to keep the goose, the other gets to have more of the golden eggs, especially early on in the separation.

Typically, the person who has the children less should pay some level of child support to offset the extra money, time, and energy the primary caregiver is spending. Failing to maintain these financial obligations is most certainly a form of financial abuse. Child and spousal support are financial obligations, like any other bill, and refusing to or intentionally failing to make those payments is a violation of the other person.

NOT SHARING DOMESTIC EXPENSES

If you are not the primary childcare provider or the one primarily responsible for maintaining the home, it can be easy to underestimate daily household expenses. Even if your partner is the one doing this work and making these purchases, they are still your shared financial responsibility.

REFERRING TO "MY" MONEY INSTEAD OF "OUR" MONEY

Once you and your partner agree to a shared financial arrangement, when a paycheck comes in your name, it technically belongs to both of you. You are expected, in good faith, to honor that agreement. Part of that is acknowledging the joint ownership of the income by describing it as "our" money, not just yours.

REFUSING TO GET A JOB

Intentionally choosing not to work or try to find work and instead living off the family income against your partner's wishes is abusive. You have the freedom to choose which job you take, but refusing to work at all is abusive if the arrangement is not mutually agreed upon. This form of financial abuse tends to lead to others, such as financial exploitation.

REGISTERING ASSETS IN ONE NAME

Once you and your partner make the economic shift from separate to shared finances, it is typically appropriate to register shared property such as a car or a house in both names. Occasionally, for various reasons, you may agree to keep something in only one name, but this is only okay if you both genuinely agree to it. Otherwise, all substantial items should be registered in both names.

REQUIRING YOUR PARTNER TO GET A JOB

Since financial decisions need to be mutual, you cannot insist that your partner has to get a job. It may be your preference, and you can advocate for your perspective, but requiring it makes you controlling. If you believe it is absolutely necessary for your partner to work and they refuse to, you can set appropriate limits, such as potentially ending the relationship.

SCRUTINIZING YOUR PARTNER'S SPENDING

Everyone has a right to decide how they spend their money. In a relationship, this can include setting a budget together to agree how much money to spend in designated areas. However, within those general areas, each person has the right to freely choose how they spend money. It is not okay to make them account for every penny, or to make them explain why they chose one brand over another or went to this store rather than that store. This is micromanaging applied to money, and it is financially abusive.

SETTING THE FINANCIAL AGENDA ALONE

While you certainly have a right to assert your financial priorities, you cannot unilaterally set those priorities for your partnership. Even if you can come up with a variety of reasons that you and you alone should be in charge of the money—perhaps you are the primary wage earner, or you handle money better—none are legitimate reasons for setting the economic agenda alone. Unilaterally deciding how much to set aside for retirement and ignoring your partner's requests to spend more or less on a certain budget item are examples of this type of financial abuse. Only when money is truly yours alone, and your partner agrees, as in the case of a gift card from a friend, can you make decisions independent of your partner.

SPENDING EXCESSIVELY
Spending way more than your partner would expect you to or would approve of is a violation of financial agreements—whether they are explicit or implicit.

THROWING OUT OR GIVING AWAY YOUR PARTNER'S PROPERTY
You have no right to discard or give away items that belong to your partner without their permission. Doing so is a form of financial abuse because it creates a financial burden on your partner to replace those items. You are welcome to share concerns, make requests, and negotiate agreements around their belongings, but you do not have a right to handle them, give them away, or throw them out without your partner's permission.

UNDERMINING YOUR PARTNER'S FINANCIAL DECISIONS
If you don't agree with a financial decision your partner has made, you need to talk with them and negotiate a new mutual agreement. Until then, respect your partner by not going against their decision. For example, do not give the children extra money if your partner has said no, even if you disagree. Do not cancel or return goods or services they purchased. Do not take money they set aside for one item and spend it on something else.

UNDERVALUING DOMESTIC WORK
It is easy to value paid labor above domestic labor because it generates income, but domestic work also has significant value. If you lived alone, who would do all the domestic work? If you have kids, who would take care of them? You could do it yourself, but what is your time worth? You could pay a housekeeper or a cook, or just not clean or cook at all, although

eventually you'll need clean clothes and food to eat. Having a partner who does the housework means you don't have to, and that you don't have to pay someone else to do it. A fairer way of thinking of it is not in terms of how much income each partner generates, but rather how many hours of work each partner does, whether in or outside of the home.

USING HIGHER INCOME AS LEVERAGE

It can be easy to fall into thinking that the person who contributes more money to the shared household is more important. This is especially common in families where the head of the household is automatically assumed to be the person generating more of the income. But making more money than your partner does not make your opinions and perspectives more important than theirs. The fact that the checks technically come in your name does not give you the right to threaten to withhold that money to get your way. Examples of this form of financial abuse include saying things like "I'm the one who keeps the lights on around here," threatening to leave or quit your job, or threatening not to deposit your check into the account.

WHINING, COMPLAINING, BADGERING

Any time you use controlling behaviors to satisfy your own financial interests or desires, you are being economically abusive. The appropriate way to advocate for yourself is to be assertive, problem-solve, and negotiate—all of which are covered in Chapter 24: Practicing Conflict-Resolution Skills. Although controlling behaviors may get you what you want, they do so at the expense of your partner, who has not freely given their consent or supported your decision.

WITHHOLDING FINANCIAL INFORMATION

Your partner has as much right to the family's financial information as you do. Not sharing what they might want to know is a violation of their right to know the state of the finances. Your partner must not only give consent to financial decisions, but give informed consent. In other words, it is important that they have a full understanding of any relevant information before making a decision.

Examples of withholding financial information includes not telling them about your unexpected bonus, not informing them that the heating bill is going way up or way down, and not providing updates on the general state of the finances.

IMPOSING FINANCIAL DEPENDENCE

Limiting your partner's ability to be economically independent and self-reliant typically leaves them more dependent on you, which can make it easier for you to be abusive and controlling. If you truly love and care for your partner, part of that is supporting them in achieving the level of professional success that they aspire to. The behaviors listed below are all types of financial abuse that limit their professional development.

BEING DISMISSIVE ABOUT YOUR PARTNER'S WORK

Regardless of your opinion about your partner's ability to get a job, or a particular job, you should only share those opinions if your partner will find them helpful. Put-downs and other derogatory remarks can be discouraging and demoralizing, and can interfere with their ability to get the job that they want. A loving partner will do their best to be supportive even if they have concerns about a partner's ability for a particular kind of job.

HARASSING YOUR PARTNER ABOUT BEING AWAY FROM HOME

You are welcome to communicate your objections and concerns about how available your partner is at home or for the children, but once you have shared them, repeatedly continuing to do so becomes harassment. Examples include badgering, verbal harassment, and inflicting guilt trips.

ISOLATING YOUR PARTNER FROM A SUPPORT NETWORK THAT COULD ENABLE THEM TO WORK

People often find jobs by talking with others and making connections with them. If you interfere with your partner's social connections, you may be interfering with their ability to find a job or advance their career. Examples include preventing them from going to work events, not letting them network with others in person or via social media, and not allowing them to do informational interviews.

KEEPING YOUR PARTNER FROM GETTING A JOB

The right to work to generate income is a basic human right. You may not approve of your partner working out of the home or doing the particular work they prefer, but you do not have the right to prevent them from pursuing that work. You can share your concerns, but ultimately it is their choice whether they work outside of the home and what particular work they do.

RESTRICTING YOUR PARTNER'S ACCESS TO TRANSPORTATION

Just as you may need a vehicle to get to work or money to pay for public transportation, so does your partner. Blocking their access to transportation to or from work undermines their attempts at success and is therefore financially abusive.

RESTRICTING YOUR PARTNER'S EDUCATIONAL DEVELOPMENT

Your partner has the right to pursue the level of education that they wish. Restricting their access to education might include preventing them from applying to a program, not being financially supportive of their educational aspirations, not providing emotional support, and not providing logistical support like helping offset domestic and family demands that are difficult for them to meet while in school.

SABOTAGING YOUR PARTNER'S JOB OR DOING THINGS THAT COULD GET THEM FIRED

Harassing your partner via phone or text while they are trying to work, showing up and being disruptive, and making false reports about them are all examples of attempts to alienate them from their workplace and coworkers.

TAKING ACTIONS TO PREVENT YOUR PARTNER FROM GETTING A JOB

Anything you intentionally do to try to prevent your partner from getting a job is considered financial abuse. Examples include hiding important documents like social security cards, failing to pass on messages from a potential employer, and interfering with their ability to attend an interview.

***

The above is not a complete list of all the types of financial abuse, but it does cover many of the most common ones. If you do not understand or do not agree with some of the examples above, we encourage you to ask about them in your group, if you are attending one.

PART TWO

THE CAUSES OF ONGOING ABUSIVE AND CONTROLLING BEHAVIOR

CHAPTER 5

ABUSIVE THOUGHTS AND BELIEFS

It is easy to think that events lead to emotional reactions. When you get behind a slow driver in the fast lane on a highway, you feel angry. When your partner doesn't greet you when you get home because they are on the phone with a friend, you feel offended.

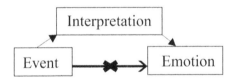

But it's not actually the event that leads to the emotional reaction. It is your *interpretation* of the event that leads to the emotional reaction.

Consider the example of getting behind a slow driver in the fast lane. Here's one way you can think about it: "What an idiot. Get moving or get out of the way! I'm *never* going to get there." And you'd quickly become angry and agitated. On the other hand, if you thought things like, "It's not personal. I'll get around them eventually. It's not that big a deal, it's just slowing me down a little," you'd feel only slightly annoyed. The exact same situation can lead to a quite different reaction, depending on how you interpret it.

In the second example, where your partner doesn't greet you because they are on the phone, you could think, "They care about their friend more than me. They just take me for granted. Well, hello to you, too," and feel offended and put off. On the other hand, if you thought things like, "It's not personal. They'd say hello if they weren't talking on the phone. Their friend means a lot to them, but I know I mean a lot to them, too," you would feel happy to be home and to see them, even if they are not able to immediately greet you.

YOUR SELF-TALK EITHER PROMOTES OR DISCOURAGES ABUSE

How you think about and interpret the things that happen in your life has a huge impact on how you feel about those things. As the maxim goes, we don't see the world as it is, but as we are.

Those thoughts and interpretations run through our minds in an ongoing internal conversation called **self-talk**. Self-talk is not just what you think about yourself, but what you think or say *to* yourself about anything and anyone.

Self-talk comes in two varieties: negative and positive. Negative self-talk tends to escalate intensity and positive self-talk tends to lower intensity. Negative self-talk is like throwing gasoline on a fire—it makes it worse. Positive self-talk is like throwing water on a fire. It may not put it out, but it contains it. Even more importantly, though, negative self-talk is inaccurate and involves distorted perceptions, whereas positive self-talk is more accurate, and truer to what is really going on.

NEGATIVE SELF-TALK REFLECTS DISTORTED THINKING

Negative self-talk distorts situations in three basic ways: through exaggerations, assumptions, and unrealistic expectations. We will elaborate on each of these below.

EXAGGERATION DISTORTS THE TRUTH

Negative self-talk tends to overstate what is going on. Words like *always*, *never*, and *everyone* are commonly involved—*"they're always late," "they never help out," "everyone is against me."* It takes a complex situation and makes it a simpler and less accurate black-and-white situation. It turns molehills into mountains, like seeing someone who is only late about half the time as someone who is always late, or someone who sometimes helps

out as someone who never helps out. It interprets a few]
as everyone criticizing them. It amplifies an accurate per:
more negative one that is no longer true.

Life is hard enough already. Why make it worse b)
worse than they are? Positive self-talk still acknowledges the bad, but keeps
to what is true, rather than adding to the misery.

ASSUMPTIONS LEAD YOU TO THE WRONG CONCLUSIONS

The second way negative self-talk distorts situations is by working with
false assumptions. With limited information, it jumps to the worst
conclusions and assumes the worst motives.

If your friend was supposed to meet you fifteen minutes ago to see a
movie, negative self-talk might assume they have a low opinion of you, or
they don't like your company, or that they're a selfish asshole. So you
become increasingly upset, then agitated, then angry. But the only cause of
your anger is your imagination and self-talk. The only cause of your anger
is that you waited fifteen minutes.

Positive self-talk, on the other hand, is like a good attorney or detective:
it keeps to what is known and doesn't jump to conclusions. Positive self-
talk uses all the available evidence to support a conclusion. It remains open
to alternative explanations. Positive self-talk would acknowledge that one
of many possible explanations for your friend's tardiness could be that they
don't care about you or want to spend time with you. But it also identifies
other possibilities—car problems, needing to get gas, unusually bad traffic,
miscommunication about the time, forgetfulness, or some sort of
emergency. Since these are all viable explanations, none can be ruled out
until more information is gathered. With that positive attitude, there is still
some agitation, but a stronger emotional reaction can wait. When your
friend shows up and you find out why they were late, whatever emotional
reaction you have will be based on what you learn, rather than on what you
speculated.

UNREALISTIC EXPECTATIONS LEAD TO DISAPPOINTMENT

Negative self-talk is also inaccurate when it involves unrealistic
expectations. Expectations tend to operate in the background of your
awareness; they are automatic and a product of your worldview.

realistic expectations do not accurately reflect the real world, but they feel believable. Because they do not correspond with reality, they lead to disappointment, frustration, and aggravation.

You might unrealistically assume that everyone will be a good driver and that you won't encounter construction or accidents, but when you say it out loud, the absurdity is obvious. Of course there are bad drivers. Of course there will be accidents and construction. Your unrealistic expectations are revealed when you encounter those situations and become agitated by them.

Positive self-talk, on the other hand, strives for realistic expectations that reflect the way the world actually works. It is reasonable to expect that some people will not be good drivers and that accidents and construction will occasionally slow down your drive. For people who accept life's imperfections, frustrations are much more manageable.

You can think of negative self-talk as the devil on your shoulder— egging you on, getting you all worked up, and encouraging you to see the worst in people. Positive self-talk, on the other hand, is like the angel on your other shoulder. It offers encouragement, perspective, a calming voice, and a more positive but still realistic perspective.

Because negative self-talk escalates and distorts the world, it increases your likelihood of being abusive and controlling. On the other hand, positive self-talk, because it is calming and seeks perspective, tends to decrease your likelihood of being abusive and controlling.

Research has shown that people who are prone to anger and abuse tend to see the world and people in a more distorted and negative manner, which significantly contributes to their anger and abuse. In other words, a significant contributor to your anger and abuse is not what happens to you, but how you think about what is happening to you. Therefore, a key aspect of becoming nonabusive is not necessarily changing what is happening to you or how others behave, but changing how you think about those things. How to change those thoughts will be discussed in Chapter 15: Becoming Aware of Your Thoughts, but the first step is realizing the role your thinking plays and to start noticing the role your thoughts play in your responses.

YOUR BELIEFS EITHER PERMIT OR PROHIBIT ABUSE

While your self-talk plays a significant role in ho\
behave in the world, your *beliefs* are even more funda
determine the core ways you interpret the world. Wh
to your thoughts in the moment about each moment,
you view the world in general. Beliefs are often unconscious; you may
rarely consciously consider them, but they are always there. Your self-talk
emerges from your beliefs like a plant emerges from its roots—it depends
on your beliefs like the plant depends on its roots for survival.

Your beliefs influence your self-talk. If you have a belief that most
people are good, your self-talk is likely to give other people the benefit of
the doubt. *"They didn't do that on purpose," "they probably don't realize
how difficult that makes it for me."* On the other hand, if you have a belief
that most people cannot be trusted, you are more likely to have self-talk
that is much more critical of others. *"They don't care about me," "they are
just trying to get everything they can, regardless of how much it hurts me."*

If you want to change how you experience the world, it is not enough
to change your self-talk in the moment. You need to change your
underlying beliefs, which form the roots of your thoughts and your
behaviors. Because they are less conscious and not always explicitly
identified, they can be more challenging to identify and change. But if you
don't change them, the changes you make to your self-talk and behaviors
will be superficial and temporary, like plucking a dandelion out of the
ground. It may appear to be gone, but if the roots remain, more dandelions
will appear. Until you change your underlying beliefs, you will not
experience true change.

Think of a house with smoke pouring out of the chimney. The smoke,
which stands out and is easy to see from a distance, represents your most
overt and extreme abuse. But the house was constructed with wood, bricks,
and drywall. Those materials, which the house is primarily built of,
represent your verbally abusive, emotionally abusive, and controlling
behaviors. The foundation of the house, which is the least visible part,
represents the belief systems that govern your behavior. If you focus only
on changing your behaviors, and ignore your beliefs, it's like building a

house on an old foundation: any cracks and leaks will compromise the integrity of the house that's built upon it.

COMMON EXCUSES FOR BEING ABUSIVE

It is important to acknowledge that people make the choice to give themselves permission to be abusive. It may be a split-second decision, but it is still a choice. In other words, when you are abusive, you are giving yourself permission to be abusive. When you are not abusive, that too is a choice: you are not giving yourself permission to be abusive in those moments.

There is plenty of evidence that you are in control of your abusive behavior. You choose when, where, and with whom to behave abusively. Many abusive people are only abusive to their immediate family members, such as their partner and their children. Others will not give themselves permission to be abusive to their children—at least not directly, since any abuse of one parent is indirectly hurtful to the children. Most people are almost never abusive to anyone outside their family. And most abusive behavior is displayed in private, where it cannot be viewed by others. No matter how upset an abusive person might be at their partner in public, most will wait to behave abusively until they are out of the public eye.

Whether you are fully aware of it or not, you decide what abusive behaviors are acceptable. You decide that saying "That was really stupid" is okay, but calling someone a "fucking cunt" is not. You decide that it's okay to engage in abusive behaviors in some settings and not others—at a family gathering, but not at a school event. You decide it's okay to be abusive toward some people and not others—you might tell your partner "that was really stupid," but would never say it to a sales clerk. You give yourself permission for some behaviors toward some people in some settings.

You also give yourself permission to decide which abusive behaviors are okay and which are not. Even if you feel justified in being abusive, you still limit yourself to "acceptable" vs. "unacceptable" ways of being abusive—as defined by you. What is on each list will vary from person to person. For example, a lot of physically abusive people give themselves permission to push, grab, and block people's ways, but not to use a knife or a gun. A verbally abusive person may give themselves permission to call someone all kinds of hurtful names, but may never use certain words, such as "cunt," that they consider unacceptable. The point is that people who are abusive typically do not give themselves permission to be abusive in every way. They have two lists: the abusive and controlling behaviors that are acceptable, and which they may occasionally demonstrate, and those that are unacceptable, which they virtually never exhibit. You might want to make lists of the specific abusive behaviors you think or thought were okay, and behaviors you would probably never do, no matter what. The goal, of course, is to make your list of "acceptable" abusive behaviors as short as possible.

This is a key point: when you are abusive, you typically feel justified. At least in the moment, if not in the moments after. This is why you do it, why you give yourself permission to do it in that moment. You have a reason. To stop being abusive means to remove the justifications that let you give yourself permission. If behaving abusively means giving yourself permission to be abusive, that raises the question of when you think abusive behavior is justified.

So when is it okay to be abusive? One difference between you and people who do not have patterns of abuse is that for people who are not abusive, there is basically never a time when it is okay to be abusive. On the other hand, you likely have a variety of reasons and excuses ready to justify your abuse. In fact, if you feel it is justified, you may no longer even consider it to be abuse. While we cannot list all the possible reasons you give yourself permission to be abusive and controlling, here are some of the most common ones.

"I HAD NO CHOICE."

This is a very common way for people who are abusive and controlling to think. This means you believed that in that particular situation, you had to be abusive because there were no other options. It is true that, in the moment, responding with abuse and control can be a tempting choice because it can be faster and easier than other options. And if that response is all you've ever done in that particular situation in the past, you may not have ever thought of alternatives.

"It was automatic."

Saying that your abusive response was automatic implies that you are somehow hardwired to be abusive—that it is as reflexive as kicking out your foot when the doctor taps your knee. Someone pushed you, so you "reflexively" pushed them back. They yelled at you, so you "automatically" yelled back.

"They started it."

The "eye for an eye" mentality is extremely common, even among people who are rarely abusive. The idea is that if the target of your abuse was abusive first, or was disrespectful, or otherwise behaved badly, it is okay to be abusive "back" to them. It's also common to think that as long as your abusive response is not as bad as theirs, then yours is okay. Retaliation, revenge, and justice are other rationalizations.

This way of thinking is so common and normal that it shows up in laws and movies: in a physical altercation between two people, the instigator is considered guilty, not the responder. If the person who was abusive had good reason—to respond to aggression—their abuse is justified. We see this in the movies all the time: good guys and bad guys, heroes and villains. Bad guys and villains use violence for no good reason. Good guys and heroes use violence because they have to.

People prone to being abusive can be very quick to perceive disrespect and abuse from others, especially those they are closest to. Showing up late, not doing homework, not doing chores, talking too long on the phone, and countless other behaviors are coded in their minds as disrespectful. Once someone becomes "disrespectful," abusive behavior is justified to address that "disrespect."

"It was in self-defense."

This rationale is rooted in the conviction that the target behaved abusively first, but here the justification is that it was necessary to stop someone or to keep someone safe. Of all the reasons given for engaging in abusive behavior, this is potentially—occasionally—the most legitimate. But even in situations where you are defending yourself, there are usually viable alternatives that are not abusive. If you are honest with yourself, self-defense is often less about defending yourself than defending your pride and honor. If someone attacks you, the way to get secure your safety is typically to flee. But because fleeing looks cowardly and is "unmanly" (for male-identified folk), the expectation is often to either ignore the threat or to respond in kind. If you are truly threatened, you should exert the least possible effort to defend yourself. Virtually all other animals—including the most fierce—simply flee, unless they are truly cornered or have to protect their young. If you stick around to make a point, to reestablish your honor, or to avoid being seen as a coward, you're not defending yourself for safety. "I had to defend my pride" sounds a whole lot less compelling than "I had to defend myself."

"IT'S FOR A GOOD REASON."
When people believe the end justifies the means, they think their abusive and controlling behavior is okay because it leads to a desirable outcome. This is a very common way of thinking, even among people who are not abusive: a good or positive outcome nullifies whatever harm was caused along the way.

"IT'S TO GET THEM TO DO IT RIGHT."
Employing abusive or controlling behavior to get someone to do things your way assumes that because the outcome will be better, the abuse is okay. It's intended to teach them and help them understand.

"I KNOW BEST—IT'S FOR THEIR OWN GOOD."
The thinking here is that because you're helping someone, your abusive or controlling behavior is justified. A classic example is intervening forcefully when someone has a substance abuse problem by discarding their alcohol or drugs. Some people describe this as "tough love"—the person may suffer, but the intention is to help them.

"IT'S NO BIG DEAL."
This emphasizes that because the abusive behavior was not particularly significant or damaging, it's okay. The expressions "no blood, no foul" and "what they don't know won't hurt them" are both indications that this type of thinking is in play.

"IT'S NOT REALLY ABUSIVE."

The thinking here is that if you have a good reason for doing something that might otherwise be considered abusive, your behavior is not abusive. This is sometimes called "justifiable abuse." However, there is no such thing as justified abuse. If an action is justified, it is not abusive.

Shooting someone is abusive—unless it is justified, and then it is not abusive. Calling someone a negative name is abusive—unless the name accurately describes them, in which case it's not. Labeling someone's behavior negatively is abusive—unless the label accurately describes the behavior, in which case it's not. For example, if you think someone is acting stupid, then saying "You're acting stupid" is not abusive; it's simply descriptive. People who are abusive often have all sorts of justifications for their abuse that allow them to believe it is not abusive—even though it is.

In Chapter 15: Becoming Aware of Your Thoughts, we will identify counterpoints to these ways of thinking that will make it easier for you to refuse to give yourself permission to be abusive and controlling.

THE POWER OVER MINDSET

One of the most common beliefs—or really, system of beliefs—that supports abuse and control is Power Over, a concept that is defined brilliantly by Patricia Evans in her book *The Verbally Abusive Relationship*.

A ONE-UP/ONE-DOWN VIEW OF RELATIONSHIPS

Power Over is a hierarchical, one-up/one-down mindset in which one person is considered on top and the other person on the bottom. From this perspective, you are either right *or* wrong, you either win *or* lose, you either get your way *or* the other person does. There's only one right way, one winner, one person who gets what they want. Others—especially others who are close to you, like your romantic partner or your kids—are presumed to be against you or are seen as competitors for limited resources like truth, time, and attention. Relationships are seen as ongoing power struggles for who will get their way, be proven right, or emerge victorious.

With a Power Over perspective, there is an assumption of **scarcity**: there can only be one right answer, one winner, and only one person can get their way. Power and good things are seen as hard to get and hard to keep, and there is not enough of anything for both of you, so only one of you will ultimately get what you want. Because of this external focus, the other person's choices are presumed to directly affect your options. This leads to a belief that taking care of yourself requires you to control other people. If the two of you disagree, part of proving yourself right is proving them wrong. (*"The way you drive to the store is not as good as how I do because it takes longer."*) If you're in competition, part of winning is getting them to lose. If the two of you want different things and you assume that only one of you can get your needs met, part of getting what you want is stopping them from getting what they want. (*We only have time to go to the mall or to the beach, so I have to convince you not to go to the mall.*) It's like being on a seesaw: for one side to go up, the other side has to go down.

This external focus also makes people quick to blame others for their suffering and struggles. Since you cannot always control what others do, you might feel powerless and victimized. This can bring on anger, because anger is often another feeling plus blame. (This will be explained in greater detail in Chapter 16: Becoming Aware of Your Emotions.) People who are abusive and controlling often have more anger than others, which is attributed to an "anger problem." The anger is not the cause of the abuse and control, though; it is a symptom of a Power Over mindset.

Another aspect of the Power Over worldview is the belief that there are right answers, wrong answers, and Truths with a capital T. It is only natural to want to get others to see those Truths, especially people you care about, so disagreements can get intense. With a Power Over mindset, there is little tolerance for people having different perspectives, agendas, or approaches, because these differences are "wrong" and they challenge what you know to be true. These differences need to be eliminated and dismissed for your Truth to prevail.

BELIEVING YOU'RE IN THE ONE-DOWN SPOT PERMITS ABUSE, TOO

You might think that everyone who has a Power Over mindset sees themselves in the one-up position, but many people in Power Over feel like they're in the one-down position. If you have this mindset, you may feel like others, especially your partner or children, often attack, criticize, or take advantage of you. You might feel like they are getting their way at your expense. If you think this way, you may see much of your own abusive and controlling behavior as self-defense: you are defending yourself against the perceived attacks, power plays, and transgressions of your partner.

Another reason you might feel like you are in the one-down spot is that you intentionally put yourself there intending to be nice or kind. For example, you might "go along to get along"—stop arguing and just go along with your partner even if you think they are wrong. You might intentionally lose so your partner can win. You might give in to what your partner wants, and give up what you want in the process—a kind of self-sacrifice. But although doing these things might seem nice in the moment, they are not sustainable. Typically, one of two things happens. Either you can only, or will only, do this briefly before going back to the one-up position—*"We did what you wanted yesterday, so today we're doing what I want"*—or you become increasingly resentful and bitter because it feels like your partner is taking advantage of you.

In the one-down spot, it's easy to feel like a victim and blame others for causing your pain and suffering. You may be quick to presume that any hurt done to you was done willfully, spitefully, and on purpose. It's easy to feel powerless if your suffering seems to be caused solely by the actions of your partner or child. It's easy to become passive and do little to improve your life because you think others must change for you to be happier. After all, if others caused the problem, it's up to them to correct it, right? But this way of thinking centers on feeling sorry for yourself. Self-pity, passivity, and assumed powerlessness can be frustrating and aggravating not only to you, but also to others who have to listen to it.

It is important to remember that if you are in the one-down position, you're still using a Power Over perspective. You have many of the qualities of the one-ups—an external focus on how other people get their way, being quick to blame others for your suffering, an either/or way of thinking, and so forth.

POWER OVER IS A COMMON PART OF OUR CULTURE

If you have a Power Over belief system, you may mistakenly assume that everyone—especially the people closest to you—thinks like you do. This set of beliefs is not just about the way you see the world; it's about the way you assume everyone else sees the world, too. Patricia Evans calls this mindset "Reality I."

Many of our culture's values support a Power Over perspective—especially in males. Academic excellence is achieved by getting high grades and outperforming other students. This is why you may dislike the students who study the hardest: they pull up the curve so you get a lower grade. The students who don't try hard are easier to like: they pull the curve down and make it easier for you to get a better grade. To be a good athlete, you have to finish first and beat the other athletes—you're either a winner or a loser. Professional worth (financial and figurative) is often defined by how much power you have in the workplace and how much you make compared to your colleagues. Many aspects of your life—academic, athletic, and professional— may support a Power Over worldview.

THE ALTERNATIVE TO POWER OVER: PERSONAL POWER

The alternative to Power Over thinking is a Personal Power mindset. Instead of seeing one person as up and the other as down, Personal Power assumes that both parties are equal, and equally deserving of respect. It sees other people not as better or worse, but as equal to you. In this way of thinking, you can win, and so can your partner. You can be right, and so can your partner, even if they have a different opinion. You can get your needs met, and so can they. There is a **both/and** view, rather than an **either/or** view.

Personal Power assumes abundance, not scarcity: there can be many right answers and many winners, and everyone can get what they need. This abundance view comes from drawing power from yourself rather than taking it from others. It presumes that sharing power and helping each other strengthens each individual. Safety comes from working together and pooling resources, rather than from working against each other.

With an internal focus, power is seen as coming from within yourself. It is not acquired by looking outward at other people's situations, but by understanding your own wants and needs. The key to your own happiness and well-being is in the choices you make, not the choices of others. Likewise, your wants and needs are met by your own actions, not the actions of others. It's not important how you measure up against others; only how you measure up against yourself.

Since the only true power you have in the world is over yourself, adopting an internal focus creates a sense of empowerment and strength. You cannot control your grade, but you can control how much you study. You cannot control whether you win, but you can control how much you train. To operate from a position of Personal Power is to measure your success and well-being by your own standards, with an internal focus on the process (studying, training) instead of an external focus on the outcome (grades, winning).

Because your happiness no longer depends on the actions of others when you adopt a mindset of Personal Power, there is no need for abuse or control. If you don't see other people as your opponent or competition, you won't need to defend yourself against them. This perspective presumes that most people are not trying to dominate or control or hurt you, and that any damage done is incidental, not intentional.

It might seem naïve to be so trusting of others, but it's true: most of the people you meet are not out to take advantage of you or intentionally harm you. This is even more true among the people you are closest to. Your family and friends certainly may hurt you at times, but most of the time they don't intend to. Their behavior may be hurtful at times, but most of the time, for most people, hurtful behavior is not abusive.

It is very rare for people to feel like a victim if they have the perspective of Personal Power. Even if they suffer because of something others have done, they look inward to remedy their suffering. Rather than focusing externally on what was done to you, you can focus internally on what you can do to handle it, including seeking to identify what, if any, role you played in it. Ironically, because most victims of abusive behavior are in Personal Power, they are often slow to identify themselves as victims or to say that they have been victimized. Their inclination is to presume the abuse was not intentional and to examine what they could have done differently, even though the person who is abusive is always 100% responsible for their abuse. Often, then, the person who is self-righteously saying "I'm the victim here" is actually in Power Over.

Another aspect of the presumption of abundance in a Personal Power mindset is believing there can be many paths to the same goal, many right

answers, and many right ways of doing things. Di
perceived as threats, because it doesn't matter what anyor.
only what you yourself are doing. From this perspecti
personal truths, not globally true. They are truths with a s.
capital T. What is true for you is true for you, even if it is n .. for
others. What matters is that you believe that your perspective and
experience are legitimate, regardless of whether others do. As a result, the
fact that others see things differently or having different wants, needs, or
priorities does not threaten, challenge, or invalidate you. You have a
tolerance and respect for differences.

There is a lot of cultural support for Power Over thinking, but it is
definitely possible to live in the world in Personal Power. What does that
look like? In school, being in Personal Power looks like learning the
material well. You still try for a great grade, but what matters most is that
you strive to do your best and that you know the material well, regardless
of your final grade. You help your classmates because you don't consider
them your competition. Even if helping another student means they pull
up the grading curve, you're still improving your own understanding of
the material, and that's your priority.

In sports, being in Personal Power looks like enjoying the game,
regardless of the outcome. If eight people compete in a race, a Power Over
perspective would identify one winner and seven losers. A Personal Power
perspective, on the other hand, would see that one person crossed the
finish line first, but all eight had fun running. You can still be competitive
in Personal Power. You can still try your best to win, but your focus is on
having fun and doing your best. In the Olympics, many athletes have
incredible experiences that they'll remember for the rest of their lives, even
when they don't come close to winning a medal. They might hit personal
bests, get to meet fellow sport enthusiasts from all over the world, and have
crowds of strangers cheering them on, even if they finish far from the top
spots.

If you're in Personal Power in your professional life, you're focused on
doing work you love and pushing yourself to do the best you can,
regardless of where you rank or how much you're paid. Your happiness
and personal success become far more important. As long as you're
making enough to live on, that is good enough. Your value in the

ɔrkplace is ultimately not defined by what others think of you or how you measure up, but by how you feel about your performance and your accomplishments, and whether you're meeting your personal goals.

POWER OVER IN RELATIONSHIPS

In order for a relationship to be in Personal Power, both people need to operate from a place of Personal Power. If one person operates in terms of Power Over, then so does the relationship. Think of it as trying to move a sofa by yourself: you can only do it with the full cooperation of the person on the other side. You can move a chair by yourself, but furniture that's designed for two requires you to work together to move it. *Relationships in which one person—or more rarely, both people—operate in Power Over are doomed to be combative, dysfunctional, and unsuccessful, even if the couple stays together, until both people are in Personal Power.*

A Power Over belief system is very common among abusive partners. A key aspect of becoming nonabusive is not just stopping certain behaviors, but changing your underlying beliefs. Exchanging a Power Over worldview for a Personal Power worldview is one of the fundamental shifts necessary for stopping your patterns of abuse and control. Without making this change, you may be able to stop certain abusive and controlling behaviors and patterns, but new ones will appear in their places. We will talk about how to go about changing these beliefs in Chapter 15: Becoming Aware of Your Thoughts.

Check the appendix for a handout that briefly compares the differences between Power Over and Personal Power. You can use it to help remind yourself what each looks like.

VIEWING YOUR PARTNER AS AN OPPONENT PROMOTES ABUSE

A very common belief among abusive individuals is that their partner is against them. In fact, this belief drives Power Over thinking in a variety of ways, including mistakenly assuming that your partner also has a Power Over perspective. With this assumption, your partner is quickly misinterpreted and mischaracterized as aggressive, combative, controlling, and apt to get into power struggles. You might describe situations by saying *"they're on my ass," "proving their point," "shot me* down," "had it in for me," or "gunning for me." All of these phrases indicate that you view your partner as being against you; that your partner, too, is in a Power Over mindset.

Partners are imperfect. They can have moments of behaving badly or being thoughtless, and they might be having a bad day. They can and do behave hurtfully at times without intending to. From a Power Over perspective, these hurtful behaviors might seem abusive, but your partner typically does not intend to hurt you. The hurt that they inflicted is just an unintended consequence of their struggles and shortcomings. This kind of unintentionally hurtful behavior takes place in nearly every intimate relationship. The problem is when you misinterpret them as abusive.

It is also a mistake to take your partner's behavior personally. The hurt they cause is often incidental; a result of being thoughtless, unaware, or neglectful. Their agenda is not to hurt you, and their behavior is often not about you, anyway. For example, if your partner agrees to go out with you for dinner but shows up twenty minutes late, it can be easy to assume they don't care as much about the date as you do. But in truth, a situation came up at work, and it just happened to occur on the night you two had a date. Their intention wasn't to hurt you, and their lateness didn't have anything to do with you.

But what if they are being hurtful on purpose? What if they are being abusive? The best way to find out is to treat them like they are not, to presume they are not. If they are being abusive, your trust and patience will make it increasingly apparent that they are trying to take advantage. Once that becomes clear, you can take steps to keep yourself safe from that person and their behavior. Thankfully, most of the people you meet will not be in Power Over; people in Power Over are the exception, not the rule. It's important to remember that. It's okay to be slow to trust, but once you give someone your trust, it should be steadfast. Once you choose to be in relationship with somebody, do your very best to give them the benefit of the doubt by assuming that if they cause you difficulties, they're not doing it on purpose. They will be imperfect, but they are not against you. They are on your side. They are your ally.

Another significant source of beliefs that can contribute to all this are the messages we get from society about how males and females are "supposed" to be. This is the focus of the next chapter.

CHAPTER 6

GENDER ROLES AND ABUSIVE BEHAVIOR

Many people think of gender as falling into two categories—male and female, which are referred to as gender binary because there are only two options. However, in some cultures, both current and past, more than two categories are recognized. In the Dominican Republic there is a small community where some children born with undifferentiated genitalia are often raised as girls, but then develop male genitals at puberty; they are then called *guevedoche*, which translates roughly to "penis at twelve." In Australia, indigenous transgendered people are known as sistergirls and brotherboys. In the United States, people who identify as male but were assigned female at birth are called trans men, and people who identify as female but were assigned male at birth are called trans women. People who identify as genderqueer tend to dress and behave in ways that defy categorization as male or female; they may prefer the pronouns "they" and "them," rather than "he" or "she." People who are genderfluid identify with a shifting variety of genders both binary and nonbinary. Although gender is often thought of as one or the other—male or female—these variations suggest that perhaps it is more of a continuum. Even if gender is a continuum, most cultures around the world have clear ideas about what it means to be "male" and "female," and expect that genitalia determines the social expectations for each person. This chapter outlines some of these expectations and examines their relationship to abusive and controlling behavior.

WHAT DOES IT MEAN TO BE A MAN OR A WOMAN?
"Man up."
"Be a man."
"When are you going to grow up and act like a man?"

Everyone has heard boys and men being encouraged to be "more manly"—to be more of a man. But what do they mean? What does it mean to be a man? Which qualities are they talking about? Let's be clear: they're not talking about how boys and men actually are. They're talking about how society expects males to behave.

One common misconception is that males and females are hardwired to act certain ways. That gendered behavior is in their DNA, like they're different creatures. While it is true that there are a variety of hormonal and physical differences between males and females, the sexes are far more alike than they are different from each other. For example, you might think it's "common sense" that males are taller than females, but in truth, the average height difference *between* males and females is less than the height difference *among* males and females. On average, males are taller than females, but there are plenty of females that are taller than plenty of males. The statement "men are taller than women" is incorrect a fair amount of the time, and this is true for virtually any other sex-related quality as well.

Even where there are physical and biological differences between males and females, society and culture play a huge role in how they play out. Everyone has a biological drive to eat, but what you eat, when you eat, and how you eat are strongly influenced by your cultural background. Culture can even override the hunger drive; people of one culture will starve rather than eat things people in another culture consume readily. Likewise, your culture can provide you with knowledge and understanding about food and what to eat; some cultures know that certain foods are edible that others believe are not. All humans need to sleep and have sex, but culture plays a significant role in how we manage and satisfy those drives.

The point is that what it means to be male or a man is defined by culture, not biology, and cultures vary and change. Even if we ask what it means to be a man in the United States in the twenty-first century, there are variations within subcultures. But if we look at the most common characteristics portrayed in our culture, including in mass media like movies and television, we can identify certain qualities.

a handyman
a leader
dominant
in charge
in control
independent
knowledgeable
logical
self-reliant
sexual
silent (especially about personal information)
stoic
strong
tearless
tough
unemotional (except for anger)

Beyond this, men in our culture are expected to take on three roles that all begin with *pro*: procreator, provider, and protector. We will elaborate on each of these roles below.

Procreator

A common source of esteem for men, especially younger men, is being sexually active and having great sex, regular sex, and potentially many sexual partners. Men who are not sexually active—or not sexually active enough—are characterized as less manly and less desirable. There is an emphasis on penis size (the larger, the better) and the ability to have and sustain an erection at will. Men spend large amounts of money in the pursuit of penis enlargement (which is generally impossible), and to ensure reliable erections (with mixed results). What is noteworthy is that the anxiety around having and sustaining erections is driven far more by fear than reality.

Men often rely on sex as a primary way of comforting themselves, receiving physical nurturance, and as a pathway to potential intimacy, because other avenues of physical comfort are considered off-limits to manly men. Taking a hot bath, spending time on grooming, getting a massage, being held, and giving and receiving loving nonsexual touch are stigmatized for males in our culture, as are sharing emotions, disclosing important personal information, and being nurturing or getting nurtured in nonsexual ways.

Provider

Many men define their worth by their ability to provide for themselves and their families by working and earning income. What a man does "for a living"—an expression that indicates how closely tied his work is to his basic sense of worth—is typically defined by his paid labor. In fact, that's one of the first questions people ask: "So what do you do for a living?" Losing a job can be a huge blow to a man's ego and his sense of self, one that can trigger serious depression. It is also one of the triggers that can lead abusive men to kill themselves and/or others, including family members.

Because being employed is such a central part of many men's sense of worth and esteem, they are sometimes willing to make sacrifices for their jobs, working long hours, working in unsafe conditions, and accepting dangerous assignments. Employers have long exploited men's willingness to make compromises to get their workers to work longer hours in more dangerous conditions. This is the primary way men are exploited: for their labor. This includes being drafted or recruited into the military and to fight in wars. As a result, many men make trade-offs they only fully realize or regret near the end of their lives. As many have observed, nobody says on their deathbed, "I wish I'd worked more."

When men assume their value is inextricably linked to their ability to generate income, they often come to think that their main value to their family is as an ATM. And if that's the case, the solution to any problem must be to work more and generate more income, and they end up living to work, rather than working to live.

Protector

The third role men are expected to take on is to protect their family and themselves from danger. This means creating a safe space from the outside world and remaining ever vigilant for threats to their family from the world, including from other people. This is the theme of countless movies—a man going to extreme lengths to protect his loved ones from danger. The threat could be from a criminal, a natural disaster, a supernatural threat, or a romantic competitor that could steal his partner's heart, but it is up to the man to keep his family safe and alive. If he fails, he is obligated to seek revenge and justice.

If you see the world as a hostile and dangerous place, the role of protector seems necessary; without your presence, your family will not survive. But this stance can lead to a variety of controlling and abusive behaviors, including a sense of ownership or jealousy that lets you give yourself permission to isolate your partner and children to protect them from the world. If you think your partner or your child could be stolen from you, it might seem necessary to limit where they can go, for their own safety and well-being.

Every day, males in our culture are expected to rigidly conform to these qualities. They see them in actors, politicians, family and friends, at school, and at work. Even if a male is free to behave as he pleases at home or among friends, he still is regularly exposed to the expectation to conform to "traditional" masculinity. This expectation takes effect on the day he is born: baby boys are touched less and physically comforted less than baby girls. It determines the clothes he is expected to wear, the toys he is expected to play with, and the games he is expected to enjoy. While there are some cultural variations, these patterns are fairly consistent all over the world.

PRESSURE TO CONFORM TO TRADITIONAL GENDER ROLES

In his book *Men's Work,* Paul Kivel draws a box around a list of traditional masculine qualities and dubs it the "Act Like a Man" box, pointing out that when boys and men venture out of that box with behaviors that are not traditionally masculine, they are met with disapproval. What sorts of things do people say about males who show emotions other than anger, who cry, who admit they don't know the answer? Here's what males are often called when they dare to step outside of the man box:

fag
gay
girl
girlie man (from Hans and Franz on Saturday Night Live)
homo
momma's boy
pussy
pussy-whipped, or whipped
sissy
wimp
wuss
plus many more. . . .

As you look at this list, you might see two things most of these words have in common. The first is that they are negative and insulting, and intended to make the person feel bad. Secondly, they often zero in on feminine or effeminate traits, implying that behaviors associated with women and gay men are inferior and undesirable.

The man box is more like a prison cell than a box. Males who try to step out of it may get teased, beat up, ostracized, or excluded from groups and activities. Their basic worth and competency may be challenged. On the other hand, males who stay in the man box are often admired, praised, supported, included, and rewarded with professional and social opportunities. There are many forces, both big and small, that strive to make males conform to traditional masculine qualities, no matter what. Gay men and trans women, who are even further outside the man box, are also the targets of some of the most extreme violence.

Kivel also talks about the "Act Like a Lady" box. Which qualities does our culture expect females to have? When we think about the ways women are portrayed in the media, we might come up with a list like this:
caring
chaste
compassionate
dainty
dependent
domestic

emotional
helpless
irrational
moody
needy/helpless
nurturing
passive
sociable
weak

Women are expected to play different roles than men. They are expected to be mothers, wives, and caregivers, to be comfortable domestically and able to manage the home.

When females venture out of the "Act Like a Lady" box and display behaviors that are not traditionally feminine, they might hear these names in response:
bitch
butch
dyke
feminazi
lesbo
man-hater
tomboy
and many others . . .

Like the responses to males who venture out of the man box, the words above are intended to be negative and insulting. They also imply that the female might be lesbian, playing into the stereotype that lesbians act more like men. But these insults don't quite have the edge that the others do for males. Maybe this is because traditionally male qualities are valued more highly, so it's understandable that women might want to be more like men. On the other hand, it seems inconceivable that a man would ever want to act like a woman.

The man box and the lady box are, for the most part, opposites of each other. Whereas men are independent, women are dependent. Whereas men are unemotional, women are emotional. And so on. All human qualities have been divided in two, so if you put a man and a woman together, between the two of them, you'll have a full human being. One traditional role reinforces the other traditional role.

There are a number of problems with the man and lady boxes, but perhaps the biggest is that they artificially predetermine how people should behave based solely on their sex at birth. They automatically block each gender from half of their humanity, requiring each to reject those aspects of themselves that do not conform to their gender roles.

In truth, there is not a single definition of true masculinity. Rather, there are as many definitions of masculinity as there are males. Likewise, there is not a single definition of femininity; there are as many definitions of femininity as there are females. And there are others who do not subscribe to either label. The reality is that males and females are not aliens from different planets, but humans from the same planet. Each person is a combination of masculine and feminine qualities. Some people will naturally, of their own free will, align with traditional roles, but most will become a mix and mashup of both. In fact, psychological research has found that the most well-adjusted people tend to have both masculine and feminine qualities. Think of it this way. Are you going to be better off with half a set of tools or a full set of tools?

Although society is slowly moving away from strict and traditional gender roles, there is still quite a long way to go toward true freedom.

THE PROBLEM WITH RIGID MASCULINITY

There are definitely situations in which conforming to a traditional male role is helpful and appropriate, and even necessary. At war, for instance, or in an area of town where people might try to take advantage of you. Those are great times to be tough, strong, stoic, self-reliant, independent, authoritative, and so forth. There are also certain careers that align with traditional masculinity, such as law enforcement, the military, firefighting, and aviation. Women in those professions tend to embrace traditional masculine qualities as well.

There is nothing inherently wrong with traditionally masculine qualities. In fact, they clearly have value for both males and females. The problems arise when masculinity is embraced so rigidly that any deviation from it is rejected. People of any gender who are prone to abusive behavior tend to conform to rigid masculinity that embraces masculine qualities and rejects feminine qualities.

When rigid masculinity conformity springs up, it can cause significant problems. To begin with, rigidly masculine people struggle to be emotionally close with their romantic partners and children. Emotionally disconnected and overconfident people are more likely to engage in high-risk behaviors that lead to injury and death. And their emphasis on self-reliance makes them disinclined to seek medical and mental health services, which leads to higher mortality rates due to treatable medical conditions and suicide. These are just three of many such examples.

The aspect of rigid masculinity conformity that we are most concerned about in this book, though, is that the vast majority of violent behavior is perpetrated by men. Whether the violence manifests as mass killings, murder, assault, rape, robbery, or acts of war, virtually every type of violence is perpetrated predominantly by men. The only two realms in which women come close are child abuse and elder abuse, which is explained by the fact that elder care and childcare are typically handled by women. It's hard to be abusive toward someone with whom you have no contact.

The other half of this equation is that the primary victims of men's violence are other men. The vast majority of homicide victims, assault victims, robbery victims, and war casualties are males. The exceptions to this are domestic violence and adult sexual assault, in which females comprise the majority of victims because most men are heterosexual.

What is striking is that most discussions of violence and its causes consider a variety of possible causes—mental illness, a history of being bullied, access to firearms—while failing to mention the greatest common denominator: masculinity! It is so "normal" for the perpetrators of violence to be men that masculinity is taken for granted, like fish not realizing they are in water. There is clear and compelling evidence that masculinity—particularly rigid masculinity conformity—is a key driver of violence. Given that this is the case, what can you do?

YOU CAN REFUSE TO CONFORM.

If you refuse to allow anyone else to define for you what it means to be a man, you will be able to break out of the "Act Like a Man" box. There are as many definitions of what it means to be a man as there are men in the world. There is no one right or true way of being a man, and every variation involves each person's distinct mix of supposedly masculine and feminine qualities. Only by embracing their full humanity can people reach their potential, free of others' constraints on what it means to be a man.

Breaking out of the man box takes courage. It means going against considerable social pressure to conform. It might mean dealing with put-downs and judgment from others, even people in your family or those you considered friends. This pressure can come from women as well as men. You may need to limit or stop contact with people who are not supportive of your change. You may need to make new connections with people who are supportive of the ways you are growing and evolving.

Breaking out of the man box can be a lot of work. Since so much time and energy during your growing-up years and beyond were focused on developing and strengthening those "masculine" qualities, they are often well developed. Breaking out of the man box means spending a comparable amount of time, effort, and energy developing and strengthening the other aspects of your humanity, your "feminine" qualities. It's like building up your legs when you've focused on your upper body for years: they won't change overnight, and they require different workouts. You'll have to learn to consciously use your legs instead of automatically relying on your stronger upper body.

Refusing to conform to rigidly masculine standards is less about rejecting qualities you already have and more about adding qualities you lack. All this will be examined in Chapter 13: Moving from Disconnection to Connection, as well as in the chapters that follow, which will offer you a variety of new ways to think and behave in pursuit of being more fully human.

CHAPTER 7

DENIAL

Everyone has emotions that they don't like to feel; that they want to get rid of whenever they surface. Anxiety, depression, sadness, discouragement, and shame are on a lot of people's lists. It's easy to think of them as "bad" feelings, but they actually have value, especially when it comes to helping you better understand and take care of yourself. A more effective way of thinking of them is as uncomfortable or distressing. All feelings are good and legitimate, but some are comfortable and enjoyable, while others are not. In Chapter 16: Becoming Aware of Your Emotions, we will examine the role and importance of feelings in a lot more detail, but in this chapter, we'll focus on how trying to avoid uncomfortable feelings can lead to abusive behavior.

The fact is, there are only three basic ways to make unpleasant emotions go away: we can make external changes, make internal changes, or ignore the feelings altogether. We will look at each of these options below.

MAKING EXTERNAL OR INTERNAL CHANGES TO ALLEVIATE UNCOMFORTABLE EMOTIONS

One way to make unpleasant emotions go away is to address the external cause by problem-solving. A person who feels stressed about doing their taxes can problem-solve by completing their tax return. A person who feels lonely can problem-solve by calling a friend or arranging a get-together.

Another way to make unpleasant emotions go away is to make internal changes by addressing how you cope with your experiences. A person feeling stressed about taxes can remind themselves that they've set aside a weekend to complete their return. After remembering this, they may feel less stressed, even though nothing has changed externally. A person who feels lonely can remind themselves that they'll be getting together with friends later in the week, and that until then they can work on projects around the house. They may feel less lonely, even though nothing on the outside has changed.

These two ways of dealing with uncomfortable feelings—making external changes and making internal changes—are summarized in the Serenity Prayer:

God grant me the serenity to accept the things I cannot change,
The courage to change the things I can,
And the wisdom to know the difference.

Having the courage to change the things you can is about making external changes, or problem-solving. Action often requires courage; fear can keep you from doing the difficult things that are necessary to improve your life. But making those changes is the best course of action when it comes to dealing with uncomfortable emotions, because it deals directly with the cause of your distress.

Having the serenity to accept the things you cannot change is about making internal changes, or coping. Some external factors, like traffic or weather, are beyond your control. There's nothing you could do to change the situation, so all you can do is work to accept it. One part of accepting something is by changing how you think about it, which could include talking with others about it. Physically calming and comforting yourself can help you feel significantly better even if the cause of your distress remains.

Most problems in life require a combination of internal and external interventions. Having the wisdom to know the difference acknowledges the fact that when you try to change things that are beyond your control, you might get frustrated and more aggravated. On the other hand, passively accepting things that you *can* change subjects you to unnecessary suffering. The key is to change the things you can, accept the things you cannot, and to understand which is which. These are the keys to dealing with uncomfortable and unpleasant emotions and the situations that cause them.

GOING INTO DENIAL ALLEVIATES UNCOMFORTABLE EMOTIONS, BUT ONLY TEMPORARILY

A third and very tempting way to deal with uncomfortable and unpleasant emotions is to deny that you're even feeling them. Making internal and external changes requires you to first acknowledge that you feel distressed and that you're having uncomfortable emotions—in other words, change requires you to turn toward the emotion. Ironically, that acknowledgment can initially intensify the emotion. Taking note of your depression, anxiety, or loneliness may actually make you feel more depressed, anxious, or lonely. Denial, on the other hand, lets you turn away from the emotion that's bothering you, to simply ignore it. Denial spares you the increased intensity.

This, however, is like putting a piece of duct tape over the check-engine light on your car's dashboard or taking the batteries out of the smoke alarm. If you're not aware of a problem, you won't be worried about it, right? But the problem is not really gone, it's just being ignored.

THE PROBLEM WITH STUFFING EMOTIONS

An alternative to thinking about denial as turning away from uncomfortable emotions is to think of stuffing them down instead of letting them out. Rather than thinking about them, letting them out, and expressing them, you avoid them by stuffing them down inside of you and refusing to deal with them in the hopes that they will go away.

Stuffing emotions can look like acceptance; when people shift their focus from troubling emotions or thoughts without making outward changes, they can appear to have successfully coped with the situation, let go of the emotions, and moved on. However, there are significant differences between letting go of emotions and stuffing them. For you to let go of something, you first need to hold it in your hand. In other words, you must acknowledge and accept an emotion before you can come to terms with it. If you have a chestnut in your pocket, letting it go means taking it out of your pocket, holding it, and releasing it. Stuffing, on the other hand, is active avoidance. It's like keeping that chestnut in your pocket and telling yourself that if you don't touch it or see it, you won't be troubled by it. It's still there, of course; you'll continue to carry it with you wherever you go, whether you know it or not.

As with denial, there are a number of problems with stuffing emotions. First, the emotion tends to remain raw and unresolved. Second, it is more likely to "come out sideways"—to reappear at inappropriate times or in inappropriate ways. People whose feelings come out sideways tend to externalize their emotions—to act them out and direct them toward others who are not the cause. It is a very unproductive response to emotions.

There are a couple of indicators that an emotion has been stuffed rather than appropriately processed and managed. First, recalling the situation that caused the initial emotion may make you emotionally escalated. When an emotion has been adequately processed, you can typically recount the situation without becoming particularly escalated in the present, even if you were escalated in the past. For example, think of some intense event from your past, like the first time you were fired or when your first romantic relationship ended. When you talked about it back then, you might have become quite upset over the thought of it. Now, on the other hand, however many years later, you probably feel only a small percentage of what you felt back then. If, on the other hand, you still have a strong reaction, then it's likely that you have not fully come to terms with or emotionally processed the situation.

A second indicator that you have stuffed your emotions is that you find yourself overreacting in other situations, including totally unrelated ones. A strong reaction to a relatively minor event usually indicates that something else is going on. We will talk more about how to deal with overreacting in Chapter 16: Becoming Aware of Your Emotions. The point here is that such overreactions are typically an indication that you have stuffed some unprocessed emotions.

Here are some questions to consider with regards to stuffed emotions:
- Why would you avoid emotions or expressing certain emotions? Maybe you don't know what you can do about it. Maybe you want to avoid a conflict. Maybe the emotion feels overwhelming.

- What are ways you typically stuff feelings? Maybe you ignore the issue, avoid raising it in conversation, get drunk or high, or keep yourself distracted.
- What are the consequences of stuffing emotions? Maybe the issue is left unresolved. Maybe the issue keeps coming up. Maybe it creates distance in your relationships with yourself and others.
- What are alternatives to stuffing emotions? You could more appropriately acknowledge your emotions by talking about them with others, bringing the issue up with your partner, or journaling about it.

HOW DENIAL WORKS

Denial is tempting because it does work in the short run. Turning away from an emotion *can* make it lessen, or even go away. If you are worried about your taxes and instead you watch a movie, your anxiety may go away. If you're stressed about your credit card bill and hide it in a drawer and forget about it, your stress may go away. If you are feeling lonely and get yourself really drunk or stoned, you may no longer feel loneliness in the same way. The problem, of course, is that nothing has really changed. The cause of the emotion is still there, unaddressed.

DENIAL DOESN'T FIX THE SITUATION.

The problem, of course, is that if you do not deal with the real situation, it continues to cause problems and suffering. Denial offers temporary relief, but little has changed, because you have failed to acknowledge or deal with reality.

Imagine that there is a pile of shit in the middle of the room. It's tempting to avoid it, to stay as far away from it as possible, to not look at it or smell it or touch it. If you are successful in ignoring it long enough, you might even convince yourself that it's not there. But before you know it, you've walked right through it. Now you have shit on your shoes, which you are tracking all over the place, and soon there is shit everywhere. Not a pretty picture, is it? That's how denial works.

On the other hand, if you notice a pile of shit in the middle of the room, the thing you really need to do is to look at that pile of shit. If you truly want to make that shit go away, you actually need to get closer to it, even handle it. In the short run it'll smell worse and you might have to touch it, but you'll be able to truly get rid of it. It will be temporarily unpleasant, but once you get rid of the shit and clean the spot up, you'll be rid of it for good. You'll be free to walk around the room without worrying about it at all. This captures the challenge of turning toward uncomfortable feelings rather than turning away from them.

DENIAL IS OFTEN AUTOMATIC.
You can intentionally avoid feeling an emotion, but most of the time you do it without even thinking about it. Everyone has reflexive ways of distracting themselves from their emotions and the situations that trigger them. Looking at your phone is incredibly easy way, as are reading, chitchatting, and sleeping. What are your automatic ways of avoiding your emotions? What do you do that allows you to avoid feeling and noticing what is really going on?

DENIAL IS A PART OF LIFE.
Everyone turns away from their emotions at times, but denying your feelings becomes a problem when you do it habitually or for an extended period of time. It's key to pay attention to yourself. If you avoid a bill by throwing it in a drawer for a day, it's no big deal. If you do that for weeks, it will become problematic. If you avoid your loneliness by watching television for a night, that's fine. But if you do it week after week, your loneliness will worsen over time.

UNCHECKED DENIAL CAUSES SELF-DESTRUCTIVE BEHAVIORS.
Denial is what keeps drinkers drinking, addicts using, and gamblers gambling. It is what keeps people in bad situations, bad jobs, and bad relationships far longer than necessary. It's one reason abusive partners continue to be abusive even when their behavior results in serious hardship for others and themselves.

In order to address a problem, you first need to acknowledge that there IS a problem. Only then can action be taken to address it. Acknowledging a problem, though, often brings on uncomfortable emotions. It requires courage to feel and acknowledge those emotions.

DENIAL IS A KEY BARRIER TO ACCOUNTABILITY.

The first steps toward making a real change in your life are identifying and addressing any denial you might have. Before you can change or solve a problem, you need to acknowledge that there *is* a problem. Denial prevents you from seeing that. You cannot become accountable until your denial is gone and your problematic behaviors have been acknowledged and changed.

To get yourself out of denial, you'll need to honestly acknowledge what is actually going on and what you actually feel, even if you don't like it and don't want to. It requires courage to sit with this discomfort. Getting out of denial is an ongoing process, not a one-time thing, and you'll have to learn to feel comfortable with feeling uncomfortable on a regular basis.

DEFENSE MECHANISMS SUPPORT DENIAL

Another way people avoid uncomfortable emotions is to distort how they think about or describe a situation so it won't seem quite as bad. If you can avoid looking at what you have done, you won't have to experience uncomfortable emotions about it. This is different from acceptance, in which there is an honest acknowledgment of the situation. People often use defense mechanisms when talking about their own behavior, particularly behaviors that make them feel ashamed or that reflect badly on them.

The thinking strategies listed below are called defense mechanisms because they are ways people defend themselves against uncomfortable emotions by distorting the truth. They are common ways that abusive partners avoid being accountable for what they have done. Most people use a number of defense mechanisms simultaneously, and there is some overlap between the strategies. Nearly everyone occasionally uses some of these to avoid fully sitting with the discomfort of their situation, whatever it may be.

Which of these strategies do you habitually use? Once you have identified them, the goal is to do your best to avoid using them, and to stay honest with yourself about what is really going on. Being able to name and notice your defense mechanisms can help you stay more honest about your circumstances, both with yourself and with others.

COMMON DEFENSE MECHANISMS

Simple denial: "I did not do that." The most basic way to avoid dealing with discomfort is to simply deny that it happened or exists. It is common for people who have been abusive to deny some or all of their abusive behavior.

Minimizing: "I just gave them a slight bump." Minimizing is making something seem small, inconsequential, less than it actually was. Abusive people often understate what they did, how much they did, and the negative impact of what they did.

Vagueness: "We had a disagreement last night that didn't go very well." Vagueness is speaking in generalities and avoiding specifics so something doesn't seem so bad. This includes leaving out the details and particulars that would make it seem much worse. If you put the situation "out of focus," then you can't see the ugly details.

Blaming: "They really know how to push my buttons." Blaming is shifting responsibility for what happened to someone else so it's the other person's fault and not your own.

Playing the victim, acting helpless: "They kept coming at me and wouldn't stop, even when I asked them to stop, so eventually I had to push them out of the way." Playing the victim and acting helpless involves focusing on what the other person was doing, often without mentioning how you were contributing to it. You then cast your behavior as a reaction to what they were doing, which left you with no choice and was beyond your control.

Paying or giving selective attention: "I was just sitting there at the computer when they started yelling at me." "They ended up getting super drunk and giving me a hard time all night." "I did not call them that name—you can't find it anywhere on the recording." Paying selective attention means only reporting or acknowledging certain aspects of a situation. It is leaving out important but incriminating facts. One common way people give selective attention to a situation is by starting a story partway through, leaving out their inappropriate behavior, and starting with the reactions or behaviors of others. Another common way people pay selective attention is by focusing on the inaccuracies of a story or accusation rather than on the parts that are true or relevant.

Rationalizing and justifying: "I had worked a twelve-hour day, then when I came home I spent two more hours trying to fix the garbage disposal. Then they wanted to have this discussion, at almost midnight, about how I'm not helping out enough. I just lost it." Rationalizing and justifying mean making excuses to make an abusive or controlling behavior seem like a reasonable, appropriate response. Often, anything said prior to an acknowledgment of abusive behavior is simply a rationalization or justification for it.

Insisting "I'm unique": "We don't just have 'some stress' in our relationship, we have two special-needs kids who are incredibly demanding. Anybody would occasionally lose their temper in that situation." Insisting that you're unique implies that the usual rules do not apply to you, or that you are an exception to the rules.

Intellectualizing: "You said controlling means there wasn't consent, but how do you know they weren't consenting to me acting that way?" Intellectualizing means talking impersonally, generally, or abstractly, or arguing over small points that distract attention from the main issue. It avoids talking about your personal involvement with the issue.

Diversion or distraction: "They had way too much to drink that night and had already passed out once in the middle of the living room. They get drunk most nights, but only this drunk about once a month. Yet that did not stop them from getting into an argument with me and resist me trying to help them get to bed." Using diversion and distraction means changing the subject or focusing on irrelevant details to take the attention off yourself and the issue.

Humor: "I may have yelled at my partner, but I didn't yell at the dog, so he was cool. And the cat was like, 'whatever.'" Using humor by making jokes or telling stories to draw attention away from yourself and the issue is another form of distraction. It also is a way of making the situation seem less serious or problematic.

Hostility: Staring someone down in silence rather than answering their question. Becoming escalated and abusive when someone raises an issue to avoid addressing their concern. Using hostility means using anger and intimidation to get someone to back off. It is another form of distraction.

Playing dumb: "What did I do?" "I had no idea!" "That's abusive?"
Playing dumb is acting like you don't know any better or pretending to be unaware of the situation.

Forgetfulness: "I don't remember doing that." "I can't remember what happened." Using forgetfulness as a defense mechanism is "forgetting" important information or actions and thereby avoiding accepting responsibility for or consequences of them. This is especially easy and natural, since forgetting also allows you to avoid the uncomfortable feelings that are associated with that memory. Often, if you really try to remember, you can; you simply don't want to. Other times it's a flat-out lie.

Agreeing: "You're right. I shouldn't have done that. Can we move on now?" "I already said you're right. What more is there to talk about?!" Superficially agreeing is a defense mechanism used to silence someone while not actually meaning it or being willing to have a longer conversation.

Superficial optimism: "That's water under the bridge." "It won't happen again." Using superficial optimism or staying future-focused is a defense mechanism that lets you avoid talking about past behaviors by focusing on the future or implying that things will be different without a clear plan and desire to make things different.

***

Which of these defense mechanisms have you habitually used? Keep an eye out for talking or thinking that way now, and do your best to resist falling into those old bad habits. Try to stay more honest with yourself and others. If you're in a group, listen for these defense mechanisms and respectfully point them out when you see them.

Defense mechanisms often lead to G-rated versions of abusive behaviors that don't seem so bad and are not particularly disturbing. It is important that the seriousness of abusive behaviors, including the negative impact they have had on others, is fully acknowledged in all its ugliness and unpleasantness. The R-rated version of the same events is clear, concrete, explicit, honest, and graphic. Acknowledging the gravity of your behavior and the damage it has caused can provide strong motivation to change. Denying or minimizing them, on the other hand, makes it easier to stay stuck where you are.

DENYING YOUR PROBLEM BEHAVIORS CAUSES MORE PROBLEMS

Sometimes your uncomfortable feelings are caused by events outside of your control—what other people say and do to you (a coworker makes fun of you, somebody sideswipes your car) or things that happen to you (you don't get the promotion, you owe money on your taxes). On the other hand, sometimes your uncomfortable feelings are caused by your own behaviors and choices. When your own behavior is the cause of your discomfort, it is both better and worse.

On the upside, because you do have control over your behavior, there are often things you can do to address your discomfort. You can make real changes to get your behavior more in line with your values. On the downside, a whole other layer of uncomfortable emotions can come up (especially shame) because you did this to yourself. Getting into a car crash is upsetting enough, but if it was caused by your own actions, it's even more troubling. Not getting a promotion is painful enough, but realizing that it was partly caused by your own actions on the job makes it even worse.

People often avoid uncomfortable emotions by going into denial about their behaviors and using defense mechanisms to explain the role they played. You minimize how many cookies you ate, you rationalize why you put off getting your car fixed until it actually broke down, you blame the dog for eating the food you absentmindedly left out. Changing how you view your behavior lets you feel better about what you actually did, at least in that moment.

Denying your own behavior may provide some comfort in the moment, but not only are you turning away from your emotions, you are turning away from your own problematic behavior. Sustained denial is problematic in general, but it's even more problematic when it's denial about your own behavior, because it keeps you from making the changes necessary for becoming a happier person. It allows a fixable problem to remain in place.

Everyone makes mistakes. That's part of the human condition. Mistakes provide an opportunity to learn and grow. They help you get better and improve. But if you don't acknowledge and admit to the mistakes you make, then you cannot learn and grow from them, and you'll probably continue to make the same mistakes over and over again until you listen to what they have to teach you.

DENYING YOUR ABUSIVE BEHAVIOR ENCOURAGES MORE ABUSE

The behavior that you engage in that we are most concerned about in this book is your abusive and controlling behavior. Because abusive and controlling behavior is inherently hurtful of others, it often causes uncomfortable emotions like guilt, sadness, remorse, and regret. If you are able to sit with those emotions, you can use them to motivate you to make changes, including not repeating those behaviors. On the other hand, if you struggle to be honest with yourself about how you behave and how it affects others, those behaviors are likely to persist and become patterns of abuse and control. Only when you break through your denial and honestly and courageously look at what you have actually done can any true change take place.

Listed below are some of the most common ways people avoid looking at their abusive behavior. As you read them, keep an eye out for things you have said or thought yourself.

WHAT DENIAL SOUNDS LIKE

"I am not a violent person." "I would never hit my partner." "I have never punched anybody." "I'm not a wife-beater." These are the most common justifications we hear. They define abusive behavior as exclusively involving physical violence, or even extreme physical violence that causes serious injury. By that standard, you may well not qualify as violent—if you ignore physical abuse like pushing or blocking someone's way, and verbal, psychological, and other forms of nonphysical abuse that you have repeatedly exhibited. In reality, most abusive partners exhibit little to no physical abuse. Most abusive behavior is verbal and psychological. Just because you have never physically assaulted your partner does not mean you have not been abusive to them in other ways.

"I'm a nice/good person." "Everyone likes me." "I've never had any problems at work." "I get along with my neighbors, coworkers, and everyone else." This justification implies that people who are abusive are abusive to everyone. The assumption is that if there are lots of people you are respectful toward—probably almost everyone—then you don't qualify as an abusive person. In reality, most abusive partners are only abusive to their immediate family—sometimes not even directly to their children—and not toward anyone else. The problem is that being repeatedly abusive to anyone is a concern, regardless of how many others you treat well.

"I'm a great partner." "I'm a great parent." "Look at all the kind and loving things I do for my partner and kids." This justification implies that people who are abusive are bad and mean people and only do bad and mean things. It plays into the stereotype that abusive partners have no redeeming qualities and are not liked at all by their families. The assumption is that if there are a variety of ways that you are kind and behave well with your partner, even ways that they themselves acknowledge and endorse, then you cannot be abusive. In reality, most abusive partners have a variety of positive and desirable qualities. Most abusive partners do a variety of good and kind things. The problem is not a lack of goodness or kindness, it is the presence of patterns of abuse and control.

"I'm not an angry person." "I'm a happy person." "I'm very calm." This justification plays into the stereotype that abusive partners have a lot of anger or are angry or reactive most of the time. The stereotype is that they are continually agitated and have angry outbursts on a regular basis. The assumption is that if you rarely get intense or angry or lose your temper, then this is not an issue for you. In reality, much abusive and controlling behavior is done when a person is quite calm and not necessarily agitated. Radiating intensity, which we mentioned in the first chapter, is one example of this. While outward anger is a symptom of the problem for some abusive partners, others rarely experience or express it.

"I'm not like those other guys." "I've never been arrested before." "I'm not a criminal." There are a variety of negative stereotypes about abusive partners: they break lots of laws, they have chips on their shoulders, they have a bad attitude with everyone, they're poorly groomed, they are poor or underemployed, etc. Abusive partners are often characterized as being working-class, drinking too much, and having had multiple brushes with the law. The assumption is that if you don't fit the stereotype—you are generally law-abiding, well-dressed, a hard worker, no criminal history, etc.—then you are not an abusive partner. In reality, abusive partners are as diverse in their backgrounds as anyone else. They come from every social class, occupation, religion, age, sexual orientation, and so forth. There is no one profile or personality of an abusive partner. Many abusive partners have never been involved with the criminal justice system. While some do abuse alcohol and other drugs, many do not.

"I come from a good home." "My parents raised me right." "I had a great upbringing." This justification draws on the assumption that abusive partners come from abusive homes in which they learned their bad behavior from a parent or other adult who behaved at least as badly as they do. The assumption is that if you had a relatively good upbringing and grew up in a loving home, then you cannot be an abusive partner. In reality, while it is true that some abusive partners—especially those with the most severe forms of abuse—grew up in abusive homes, many did not. Many abusive partners were brought up well by parents who got along and treated them fairly well. Your childhood experience is not the only factor that determines whether you will be abusive or controlling.

"I would never do the awful things my parents did." "I vowed to never be like my father/mother." "I would never treat my partner the way my father treated my mother." It is common for people who grew up in abusive homes to promise themselves they'll never behave the way their abusive parent did. The people who make that promise to themselves usually have at least some success, in that they are often not as extreme in their abuse as their parent was. The assumption is that if you have not done the kinds of things your abusive parent did, then you are not abusive or that bad. In reality, although you may not go to the extremes your parent did, less severe forms of abuse are still not okay. Every kind of abusive behavior can inflict deep suffering on others that is as bad or nearly as bad as more extreme forms of abuse.

"It was all a big mistake." "It was just a misunderstanding." "I should not have done that and never have before and never will again." The implication here is that whatever was done was a one-time thing that can be easily corrected. The assumption is that if it was a mistake, then all you need to do is avoid making that mistake again, and everything will be fine. In reality, it might be true that a particular incident was truly a mistake that you will never make again. However, the specific incident is typically just one example of a much larger pattern. Behaving better means not just avoiding repeating that particular behavior, but also stopping the less extreme but more common and significant underlying patterns of abuse and control that you have. To do that means changing your belief system, not just your behavior. The most extreme behaviors are often the easiest and quickest to stop. The harder work is stopping the less extreme behaviors and changing the beliefs that support them.

"I did not do what they said I did in the police report." "Child Welfare has got it all wrong." "That police report is filled with falsehoods and inaccuracies." This justification involves disputing the accuracy of the accusations made about you. The assumption is that if some part of an incident was inaccurately recorded, then it invalidates the entire report and you are therefore not abusive. In reality, a partly inaccurate incident report does not erase the abusive behavior you actually engaged in, and the specific incident that led to agency involvement is not the only abusive behavior you have exhibited.

"My partner is bipolar." "My partner is Borderline." "My partner has a substance abuse problem." The justification here is that if your partner has issues that make them challenging to get along with at times, you either "had" to be abusive or controlling for their own good, or their behavior was so out of line that "anyone" would have behaved the way you did. The assumption is that if their behavior caused you to behave poorly, then their behavior is the true problem; if they behaved well, you would never have behaved badly. In reality, most abused partners do not have mental health issues that are not caused by the abuse they have experienced from you. They can behave and function relatively well when they are consistently treated respectfully. Furthermore, no partner is perfect. Whatever your partner's imperfections may be, none of them cause you to be abusive. Most people are not abusive with their partners—even people who are in relationships with deeply flawed and troubled partners. Regardless of your partner's flaws and psychological issues, you are 100% responsible for any abusive behavior you exhibit toward them. None of it is justifiable.

"They're super sensitive because they used to be with an abusive partner." "They grew up in an abusive home, so they're very sensitive." The justification here is that if your partner was abused as a child or by a previous partner, then they are quick to assume behavior is abusive, even when it is not. The assumption is that you didn't do anything wrong—they simply misperceived, misinterpreted, or overreacted to what you did. The problem is not anything you are doing, it is their past trauma. In reality, while abuse survivors can be extra vigilant and aware of abusive behavior, it is rare that they mischaracterize behavior that is not abusive as being abusive. Even if they do, a partner who is not abusive will do their best to change the concerning behavior (not speak as loud, offer more kind reassurance), rather than be dismissive of their partner's experience.

"I grew up in an abusive home and it is a trauma response." "I have PTSD." The justification here is that if you grew up in an abusive home or otherwise are a trauma survivor yourself, your reactivity or abusiveness is understandable—it is just part of your condition. There is also an implication that you cannot help being that way because of what was done to you in the past. In reality, any trauma you have experienced can cause a variety of internal reactions, but it is not the cause of your abusive behavior. Most people who grew up in abusive homes or survived other forms of trauma are not abusive, even when in a triggered state.

"I had too much to drink." "I have substance abuse issues." "This only happens when I have been drinking/using." There are two separate but related ways of thinking at play in this justification. The first is that the alcohol or drugs you were using made you act that way, so it wasn't really your fault. As long as you don't drink or use like that again, you'll be fine. The second is that your substance abuse is the cause of your abusive behavior, so if you get clean and sober, then you will not act that way again. In reality, alcohol and drug use and abuse do not cause abusive behavior. They can escalate it and trigger certain abusive behaviors that only occur when you are intoxicated, but the problems remain even if you get sober or are not intoxicated. Substance abuse treatment alone may lead to a reduction in the most severe and extreme abusive behaviors, but it does not usually stop all of the abusive behaviors, because the abusive behaviors are not caused exclusively by substance abuse.

"My partner didn't even want me to be arrested." "They pled with the police not to arrest me." "They asked the court not to prosecute me." Abused partners often object to police involvement or afterward express regret about calling the police or getting the court involved. This is then used to support the justification that no abuse happened in the first place or that it was really no big deal. In reality, even if your partner did not want you to be arrested or prosecuted, you are still responsible for being abusive in the first place. It is common for abused partners to recant their testimony, not because the abuse did not take place, but because they are concerned about the consequences, legal and otherwise. The fact that they don't want you in the criminal justice system does not mean that you have done nothing wrong.

"My partner really knows how to push my buttons." "They really know how to set me off." "They are a really difficult person." There are a couple of separate but related thoughts involved in this justification. The first is that your partner provoked you into behaving badly. The implication is that anyone in your shoes would have acted similarly. If your partner doesn't act that way again, you will not be abusive. The second is that you and your partner were acting equally poorly, and therefore the behaviors should cancel each other out, like offsetting penalties in a football game. Because they behaved badly, your bad behavior doesn't count. In reality, there are plenty of people with difficult partners who do not become abusive when their partners are behaving poorly. Even if your partner behaved poorly, there is no excuse or justification for the abuse that you engaged in. Regardless of how you were feeling, you gave yourself permission to be abusive, and you didn't have to.

"My partner is lying about this." "My partner set me up." "My partner is just trying to get custody of the kids." One implication of this justification is that your partner in some way manipulated you into becoming abusive. Another is that they were not fully honest with the police. The assumption is that if your partner lied about the incident, then it didn't happen and you have done nothing wrong. In reality, people who are abusive are quick to view their partner as being against them, which is often not true. Such statements may be a result of a distorted view of your partner. Even if your partner did behave in a deceptive or manipulative way, it is important that you look at what you actually did that was inappropriate and take responsibility for it. Focus on what you did—the part that is true—rather than on what you did not do.

"My partner bruises easily." "I hardly even touched them." "They were clumsy and they fell." "I didn't mean to hurt them." All of these justifications say that you didn't intend for anyone to be injured or impacted the way they were. The assumption is that if you did not intend to hurt them or for them to be hurt, then what you did was not so bad or abusive. In reality, whether you consciously intended to hurt someone or not, you are still responsible for your actions. Abuse is abuse, regardless of whether it causes injury.

***

This chapter has presented a variety of ways that defense mechanisms and other ways of thinking can help you avoid feeling and addressing uncomfortable emotions and the behaviors that may contribute to them. Another way of avoiding those feelings and behaviors is by artificially changing your emotions through the use of alcohol, other drugs, and other mood-altering experiences; that is the focus of the next chapter.

CHAPTER 8

MOOD-ALTERING SUBSTANCES AND EXPERIENCES

As we discussed in the previous chapter, it can be tempting to avoid uncomfortable emotions by turning away from them. Although this turning away, or denial, of those uncomfortable emotions may provide temporary relief, the problems and behaviors that cause them are still there, just in the dark, like a closet full of things that haven't been dealt with: out of sight, but not truly gone. We listed a number of common ways of thinking that allow people to avoid looking at what's causing their uncomfortable emotions, but there is another way of avoiding uncomfortable emotions, which is to artificially change the way you feel. You can do this with alcohol, cannabis, and other drugs, as well as certain behaviors. These artificially mood-altering substances and behaviors are the focus of this chapter.

There is clear research that shows that substance abuse is more common among people with abuse and control issues than in the general population. There are a number of reasons this is true, but what is most relevant for now is that substance abuse makes it easier to stay in denial; to stay stuck in old, unhelpful ways of behaving; and to block positive growth and change from occurring. It is important to examine the role that mood-altering substances and behaviors play in your life, the extent to which you might have a substance abuse issue, and even if you are not abusing a substance, what, if any, problems mood-altering behaviors are causing for you and others close to you.

MOOD-ALTERING EXPERIENCES

When we think of addiction or substance abuse issues, we usually think of chemicals such as alcohol and other drugs. However, there are a number of behaviors that can also artificially change the way you feel. This is also referred to as "process addiction." Here are some examples:

food
gambling
internet
pornography
sex
shopping
television
video games/computer games
working long hours

What all of the above have in common is the ability to artificially change your mood. They might make you feel better, even when whatever is making you unhappy is still there. The problem is that the lift you feel in your mood is not caused by any real change in your circumstance, but solely due to the activity that's distracting you from your uncomfortable feelings. You can fool yourself into thinking things are better, but in truth, they are just the same. In that way they can be used like alcohol or other drugs.

"BUT I DON'T HAVE AN ISSUE WITH ALCOHOL AND DRUGS!"

Some people clearly have an addiction to alcohol and/or other drugs. They repeatedly drink or use too much and have problems that arise from that use. If that is not the case for you, it can be easy to think a discussion about mood-altering substances and behaviors is irrelevant for you. However, mood-altering substances and behaviors are something all of us encounter and wrestle with at some level. The real question is not whether you have an issue with them, but rather where you struggle with them. Hopefully by the end of this chapter you will have some beginning clarity about that. As with every other chapter in this book, we encourage you to focus your attention on what does apply, not on what does not. We guarantee that at least some of what we cover in this chapter applies to you. We ask that you keep an open mind and focus on what is relevant.

SUBSTANCE USE/ABUSE DOES NOT CAUSE ABUSIVE BEHAVIOR

If they were drinking or using at the time of being abusive, people often make the excuse that they were intoxicated and not in their right mind. We want to make it clear that although alcohol and drug use may *trigger* abusive behavior, it does not *cause* abusive behavior. While being intoxicated can make it more tempting to be abusive, in part because judgment is compromised, being abusive is still a choice. There are plenty of people who are intoxicated and/or have substance abuse issues who are never abusive. Likewise, even when intoxicated, abusive people will still only give themselves permission to do certain things. Intoxication will not make someone abusive, but it can tempt them to give themselves permission to be abusive or to be more abusive.

SUBSTANCE USE/ABUSE CAN INTERFERE WITH ATTEMPTS TO STOP YOUR ABUSIVE BEHAVIOR.

One of the things that will keep a stuck person stuck, even if they are seeking to change, is an active addiction. This is one reason that programs that seek to help abusive people stop their abuse are not always effective: because the person is still abusing substances. Ongoing substance abuse often limits the effectiveness and impact of other change processes. This is why it is important to monitor and be mindful of your substance use to make sure it is not problematic.

In this chapter we look at various ways mood-altering substances and behaviors can contribute to abuse and control. We will address the issue in three different ways. First, with a brief overview of substance abuse and addiction. Second, by helping you identify which mood-altering experiences you use to manage your emotions. Third, by identifying how even casual use of alcohol and other drugs can be problematic.

SUBSTANCE ABUSE AND ADDICTION

When it comes to people's relationships with alcohol and other recreational drugs, a person typically falls into one of four categories with each drug: abstinence, use, abuse, or dependence. Here is a simple definition for each category.

Abstinence means you do not use alcohol or a particular drug. Because you don't use it, you cannot have a problem with it. For example, if you have never used cocaine, you cannot have a problem with cocaine. That does not mean you would not have a problem with it if you did use it, just that it is unknown.

Use means that you do use alcohol or a particular drug, but do not have problems of any kind that arise from that use. For example, you might occasionally have a beer or a glass of wine with a meal, and it is never a problem or issue. You might smoke pot once in a while for fun, and it has never been a problem or issue. There are many people who occasionally drink alcohol or use pot and do not have any problems that arise from that use.

Abuse means that you use the substance and that it has caused you a problem, but you are able to consistently control or manage your use of it, so it no longer causes you a problem. For example, maybe you drank too much and got hungover or threw up. After a bad experience like that, you presumably made changes to your alcohol use so it would not happen again. You did not stop your drinking, but you modified it. This is common, especially for people in their teens and mid-twenties. Typically, people report having a few bad experiences with alcohol and then modifying their use, but not stopping it, and no longer having problems with it. For this group of people, most of their inappropriate use of a substance happened in their mid-teens and mid-twenties. It is less common for them to have issues with inappropriate use as they get older.

A subset of substance abuse that is often overlooked is **ongoing moderate use**. Typically, this is only true for widely available substances—alcohol, cannabis, and mood-altering prescription drugs like narcotic painkillers or certain antianxiety medications. People within this subset often do not have obvious problems related to their use. They are gainfully employed, are active in family and social events, and successfully manage most of their responsibilities. If you fall into this group, your substance use is rarely obviously excessive, and usually looks like this:

- alcohol: 3 or more drinks most nights (i.e., enough to catch a light buzz)
- pot: 1–2 hits most nights
- prescription drugs (painkillers or antianxiety meds): heavier use in the evenings on most nights, which is greater than prescribed

Timing is key here. Use typically occurs relatively late in the day when you are most prone to feeling emotionally connected and aware. It is typically a "winding down" time, when the day slows down but it is not yet time to go to sleep; people are often more present with their feelings now because they are less distracted by the normal routines of life. This type of use helps you anesthetize and avoid the emotional self-awareness that is easier to avoid throughout the day. There is nothing wrong with occasionally "unwinding" with alcohol or pot, but in the case of ongoing moderate substance use, it's not just occasionally, but on most nights. This level of use still achieves the dysfunctional goal of emotional anesthetizing, and in that way, it qualifies as abuse because of its persistence.

Dependence or addiction means you have a problem with the alcohol/drug, and if you continue to use it, it will inevitably cause more problems, despite any attempts you make to modify or manage your use. In other words, you are not able to consistently or reliably control your use. Dependence does not mean that every time you use you have problems; it means that sometimes when you use you have problems. It does not mean that every time you use you cannot control it, just that sometimes when you use you cannot control it. Typically, sometimes when you decide to drink/use, you do not accurately predict how much you use. Sometimes you use exactly as much or as often as you planned, but other times you use more or more frequently than planned, and it causes problems. It is like playing Russian roulette: sometimes the gun fires, sometimes it doesn't.

In younger people (mid-teens to mid-twenties), this group can look like people who abuse but are not dependent on a substance. However, people who are not dependent are able to modify their use without abstaining, but those who are dependent or addicted cannot. They continue to struggle even after they know they don't want further problems. For people who cannot reliably control their use, the only viable option is abstinence. Addicts and alcoholics fall into this group.

Most people in the US have stories to tell about drinking too much or using a drug that ended up causing them problems. For most people, this happens somewhere between their mid-teens and mid-twenties, and they eventually modify their use so that it is consistently fun and free of problems. With these substances they were abstinent when younger, had a period of use and perhaps abuse, and then shifted back to use and/or abstinence. People who are dependent or addicted to a substance often need to become abstinent to prevent further problems. They never know for sure if their use will lead to a problem, so use is not an option. In general, if people are still reporting repeated issues or problems caused by substance use in their thirties or later, they are often dealing with dependence or addiction.

Based on these four categories—abstinence, use, abuse, and dependence—where does your alcohol and drug use fall? You need to answer this for each substance that you have ever used. Do your best to be honest with yourself about this. Have other people in your life expressed concerns about your use? Why do you think that is? If you are uncertain about whether alcohol and drug use is an issue for you and you are attending a group, ask your group. It is also important that you stay honest with yourself and the group about just how much and how often you are drinking and using drugs. If you are not staying honest with yourself and the group about your frequency and level of use, it is almost certainly a problem.

Examining your relationship with mood-altering experiences can be complicated because some, like food, sex, and shopping, are difficult or impossible to truly abstain from. Furthermore, virtually everyone engages in some mood-altering experiences. Just like with alcohol, these experiences are not a problem in moderation. The relief is temporary and you ultimately deal with the true causes of your distress. They become a problem when they are engaged in repeatedly to avoid the same uncomfortable emotions. A little denial is not a problem; ongoing denial is. These behaviors become a form of substance abuse when they are used to excess—to the point where they are causing a problem, like costing too much time, money, or energy. Something becomes an addiction when your use of it becomes habitual and uncontrollable.

When it comes to mood-altering experiences, the question is not just "Am I addicted?" but "Which mood-altering experiences do I most typically resort to?" Everyone has certain experiences that they use to comfort themselves and self-soothe, and which, on occasion, they may overuse. What do you use to help settle yourself and comfort yourself when you're feeling uncomfortable? These are the experiences you need to monitor. If you're using them more than usual, you may be experiencing greater emotional distress. Be careful not to go down that road too long or too far; it can lead to greater problems.

PROBLEMS WITH CASUAL ALCOHOL AND DRUG USE

Intoxication refers to feeling the effects of alcohol or another drug. Even a single drink can lead to intoxication. Although it is not necessary to practice abstinence if you are not addicted to or dependent on a substance, even intoxication due to casual recreational use can contribute to abusive behavior. Below are some of the effects of casual use.

IMPAIRED JUDGMENT

One of the first things affected by intoxication is a person's judgment. Because your thinking is typically clouded when you are intoxicated, you may make poor choices about what you say and do not say, how you say it, and what you do. You may give yourself permission to make a choice that you wouldn't if you were completely clear-headed.

LOWERED INHIBITIONS

Impaired judgment can give you false courage and lead you to give yourself permission to do things you might not otherwise do. Sometimes this might be positive, like having the courage to ask someone to dance or sharing how you really feel. On the other hand, it might be negative, like having sex with someone you otherwise wouldn't or saying things you later regret. People who are intoxicated tend to be impulsive, which can cause problems; drunken phone calls and texts are a good example of this.

146

IMPAIRED JUDGMENT OF THOSE AROUND YOU

If you are drinking or using with other people, you'll also have to deal with their intoxication. They too have compromised judgment when under the influence, and may do or say things they otherwise would not, which could make it more tempting for you to respond in abusive or controlling ways.

DISTORTED PERCEPTION

Intoxication causes clouded thinking and distorted perceptions that can lead you to respond inappropriately. You might be more likely to engage in negative self-talk and negative and distorted thinking.

INCREASED DENIAL, STUFFING, AND EMOTIONAL AVOIDANCE

One goal of intoxication is to avoid uncomfortable feelings. This is not necessarily problematic in moderation, but in combination with other forms of emotional avoidance and denial, it can become so.

REDUCED SELF-AWARENESS

When you numb out, you may be less aware of when you are getting escalated. You may not notice ways you are feeling escalated or becoming more agitated. Because of this lack of self-awarenss, you may be slower to do what is necessary to help yourself settle.

COMPROMISED SELF-CARE

When you are less self-aware, you may be less likely to take good care of yourself. You may overlook your need to eat, sleep, spend time alone, etc.

IMPAIRED COMMUNICATION SKILLS

Clouded thinking may make it harder for you to use effective communication skills, especially those that are newer to you, and easier to go back to saying things the way you have in the past. It is vital that you and your partner are both clear-headed for any difficult conversations you might have.

REDUCED AWARENESS OF OTHERS

When you are in an altered state, you may be less aware of how others feel, and may not fully understand what they are saying or doing. This makes it easier to misunderstand or neglect others, which can lead to problems.

INCREASED RISK OF INAPPROPRIATE BEHAVIOR

Even when people are intoxicated, they still give themselves permission to do what they do. This is why people who are generally not abusive will not become abusive when intoxicated: even in an altered state, they believe it is unacceptable to be abusive. On the other hand, you may be tempted to behave abusively when you are intoxicated because you can later blame the intoxicated state for your abuse. It can almost become a "get out of jail free" card.

REDUCED EMOTIONAL AWARENESS OF INAPPROPRIATE BEHAVIOR

After a difficult interaction with your partner, particularly if you behaved inappropriately, it can be tempting to use a substance to help you to calm down and settle. The problem is that it may also help you avoid feeling an appropriate sense of guilt and discomfort about what you have done. Part of being accountable includes being honest with yourself about how you feel about what you have done, even if it makes you feel uncomfortable. That discomfort can be a significant motivation to change or stop the behavior. If you avoid the emotional discomfort, you may be less motivated to make the necessary changes.

INCREASED RISK OF CONFLICT WITH YOUR PARTNER

Sometimes partners have concerns over even a low level of substance use. They may be afraid that it will not stay low-level, perhaps because of their own family history, or they may experience you as behaving differently even at this level. This may lead to arguments that are difficult to navigate.

INCREASED EXPOSURE TO NEGATIVE INFLUENCES

If you are drinking or using, there is a good chance other people around you are doing the same. Even if you are managing yourself well, others may not be, and their impaired judgment can become your problem.

***

In reviewing the list above, how might casual substance use and low-grade intoxication be problematic for you? Which of the above can you relate to? If you want to protect your work toward being a respectful, nonabusive person, you need to do everything you can to make sure your substance use has as few negative consequences as possible, regardless of your level of use.

A variety of uncomfortable feelings can encourage substance use and abuse, but one of the most uncomfortable is **shame**. Shame is a particularly damaging and problematic emotional state that can significantly contribute to denial and substance abuse. We will examine shame in the next chapter.

CHAPTER 9

ADDRESSING SHAME

Shame is one of the few emotions that is rooted in concerns about how others think and feel about you. It is a strongly unpleasant emotion that often leads to denial, and it can prevent you from doing the introspective work that helps you become nonabusive and noncontrolling. Even when people have made significant positive improvements, unaddressed shame can push them back into destructive behaviors. For all of these reasons and more, it is vital that you identify and address any significant shame you might have. This chapter is intended to help you do that.

Recall something that you have done in the past for which you feel ashamed, perhaps even one of the things you feel the most ashamed of. What are you concerned would happen if people learned that you had done that shameful thing? If you're like a lot of people, you might fear that others would:

- judge you harshly
- think less of you
- punish you
- not want to be around you
- no longer want to be your partner or your friend
- exclude you
- shun you
- want you to lose your job
- label you
- devalue you

- see you as nothing but that behavior
- stop liking you or caring about you

These fears do not always come to fruition, but sometimes people do respond like this. This is one reason some cultures use shame to discourage undesirable behaviors; the thinking is that if people are shamed for them, they won't engage in them. That is certainly true some of the time, but other times, for a variety of reasons, people do those things anyway—but they keep quiet about it. Shame silences people and pushes behaviors underground, where they continue unaddressed and unacknowledged.

When talking about something introduces a real risk of negative repercussions, it may seem better not to admit to, talk about, or even think about it. But if you can't even think or talk about something, how will you change it? If you handle behavior you feel ashamed of by pushing it "into the closet" or sweeping it "under the rug," never to be addressed, it cannot be examined, addressed, or changed.

THE DIFFERENCE BETWEEN SHAME AND GUILT

Many mental health professionals consider shame an unhealthy or less healthy emotional state, describing it as unhealthy shame or being shame-prone. We (and many others) believe the healthier emotional alternative is guilt, or healthy shame. Like shame, guilt arises when you do something wrong or bad or contrary to your morals, values, and self-image. Like shame, guilt is an uncomfortable feeling that you want to get rid of, but guilt is a more helpful, effective emotion that does not interfere with the change process like shame does. Guilt is far more likely to lead to true behavior change than shame, which may simply push the behavior underground. Let us compare how shame and guilt are different from each other and why guilt (or healthy shame) is preferable to shame (or unhealthy shame/being shame-prone).

CONDITIONAL LOVE

The key difference between shame and guilt is that shame is rooted in conditional love, whereas guilt is rooted in unconditional love. Understanding the difference is vital to understanding why a shame state is so destructive.

Conditional love means that you are only lovable under certain conditions, that you only deserve love if you act certain ways. It means that you can earn or lose love as a result of the way you behave. On the surface, this make sense: if someone wrongs you, you very well might stop liking them. However, living in a state of conditional love means believing no one will ever love you if you do certain things. Not just one person—no one. It means feeling like no one will ever love you.

Conditional love also means that love can disappear at any moment if you do the wrong thing, so you need to be forever vigilant. Conditional love presumes that you are not inherently lovable and you do not inherently deserve love. You are only lovable if you behave in certain ways; you only deserve love if you do certain things. Love is earned, not given.

The feeling of shame is rooted in a belief in conditional love. Shame makes you feel bad about who you are as a human being. It makes you feel like you no longer deserve love because of what you have done, like you are no longer lovable. It makes you feel unlovable and undeserving of love because of your actions, and it often leads to a strong sense of isolation. Since you cannot undo what you did, if and when others find out, you will lose their love and regard. Shame invites fears about how others will perceive you, and since there is nothing you can do to change the past, the next best thing is to deny it and do everything you can to hide it from others—and from yourself. Shame encourages a focus and preoccupation with how others perceive you rather than how you truly are. It can deter you from being true to yourself and instead "act" how you think others want you to behave. Because the behavior is not genuine, it may be difficult to sustain.

For many people, the fear of being discovered and the shame of knowing what they have done are never resolved. With shame there is no way to ever get past the bad behavior, even if you never do it again. With shame you are doomed to be judged by your past, no matter how different you may be in the present. As a result, people are often labeled and defined, forever, by their past behavior—as an "alcoholic" or as an "abuser," for example.

UNCONDITIONAL LOVE

Unconditional love, on the other hand, means that you are lovable no matter what. Although you may do unlovable things, they do not make you an unlovable person. Unconditional love means you cannot lose the right to deserve love, no matter what you do. Your actions may lose you the love of a specific person, but you can never lose the right to be loved in general.

Unconditional love also means that although you may not be able to undo the things you have done, they do not need to define you. By behaving differently in the present, you can still experience love and acceptance, although not necessarily from someone you wronged in the past. Your past behavior matters, but it does not define you, especially if you behave differently in the present.

The feeling of guilt is rooted in unconditional love. When you feel guilty, you feel bad about something you have done, rather than about who you are. You may have done bad things, but you are not unlovable. Guilt does not feel as isolating as shame does. Guilt focuses more on how you see yourself than on how others see you. Guilt acknowledges that you have done something wrong, and that there is hope for the future because you can change things going forward. Guilt does not label people or define them by their past. Guilt allows you to have a different future that's based on your present. As they say, "All saints have a past and all sinners have a future."

The truth is that everyone deserves love and everyone is lovable. Not everyone will love you, and you might lose someone's love because of how you behave, but you won't lose the love of everyone, and you can be loved again.

Shame focuses on the whole person, saying you're a bad person who is underserving of love. Guilt focuses on the bad behavior, acknowledging that the behavior is unlovable, but the person deserves love. Your behavior may have been bad, but it's not all that you are. Shame presumes that bad people do bad things, but guilt acknowledges that good people can do bad things.

Shame makes people less motivated to change, because it believes the behavior is consistent with the person. Guilt, on the other hand, pushes for change, by acknowledging the dissonance between the good person and their bad behavior. Guilt inspires people to stop behaving badly and be the good person they are. With shame, the message is "You are not welcome here. There is no place at the table for you." With guilt, it's more like "You are welcome here. You can join us, but you need to check your bad behavior at the door."

SHAME AND ABUSIVE BEHAVIOR

Violence and abuse are viewed very negatively all over the world; most people agree that being violent is a bad thing that is to be avoided as much as possible. Many people have a negative judgment about people who are violent. As a result, it is common for people who are abusive to want to deny it. Some level of shame about their abuse is common, and typically, the greater their shame, the greater their denial and refusal to acknowledge and examine their abusive behavior. It is just too much to admit to; it is too painful and uncomfortable.

It is quite appropriate to feel guilty about your abusive behavior and how it has hurt people you love and care about, but it is not helpful at all to feel shame over it. In order to move forward and become nonabusive, it is necessary to move past your shame. It is okay to feel guilt, remorse, sadness, and other uncomfortable feelings, and even to feel ashamed (which is actually closer to guilt than shame)—but not shame. The goal is to shift any shame you are feeling about your abusive behaviors to guilt.

It is vital to remember that although you may have done some bad things, you are still a good person. You can pull your behaviors more in line with the good person you truly are, and the first step toward doing that is to move past and heal any shame you have about what you have done.

Before Alcoholics Anonymous was founded, alcoholism was as seen as a moral failing in the United States, and strong judgment was placed on alcoholics. The goal of AA is to reduce the shame so something can actually be done about the addiction. The program features disclosure of the issue and being welcomed into the group by other alcoholics—which in itself is a shame-reducer. Today, there is much less shame around alcoholism and other addictions. People who are alcoholics are seen as whole people now, rather than being solely defined by and judged for their drinking. People are quicker to acknowledge and address problems with substance abuse. Some people still feel ashamed of being an alcoholic or an addict, but they are far more willing to address the issue than before.

Abusive behavior, on the other hand, still stirs up a great deal of shame and fear of judgment. People who are identified as having been abusive are typically vilified. As a result, it is rare for people to acknowledge their abusive behavior, even to themselves. They use other words that don't sound as bad (or shameful), like "anger" or "reactive" or "intense." The problem is that pushing it underground lets it go unaddressed. If it is not accurately named, it is unlikely to be effectively addressed.

Shame does not cause abusive behavior, but it can contribute to it, most commonly through denial. The more shame you feel, the more difficult it is to examine it, admit to it, and change it. As they say in AA, you can't heal what you can't feel, and you're only as sick as your secrets. Your feelings of shame about the abuse is likely to keep it in the closet where it is unacknowledged and unaddressed.

Beyond that, shame will also block helpful interventions like engaging with a group to address abusive behavior. For some people, being in a group triggers so much shame that they drop out—although they typically give other reasons, like "it wasn't a good fit," "I'm not like the other people in the group," or "they're much worse than me."

Feeling strong shame about *anything* can trigger abusive behavior, just as any kind of distress can trigger abusive behavior in someone prone to abuse. Because shame is a particularly uncomfortable and unpleasant emotion to experience, it can be particularly triggering.

Shame can also interfere with your ability to address problematic behaviors that play a role in your abusive behavior. For example, if shame prevents someone from addressing their substance abuse, it's that much more difficult for them to address their abusive behavior.

COMMON INDICATORS OF SHAME

People are not always aware of or willing to admit to their shame. Listed below are some common indicators that you are struggling with significant shame.

IMPRESSION MANAGEMENT

This refers to trying to present yourself in as positive a light as possible. It includes talking up your achievements, talking about how well-liked you are, dressing more professionally or elaborately than necessary, and denying your imperfections. Because you fear that others will evaluate you negatively, you work extra hard to convince them otherwise.

SPEAKING WITH DISGUST ABOUT EVEN THE POSSIBILITY OF BEING ABUSIVE

For people prone to shame, even the suggestion that you might have been abusive is abhorrent and inconceivable. If someone raises the issue or asks a question, it can be deeply disturbing. Listen for responses like "I can't believe you would even ask me a question like that!" or "What kind of a person do you think I am?"

BECOMING IMMEDIATELY DEFENSIVE

People prone to shame struggle to consider the possibility that they are abusive. They are very quick to assume accusations are being made, and quick to defend themselves. Ironically, this response itself is a form of controlling behavior.

SPEAKING HARSHLY ABOUT PEOPLE WHO ARE ABUSIVE, WHILE DENYING THEY COULD EVER BE LIKE THAT

For people prone to shame, it is not enough to deny that they engage in a shameful behavior; they feel a need to go further and denigrate others. Listen for put-downs, name-calling, and statements like "People who abuse their partners are really sick."

DESCRIBING ABUSIVE AND CONTROLLING BEHAVIOR IN SOFTER LANGUAGE

Another common quality of people with shame is using euphemisms like "anger," "conflict," and "arguments" to describe their abuse and control. Even after it is pointed out how certain behaviors are abusive or controlling, they will continue to refuse to use those terms, even in private.

REFUSING TO GATHER INFORMATION ABOUT WHETHER ABUSE IS AN ISSUE FOR YOU

For people with significant shame, the possibility that they might have issues with abuse and control is unthinkable, so they typically refuse to research or seek consultation about it. Even the thought of that possibility is more than they can bear, and they are often quite resistant to examining it. This lack of self-examination prevents them from realizing what is actually going on.

HEALING FROM SHAME

There are many ways to move through and heal from shame, but none are quick or easy. There are countless books written about it; John Bradshaw and Brené Brown lead the pack. Individual therapy can be helpful. Some people draw on spiritual practices or the loving support of friends and family.

Although healing shame can help you to become nonabusive, you can stop your abusive behavior without doing so. In fact, if you don't focus on stopping your abuse and control, shame work alone will not stop the abuse—and it may even escalate it because of the uncomfortable feelings it raises.

MOVING PAST THE SHAME YOU FEEL ABOUT YOUR ABUSIVE BEHAVIOR

You do not need to heal *all* of your shame to stop your abuse and control, but you *do* need to address the shame you have over your abuse. If you don't, it may keep you from making real change in this area. Below are some common ways people who have been abusive and controlling have been able to move through their shame about their behavior.

TALK ABOUT IT WITH SUPPORTIVE PEOPLE

The simplest method is to talk about and acknowledge the behaviors that continue to cause you shame in a safe and supportive environment. This is something you might need to do repeatedly to truly banish your shame. This could be with friends, a therapist, or the people in your group. The more you talk about it, the easier it becomes to talk about it. It's like building up a muscle: you might start out weak, but with practice, you get stronger.

ENROLL IN AN ABUSE-INTERVENTION GROUP

One of the many reasons a group for abusive partners can be so helpful and transformative is that it reduces the shame that keeps people from talking about and examining their abusive and controlling behavior. It is the only place where these conversations are normal, routine, and conducted without judgment. As people go through the process of disclosing their abusive behavior to the group, they see that although the behavior is not okay, they are still okay, and they have the assistance, guidance, and support from the group as they begin to change their behavior.

DO AN ACCOUNTABILITY STATEMENT

Near the end of the book, we will review a written assignment called an Accountability Statement. Many people who do this assignment find that it reduces the shame they feel about their past abuse and control. It is especially effective when it is shared out loud in a group, but even the process of writing it can help.

PRACTICE SELF-COMPASSION

Self-compassion is the antidote to shame. Actively practicing self-compassion can significantly reduce shame and prevent it from showing up in the first place. We will review this in greater detail in Chapter 18: Learning to Self-Soothe.

PART THREE

THE PATH TO BECOMING NONABUSIVE

CHAPTER 10

START WITH ACCOUNTABILITY

It is common for people who have been abusive to deny their abusive and controlling behavior and make excuses for it, which makes the behavior difficult to address and change. This refusal to acknowledge the abuse significantly increases the damage that it causes, like a disease that is left untreated.

If you say good morning to a coworker and they respond with "What's good about it? That's a big assumption you just made! I don't want or need your 'good morning.' You can just take that and shove it up your ass!" before storming off, it might leave you feeling surprised, hurt, and confused. You may have a variety of other thoughts and emotions, wondering what is going on with them, whether you did anything wrong, and how to deal with them in the future. You might feel uncomfortable, troubled, and pretty upset at them for talking with you that way. Now imagine that two different scenarios follow.

In the first scenario, they check in with you later about a work-related issue and make no mention of the earlier exchange. They act as if it never happened; they seem perfectly normal. How would that leave you feeling? How validating would that be? Would you feel better or worse?

Say you try to bring it up and they act like they don't know what you're talking about. Maybe they mention that you seem awfully sensitive. Or maybe they acknowledge it, but dismiss it as no big deal and suggest moving on. How would those responses leave you feeling?

Most people would feel even more confused, hurt, invalidated, and uneasy than after the initial exchange, because your coworker's refusal to acknowledge (let alone apologize for) what happened implies that your feelings and your experience do not matter. Bringing up the initial exchange only to have it dismissed or denied would probably leave you even more troubled and disturbed than you were to begin with. It was already a problem before, but now you feel even worse.

In the second scenario, your coworker finds you a short time after the original incident. They come up to you and immediately apologize for their behavior. They acknowledge that how they behaved with you was completely inappropriate and out of line. They make it clear that you didn't do anything wrong, and that they were having a difficult day and took it out on you. They say there was no call or justification for how they acted and they will do their best not to be that way with you again.

How would that make you feel?

For many people, it would feel validating. If the coworker takes full responsibility and acknowledges that their behavior was not okay, it is easier to forgive them. Their decision to talk with you implies that you matter; your feelings and your experience of the situation matter. It also validates your experience rather than leading you to question yourself. Talking to you makes it clear that they believe you deserve to be treated with respect, and they are calling themselves out for not doing so. It creates an opportunity for you to talk about your feelings and your experience, which makes it more manageable in your head. It may even let you feel closer to them than you did before. And it makes it more likely (but doesn't guarantee) that they won't do the same thing again in the future.

As they say, "It's not what you do, it's what you do next." Abusive behavior that is accountably acknowledged in a timely, affirming way is far less damaging than abusive behavior that is followed by silence and denial. It's like falling and scraping your knee. If you clean it up, it's more likely to heal better and faster. If you ignore it, it's more likely to get infected.

Sometimes, when someone admits to being abusive, they still justify and rationalize their abuse. They might make excuses (*"I was drunk"*) or blame the other person (*"You started it!"*), believing that justified abuse is simply appropriate and acceptable behavior. We see this in movies all the

time. The difference between heroes and villains or goo
guys is not that one group is violent and abusive and the c
are often abusive. Instead, what differentiates the hero fr
that the hero's abuse and violence are justified, whereas the villain's is not.
A movie villain is often someone who is abusive for no good reason, but
the hero always has a good reason, or is "forced" to be abusive, or "has" to
be abusive, in order to save lives. The villain can arbitrarily kill other
people for a minor infraction, but the hero can only use violence as a last
resort, even against the villain. If the villain is about to kill an innocent
person, the hero has to choose between remaining nonviolent and seeing
somebody die, and becoming violent to save someone's life. In the moment
they choose to engage in violence to save someone's life, the violence is
justified, so it is seen as heroic. The villain had it coming.

In real life, people who are abusive (especially those with patterns of
abuse) often see themselves as a hero rather than a villain, so they come up
with lots of ways to justify their behavior. They rarely see it as a mistake,
or even optional; they see it as necessary, unavoidable, and almost
inevitable. The other person had it coming.

One very common reason abusive people offer for their behavior is that
they had no choice. This is important to note, because most people, even
abusive people, understand that unjustified abuse is a bad thing—it is what
"bad" people do. To avoid seeing yourself as a bad person, you need to find
a way to make your abuse justifiable. If it wasn't your choice, then you are
not responsible for your behavior, and you can't be blamed for it or
required to change it. If you are forced to do something at gunpoint, you
are not really responsible.

In Chapter 1: Abusive Behaviors, we made a distinction between
hurtful behavior and abusive behavior. Hurtful behavior unwittingly and
unintentionally causes harm to another—like accidentally stepping on
someone's toe or making a comment that inadvertently hurts someone's
feelings. Almost everyone is occasionally hurtful, especially to those closest
to them, but they are quick to take responsibility, quick to apologize, and
determined not to do it again. They are not in denial about their behavior.
They can acknowledge that it hurt someone.

Abusive behavior, on the other hand, is intentional. It is a willful violation of another person's boundaries. It is part of a pattern, it is a result of a belief system, and denial allows it to continue.

Denial keeps the engines of abuse running by preventing you from feeling the discomfort your hurtful behavior causes. It is what turns accidental hurtful behavior into intentional abusive behavior. It is what allows you to behave in ways that are not true to your core values. It is what keeps you from being the kind of partner and parent that you truly want to be. It is what keeps you from changing. It is what keeps you stuck as you are instead of becoming a better, fuller you. If you are serious about stopping your behaviors, improving your relationships, and taking better care of yourself, then you need to find the courage to face your uncomfortable emotions and behavior and muster up the courage to change. You need to become accountable. Accountability is the key pivot point that will move you away from being abusive and controlling and toward being a better partner.

ACCEPTING RESPONSIBILITY FOR YOUR ACTIONS

Accountability is accepting responsibility for what you say and do. You are accountable when you acknowledge that your actions reflect your conscious choices. When it comes to being abusive and controlling, accountability means taking responsibility for your behavior. It means casting aside your excuses and justifications and acknowledging that you made the choice to be abusive and controlling. It means acknowledging that your abuse and control are 100% your fault.

By doing this you open yourself up to the possibility of change. If it is true that you chose to engage in abusive behavior, it is true that you could make a different choice. You could choose not to be abusive instead. The only person who can truly stop the abuse is the person who is abusive: you. You are not abusive because others make you abusive, but because you choose to be. Other people may be able to influence or affect your choice, but it is ultimately your choice, and yours alone. Let us look at this in more detail.

ABUSIVE BEHAVIOR IS NOT HARDWIRED OR REFLEXIVE

While being abusive and controlling is a conscious choice you make, it can be a habit and even pretty automatic. One very common excuse abusive individuals make for their abusive behavior is that they "couldn't help it." This implies that they had to be abusive, almost in the same way they have to breathe or swallow or blink. You can resist doing any of these things for only so long before you "can't help it," and do it. Although everyone breathes, swallows, and blinks their eyes, most people are basically never abusive, even in the most difficult and exasperating situations.

ABUSE AND CONTROL ARE ABOUT TAKING CONTROL, NOT LOSING CONTROL

Another common justification that abusive people give for their behavior is that they simply "lost control." The implication is that while normally you can control yourself and be nonabusive, in this particular situation your abusive behavior "got out"—like a dog breaking free of its leash. What is striking is that while you may "lose control" with your partner or children, you probably do not "lose control" with anyone else.

Similarly, even when you "lose control," there are many things you will not do. You might throw something, but probably not something of value; if you damage property, it is probably not your own. When abusive partners are asked about property abuse, many say they never have done significant damage because "it costs too much to replace things."

Likewise, it is common that abusive individuals who are "out of control" suddenly immediately get "in control" if an outsider—particularly law enforcement—shows up at the door.

A more accurate account is that when you were "losing control," you were not losing control of yourself; you were losing control of the situation. The situation was not unfolding the way you wanted it to, so you tried to take control of it by becoming abusive.

YOU ARE ALWAYS RESPONSIBLE FOR YOUR CHOICES

It is true that people and circumstances can negatively contribute to your life experiences. Someone can be hurtful to you and cause you suffering. Someone can cut you off on the highway. Others may contribute to your struggles and emotional state, but you choose how to respond. You may not be to blame for what was done to you or what happens to you, but you are responsible for how you respond. Even though other people can impact and influence you, they are not responsible for your choices or your behavior. Only you are. No one can make you abusive.

YOU GIVE YOURSELF PERMISSION TO BE ABUSIVE

People who are abusive not only think about being abusive, but also allow themselves to act on those thoughts. People who are not abusive may at times have abusive thoughts, but they do not give themselves permission to act on them. You need to strive to do the same thing: never give yourself permission to behave abusively. This may seem difficult, but even abusive people don't usually give themselves permission to be abusive—even when they are tempted.

For example, you probably don't give yourself permission to be abusive outside of your immediate family. You have not been abusive to neighbors, coworkers, strangers, friends, retailers, and so on. You may have wanted to—you might have thought they "had it coming" for some reason—but you didn't give yourself permission, because doing so could invoke significant consequences including arrest, public humiliation, and being seen as a bad person.

In the outside world, your control over others (drivers, merchants, neighbors, coworkers) is limited; you have little say over how they behave. But in your own home, you may feel more entitled to dictate how people act toward you. You may give yourself permission to act in abusive and controlling ways to achieve that goal. If your abuse only takes place in the privacy of your home, only your victim sees it—and they "had it coming" anyway.

ALL OF YOUR ABUSIVE BEHAVIORS ARE UNACCEPTABLE

Just as you give yourself permission to be abusive to only a few select individuals, you give yourself permission to engage in only certain kinds of abusive behaviors. Typically, the more extreme the behavior, the less likely you are to give yourself permission to use it. There are some abusive behaviors that you consider acceptable, and others you would truly never do.

Consider the following actions on a continuum: getting sarcastic with someone, calling them stupid, calling them an asshole, pushing them, hitting them, stabbing them, shooting them in the head. Chances are, you'd be far less comfortable engaging in the more extreme behaviors.

For another example, say you're sitting at the breakfast table when your partner makes a statement you disagree with. Could you imagine responding with "That's stupid"? Perhaps you actually have, and felt it was justifiable. But have you ever taken your fork and plunged it into their eye? It's likely that even thinking about that disturbs you.

When abusive partners in our groups are asked to consider that scenario, most respond with disgust, stating emphatically, "I would never do that! That's horrible!" Perhaps you would agree.

While plunging a fork into someone's eye is horrible and abusive and unacceptable and something you would never do, calling someone stupid is not horrible, and is perhaps a justifiable option. In other words, even for abusive people, including you, there are many abusive behaviors that are unacceptable. The goal is for you to not give yourself permission to do any kind of abusive behavior.

There are nearly always realistic alternatives to being abusive, but sometimes it's difficult to identify them, and being controlling can be quicker and easier, especially in the heat of the moment and when nonabusive behaviors are new to you. You'll need to commit to choosing to do what is right, rather than what is easy. Time-outs, which will be explained in a later chapter, can help buy you some time to come up with alternatives when you don't know what to do.

TAKING AN HONEST INVENTORY OF YOUR ACTIONS

In addition to taking responsibility for your actions, being accountable means to actually count those actions up. It is vital that you account for the full range and frequency of your abusive and controlling behaviors. Completing an honest inventory of your actions can help you see that your behaviors pose a serious problem—and motivate you to put an end to them. This is similar to the Fourth Step in AA and other twelve-step programs.

At first, nearly everyone who has been abusive is in some denial about the extent and effects of their abuse, but when accountability is coupled with true change, it can significantly contribute to healing and recovery in the people you have harmed.

In a later chapter, we will guide you through writing an Accountability Statement and a Letter of Accountability that not only acknowledge what you have done, but also how you have changed. It is an important and powerful set of exercises that essentially summarizes your entire program.

ACCEPTING PRIMARY ACCOUNTABILITY

Although many programs for abusive partners limit the discussion of accountability to abusive and controlling behavior, we believe you are responsible for ALL of your choices, as well as your emotional states, your needs, and your general well-being. We call this **primary accountability**.

Primary accountability doesn't mean you're responsible for everything that happens to you, but that you are responsible for how you respond to what happens to you. Things happen and people behave in ways you can't control, but you still have the power to determine how you handle them. For example, you can't control whether it rains, but you can usually control whether you get wet.

Primary accountability means taking responsibility for your own well-being. If you are unhappy or dissatisfied, it is ultimately up to you to do something about it. (And there is usually something you can do about it.) The coping and problem-solving skills named in the Serenity Prayer are typically involved. You can certainly enlist the help of others, but you're ultimately responsible, and you'll need to shift from an external to an internal focus.

SHIFTING FROM AN EXTERNAL TO AN INTERNAL FOCUS

It is very common for people who are abusive to have an external focus. An external focus inclines you to pay more attention to others than to yourself. For example, when you describe a situation, you tend to spend more time talking about what others did than what you did. An external focus presumes that your current state is the result of other people's actions, so in order to change how you feel, you'll have to manage others.

This leads to abuse and control: the belief that in order to take care of yourself, you need to make other people behave differently.

It's not surprising that people who are abusive typically experience a lot of anger. An external focus lets you blame others for your distress, and inappropriate anger is often caused by blame plus another emotion.

Traditional masculinity encourages an outward focus and discourages an inward focus. People who embrace traditional masculine qualities, regardless of their gender, tend to be disconnected from their emotions, wants, and needs, and to stay guarded, self-reliant, and not too trusting in order to prevent people from taking advantage of them. An external focus is very consistent with Power Over and the need to monitor and control others; both mindsets presume it's necessary to control and manage what others are doing in order to meet your own needs.

Childhood trauma also can result in development of an outward focus. Children who are repeatedly abused and neglected by their families tend to become vigilant and hypervigilant, closely monitoring their environment for signs of danger. Most childhood trauma survivors are not abusive unless they have a pro-abuse belief system. Environmental factors may trigger a trauma response, but they are unlikely to lead to abusive behavior. Childhood trauma can aggravate and escalate abusive behavior, but it does not cause it.

Because they are determined to control things they have no control over, people with an external focus tend to feel quite powerless; they are basically giving their power away. This makes them quick to fall into a victim stance, in which they feel like the world is against them. They put the blame squarely out there: on their families, the justice system, their employers, and so on. This victim mindset can take any general injustice or mistreatment, even of an entire group of people, and turn it into something much more personal that is specific to them in particular. They talk in broad generalizations about the "system" mistreating them, but ironically, most people who actually are victimized—by their partners, the system, etc.,—do not adopt a victim stance. They focus on taking care of themselves rather than getting stuck on what has been done to them.

The alternative to an external focus is an internal focus. An internal focus lets you look inward at your thoughts, emotions, actions, wants, and needs. It is focused on you. It is less focused on what happens to you or is done to you, and more focused on how you are affected by and deal with what happens to you. It is rooted in accountability: the belief that it is up to you to deal with what life throws you.

An internal focus is rooted in Personal Power. This power comes from within you and determines how you deal with things, not on how you can control other people. It means being self-aware and doing more self-management.

With an internal focus, abusive and controlling behaviors tend to fall away, because being happy is no longer about managing what others say or do. Anger also tends to subside because there is a lot less blame. Instead, people with an internal focus can more easily connect with their true feelings of distress, such as sadness, anxiety, hurt, or embarrassment.

It is empowering to shift to an internal focus because it turns your attention to the only thing you truly do have power over: yourself. You may not be able to control how your children behave, but you can always control how you behave as a parent. You may not be able to control the traffic, but you can control how you deal with traffic. The more you stay focused on managing yourself, rather than the world or others in the world, the more empowered you will feel.

This is the key change that will allow you to stop being abusive and controlling: shifting from an external to an internal focus. Until you make this change, your success is likely to be short-lived. Once you start to make this shift, the other skills and tools we offer will fall into place much more easily. This is the foundation upon which to build a sound, healthy life.

THE BENEFITS OF AN INTERNAL FOCUS

Two analogies can illustrate the shift from an external to an internal focus. The first is the difference between cold-blooded and warm-blooded animals. The second is the value of having shelter rather than living outside in the elements.

Cold-blooded animals are very dependent on the surrounding environment because their body temperature is regulated by air temperature. If it's cold outside, they're cold. If it's hot outside, they're hot. To change their body temperature, they need to change their environment. The benefit of this is that they don't need much food because they don't have to burn calories to warm their bodies. The drawback is that they're at the mercy of their environment, which limits their abilities. People with an external focus can be thought of as cold-blooded: their emotional state depends on their environment. If the people around them are agitated, then they are agitated. If others are relaxed, then they are relaxed.

Warm-blooded animals, on the other hand, are less dependent on their surrounding environment because their bodies regulate their internal temperature. Although this requires more calories, it allows for far greater freedom; they can go where they want without being severely affected by the outside temperature. This is why all higher-functioning animals are warm-blooded: they can adapt and thrive in a wide variety of environments, including extremely difficult ones.

People with an internal focus can be thought of as warm-blooded: their emotional state remains more or less stable regardless of what other people are doing around them. Their kids may be agitated, but they can remain calm. Their spouse may be grumpy, but they can still be relaxed and happy. Regulating their own moods takes more work, but it affords them far greater mobility and independence.

Our second analogy compares an external focus to living outside in the elements. You might only be happy if it's the right temperature, there's daylight, it isn't raining, and there's no wind. If it's at all stormy, you may not function as well. You could relocate to where the weather is "better," but no matter where you move, the weather will sometimes interfere with what you're trying to do. People with an external focus need everything around them to be just so for them to feel okay. They mistakenly believe that if they control the people around them, they can accomplish that. That endeavor inevitably fails, which is why people with an external focus can feel so angry, frustrated, and powerless. They may not actually be trying to control the weather, but the results are the same.

Adopting an internal focus is like moving into a house that has climate control. Regardless of the weather outside, the inside environment remains stable. It may be dark, cold, rainy, or windy outside, but you can steadily continue doing what you need to in a well-lit, warm, still, and dry indoor setting. Keeping an internal focus is like creating and maintaining that home within yourself. If you maintain a good internal space by practicing self-awareness, self-management, and self-care, and by staying relational and maintaining positive, collaborative relationships with others, you will be able to find comfort and support in times of need. This is an ongoing process, as any homeowner knows; every home needs maintenance. Well-maintained homes can last indefinitely, but abandoned or neglected homes are at the mercy of the elements and will literally fall apart.

***

Primary accountability is the key to self-empowerment and to working the program well. Becoming accountable will empower you to change unsatisfying aspects of your life and to deal effectively with challenges. It will transform you from feeling like a helpless victim of circumstance to an empowered agent of change. When you accept responsibility for your power, your behaviors, your thoughts, and your feelings, you will be able to take excellent care of yourself. You will stop giving away your power by blaming external sources for your problems.

This core concept of the program ties into many other principles and concepts. All of the self-awareness, self-management, and interpersonal skills we cover in later chapters are ways of practicing primary accountability.

The next two chapters are intended to help you gain a deeper appreciation for the suffering your loved ones have likely endured. Taking responsibility for the damage and suffering caused by your abusive and controlling behavior is often the most difficult part of this work, but it is vital. Please read on.

CHAPTER 11

UNDERSTANDING THE IMPACT OF ABUSE ON YOUR PARTNER

Abusive and controlling behaviors are hurtful to other people because they violate the basic rights of others. One reason most people are not abusive is that they understand that abuse is hurtful and disrespectful, and they don't want to treat people that way. On the other hand, people who are abusive and controlling often find ways to ignore or minimize the negative impact their behavior has on others, which makes it easier to continue the behavior. An important deterrent to behaving abusively is knowing and understanding the harm it can cause. It is important to understand as fully as you can how your abusive and controlling behavior has caused harm, both in general as well as to the actual people to whom you have been abusive. Your sincere acknowledgment of the impact of your behavior on those you have harmed can contribute significantly to their healing and recovery process. Part of that is developing your capacity for compassion.

SYMPATHY, EMPATHY, AND COMPASSION
Many people think that sympathy, empathy, and compassion mean the same thing. The terms are sometimes used interchangeably, and different mental health professionals and other experts have slightly different definitions. Even so, it's important to understand the differences between them so you can see your behavior with your loved ones clearly.

Sympathy involves sharing or acknowledging the feelings someone else is having *in that moment*. If a child is crying because their ice cream fell on the ground, you might share their sadness—your heart might go out to them in that moment. When someone is grieving a loss and you acknowledge their grief, you might share their grief in that moment. You might feel sad as they are feeling sad.

The limitation of sympathy is that it only exists in the moment. When you stop sharing the other person's emotion, you may no longer think about it or feel what that person is going through. It's kind of like, "Oh, that's too bad. Well, I'm off to run errands!"

The opposite of having sympathy is feeling numb and emotionally detached in the moment. When you are unsympathetic, you don't really care about someone's emotions in the moment. It's not that you don't care about the person; it's just that you don't care about the particular emotion they're having in the moment. If you're pulled over for speeding and you break down in tears, the police officer might be unsympathetic as they give you your ticket. It's not that they don't care about you, but they don't particularly care about the sadness and frustration you feel in that moment over the consequences of your choice to speed, and they know that helping you drive slower could save your life or the lives of others.

Empathy is the ability to understand the emotions of another person *in general*. It often involves imagining how you might feel if you were in their shoes. You can have empathy for someone even if you don't know how they actually feel. For example, if you hear that someone is losing their job, you can imagine what that might be like for them. Empathy is an ongoing process of seeking to understand someone else's emotional space.

An absence of empathy means you are unable to recognize someone as experiencing emotions in the same way you do. Without empathy, there is a general emotional detachment from the other person. Without empathy, you fail to see someone else as having human struggles, and you fail to consider and connect with their struggles. To you, they seem more like things than like people; more like a statistic than a person. Put simply, an absence of empathy means not caring for the other person or their emotional state in general.

This may sound harsh, but most people lack empathy sometimes, and there are times when it is even adaptive to not have empathy. A surgeon works better when they focus on their "case," rather than on a human being who might live or die on their operating table. If you continually had empathy, it would be almost impossible to read the news without being overwhelmed by the pain and suffering in the world.

Compassion is sympathy plus a desire to alleviate someone's pain. It goes beyond empathy. When you have compassion, you are able to understand what someone else is feeling, you care about it, and you want to help. Compassion is what shifts you from a passive stance to active engagement. You can have empathy or sympathy and remain an observer, but compassion pushes you to help. When you feel compassion, you don't just understand how someone is feeling; you want them to feel better.

The opposite of compassion, to be uncompassionate, means that you have no desire to help the other person feel better. You might worry about a friend who is really struggling in a relationship, but you have seen them do this so many times that you don't really want to help them. The thinking is "They got themselves into this mess, and they can get themselves out of it."

Be careful not to confuse your emotional discomfort about how someone else is feeling with compassion. Some people get very uncomfortable when they see someone—especially someone close to them—in distress, and they want to get away from that feeling. With compassion, you want to help the other person stop feeling bad; without compassion, *you* want to stop feeling bad. This can lead to superficial interventions like telling someone to "cheer up," or "look on the bright side," or "just smile—turn that frown upside down," or "could be worse,"—or problem-solving when the other person hasn't asked you to. Compassion is primarily driven by a concern for others and their distress, not for yourself and your own distress.

Let's go back to the young child who is crying over a dropped ice cream cone. Sympathy means noting, and possibly sharing, how sad it is that they lost their ice cream before they were able to fully enjoy it. Empathy means continuing to be aware of how they were affected by that event, and knowing that it made for a tougher day for them and they still might be upset about it later on. Compassion means feeling a desire to help them feel better, maybe by giving them a hug or buying them a new ice cream cone in the moment, and later by acknowledging to them that it's tough when your ice cream falls on the ground, and it certainly was a bad day in that way. It might mean giving them a little extra acknowledgment and love later.

Most people think sympathy, empathy, and compassion apply only when someone is distressed, but they apply to positive and comfortable emotional states as well. If a good friend has just started a new and exciting romantic relationship, sympathy is being happy with them in the moment when they share the news with you. Empathy is continuing to hold warm thoughts toward them about their excitement in the coming days. Compassion might be making a toast when they share the news, checking in with them in the coming days on how the relationship is progressing, or sending them a quick text later about how happy you are for them. Validation and acknowledgment of all of someone's emotions, not just their distressing ones, is vital to being truly supportive.

Sympathy, empathy, and compassion are all deterrents to abusive and controlling behavior. The more you connect with and care about how someone is feeling, the more disturbing their suffering from your abuse will be to you. Multiple studies have shown the important role empathy plays in discouraging abuse; the more compassion one person feels toward another, the less likely they are to be abusive or controlling with them.

On the other hand, an absence of sympathy, empathy, and compassion make it far easier to be abusive and controlling toward others. This is one reason the military teaches soldiers to objectify and dehumanize the enemy. It's a whole lot easier to shoot at an "invader" or "terrorist" or "enemy" than to shoot at someone's son or daughter or the parent of a young child. Likewise, taking advantage of someone criminally—robbing them, for example—means not seeing them as a person, but simply as a "mark," a "target," a "meal ticket."

While all three of these are important, compassion is at the core. An active desire to care for others (and for oneself, with self-compassion) is a key motivator for people to want to stop their abuse and control.

A panel from the comic strip *Dilbert* beautifully illustrates the importance of sympathy, empathy, and compassion. Dilbert is talking to his mother about his work, and he is stunned to find out that she doesn't really care. He tells her that since she's his mother, she should automatically care. She points out that the electrical impulses in his brain can't fly across the air gap to her brain. "You could be writing in agony," she says, "and I wouldn't feel a thing." "Ouch," he says, to which she replies, "Air gap."

There are not wires to connect your brain together with others. You do not automatically feel what someone else is feeling, but this is where compassion comes in. Although you cannot literally feel what someone else is feeling, you can imagine what they are feeling. You cannot feel their hurt, but if you can connect with your own past hurt, you can have some understanding, and compassion, for what they are going through.

If you don't know and connect with your own emotional experiences, it's much more difficult to connect with the emotions of others. For example, say a friend informs you that their romantic partner of the past five years has just unexpectedly broken up with them. Because you care about them, you try to imagine what they're going through. If you have never been in a serious romantic relationship and never experienced the pain of an unexpected breakup, you might say something like, "That's too bad, but there are plenty of other fish in the sea. You have plenty of desirable traits. I'm sure you can find someone else in no time at all." You are being supportive the best you know how, but you clearly don't understand what it's like to go through a painful breakup. On the other hand, if you do, you will recall the sadness, disbelief, hurt, anger, and discouragement you felt when it happened to you. You can imagine that your friend might be having similar feelings, and reply, "What?! Oh, I am so, so sorry to hear that. That's so surprising—how are you doing?" Your compassion and concern will be evident in your tone of voice and your facial expressions. You may not literally be able to feel what your friend is feeling, but through compassion, you can be there with them.

OTHERS HAVE SUFFERED FROM YOUR ABUSE AND CONTROL

Part of the abusive cycle is to come up with justifications and excuses that distract you from understanding the consequences of your abuse, but doing this lets you continue to be abusive. It allows you to avoid the discomfort of your actions, but also prevents you from understanding how others are suffering from your abuse. But it is that very discomfort that motivates people to change. If you stay connected with the damage and suffering further abuse would cause the people you love and care for, it is easier to stop being abusive. It is also easier to have compassion for those you have harmed.

If you are serious about stopping your abusive and controlling behavior, it is vital that you get honest with yourself about the damage it has caused to the people you love. The goal is not to beat yourself up or wallow in shame, but to help you stop your abuse. Honestly looking at the damage your abuse and control have caused is important for several different reasons. First, sitting with the discomfort of the pain it has caused others is a great incentive to stop doing it. Second, getting honest with yourself about the damage you have caused is a key aspect of being accountable and validating another's experiences that you invalidated in the past because you were in denial. Third, connecting with the hurt you have caused builds empathy and compassion for those you have hurt and makes you less inclined to continue to hurt them. Finally, becoming accountable for your past behavior and compassionate for the people it has hurt can help your loved ones heal and recover from the hurt you have caused.

Honestly looking at the damage your abusive behavior has caused requires a tremendous amount of courage. It means being able to sit with the discomfort and guilt of what you have done. This is typically the most emotionally demanding part of the work—the part that is hardest for people to do and leaves them feeling the most uneasy. It is also vital for making true change. If you are serious about stopping your abusive behavior, then you need to intentionally turn toward the people you have hurt, to connect with their hearts, and to actively foster compassion for them.

All abusive behavior is damaging in some way, but the harm it actually does can be quite different from person to person. As you read through the rest of this chapter, you can be certain that some things will apply and others will not. Try to focus as much as you can on what does apply rather than what does not. Be extra careful that your denial and defensiveness do not start to creep in to minimize the suffering you have caused. If it gets to be too much for you, consider taking a break from reading this chapter until you are in a more grounded and receptive space.

IMMEDIATE EFFECTS OF ABUSE

The most obvious impact of your abusive behavior is how others were affected in the seconds and minutes after you did it. Listed below are the most common ways this manifests.

EMOTIONAL DISTRESS

The most obvious immediate effects are uncomfortable emotional reactions. Common emotional responses to being abused include feeling afraid (or scared, worried, or anxious, to name a few), shocked, sad, depressed, discouraged, confused, and angry. Some of these emotions pass quickly and others linger for days afterward or even longer. These emotions may have corresponding behaviors, such as crying, sobbing, being skittish or jumpy. In addition to feeling emotionally distressed by the abuse, some people may feel emotionally overwhelmed; this leads to other consequences.

EMOTIONAL OVERWHELM

Strong emotions release adrenaline into the body and can trigger the fight, flight, or freeze response, which has a number of consequences, including racing thoughts, difficulty concentrating, and distractibility. The raised adrenaline level in their body can make it difficult for them to sleep. It can also disrupt their appetite or make them feel sick to their stomach. They may become hypervigilant, which means being overly tuned-in to everything happening around them, which makes it difficult to settle. They may feel physically agitated and struggle to sit still or stay in one place. As the overwhelm passes, they may become physically exhausted and fatigued.

PHYSICAL DISTRESS

They may be in physical pain and have physical injuries from times when you were physically abusive. They may get a headache or have other muscle pain (jaw pain, shoulder pain, back pain) from the high level of tension and emotional distress they are experiencing.

COMPROMISED DECISION-MAKING

People who have just been abused may make compromised choices and agree to do things they do not really want to do. There are at least two reasons for this. The most obvious is to avoid being further abused in the moment. The less obvious reason is that even if the abuse has stopped for now, they may be so distraught and overwhelmed that they cannot think clearly enough to fully think through what they truly want. They may also not have the energy and internal resources in the moment to express what they want. They might say things they don't really mean or believe, agree to sexual contact they don't really want, and agree to other activities they don't really want to do, like housework or a social event. Their agreement may appear to be consent, but because of their immediate distress, that consent is coerced or uninformed.

INTERPERSONAL WITHDRAWAL

The immediate trauma caused by abusive behavior may lead someone to withdraw from interactions from others. They may become silent and uncommunicative or have difficulty speaking. They may be quite distracted, struggling to tune into and be aware of others around them, including their own children.

EMOTIONAL FALLOUT

Even after the abusive episode ends and they begin to settle a bit, there may be additional emotional fallout. They may feel embarrassed about the situation. They may worry about how the children or others were affected by being exposed to it. They may blame themselves or get self-critical, in part because the abusive person often blames them for the abuse even as it happens. Because the abusive behavior was completely dismissive of their boundaries and disrespectful of them, they may feel inadequate and insignificant.

DELAYED EFFECTS OF ABUSE

Although it may be easy for you to forget about your abusive behavior and move on after the moment, that is often not the case for the person you have been abusive toward. Even days later, they may continue to struggle. Listed below are some of the most common ways this is experienced.

EMOTIONAL DISTRESS

Even days later, the abused person may still be troubled by the incident. It is common for emotions to linger, including sadness, depression, anxiety, anger, disappointment (with themselves as well as with you), and shame. They may continue to be hypervigilant and to feel like they have to walk on eggshells.

MOOD PROBLEMS

The general mood of an abused person can be affected for many days after the incident. They might feel depressed, more anxious, more irritable, or experience significant mood changes and mood swings.

PREOCCUPATION

An abused person may spend a lot of time—days and weeks, even— thinking over the abusive episode as they try to make sense of it. They may be trying to understand what happened, think of what they could have done differently, and figure out why it even happened. This preoccupation can interfere with their daily activities and other aspects of their life.

AVOIDANCE

It might be so unpleasant for the abused person to think about what happened that they try to avoid thinking about it or remembering it. They might try to numb out with alcohol, drugs, or other mood-altering activities like overeating or screen time. They might avoid interacting with you or talking about it with you. They might stay away from their friends so they won't have to deal with it. They may become spacy and seem out of it as they dissociate from the memory. They may fall into denial about what you did to them to minimize the pain.

REDUCED TRUST

Because abusive behavior is such a violation of trust, it can take days, or longer, before they trust you again. They may be more cautious around you—careful about what they say and do. They may be more hesitant to share with you what they are thinking, feeling, or wanting. They may be more withdrawn or superficial in what they share.

PHYSICAL ISSUES

An abused person may experience lingering physical pain and discomfort from physical abuse or from high levels of emotional distress. This tension causes headaches, backaches, and other muscular pain, and can aggravate preexisting conditions, particularly those affected by stress, such as digestive issues and IBS. They may have continued fatigue, nausea, and reduced appetite.

INTERFERENCE WITH ROUTINE ACTIVITIES

Being abused often makes daily life more difficult. An abused person may struggle with motivation. They may not be as productive. They may not be able to complete certain tasks, or take much longer than normal to complete them. They may struggle to concentrate.

INTERFERENCE WITH OTHER ASPECTS OF THEIR LIFE

They may end up missing work and not being as productive when they are there. They may be less attentive as a parent. Their sleep may be disrupted, whether they are sleeping less or sleeping more. They may struggle to fall asleep, wake up repeatedly during the night, and have nightmares.

SELF-NEGLECT

Being mistreated by you can lead someone to treat themselves poorly. They may blame themselves for the abuse. They may have lowered self-esteem. They may struggle with shame and embarrassment. Their self-care may suffer.

CUMULATIVE EFFECTS OF ABUSE

All of the consequences of abuse listed so far have been bad, but they are nothing compared to the cumulative effects of repeated and persistent abuse. The fact that you were not just abusive to your partner once or twice, but over and over and over again, amplifies and deepens the effects. This is where the worst, deepest, and most enduring damage occurs. The reality is that you did not just commit individual acts of abuse, you followed patterns of abuse. These patterns are even more damaging because it communicates that the abuse is likely to happen again. The person who is abused feels (justifiably) like the abuse will never end, like the abuse is simply part of the relationship. The abuse stops being the exception and becomes the norm. This is where things shift from you being an imperfect partner to being an abusive partner.

It is important to keep in mind that these cumulative effects of your abuse can persist even if you stop being abusive, and even if the relationship ends. This is one of the many reasons it is not enough to simply stop your abuse and control, but to do what you can to repair the damage that your abuse and control have caused.

VOCATIONAL DIFFICULTIES

Over time, abusive behavior can affect a person's ability to fulfill their professional ambitions. They may have to take time off to recover from physical or emotional injuries. Their work performance may suffer, which could lead to being fired or reprimanded. They may miss out on promotions and pay raises. They may need to quit because they don't have the internal resources necessary to keep working. They may lose their ambition, get distracted from their professional goals, and settle for unfulfilling work, All this is true even if you are supportive of their work; if you are abusive and controlling about their work, it is even worse.

INTERPERSONAL DIFFICULTIES

As you might imagine, being repeatedly abused by someone you love and who says they love you can undermine your ability to trust people. A person who has been abused may struggle with intimacy, even in subsequent relationships, because they are afraid that being vulnerable could lead to more abuse. It is common for people who have been abused to fail to stand up for themselves to get what they really want or need, especially in areas where there has been abuse or control. They might become passive and unassertive.

For a number of reasons, many victims of abuse become socially isolated. It may be because you have exerted control over who they communicate with or what they're allowed to do when they're not with you. But even if you have not controlled your partner's social life, they may have less time and energy for their friends because they are embarrassed or ashamed and don't want to burden anyone. They may fear judgment from their friends, especially if they stay with you after they disclose that you have been abusive. Their friends may pull away if they feel burdened or burned-out by the latest episode, or because they feel powerless to help. It is emotionally difficult to see a friend suffering.

SEXUAL ISSUES

One of the more common complaints abusive partners have about their partners is their partner's reduced interest in sexual connection. This really should not come as a surprise. For most people, an important precursor of being sexual with someone is feeling emotionally safe with them. Abuse often leaves people feeling anxious, afraid, and on eggshells—the opposite of emotionally safe—which can have a significant impact on their desire to be sexual with the abuser.

Another common consequence is that the abused person ends up having sex when they don't really want to, or for the wrong reasons, such as to placate and pacify the other person. Sometimes "makeup sex"— sexual contact after an abusive episode or an argument—is less about a genuine desire to connect than an attempt to make things better in any way possible.

Many of the other consequences of abuse listed earlier in this chapter also contribute to a reduced interest in sex and affection.

MEDICAL ISSUES

The most obvious physical problems caused by abuse are injuries and the chronic pain that can persist for years afterward. Even more common, though, are ongoing physical issues caused by abuse-related stress, even if the abuse never became physical. This includes irritable bowel syndrome (IBS), indigestion, asthma, and stress-related disorders. Medical research has found that even years after abusive behavior stops, abused partners have significantly more medical issues than patients of the same background who had not been in an abusive relationship.

Abusive behavior aggravates preexisting medical conditions in several different ways. First, the ongoing stress of being abused can compromise the body's immune system, making healing and recovery take longer. Second, the negative emotional and cognitive impact of the abuse can make it difficult to consistently take prescribed medications, see health care professionals promptly, and otherwise take good care of themselves. If a chronic medical condition like diabetes is not managed well, it can lead to additional complications.

PSYCHOLOGICAL ISSUES

Even more common than long-term medical issues are long-term psychological issues. Abusive partners most frequently complain about their partner's low self-esteem. While this is true, it is important to unpack this to understand what it means.

People who have low self-esteem feel like they are not as good, capable, or deserving as other people. But it goes beyond that: low self-esteem also affects how people behave. Their low self-confidence and chronic self-doubt may lead them to feel unmotivated, which leads to underachievement. They may neglect their self-care and isolate themselves from others. Low self-esteem can be strengthened over time, but not overnight or all at once. It can linger long after the abuse, and the abusive relationship, has ended.

Just as preexisting medical conditions can be aggravated, so can preexisting psychological conditions. Someone who already has a history of depression may fall into a more severe depression. Someone who has previously struggled with addiction may start using again. Someone who experienced earlier trauma may have that trauma reactivated.

It is widely known that a long-term consequence of being abused is depression, but this is another term that needs to be unpacked. Depression can involve a lot more than a depressed mood. It can include negative thought patterns like being more pessimistic and cynical, and not feeling as hopeful or optimistic about life in general. It can spiral into true clinical depression, which includes disrupted sleep, reduced energy, changed appetite, general apathy and disinterest in life, no longer enjoying activities they once did, and hopelessness that can become suicidal. Clinical depression can feel like carrying around a 100-pound backpack or moving through molasses. Even the smallest task requires a ton of effort and energy.

Anxiety is common in people who have been abused, but when it persists, it can spiral into a full-blown anxiety disorder. With an anxiety disorder a person feels anxious even when they have no reason to. It may become difficult to leave the house or be around other people. It can trigger panic attacks, which can feel like heart attacks. It can lead people to ruminate, or think repeatedly and seemingly endlessly about something. They can become preoccupied with minor issues or concerns or spend far more time than they should preparing for an activity or an event. Anxiety disorders, like clinical depression, can be quite disabling.

The most common diagnosis received by people who have been in abusive relationships is probably post-traumatic stress disorder, or PTSD. This condition was originally diagnosed in combat veterans, but it is evident in survivors of natural disasters, sexual assault, and abusive relationships. Symptoms of PTSD include nightmares, flashbacks (intense waking memories), hypervigilance (scanning the environment intensely), and an overactive startle response (being jumpy, scaring easily). It can include rumination and intrusive thoughts that are difficult to get rid of. A person with PTSD can have wild mood swings, shifting between intense distress and anxiety to numbness and complete emotional disconnection. Note that PTSD is only diagnosed after the person is no longer in the abusive relationship; only people who are no longer experiencing trauma can be given this diagnosis of post-traumatic stress disorder.

SUBSTANCE ABUSE AND OTHER NUMBING BEHAVIORS
People may cope with the intense distress of abuse by trying to self-soothe in unhealthy ways, such as abusing alcohol and other drugs. They may also strive to numb out by overeating, overspending, spending way too much time in front of a screen or on their phone. As we discussed in Chapter 8: Mood-Altering Substances and Experiences, differing levels of use can cause different problems.

BEHAVIORAL ISSUES

In addition to extensive internal problems, abuse can lead to persistent behavioral issues. Your partner may struggle to manage their finances, failing to pay bills on time or do their taxes. They may struggle to manage domestic and household tasks, forgetting to do things or being inattentive. They may display poor decision-making, not thinking things through or being unable to concentrate. They may be impulsive, unable to weigh the pros and cons or consider the consequences of their choices.

There are four final consequences of the cumulative effects of your abusive behavior that we want to address below: the Bully Effect, underachievement, emotional homelessness, and loss of spirit. Each of these negative effects is present in nearly all abused partners, although how extensive they are can vary a great deal.

THE BULLY EFFECT

Chances are, you had experiences with school bullies when you were growing up. Most bullies only have to beat up a few people (it doesn't really matter if it's with fists or words) to be established as a bully. Once people know someone is a bully, almost anything that person does can put people on edge. They don't have to actually beat people up; they can scare people just looking at them, walking by them, or sitting by them. They may not be trying to intimidate you, may not even notice you, but you're still scared.

The Bully Effect describes how once a pattern of abuse has been established in a relationship, even benign behavior is experienced as abusive. For example, simply arriving home, walking into the room, clearing your throat, getting quiet, or giving a certain look or gesture can put your family on edge. This is because your family has been traumatized by a wide variety of your behaviors, even things you did when you felt fine and did not intend to be abusive! This means an exponential increase in the abusive behaviors people in your family experience. Think of it like this: in a regular house, you might hear wind blowing, doors creaking, and the sound of footsteps and think nothing of it, but in a haunted house those sounds can invoke great fear. That's what happens in an abusive relationship. There is only one way to stop the Bully Effect: stop the pattern of abuse. Only after a significant period of time has passed without any significant abusive behavior will the Bully Effect subside.

EMOTIONAL HOMELESSNESS

For some people, ongoing abusive behavior leads to literal homelessness; they choose to leave simply to get safe, even though they have nowhere to go. In fact, domestic violence is the leading cause of homelessness among women and children in the United States. More common than physical homelessness, though, is emotional homelessness.

A home is not simply a living space, but a place where people feel safe, comfortable, and free to be themselves. For many people, home is the only place they can act the way they truly want to. In public, you have to dress a certain way, act a certain way, and be much more careful about what you say or do. But at home, you can talk, dress, and act however you wish, as long as you are not hurtful to the people around you. Home is also typically the place you feel safest. That's what makes a house or an apartment a home, and not just a living space.

In an abusive home, people have to be careful how they act. They may have to avoid talking about certain topics. Certain behaviors may be forbidden, like leaving dishes in the sink or leaving the lights on. Other behaviors may be required, like responding with "sir" or always speaking in soft tones. A variety of restrictive rules and expectations may be in place, and failure to comply results in abuse or control.

As a result, many abused people cannot truly be at home in their own living spaces. In that way, nearly every victim of abuse is emotionally homeless. They have no safe space in which to truly be themselves, no place where they are truly at home.

UNDERACHIEVEMENT

Abusive and controlling behaviors are inherently invalidating. They can involve overt criticism and denigration, such as put-downs, name-calling, demeaning remarks, and harsh criticisms. They may be more subtly controlling but still dismissive of the thoughts, feelings, and behaviors of others. This is draining and exhausting to deal with. It consumes energy, motivation, time, and attention that would otherwise be available for employment, parenting, socializing, and other pastimes. The fallout from abuse can also be incredibly distracting, making it difficult to focus on other tasks. Just as a person does not function as well when they are sick, people do not function as well when they are repeatedly abused. Many victims of abuse and control can still be capable and skilled employees, parents, and friends, even despite the extra time, energy, effort, and attention they have to devote to coping with abuse. Imagine what they could accomplish if they didn't have to deal with being abused—if they'd had a consistently supportive and respectful partner!

LOSS OF SPIRIT

One fear people have about domestic violence is that it will end with someone's death. Fortunately, the vast majority of abusive relationships will not lead to actual murder. What is far more common is the slow killing of someone's spirit.

One way to think about spirit is as the essence of who a person is—the combination of qualities that makes them distinct and unique. Some people, when asked the meaning of life, would reply that it is to be as true to themselves as they can be. In other words, to live with integrity; "To thine own self be true." The more a person strives to be true to themselves, the more connected they are with their spirit.

Every act of abuse and control cuts away at a person's connection with themselves by pushing them into behaviors, thoughts, or feelings that are different from how they truly want to be. Each act of control makes a person act or think or feel in a way they would not otherwise choose, that is not right for them. Each act of control cuts away a little at a person's connection with themselves—their spirit. Preventing a person from honoring themselves and being true to who they really are is spirit-killing. Some would argue that there is nothing worse that you could do to a person.

***

This list of ways your partner may have suffered from your abuse and control may seem long, but it is by no means exhaustive. We encourage you to do your best to fully understand how your partner has endured your abuse. Thinking about all this may leave you feeling quite uncomfortable and upset. That is a good and appropriate reaction. Use that discomfort as motivation to stop—for good—your abuse and control.

CHAPTER 12

UNDERSTANDING THE IMPACT
OF ABUSE ON CHILDREN

In the last chapter we examined ways that your abusive and controlling behavior might have hurt your partner. This chapter focuses on the collateral damage to people who were not the intended target but who saw, heard, or learned of your abuse. This might include your children, family members, friends, and neighbors may have been exposed to your abuse, as well as your partner's and children's friends and coworkers, and strangers of whom you might not have been aware.

The most significantly and commonly impacted people in this category are children. This includes your children, your partner's children, and any other children who spend time in your home. It includes children who were present in your previous abusive relationships, as well.

EXPOSURE TO ABUSE IS ABUSIVE

Although some abusive partners have been directly abusive to their or their partner's children, some have not. However, even when children are not direct targets, they are significantly affected by being exposed to abuse. If there are children in the home, they have almost certainly been exposed to the abuse—either by seeing it or hearing it in the moment or by witnessing its aftermath.

Extensive research has shown that children who are exposed to abuse can be as negatively impacted as those who are directly physically and emotionally abused. The main difference is that one group was directly and willfully abused and the other was not. The bottom line is that there is virtually no difference between children who are directly abused and children who are exposed to abuse.

HOW CHILDREN ARE EXPOSED TO ABUSIVE BEHAVIOR

SEEING ABUSE
The most obvious way a child is exposed to abusive behavior is when it takes place in front of them. They might have been in the room when it was happening. They might have come into the room while it was happening, since abusive behavior often draws attention. It is possible that they entered the room and then left before you realized they were there.

OVERHEARING ABUSE
Many children are exposed to abusive behavior when they overhear it. Yelling and loud voices carry, especially in small living spaces or at night after the children are in bed. Sometimes a child will listen after being ordered to leave the room. Unusual sounds like intense voices, crying, objects being dropped or thrown or struck, and doors slamming are sure to draw attention and even wake children up. They may pretend to be sleeping when you check on them, or have fallen asleep after hearing part of the episode.

DEALING WITH THE AFTERMATH
Even if a child is not directly exposed to an abusive episode, they can be negatively affected by its aftermath. Their parent might be visibly distressed, perhaps crying, spacy, distracted, or agitated. They may act in unusual or unsettling ways.

If there was property abuse, a child might see the hole in the wall, the smashed phone, broken remote. The abused parent might have been too distraught to conceal the signs of the abuse.

FEELING THE TENSION
Children can be negatively affected by witnessing the emotional aftermath of an abusive episode. Even though you are no longer being abusive, you

might still be upset and agitated, and there may be significant coolness or distance between you and your partner. That tension can cause children to feel anxious and uncomfortable.

EXPERIENCING NEGLECT

After an abusive episode, you and your partner may need time before you're ready to parent again. You may have follow-up conversations or arguments. You may be agitated or distracted. As a result, your children may experience neglect. They may not get the attention or assistance they need. They may not be fed in a timely way. They may not have their questions answered. They may not get assistance with homework or struggles. They may be less supervised and more likely to get into trouble by going places or doing things they should not. With multiple unsupervised children, there is an increased risk that they could act inappropriately with each other. Their other wants and needs—to be read to, to play with you, to spend time with you—may be put off or overlooked. Any of this can be damaging, but it's especially so when it happens repeatedly.

It is important that you consider and acknowledge the ways your abusive behavior may have impacted any children you were in contact with during your relationships. This includes sons or daughters of yours or your partner's, regardless of their age, even if they are adults. In general, the younger they were when they were exposed to your abuse, the more severely it would have affected them. In some cases, though, especially if the abuse is more subtle (as with financial abuse or controlling behaviors), only older children may even realize that it was abuse.

THE IMMEDIATE IMPACT OF EXPOSURE TO ABUSE

Children who are exposed to abuse have very similar immediate reactions to children who are directly abused. Their reactions vary depending on the child's age, but they include emotional distress, emotional overwhelm, physical distress, compromised choices, interpersonal withdrawal, and emotional fallout. We will examine each in detail below.

EMOTIONAL DISTRESS

Just as with adults who are abused, children who are exposed to abuse are likely to feel afraid, shocked, sad, depressed, discouraged, confused, and angry. However, children tend to feel things more intensely and become more easily overwhelmed by their emotions, and during an episode of abuse they may feel terror, horror, and utter despair. They may cry and sob. They may self-soothe by clutching a blanket or beloved stuffed animal or toy, suck their thumb, rock, or curl up into a ball, hugging themselves.

EMOTIONAL OVERWHELM

Because they have fewer internal emotional resources to deal with their intense emotions, children are very likely to become overwhelmed by an abusive episode. They can display all the classic signs of emotional overwhelm: distraction, agitation, difficulty sleeping, and concentration problems. They may lose their appetite. They may literally flee the situation—or hide. Some children have favorite hiding places where they go to keep themselves safe during abusive episodes, such as under their bed or in a closet.

Because their agitation is so great, children may become nauseated to the point of vomiting. They may wet themselves or their bed or soil their clothing. They may destroy or deface toys or other belongings to relieve their feelings of agitation and powerlessness.

Some children may appear to be quite calm and unaffected, but this may be because they are going numb or dissociating. Dissociation is a mental disconnection from the moment in which a person is not emotionally or cognitively aware of what is happening—they "go away" mentally and emotionally. They may appear to be "out of it" or "spacy." They may appear to be okay in the moment, but later reveal that they have no memory of a period of time. This is most common in children who experience extreme distress that they are powerless to stop.

PHYSICAL DISTRESS

When children are inadvertently physically abused or injured because they tried to intervene, they may experience pain and discomfort. More common, though, are stomachaches, headaches, and other kinds of physical distress caused by their intense emotional response to the abuse.

COMPROMISED DECISION-MAKING

In the moment, children might do whatever they can to stop the abusive episode they are witnessing. They may make promises or agree to do things they don't actually want to do. They may have temper tantrums or act out in the moment. They may try to distract the adults with attention-seeking behaviors like crying, injuring themselves, becoming aggressive, or breaking things. They may believe they are the cause of the abuse and make promises to God or imaginary others in hopes of stopping the abuse.

WITHDRAWAL

Children who are exposed to abuse may run away from home, isolate in the home, or refuse to talk to anyone. Others may refuse to leave home, even to go to school, out of concern for what might happen when they are gone. They will do what they can to distract themselves from what is going on: listen to music, watch videos, spend time online. They may use headphones or earplugs to block out the sounds of abuse.

Some children become highly needy, wanting to be in the abused parent's presence 24/7. They may follow them everywhere, from room to room, like their little shadow. They may refuse to sleep in their own beds or let the parent leave their sight.

EMOTIONAL FALLOUT

Children may continue to struggle with the emotional aftermath of abuse as hours and days go by. They may blame themselves, feel guilty, be inconsolable, and feel embarrassed. They may feel generally out of sorts and have a hard time getting back into their routines.

THE DELAYED IMPACT OF EXPOSURE TO ABUSE

EMOTIONAL DISTRESS

The memories of a parent that they love being mistreated and abused are likely to haunt children for a long time to come. They may continue to feel sad, depressed, worried, angry, heartbroken, troubled, confused, and uncertain for days afterward. They may be hypervigilant, monitoring everything that is going on around them.

MOOD PROBLEMS

Children may be in a bad mood for days after being exposed to abusive behavior, and feel depressed, anxious, and uneasy. They are more likely than adults to have behavioral issues when they are sad, depressed, or anxious, and they may be uncooperative. They may not follow rules. They may be unmotivated or lethargic, irritable or angry. They may have conflicts with siblings and peers. They may have temper tantrums.

By contrast, some children become less emotional. They may become numb and emotionally unexpressive. They may become passive and unable to express themselves and what they want. This is one way depression in children appears—as checking out.

PREOCCUPATION

Children may repeatedly think about what happened, trying to fill in the missing details so they can make sense of it. They may have many questions even if they don't ask them. This distraction may show up in their play. Older children and teens may struggle to be fully present with their friends, in their classes, or during other activities as they continue to go over what happened.

GUILT AND SELF-BLAME

Children are often quick to blame themselves for all kinds of things, including abusive behavior, especially when a behavior of theirs (getting a poor grade, not finishing a chore, etc.) was the initial trigger of the abusive episode. Even if there isn't an obvious connection, they may think they caused the abuse by not getting better grades, listening better to their parents, or treating a sibling better.

Self-blame can be a result of superstitious thinking, particularly in younger children. Superstitious thinking refers to the false presumption that because a behavior happened at the same time as or just before an event, it somehow caused the event. For example, if the child was playing with a particular toy just as the abusive episode began, they might assume that doing so caused the abuse, and avoid playing with that toy again out of fear that it was their fault.

Children who blame themselves for abusive behavior can feel an incredible burden to prevent further abuse, and a heavy responsibility for the negative fallout. None of this is true, of course, but it is a heavy load to carry. It can lead to all sorts of struggles, including depression, guilt, and acting out.

AVOIDANCE

Just like adults, some children do what they can to distract themselves from what happened or deny it altogether, perhaps by losing themselves in imaginative play, spending excessive time online, or playing video games. Older children and teens may avoid being at home, spending more time at school or with friends so they will not be exposed to abusive behavior again. They may use alcohol or other drugs to avoid their feelings.

Children and teens often avoid an issue by misbehaving, hoping to distract, and possibly reunite, their parents by taking on the role of the problem child or scapegoat. Others try to lift their parents' mood by being funny, taking on the role of the clown. Still others hope that if they excel at school or in other activities, their parents will feel better, happier, and less likely to have further issues, taking on the role of the hero. Finally, they may choose to keep as low a profile and to be as small a burden as possible, being the lost child. These are common roles for children in dysfunctional families, including families in which there is abusive behavior. These roles may remain with the child even into adulthood, causing them to struggle long after they have left home.

REDUCED TRUST

Exposure to abuse may lower children's trust in their parents. They may be reluctant to share information about themselves, especially if they think it will be troubling to either parent. They may feel responsible for making sure things are going well by staying close by, keeping an eye on their parents, and helping them out before things get too bad.

PHYSICAL PROBLEMS

The stress children experience can lead to physical problems. They may complain of stomachaches or a reduced appetite, or have general complaints about not feeling good even though there is nothing demonstrably wrong with them. If they have a history of physical issues like headaches, asthma, or a sensitive stomach, those issues might flare up.

DISRUPTED ACTIVITIES

For many of the reasons listed above, children who are exposed to abuse may experience difficulties with daily life. They may want to spend more or less time with their parents, or away from home. They may feel the need to behave differently. If their parents are less available to them, they may have to figure things out on their own, which makes taking care of responsibilities like chores and homework more difficult.

NEGLECTED SELF-CARE

Children may neglect their own needs more when they are feeling distressed, and they may take on a caregiving role with either or both parents. They may downplay their own wants and needs to avoid burdening either parent. They may try to take on more responsibilities for themselves or for younger siblings.

Unlike adults, juvenile children are not fully responsible for their well-being. They are dependent on adults, and if the adults are less able to meet the children's needs, the children continue to suffer. The younger the child, the more problematic this is.

EMOTIONAL REGRESSION

Developmental milestones a child has achieved may fall away in the aftermath of exposure to abuse, leading children to revert to a younger age and become less mature and capable of taking care of themselves. A child who has not wet the bed in many months may start again. A child who had stopped sucking their thumb may start again.

CUMULATIVE EFFECTS OF EXPOSURE TO ABUSE

BEHAVIORAL ISSUES

Even more so than adults, children and teens may act out their distress through problematic behaviors including getting in trouble at school, getting into fights with peers, and having problems with authority figures and other adults. They may become oppositional at home and refuse to follow rules and expectations. Teenagers become more likely to run away and are at risk of becoming homeless; they may live at another person's house or on the streets. They may engage in criminal activities like vandalism, theft, or drug dealing. They are at significantly greater risk of finding themselves in an abusive relationship themselves, as either the abusive partner or the abused.

INTERPERSONAL DIFFICULTIES

Children may struggle to keep friendships if they exhibit behavioral problems that scare off or alienate their peers. They may be so caught up in the struggles at home that they rarely reach out or put energy into friendships, which subsequently fade. They may end up in the company of other children who act out, which can lead to a circle of peers who support and reinforce bad behavior—the "wrong crowd" that parents fear.

Adolescents who are exposed to abusive behavior are at greater risk of being in abusive dating relationships, replicating (sometimes unintentionally) what they have seen at home. When they are adults, they may experience significant problems with intimacy. They may be slow to trust others and struggle to stay in a healthy relationship, keep a good partner, or maintain healthy friendships.

SEXUAL ISSUES

Sexual issues arise as children who have been exposed to abusive and controlling behavior enter adolescence and beyond. The greatest danger is that they will start to act out sexually by prematurely seeking out sexual partners or seeking those who are not loving and supportive. They may be more vulnerable to sexually abusive people. They are considerably more at risk of teen pregnancy.

MEDICAL ISSUES

Exposure to ongoing abusive behavior can cause ongoing emotional distress that wears down the body and makes it more prone to physical issues like stomachaches, headaches, and accidental injuries.

PSYCHOLOGICAL ISSUES

All children who are exposed to abusive or controlling behavior, regardless of their age, are at risk for developing a wide range of psychological issues. One way of thinking of it is that repeated exposure to abusive behavior compromises someone's psychological immune system.

Children, like adults, may experience clinical depression, anxiety disorders, and PTSD. In children and teens, the symptoms look a little different. They may seem more irritable and angry than depressed. They may show developmental regression (as mentioned above). They may show physical agitation.

As with adults, low self-esteem is common. This is often fueled by self-blame as well as the emotional neglect from adults locked in an abusive relationship. This is more than just feeling down about themselves, and can lead to a wide variety of struggles mentioned elsewhere, including underachievement, unhealthy relationships, and other psychological issues. Low self-esteem can significantly contribute to a compromised life where a person struggles to make choices that honor who they truly are.

Teenage girls in particular who have been exposed to abuse are at greater risk of developing an eating disorder by going on extreme diets, purging food after eating it, or overeating to the point of obesity.

NUMBING BEHAVIORS AND SUBSTANCE ABUSE

Just like adults, children and teens may try to avoid their uncomfortable emotions by numbing out with alcohol and other drugs. This may be a temporary solution that they grow out of, or the start of long-term struggles. People who grow up being exposed to abusive behavior in the home are at greater risk of developing ongoing substance abuse issues; many of them end up in substance abuse treatment programs.

Other ways that children and teens avoid their distress is by losing themselves in fantasy worlds, whether in their imaginations, in books, or with online gaming. They may develop interests that verge on obsessions. Some children become academic overachievers who spend much of their time trying to get the best grades possible. Because getting good grades is generally a positive thing, the obsessive aspect of it can be overlooked.

THE BULLY EFFECT

Just like your partner, your child may be put on edge simply by your presence, even when you behave appropriately. They may become anxious if you are upset in any way, even when you appropriately express and manage your distress. Ultimately, only repeated positive experiences with you over time can help this go away. The longer your child has experienced or witnessed your abuse, the longer they are likely to be on edge after you stop behaving poorly.

EMOTIONAL HOMELESSNESS

For children who have been exposed to ongoing abusive behavior, the family house may not feel like a home. They may not feel comfortable or safe being themselves, or able to and fully express themselves. They may feel like they have to act a certain way, whether around you or in general. They may avoid home and spend extra time with friends, at school, on the streets, at the library, in stores or shops or cafés. Even if they enjoy being elsewhere, it's not the same as being in their own room or at home with their own belongings. If they don't spend time elsewhere, being at home may be uncomfortable and unsettling. They may not feel emotionally safe there. It may be where they live, but it doesn't always feel like a home.

UNDERACHIEVEMENT

It is difficult for children who are exposed to abusive behavior to perform at their best. Some of the immediate consequences—disrupted sleep, concentration problems, appetite issues, etc.—can interfere with their ability to perform. They are probably getting less help and support from their parents with homework, events, emotional support, etc. They may lose the motivation, drive, focus, and energy to do their best.

Teens and adults may drop out of school or get a low-paying job instead of pursuing their professional ambitions. They may not develop a fulfilling career or pursue an advanced education that leads to work they are truly passionate about. How much better could they do if they had grown up in a home without any abusive behavior?

LOSS OF SPIRIT

Just like abused adults, children who are exposed to abuse may lose some of their connection to themselves—what they like, what they are passionate about, what they want to do, and who they want to be. The more energy and attention that are drawn to the abusive and controlling behavior, the less a child has for themselves. In a functional home, children have a lot of room and space to just be kids, without getting drawn into adult concerns. In an abusive home, there is less room for kids to be kids.

They may have less of a sense of who they are, what they love, and what they are passionate about. They may compromise themselves in a variety of ways to pacify the abusive parent.

PARENTIFICATION

Parentification is when a child prematurely takes on the responsibilities and mannerisms of an adult (or older child) at the expense of their own childhood. They may become more serious, do more caretaking of other family members, take on adult responsibilities, and do tasks they are not developmentally prepared for (e.g., making meals, providing care to younger siblings, doing chores that were previously done by an adult). This can lead them to become quite responsible but not very happy adults who prioritize others over themselves to their own detriment. Their inner child is locked up and rarely comes out to play.

***

Some of you will recognize these consequences because you, yourself, grew up in a home in which you were exposed to abusive behavior. Everyone's experience is a little different, so you might want to reflect on other ways that you suffered from that experience and how your own children may have experienced similar things. You are welcome to add your experiences to each of these lists, which are admittedly incomplete.

Children can be affected very differently depending on their age and their temperament, but what remains constant is that every child who is exposed to abusive or controlling behavior suffers to some extent, in some ways, over time. Some are remarkably resilient and largely unaffected by their experiences. Others struggle mightily. Even among those who are significantly affected, many find ways to heal and recover over time, in part with the help and support of adults and peers. But the very first thing they need is for their exposure to abusive behavior to stop.

Our hope is that reading the past two chapters has troubled and disturbed you. You might find yourself feeling sad, depressed, guilty, ashamed, and troubled, among other things. What is important, though, is not that you beat yourself up about it, but rather that you use your distress to motivate you to change. The first thing you can do to alleviate the suffering of those close to you is stop your abuse and control. The more upset you are by thinking about how others have suffered as a result of your abusive behavior, the more you can use that to energize making real changes.

The remainder of this book is focused on this change process, on how to become and stay nonabusive. It offers multiple concrete skills and, even more important, core ways of thinking and seeing the world and your relationships differently. In a later chapter we will outline ways that you can mend and repair the damage to relationships, but your first priority needs to be not doing any further damage.

CHAPTER 13

MOVING FROM DISCONNECTION
TO CONNECTION

In the previous chapters we outlined different forms of abuse and control, the thoughts and beliefs that drive them, and the denial and avoidance that allows those thoughts and behaviors to continue. Now we are finally ready to pull it all together into a single model. If you think of each of the previous chapters as describing individual trees in the forest, now we are ready to describe the forest—all of those trees put together.

RIGID MASCULINITY CONFORMITY
We believe that a strong embrace of traditionally "masculine" qualities and a simultaneous rejection of traditionally "feminine" qualities drives many of the underlying beliefs that support abusive behavior. This is why the vast majority of abusive behavior is displayed by men and a disproportionate number of those who embrace nonviolence are women. However, the tendency toward abusive behavior is not due to gender, but to a narrow embrace of traditional male behaviors and broad exclusion of traditional female qualities that lead to problematic outcomes, including violence. This appears to be true for women who are abusive as well, and is sometimes described as "rigid masculinity conformity."

Human qualities that are typically considered to be more masculine than feminine—being strong, unemotional, self-reliant, independent, etc.—are not random. They are seen as necessary for survival in a hostile environment, and certain people require this skill set: pilots, police officers, surgeons, soldiers. In these occupations, being cautious, vigilant, and stoic are helpful—but it is not necessary for people who embrace those more "masculine" qualities to be male.

Embracing these qualities in moderation can be helpful, but it becomes problematic when they are embraced to the exclusion of all others. For example, someone who is not just vigilant while working as a police officer, but remains in a continued state of guardedness off the job as well, may struggle in their personal relationships. If you think of the "man box" as a suit of armor, these people wear their armor all the time, even when they are safe at home. The problem is that the same suit of armor that protects them in a dangerous situation can interfere with their ability to connect with others—and even themselves—if they wear it all the time. The single word that best describes this psychological suit of armor is **disconnection**.

DISCONNECTION

Disconnection is a powerful resource in dangerous situations. In a life-threatening situation, disconnecting from yourself and your hunger or fatigue or sense of pain can allow you to focus on surviving—you can deal with your discomfort when the threat to your life has passed. Disconnecting from others can be necessary if your job is operating on a patient or safely flying a plane through a storm—worrying about the person on the operating table or the people on the plane can distract you from doing the job that needs to be done. Disconnecting from a relationship is necessary if you have to end it because the other person is not good for you or is taking advantage of you.

While there are times when disconnection is helpful and adaptive, it is problematic if you are disconnected in general. You need that suit of armor when you are going into battle, but not when you are with your partner or children. Those thick work boots may protect your feet on the job, but they are not great for dancing or sleeping. Focusing on survival is maladaptive when the situation does not demand it. The world can be dangerous and others can hurt you, but much of the time, most people are trustworthy and well-meaning. From the very beginning of human history, human survival has depended on forming close, trusting relationships with other people. That is still true today. Connection with yourself, your romantic partner, and others is vital for living happily and effectively in the world.

People who are prone to abusive behavior struggle to form these connections, and their disconnection drives their abusive behavior. To truly stop abusive behavior at its roots requires connection. In a nutshell, we believe disconnection drives abusive behavior and connection is key to stopping abusive behavior.

We have found three specific domains of disconnection that are problematic: disconnection from yourself, from others, and from intimate partners. We will examine each in more detail below.

DISCONNECTION FROM YOURSELF

Disconnection from yourself is ignoring or avoiding thinking about your body, your mind, and your heart. It means ignoring what your body needs to function, such as food, rest, or comfort, as well as basic human needs such as the need to play, socialize, and relax. It involves ignoring how you view and think about situations, then determining how you want to respond to them. It involves ignoring your emotions, which are key to helping you live true to yourself in the world.

Temporarily ignoring and disconnecting from yourself is okay, and even necessary at times. People do it all the time to devote their full attention to something like a task at work, a friend in need, or a movie. This is like temporarily putting something on a shelf until you're ready to attend to it. You may have a busy day at work, but at your midmorning break you go to the bathroom, respond to a text from a friend, and add a few items to the grocery list. With those quick needs checked off, you go back to work. That evening after work, when you have time to connect more deeply with yourself, you notice how you feel, reflect on your day, and think over the days ahead. You realize that the full days at work are wearing you down and you start to think about when you can take a day or two off just to recharge. Although you didn't spend much time during your workday thinking about or connecting with yourself, you remedy that on the drive home and beyond.

Disconnecting from yourself becomes a problem when you do it continually—putting everything on the shelf and never taking anything off. The longer you ignore and neglect yourself, the more intense and urgent your needs become. Even so, it's possible to ignore those warning signs, and unmet needs can significantly interfere with your ability to be happy and function well. Certain unmet needs, like an untreated medical condition, could lead to your death, but usually they cause less severe problems that you might continue to ignore.

If you spend your day ignoring what is going on inside you, how would that look? As soon as you wake up, you'd get going with your day, busying yourself with tasks. During your morning break you might still go to the bathroom, but you would numb out by playing a game on your phone. After work, you might listen to a podcast the whole way home and spend the evening distracted, not really checking in with or thinking much about yourself. You would go to bed physically exhausted but unaware of any particular emotion. You would wake up the next morning and do it all over again. If you give no thought to taking a little time off, have limited interaction with friends, and are unaware of how burned-out you're getting, you might tell someone you're just fine, and even believe it. But ignoring something doesn't make it go away, as we discussed in great detail in Chapter 7: Denial.

Intentionally ignoring your needs every now and then, perhaps by putting off sleep until you finish a task or postponing lunch until you have made an important phone call, is appropriate. But when you ignore your needs automatically and unconsciously, it's like you're wearing an invisible suit of armor that you've forgotten how to take off. You may mistakenly believe the armor is your skin, a natural part of you—but it's not true. You were not born this way. You became this way. This armor is something you learned to put on and wear, and therefore, you can learn how to take it off. We will discuss how to do this in later chapters.

Your disconnection from yourself does not only affect your level of self-awareness, but your ability to self-soothe and self-manage as well. Without self-awareness, it is difficult to comfort and take care of yourself, and to have compassion for yourself. Taking poor care of yourself can have a negative impact on those closest to you, who may feel like they need to step in to take care of you. They may do this on their own or in response to pressure and blame from you. You may consciously expect and demand it of your partner (and sometimes your children, too) and blame them for not taking adequate care of you when you are not feeling or doing well.

Either way, this disconnection from self is unnecessarily burdensome to others, particularly those closest to you.

Abusive behavior is one serious consequence of this disconnection from and neglect of yourself. Internal distress often becomes external distress, especially when it is unaddressed. Appropriate emotional expression typically involves using words and assertiveness. Inappropriate emotional expression involves externalizing with reactive and immature behaviors, including abusive and controlling behaviors. Externalizing often involves misplaced emotional intensity. You may act out with situation A (yelling at the children for having a messy room) when in fact you are upset about situation B (not having enough money to pay your credit card bill). Overreactions and overly intense emotions can be indications of externalization.

The inclination to externalize can be compared to an overflowing garbage can that is never emptied or a balloon that expands until it bursts. Typically, what happens is that you feel generally or broadly unhappy and then vent it or act it out with others, usually those closest to you. This can be called being grumpy or in a bad emotional place; this is when you **radiate intensity** and the people around you feel like they're walking on eggshells, worried that you may blow up. The more distressed you are by the external events that you haven't managed and the internal neglect you've inflicted on yourself, the more likely you are to be abusive and the more severe the abuse is likely to be. The less distressed you are, on the other hand, because of your better self-care and better management of external problems, the less likely you are to be abusive. There is plenty of research to support this, including the connection between being unemployed or financially distressed and being abusive, or having a co-occurring substance abuse problem and being abusive.

When this is an issue, your family learns to watch you for signs of distress. They have learned the hard way that when you are feeling distressed on the inside you are much more likely to become abusive on the outside. For their own safety, your family may do their best to pacify and comfort you, to lower your distress so you do not become abusive. However, because your distress is not primarily about your family members but about your own self-neglect, no matter what they try to do to help, it ultimately fails and there are abusive outbursts.

DISCONNECTION FROM AND DISREGARD OF OTHER PEOPLE

As important as it is for you to be aware of yourself, that's not enough, unless you live alone and are not in a relationship. It is important to be aware of and considerate toward the people with whom you are in relationship.

Being disconnected from others means being not particularly aware of or tuned-in to the people around you. It often means failing to consider what they need, want, or are feeling. This is particularly problematic when their wants, needs, or perspectives are different from yours. If you're not aware of those differences, you may neglect them; they may be overlooked or unaddressed. This has a particularly negative impact on the people you live with since your lives are so intertwined. This disconnection also makes it more difficult to treat them with compassion.

Being disconnected from others might result in the schedule, budget, and quality of life in your household being based solely on your needs and wants, to the exclusion of everyone else's. You might only consider your own physical comfort when you set the thermostat, your own hunger when it comes to meals, or your own priorities for how to spend the day. All this is fine if you live alone, but it is problematic if other people live with you in relationship. Relationships are living, growing, changing things that need regular care and attention. Left unattended, they can fade and weaken, and as people fade from your awareness you may increasingly act as if you live alone.

Disconnection from others can develop out of disconnection from yourself. If you are unaware of your own emotions and needs, you'll have a hard time connecting with those of others. Disconnection from others can also develop out of self-absorption, in which you are overly caught up in your own wants, needs, and feelings, to the exclusion of those of others. Terrence Real calls this "grandiosity" in his book *I Don't Want to Talk About It*; we call it egotism. Egotism can lead you to neglect and dismiss others, particularly when their wants, needs, and perspectives are different from yours. This is a form of relationship neglect.

Relationship neglect typically involves very little overt abuse. In fact, it is often about not about what you are doing to others, but about what you are *not* doing for them. It is about *not* thinking about the other person, *not* remembering them, *not* including or considering them in the decision-making process. Unlike overtly abusive behavior, which often scares others and leaves them walking on eggshells, neglectful behavior may leave them feeling depressed, discouraged, and disregarded. People who are being neglected often feel invisible and voiceless. This is particularly destructive coming from someone they love. The opposite of love is not hate, but indifference. Being neglected feels like you do not matter, like you are unimportant.

One particularly damaging way this disconnection shows up is when abusive partners deny their abusive behaviors and the damage they have caused. No one is perfect; everyone is occasionally inadvertently hurtful to their partner. Much can be forgiven and healed if it is acknowledged and addressed. But if the bad behavior is followed by denial, it is more damaging, like a spill that is left to soak in and becomes an indelible stain. Much of the damage of abuse is inflicted not in the moment, but in the silence, refusal to acknowledge what happened, and denial about the consequences that follow.

DISCONNECTION FROM AND DISTRUST OF INTIMATE RELATIONSHIPS

The final form of disconnection is from the romantic partnership. A basic assumption of partners in close relationships is that each person is lovable, trustworthy, and on the other's side: they are on the same team. However, people who are prone to being abusive tend to be quite mistrustful in their primary relationships, and quick to question whether their partner is truly on their side.

To what extent do you honestly view your partner as being on your side, particularly if they have hurt you before? Getting close to someone and being vulnerable with them means that they can hurt you. They may misunderstand you, or forget to do something, or say the wrong thing, or behave in a thoughtless manner. Although this sort of hurtful behavior is common and inevitable in most close relationships, it can still hurt. People who are prone to being abusive tend to misinterpret their partners' hurtful behavior as abusive and intentional. You may be quick to take offense, quick to take things personally, and quick to view your partner's behaviors as aggressive. As a result, you may be quick to protect yourself by becoming defensive, withdrawn, or aggressive. This is where the Power Over belief system described in Chapter 5: Abusive Thoughts and Beliefs shows up.

This way of thinking is either/or: only one person can be right, only one can get their need met. In any given moment, for one person to win, the other must lose; for one to get what they want, the other must go without; for one to be right, the other must be wrong. It is not surprising that controlling behaviors often show up here. They are driven by an external focus and a belief that to meet your own needs, you must control how others behave. If they are not kept in line, they will dominate and take advantage, and you won't get what you want and need.

To summarize, we believe the root cause of abusive behavior is disconnection: from yourself, from the people you live with, and from the implicit partnership of an intimate relationship. Disconnecting from yourself allows you to externalize your unmanaged distress as abusive behavior toward others. Disconnecting from and disregarding others allows you to neglect them. Disconnecting from and distrusting your primary relationships allows you to abuse and control the people closest to you in order to keep them in line. Although most abusive partners exhibit abusive behavior in all three realms, some struggle with just one or two. All three are problematic and they each need to be addressed.

CONNECTION

Stopping abusive and controlling behavior is less about learning specific skills or stopping certain behaviors than it is about changing the way you see the world. Once you change your core beliefs regarding how you see yourself and relate to others, many of the necessary behaviors will fall into place. On the other hand, any skills you learn before you make this shift are at significant risk of misuse. What makes someone a carpenter is not a set of tools, but the knowledge of a carpenter. What makes a person a doctor is not a stethoscope or a bunch of medical terms, but the knowledge of a doctor. Learning how to see the world differently involves not just changing your self-talk, but changing your deep core values that may not always even be conscious.

The central core value necessary for making real, sustained change is connecting and turning toward yourself and others—which is the very opposite of what you were learned from the "Act Like a Man" box. You need to be willing to connect with yourself, with other people, and with your intimate partner and children. This requires courage because connecting opens you up to being hurt and to feel that hurt more deeply. It takes courage to be vulnerable with yourself, with others, and with your intimate partner and children. The rewards are great, but the process is neither easy nor well-supported by society, particularly for males.

SELF-COMPASSION: CONNECTION WITH SELF

Connection with self involves three steps. The first is to become more self-aware. You need to be willing to be open to and curious about your emotions, which shift and change from moment to moment. Understanding your emotions is key to understanding yourself in all your uniqueness. You need to notice and connect with your thoughts and how you perceive the world. You need to realize that how you *think* about the world is more important than how the world affects you. When you become able to step back and examine your thoughts, you will realize you don't have to be at their mercy. You can change your thoughts so they align with your core beliefs and values. You need to connect with your body and its physical sensations and needs, which can help you better understand your emotional and cognitive states. This includes muscle tension, energy level, temperature, agitation, hunger, and fatigue, as well as discomfort and injury. Just as negative thinking and uncomfortable emotions can increase the temptation to be abusive and controlling, so can uncomfortable physical states.

Once you are more aware of yourself—your body, head, and heart—it's up to you to do what you can to take care of yourself, to use that information to figure out what you want and need and then do your best to get it. This often means realizing that you are not just a worker or employee and that you have a variety of wants and needs that cannot be met in the workplace. It means being willing to seek out what you want, ask for it, and appropriately advocate for it using appropriate assertiveness and negotiation. It means admitting that you cannot be fully self-sufficient and self-reliant, but need others as well. It means admitting that you are not an emotionless, invulnerable robot, but a human being with a variety of wants and needs. It means realizing that most of your true power is over yourself—your thoughts, emotions, and behaviors. By focusing on this true power, you will actually feel more empowered.

When you are unable to adequately or immediately meet your wants and needs for whatever reason, you need to be able to comfort and soothe yourself in the moment. This means learning how to tolerate and manage distress until you can more permanently or appropriately address it. One important part of this is practicing self-compassion: to acknowledge yourself with lovingkindness and without strong negative judgment or mental self-abuse.

REGARD: CONNECTION WITH OTHERS

Connecting with others involves willfully and consciously considering the people around you, especially the people you live with. It means intentionally regarding them and considering how they will be affected when you make decisions. It means seeking to understand them, especially when they are different from you. It means striving to see the world through other people's eyes and loving them as they wish to be loved (the Platinum Rule) rather than how you wish to be loved (the Golden Rule). It is believing that you can honor and acknowledge the people you love without compromising your needs or your integrity. It means being open to their influence and giving serious consideration to what they think, want, and perceive rather than focusing exclusively on your experience, priorities, and perceptions.

Another skill that is key to connecting with others is learning to be **relational**. This means being mindful of others around you and giving weight to their thoughts, feelings, and needs. It is remembering that you are not alone in the world (or in the home!) and that your choices affect those around you and making decisions accordingly. Developing compassion and empathy are vital. Compassion and empathy are key to treating the people around you like people and not like things or objects.

Connecting with others requires humility, a concept that is rarely talked about in American culture. Humility means remembering that you are literally just one of billions of people in the world and that the world does not revolve around you. You matter, but you matter no more and no less than anyone else. It is remembering that you are often not the only one in the room or home and you need to be mindful of everyone present. If you wish to consider only yourself, it is best for you to live and be alone. To consider only yourself when others are around is selfish.

TRUST: CONNECTION WITH THE INTIMATE RELATIONSHIP

Finally, you need to trust others, especially the people who are closest to you. This means reminding yourself that most relationships are collaborative and cooperative, and even though some people have bad intentions, you will intentionally not jump to conclusions until you have clear and compelling evidence. You need to presume that the people who love you are on your side; that they are on your team. Assume that they are your allies!

Connecting with your loved ones means presuming that if they hurt or neglect you, it's unintentional and thoughtless, not on purpose or willful. It means giving them the benefit of the doubt and being gracious and understanding. It also means not taking their behavior personally—they are not intentionally targeting you with the hurtful things that they do. It means acknowledging that no one is perfect, that everyone makes and will make mistakes. It means presuming that they are hurting you on accident, not abusing you on purpose, until there is clear evidence otherwise.

Connecting with the people you are in intimate relationships with means working with an **abundance mindset** that assumes everyone can get what they want most of the time. Neither you nor the other has to sacrifice for both of you to get what you want. It means looking for win-wins instead of presuming that someone has to lose.

THE CHANGE PROCESS

In order to move from disconnection to connection and to stop your abusive and controlling behavior, you need to take a number of steps.

1. Break through your denial and get honest with yourself about what you did in the past, what you may continue to do, and how you feel on a day-to-day basis in the present.

2. Admit that you have been abusive and controlling and acknowledge the full extent of it over time and throughout your relationships. Do this without engaging in shame.

3. Take responsibility for what you have done, own it, and become accountable for the abusive and controlling choices you have made.

4. Immediately stop the abusive and controlling behaviors that you can. Interrupt and contain the ones you cannot immediately stop.

5. Change your core beliefs and thinking. Change the way you see and think about the world.

6. Develop a new way of living that is rooted in an internal and Personal Power focus.

7. Make amends and repair relationships where you can.

8. Build intimacy in your closest relationships to the extent that you and your partner want.

9. Watch out for relapse and the tendency to drift away from this work.

The rest of this book examines how you can change your patterns of abuse and control to fulfilling connections with yourself and others. Read on to learn how to build a better life within yourself, your home, and the world in general.

CHAPTER 14

LEARNING TO STOP YOUR ABUSE
IN THE MOMENT

Stopping your abusive behavior for good typically means shifting the way you think and live in the world. It includes changing the relationships you have with yourself, your romantic partner, and your children. It means embracing a new belief system and developing a new lifestyle. This takes time. You didn't get this way overnight and you're not going to change overnight. It takes time, energy, effort, and practice to change habits. Since you cannot make all of these changes immediately, what can you do in the short run to stop your abusive behavior in the moment?

This chapter offers immediate and short-term solutions for stopping your abusive behavior in the moment. The suggestions below are all things you can do pretty much immediately. They are mainly intended to be band-aids and temporary solutions while you are working to make the deeper and more enduring changes outlined in later chapters. They are similar to techniques used early in recovery by people who are learning how to deal with temptations to drink or use. Later in their recovery process when they have incorporated many lifestyle changes, they may rarely, if ever, feel tempted to drink or use, but early on, such temptation is real and dangerous. Dealing with the temptation to be abusive and controlling is the first—but certainly not the last—step toward being different and behaving better. These are the things to do while you make deep, long-term changes or are getting back on track after relapse, which we will explain in Chapter 26: Learning to Sustain Your Positive Changes.

If you think of your abusive and controlling behavior as a fire, then this chapter's tools are fire extinguishers. Chapters after this will focus on fire prevention: how to avoid fire in the first place. Listed below are some tools you can use to keep a fire from getting out of hand.

USE SHEER WILLPOWER

The first step many abusive partners take is to use sheer willpower to stop their abusive behavior. No real changes support this, just a vow that they will never be abusive again—or at least not right now. This is similar to "white-knuckling" sobriety. While this can work temporarily, your bad behavior will return if you don't make substantial underlying changes.

DON'T GIVE YOURSELF PERMISSION

Abusive behavior is always a choice. It involves giving yourself permission. When things are not going your way and you're getting escalated, intense, and angry, it can be extra tempting to become abusive and controlling. Believe it or not, even people who are not abusive are sometimes tempted in moments like these, but they don't give themselves permission. You can do the same thing. You can make a different choice.

INTERRUPT IT IN THE MOMENT

Even if you choose to become abusive in the moment, you can choose to stop being abusive at any moment. Your goal is to stop the behavior, in the moment, as soon as possible. The sooner you can stop it, the less damage you will cause and the less you will have to apologize for and repair later. Once you start, STOP IT as soon as you can. Do damage control and disengage as quickly as you can. The goal is to not be abusive at all, but reducing the duration and intensity of your abuse in the moment is still progress in the right direction.

ZIP YOUR LIPS

When it comes to verbal abuse, the simplest technique to use in the moment is to keep your mouth shut. Just do not say—or write or text—the abusive thing you want to say. You may be thinking it, but do not say it. Do not hit send. As Dr. Evil in the *Austin Powers* movies puts it, "Zip it!"

For a variation of this, slightly delay your responses. Mentally count to five before you respond to engage your brain before you move your lips. If you pause before responding—verbally or by hitting "send"—you may be able to catch yourself before you do or say something abusive.

PUT IT ON THE SHELF

Another short-term solution is to temporarily shelve the issue or situation until you can calm yourself or are in a better space. This is different from a time-out (which is explained below) because you are not trying to immediately return to the situation or even to immediately prepare yourself to deal with the situation. Instead, you are walking away from the situation for now because you are not ready or able to deal with it well. The idea is to return to it when you are in a better headspace.

If you are communicating via text or email, take some time before hitting "send." If it's a good idea now, it will still be a good idea in five or thirty minutes. Briefly delaying your message allows you more time to get calm and make sure you really want to say it before you send it.

Keep in mind that you can only walk away from things or put them on the shelf for so long before they come up on their own. This can be an unhealthy way of avoiding issues and concerns that others need you to address. As a short-term, immediate solution, this works fine, but it is not a good long-term or permanent solution.

LIMIT CONTACT

It is much harder to be abusive to someone if you have no contact with them. If you are serious about stopping your bad behavior but are struggling to do so, temporarily limiting your contact with someone is an artificial but effective solution. Abusive partners who are mandated by probation or child welfare to attend a program might already have been ordered to limit or cease contact.

Even if you are able to have contact with or are living with your partner, you might consider limiting contact, especially if your partner wants to. This might include limiting your interactions, agreeing not to address intense issues until you can better manage yourself, and temporarily moving out. Controlled separation (explained below) is one specific intervention.

Although not having contact with your loved one can feel like punishment, its intention is to reduce the risk of abuse until you learn to behave differently. The hope is that you will change how you think and develop new skills that increase your chances of success later. Limiting contact now may save the relationship later.

You may have already lost your relationship because of your abuse and control or for other reasons. If you haven't, every new episode of abuse incurs more damage and increases the likelihood that your relationship will end. As the saying goes, "If you want to get out of a hole, the first thing to do is stop digging."

PLAN A CONTROLLED SEPARATION

A controlled separation is not quite the same as a separation. Many times, when couples separate, they are headed toward divorce or a permanent breakup. As a result, even during the separation they may act like they are no longer together: they separate the finances, make decisions independently of each other, and even date other people. A controlled separation is different in that both people are expected to maintain the committed relationship: they share finances, they make important decisions together, they do not date anyone else. The hope is that a controlled separation will lead to reconciliation and a stronger relationship. Even if it doesn't, it creates a pause before a breakup.

In a controlled separation, there is initially little to no contact, but contact gradually increases over time as you consistently manage the current level well. Doing this increases the chances that you are not abusive or controlling while you learn how to behave differently. The idea is to never have more contact than you can handle without becoming abusive or controlling. Early on, it is unrealistic to expect you to be on your best behavior 24/7, but you probably could be on your best behavior with email contact or limited texting, provided you think about what you have written before you hit send. A little more challenging might be a brief phone conversation or a short visit in public. Still more challenging would be spending several hours together in public. More challenging still would be spending a few hours together in private, and so on. The limits are set solely by your partner and reflect their comfort level. One of the very first tests you'll need to pass in order to start rebuilding trust is to show that you can respect their boundary around this, even if you do not like it.

Controlled separations vary depending on the couple and the situation. They often last for a number of months. When successful, they spare the relationship additional hardship while you are making changes. The most common fear is that a controlled separation is a significant step toward breaking up. That is a possibility, but this is actually intended to be a step toward saving the relationship and reconciling. Most of the time, controlled separations lead to reunification, especially when abusive partners make significant positive changes to their behavior in the meantime.

For more information on a controlled separation, review the handout in the appendix. You might also want to share a copy with your partner.

BE OPEN TO PROMPTS FROM YOUR PARTNER

Sometimes your partner will be able to pick up on your escalation and agitation before you do. At such moments it is not unusual for them to speak out about where things seem to be headed. They may share their observations and concerns, ask if you need a time-out, or ask about your intensity. In those moments, when you already feel escalated, it may be hard to hear your partner's words or take them seriously, but it is particularly important that you do so. If you can respond to their concerns, take the time-out they are asking you to take, or otherwise calm down as they are requesting, you may prevent yourself from become abusive (or more abusive) and spare additional hardship for each of you. One way to increase the likelihood of that happening is to make a firm commitment to yourself that any time your partner expresses a concern about your behavior in the moment, you will trust them completely in that moment, not question their concern, and do whatever is necessary to keep things from getting further out of hand, perhaps by taking a time-out or otherwise calming yourself and disengaging.

TAKE A TIME-OUT

One of the most common tools for stopping abusive behavior, especially early on, is a time-out. A time-out is like an emergency brake: when all else fails, you can always pull the emergency brake. It is also an emergency break from the situation—although it is far more than just a break. A time-out is intended to interrupt your behavior *before* you become abusive.

Typically, your internal physical sensations and your external behaviors will let you know when you are becoming escalated. There is nothing wrong with this if you are managing yourself well—if your thinking is solid and you are behaving appropriately. But if you are concerned that you might start making poor choices—that you are headed in a negative direction—a time-out can help you change direction in almost any situation, whether you are alone or with others.

The time-outs we describe are similar to the time-outs used in some sports. In professional basketball, when is a time-out usually taken? Not necessarily when the other team scores a basket, but when the other team is scoring a *series* of baskets. Not necessarily when your team makes a mistake, but when your team *keeps* making mistakes. When you want to interrupt the other team's momentum.

Likewise, people typically don't need a time-out just because they are feeling anger, but rather when their anger is gaining momentum. It is not when they get a little spiked, but when things are spiraling. The goal of the time-out is to interrupt that spiral before things get too bad or the situation gets away from you. You can usually tell you need to take a time-out by how you are feeling physically, your internal self-talk, and how you are behaving. If your intensity is getting too high or your thoughts are filling with negative self-talk, a time-out can get things headed in a better direction.

When a basketball team wants to take a time-out, what is the very first thing they need to do? They need to announce it. They cannot just all of a sudden walk off the court. They need to let an official know that they wish to take a time-out. That is true for you as well, especially if you are with people who know you well, like your family. You should not just walk off; you need to let the people around you know that you are taking a time-out. It is important that they know why you are leaving and what it means.

If you don't tell them, they may jump to the wrong conclusion and it may actually make things worse.

How does a basketball team announce they want a time-out? Someone typically forms their hands into a "T" or they say it out loud. They need to announce it, but they don't spend a long time explaining why. You should announce when you are taking a time-out, but you shouldn't spend a lot of time explaining why. The more time you spend talking about it the more likely you are to say something you shouldn't. For example, "I'm going to take a time-out because I'm starting to get escalated. If I stay here I'm afraid I'm going to start calling you names, like you're a bitch. So before I start calling you a bitch, I'm going to take a time-out." Instead, say simply, "I'm going to take a time-out and I'll be back in X minutes." Anything else is better said after you've had a chance to think things through. If you are with people who know you well, it's important that you call it a "time-out" instead of saying "I'm leaving," "I'm out of here," or "I'm taking a break," especially if you say those things at other times. It is important that they understand you're taking a time-out, not just walking away. If you're with people who don't know you well and the phrase "time-out" would be confusing or embarrassing, it is okay to say something like "I'm going for a walk," "I'll be back in a few minutes," "I'm going to take a quick break," or "I need to go to the restroom." You might not have to say anything at all, since they may not even notice your brief absence.

In professional basketball, it used to be that not all time-outs were the same length. There were twenty-second partial time-outs and full time-outs. Likewise, your time-outs can vary in length. Sometimes you may need only a few minutes to work through all the steps. Other times you may need longer to get yourself calmed down. In some situations it is only possible to take a brief time-out, like when you're caring for young children. Time-outs are typically measured in minutes, not seconds or hours or days, and should be at least a few minutes long. Less than that is more like a brief interruption than a true time-out because you have probably not had time to do all the steps. Keep in mind that it takes the body a minimum of twenty minutes to physiologically calm, so if your time-out is shorter than that, you may still feel some physical agitation. Likewise, time-outs should not be longer than an hour or two. If it is longer than that, it is probably more of a true disengagement from the situation than a time-out. When you announce your time-out, do your best to give the other a sense of how long you will be gone. That lets them know that you will be back and about when they can expect you.

After a time-out is announced in basketball and the officials blow their whistles, what is the very first thing the players do? They stop the game and walk off the court into a huddle. It is very important that you physically leave the situation. If you stay in the room or in the situation you are at much greater risk of getting hooked back into the situation before you are ready. If possible, move out of earshot.

Sometimes it is not possible or practical to leave the situation. If you are home alone with your young children, you could take a brief time-out in the bathroom. If it is impossible to physically leave a situation, for instance because you are stuck in a car in traffic, you can try to mentally leave it by temporarily shifting your attention inward, away from the external situation, and mentally working through the time-out steps. Make sure to request that others not engage with you while you are on your mental time-out.

There are three main things you should be doing during your time-out: calm down physically, improve your attitude, and strategize how to turn the situation around. This is what basketball teams typically do during time-outs. They catch their breath and drink fluids, get a pep talk from the coach that replaces their negative self-talk with positive self-talk, and draw up a play to turn the game around. Let's look at each of these steps more closely.

1. CALM YOURSELF

One reason you may have needed a time-out is that you were getting emotionally intense and agitated. When a person gets emotionally aroused, adrenaline is released into the body, which creates this condition. While adrenaline can be helpful in some situations, it can interfere with thinking and speaking clearly. It is probably not helping if you need a time-out.

Three common ways of helping your body to physically calm down are exercising, relaxing your muscles, and consciously changing your breathing. Let's look a little more closely at each of these.

Exercise

Exercise has tons of benefits, one of which is to calm the body down by metabolizing adrenaline. Chopping wood, taking a brisk walk or run, and mowing the lawn are all examples of exercise. If you are agitated, you should avoid exercise that is related to aggression, such as boxing, certain martial arts, or punching a pillow. Many therapists used to think that physical aggression helped people vent their anger, but research has since shown that it often actually escalates people's anger. The helpful part is the exercise, not the venting. It's fine to do aggressive exercise when you are not feeling agitated or taking a time-out.

Relaxation

A second way to physically calm yourself down is by willfully relaxing your muscles, which become tight and tense in response to agitation and emotional arousal. Relaxation calms the body and slowly lowers its adrenaline levels.

One specific way of relaxing the body is with progressive relaxation. This involves slowly working your way up or down your body, turning your attention to each muscular area, noticing how it feels, and willfully relaxing it. You might start with your toes and move up to your feet, then your calves, then your thighs, and so on. A variation of this is to first tense an area so you can notice it more clearly before you relax it, then notice the contrast between tension and relaxation. Progressive relaxation is often used to help people fall asleep. A variety of apps and programs can guide you through this process.

Conscious breathing

The easiest way to calm down requires the least effort and can truly be done anywhere. Conscious breathing involves noticing your breath and consciously changing it. When a person is physiologically aroused, their breathing tends to become rapid, shallow, and irregular. Conscious breathing willfully does the exact opposite—slows your breathing, deepens it, and makes it more regular. The process triggers the parasympathetic nervous system, which helps the body return to a calm state.

Although we are always breathing, we rarely pay attention to it. To do conscious breathing, simply turn your attention to your breath. Slow your breath down so you are gradually taking in and releasing air rather than gulping it in all at once or releasing it all at once. You want to deepen your breath as well, fully expanding your lungs. Shallow breathing primarily expands your upper chest. Breathing deeply, like singers and wind instrument players, expands the lungs as well as the abdomen. Finally, you want to make your breath more even and regular by inhaling for a set period of time (for example, breathing in to a count of 4) and exhaling to the same count. Even a single slower, deeper, more regular breath can help you feel more calm, and you can do this discreetly virtually anywhere—during a conversation, in a meeting, in traffic, wherever.

There are a number of variations of conscious breathing that accomplish the same result. For example, square breathing or box breathing has you breathe in for a count of 4, hold your breath for a count of 4, breathe out for a count of 4, and then pause for a count of 4 before starting over again. Triangle breathing has you breathe in for a count of 3, hold for a count of 3, and then breathe out for a count of 3.

If you think of your adrenaline as water in a sink, physically calming yourself with any of these techniques is like pulling the plug and allowing the sink to drain.

2. IMPROVE YOUR ATTITUDE

Although calming yourself can help, you also need to address what got you worked up in the first place: your self-talk. The second step of the time-out is to improve your attitude by noticing what your self-talk is, identifying which of it is negative, and challenging it.

As mentioned in Chapter 5: Abusive Thoughts and Beliefs, what gets you emotional is not just what happens to you, but how you interpret what happens to you. Negative self-talk reflects an inaccurate and distorted view of the situation. Positive self-talk, on the other hand, reflects a more accurate and reasonable perspective. Negative self-talk gets you more escalated; positive self-talk helps you calm down.

When your emotions are escalated , your body releases adrenaline into your bloodstream. If you think of adrenaline as water pouring from a faucet, negative self-talk turns the faucet on. If you need a time-out, your sink is probably overflowing. When you calm yourself physically, you're essentially pulling the plug. But until you turn off the tap, the sink will keep filling up. Positive self-talk turns off the tap and helps you calm yourself mentally. The goal is to interrupt and contain your negative self-talk by improving your attitude and your outlook on the situation.

One way to help your mind settle is to clear it of all thoughts using the progressive relaxation and conscious breathing techniques described above. When you focus on your body or your breath, you stop focusing on the negative self-talk that is contributing to your agitation. Meditation and mindfulness practices are other ways to clear your mind; we will discuss these techniques in later chapters.

3. MAKE A PLAN

The third thing to do during your time-out is make a plan. In the midst of the situation, particularly if things were moving quickly or unexpectedly, you may not have known how to respond appropriately. When tensions are high, it's easy to fall into old habits and old ways of being, and you could become abusive and controlling. Taking a time-out lets you pause the situation to gather your thoughts so you can respond in a more thoughtful, considerate manner.

As you reenter the situation, how might you respond differently? You might want to plan for several different possibilities, anticipating how things are most likely to go or how the person is most likely to respond.

Once you have calmed yourself, cleared your thinking, and made a plan, you need to *return to the situation*. In basketball, no matter what the score is or how much time is left, the teams have to get back out on the floor and pick up where they left off. You need to do the same thing. If you don't return to the situation when you can, calling your avoidance a time-out is simply manipulative. This is one of the most common ways people misuse time-outs: by leaving and not returning.

The goal of returning to the situation and picking up where you left off is to feel calmer, think more clearly, and be more respectful so you can work things out. This could include continuing a conversation or completing something you started. On the other hand, although you have to return to the situation, you do not have to resolve it. There are a number of reasons for postponing a resolution: it's too late, you need a true break, you don't know how to move forward, other things need your attention, the other person isn't ready or willing to talk yet, and so on. It is possible that you will return to the situation only briefly to reach an agreement that you will deal with it later. But if it involves another person, you should try to reach an agreement about how to proceed, not make a unilateral decision.

MISUSE OF TIME-OUTS

When time-outs are misused, it's usually because people fail to do all the steps and spend the time doing other things. Things that are not time-outs: sleeping, watching television, reading, talking with friends, having a meal, working on a hobby. Any of these activities might help you calm down, but none of them are part of a true time-out.

Another common misuse of a time-out is to leave the situation and not return promptly. This silences the other person and lets you avoid the situation.

Leaving without announcing that you're taking a time-out is ineffective, too. If the person you're walking away from is close to you, it's important that they know you're not just walking away (as you might have done in the past), and that you will be back to continue the interaction when you're in a better headspace.

Finally, you cannot give your partner a time-out; you can only take one for yourself. If you think your partner is getting escalated, you can share your concern, but you cannot tell them to take a time-out. Likewise, it's not okay to say "we" need a time-out; that's just another way of telling your partner that they need one.

PRACTICE TIME-OUTS

Early on, it's important to do trial runs when you are not escalated. To take a practice time-out, simply announce that you are doing so, and that you're not angry or agitated. Then follow the rest of the steps (leave, calm, improve your self-talk, make a plan, return) just as if it were a real one. Some people imagine a situation in which a time-out would help, then practice using that scenario. There are several benefits to practice time-outs. They can help you remember to take them and how to take them. They can familiarize your partner with the practice. And they let you troubleshoot practical challenges. What if it's raining? What if you can't leave the house?

People often complain that their partner will not let them take a time-out or will follow them when they try to leave. In this situation, you can try a few things. First, explain to them in advance what a time-out is, what it looks like, and what the steps are. Second, take practice time-outs when they are around so they can see what it's like. Third, make sure to return to the situation and follow up with your partner. When you do these three things—explaining time-outs, practicing them in front of your partner, and returning from them in a better space—partners are usually cooperative, since they benefit as well.

PARTIAL TIME-OUTS
Although it's not the same as a time-out, you can use parts of the time-out to help stop abusive behavior in the moment. Examples include calming yourself or changing your thinking while remaining in the situation, or briefly leaving the situation to clear your head a bit by going to the bathroom. It can be helpful, but a time-out is more extensive.

OTHER INTERVENTIONS THAT INVOLVE LEAVING A SITUATION
There are other helpful interventions besides time-outs that involve leaving a stressful situation. One is to simply take a break to do something else. A break does not involve all the steps of a time-out and can be taken anytime, not just when you are escalated. Breaks can allow you to rest, get new perspective, do something different, deal with other things, and just mix things up.

Another intervention that could involve leaving a situation is setting a boundary by warning someone that if they don't stop a particular behavior (teasing you, raising their voice, refusing to drop an issue you don't want to talk about) you will leave the situation. You can't make them stop, but you don't have to stick around. Boundaries are explained in greater detail in Chapter 24: Practicing Conflict-Resolution Skills.

Finally, you and the other person could agree to shelve an issue and come back to it later—whether that's minutes, hours, days, or longer. This can be particularly wise if no constructive progress is being made. Sometimes issues are shelved for practical reasons; perhaps it's getting late or other tasks need your attention. Shelving will be discussed in more detail in Chapter 23: Learning to Communicate Effectively.

***

APPROPRIATE WAYS TO LEAVE AN UNRESOLVED SITUATION

- Temporarily step away from the situation.
- Shelve the topic until a better time.
- Take a time-out when you are becoming escalated.
- Set a boundary when someone else is becoming escalated and inappropriate.

HOW TO TAKE A TIME-OUT

1. Announce it briefly, giving the other person a sense of how long you will be gone
2. Leave or disengage from the situation (physically, if at all possible)
3. Do these (and only these) three things:
   a. Physically calm yourself down
   b. Improve your thinking by clearing your head of negative self-talk as much as possible and increasing your positive self-talk
   c. Make a plan for how to handle the situation more appropriately
4. Return to the situation and follow up on the issue

WHAT TO DO IF YOU HAVE BEEN ABUSIVE AGAIN

Try as you might, it is likely that you will exhibit abusive behavior again. But you can significantly reduce the negative impact if you address it quickly. Abusive behavior is made far more damaging when it is not acknowledged afterward—when it is met with excuses, denial, blaming, rationalizations, and so on. Although you may have failed to avoid abusive behaviors, you can still accountably acknowledge it, apologize for it, and make reparations for it. Each will be explained in more detail below.

ACKNOWLEDGE YOUR ABUSIVE BEHAVIOR

First, you need to admit and acknowledge that you were abusive and controlling. Even if you didn't intend to do it, you either did—or your partner experienced what you did as being so. We will discuss this second point further in Chapter 21: Learning to Regard Others when we talk about intention vs. impact.

Accountable acknowledgment means naming the behavior as abusive or controlling and taking full responsibility for it—not offering excuses, justifications, or rationalizations. Regardless of what else may have been happening or what else your partner or child may have been doing, you were abusive or controlling, and that was not okay. Typically, your acknowledgment should be brief and to the point. The longer you talk about it, the more likely you are to drift into rationalizing or justifying it.

It is vital to do this as quickly after the incident as you can. The more time passes, the greater the damage. Within seconds is best, minutes good, hours adequate, and days barely acceptable. Even so, don't acknowledge the behavior until you can do so genuinely. An insincere acknowledgment or one that involves blaming or excuses just makes things worse, literally adding insult to injury.

MAKE AN ACCOUNTABLE APOLOGY

An apology is more elaborate than an acknowledgment. It expresses remorse and empathy as well as accountability, and it is done solely for the other person, not for yourself. Don't expect anything in return—even for them to accept your apology or forgive you. There are basically five steps in an accountable apology.

1. Adopt an appropriate attitude and stance. Be sincerely apologetic and remorseful for whatever harm was done, whether it was intentional or not. If you lack that attitude, it's generally not a good idea to apologize.
2. Offer a simple summary in an accountable manner. Be specific about what you did without offering excuses or justifications. Use "I" statements and leave out blaming, judging, or accusing statements about the other person.
3. Speculate on how the other person was negatively affected by your behavior by showing empathy and compassion for them.
4. Express your feelings of remorse for what you have done. Make it clear that what you did was not okay and that you intend to behave differently in the future.

5. Determine whether you need to make further repair or amends. This could include an explanation (not a justification) of why you did the thing that hurt the other person if that's something they want. It often includes listening compassionately and fully to what they have to say about their own experience of your behavior and the way it may have rippled through their life and day.

For example, say you and your partner are preparing to go on a hike on a summer Saturday. You hoped to get an early start, but you end up leaving fifteen minutes later than planned because your partner needed extra time to get ready. As you get on the highway, traffic is bad. You glare at your partner and say in an angry tone that if they had been ready on time you would not have to deal with so much traffic; you call them selfish and thoughtless.

An accountable apology would look something like this: After just a few moments of uncomfortable silence, you realize that you took out your frustration with the traffic on your partner and were verbally abusive with your tone, your glare, and your words. You settle yourself for a moment and then say in a much calmer, gentler, kinder tone, "I'm sorry for speaking that way to you. I know you got ready as quickly as you could and even cut short your preparation so we could get an early start. You were not behaving thoughtlessly or selfishly and it was not right for me to say those things. I was frustrated that even with this early a start there was still traffic and took my frustration out on you. That was not okay. I imagine that hurt your feelings and may leave you anxious that I might continue to be in a bad mood the rest of the drive and beyond. I wanted us to have a nice day trip together. I am unhappy about the traffic, but my intense reaction is only making it worse. I can't control the traffic, but I can control my reaction to it, including NOT taking it out on you. I will be more settled now and accept that we aren't going to get there as quickly as I had hoped. What matters is that we get to spend time together, even if part of it is in the car in traffic. I apologize for acting that way. If there is anything else you want to say to me about this, I am open to hearing your experience." Your partner might have a few other things they want to share with you about what it was like for them, which you listen to and acknowledge. Seeing the clear shift in your tone and demeanor as you acknowledged and owned your abusive behavior lets them settle, and things go much better after that. It was only briefly difficult, rather than being difficult for much longer than that. Besides stopping your escalation, your accountable apology helped you make things right again.

TRY TO REPAIR THE DAMAGE

Repair attempts are similar to amends, but amends are made for damage done some time ago, while repair attempts are made for damage that was just incurred. They can be fairly brief and simple, especially if the abuse or control was not extensive. Examples include apologies, listening to and acknowledging the other person's thoughts and feelings, having a do-over in which you behave more appropriately, and asking for what the other person needs to make things right—and following through on their requests.

In his extensive research on what differentiates successful from unsuccessful romantic relationships, John Gottman found that people in successful relationships made far more frequent repair attempts than people in unsuccessful relationships. In other words, people get hurt even in healthy relationships; what matters is how those moments are handled.

Partners do not expect perfection, but they do need accountability. Think of moments in your own life when others have behaved rudely or disrespectfully toward you. Now think of times when they came back shortly afterward to acknowledge what they did and apologize. Think of how much less hurtful it felt afterward. The next best thing to not being abusive or controlling is to make timely and accountable attempts at repair if you are.

As with acknowledgment, attempts at repair should be made promptly—the longer the delay, the more damage has likely been incurred. But it is important that they are genuine and accountable. In addition, the other person must be willing to consider your attempt at repair. If they are not ready, then wait until they are. It is for them, after all.

WHAT NOT TO DO AFTER AN ABUSIVE MOMENT

Listed below are some of the most common mistakes made by people who have been abusive as they try to make things right. These will only make things worse.

DON'T MAKE PROMISES YOU CANNOT KEEP.

As much as you might want to promise that you will never engage in an abusive behavior again, don't. A broken promise makes abuse even worse. Be very certain, with very clear reasons and plans, that you will be able to keep your promise.

DO NOT DENY, MINIMIZE, OR MAKE EXCUSES FOR WHAT YOU HAVE DONE.

It is important that you take responsibility for what you have done. If you start explaining, it's likely to sound like justification or excuses. Simply acknowledge what you have done unless the other person wants an explanation.

DO NOT GIVE GIFTS OR TRY TO "MAKE IT UP TO THEM" UNLESS THEY CLEARLY WANT YOU TO.

Gifts and other acts of kindness after an episode of bad behavior are often a covert attempt to make people feel better before they're ready. In that way, the presents are more for you than for them. Make sure your offerings are truly for the other person, and something they truly want, not just a way for you to get around your appropriate guilt or to manipulate them into feeling differently.

DO NOT TRY TO TALK THEM OUT OF THEIR HURT FEELINGS.

Because it is hard to see someone in an unhappy place because of something you did, you may be tempted to try to help them feel better. On the surface this may seem like it's for their benefit, but it tends to be for yours: to relieve you of feeling uncomfortable about their unhappiness. Your loved ones' unhappiness is a natural consequence of your hurtful behavior. If you are going to be truly accountable, you need to respect them and let them have their feelings.

Being able to feel, sit with, and process feelings is an important part of the recovery process that they were unable to do while you were abusive and controlling. Letting them have their feelings—for as long as they need to—is an important way of respecting and affirming them.

***

The tools described in this chapter are the most appropriate ones to use early in your change process, before other deeper change is present. The chapters that follow will outline tools for creating deeper, more enduring changes in yourself. It is not enough to put out fires after they start; you want to do everything you can to avoid them in the first place. If all is well, you'll never have to use your fire extinguisher.

CHAPTER 15

BECOMING AWARE OF YOUR THOUGHTS

What affects you most is not what happens to you, but how you *think* about what happens to you. If you change the way you think about the world you will change the way you experience the world, for better or for worse. Changing the way you think needs to happen on at least two levels: with your self-talk and with your underlying beliefs.

NOTICING AND CHALLENGING NEGATIVE SELF-TALK
Self-talk is the ongoing monologue or commentary in your head; it's like a sportscaster constantly describing the game of your life. It's not just about you—it is *to* you and can be about anyone and anything. Self-talk is part of everyone's inner experience.

Self-talk comes in two types: negative and positive. Negative self-talk fans the flames of uncomfortable feelings, making you feel even worse. It tends to distort and mischaracterize things by making negative assumptions, jumping to negative conclusions, and imposing unrealistic expectations. Positive self-talk, on the other hand, is more careful not to jump to conclusions and tends to stay more realistic and objective. Research has shown that people who are prone to anger and abuse tend to have more distorted perceptions of situations—more negative self-talk.

If you want to improve your experience of the world, you'll need to correct your distorted perceptions. Negative self-talk is inevitable, like weeds in a garden; the key is pulling them out before they take over. Positive self-talk pulls the weeds out.

238

The core distinction between positive and negative self-talk is not how optimistic or pessimistic it is, but how *accurate* it is. If you are inaccurately thinking something positive ("Everything is going to go perfectly.") then it is actually *negative* self-talk. On the other hand, if you are realistically thinking something negative (*"I didn't get the raise"*), then it is not negative self-talk; you have a good reason for feeling bad.

It is important to keep your mind from being dominated by negative self-talk. That means being careful not to make negative assumptions or jump to negative conclusions. It means giving others, especially those close to you, the benefit of the doubt. It means keeping to what is known rather than engaging in speculation, especially if speculation takes you in negative directions. It also means keeping your expectations realistic so they're more likely to actually be met. We will look at these points in more detail below.

DON'T ASSUME THE WORST

You will periodically find yourself in situations where you don't fully know what's going on. People may not be acting as expected or things are not going as planned, and it can be easy to make negative assumptions about what's happening. Instead, do your best in the moment to keep your mind open to a number of possibilities and explanations—positive as well as negative—and hold off on making a judgment until you know for sure what is going on. Things are often, but not always, better than you fear. It's okay to be fearful, but be careful not to presume something is true until it is confirmed. If you don't know for certain, stay open to explanations that are benign or positive.

Most people want to know things for sure. Holding onto uncertainty is difficult, and it can be tempting to resolve the situation in your mind even if you don't have proof. As much as you are able, resist jumping to conclusions. Remind yourself that things are still up in the air and unclear, and that you need more information before you know for sure.

Examples
"To assume makes an ass out of u and me."
"Let's wait and see."

GIVE OTHERS THE BENEFIT OF THE DOUBT

If you're going to jump to conclusions, give others the benefit of the doubt. People can make all kinds of mistakes. They forget, misunderstand, miscommunicate, and more. But rarely do they do it on purpose. If you do your best to presume the best about people, especially that they did not intend to hurt you or cause problems, most of the time you'll be right. On the rare occasion that you know for sure the hurt was willful, you can figure out how best to take care of yourself.

Examples

"Everyone makes mistakes—that's why pencils have erasers."

"No one's perfect."

"It's not like they did it on purpose."

KEEP YOUR EXPECTATIONS REALISTIC

Unrealistic expectations—whether they're too high or ungrounded—are a recipe for disappointment and frustration. If you always expect things to go as planned or people to act the way you want them to, you will be disappointed. You can hope for the best, but be careful not to *expect* it. Part of living well is learning to "roll with the punches" and deal with the unexpected. This requires flexibility and acceptance.

One indication that your expectations are unrealistic is being repeatedly frustrated with the same situation. When that happens, you might want to reconsider what you can realistically expect and modify your expectations accordingly. You're on safe ground when you expect people to be who they are, rather than who you want them to be. Your expectations are realistic if you expect situations to unfold naturally, rather than how you want them to. Sometimes that means acknowledging that what you want and what you can have are two different things. It can be hard to modify what you want, but you can at least get more real with yourself about what you can get. The Buddhist concept of radical acceptance fits with this: accepting things as they are, rather than as you want them to be, even if you don't like it.

Examples

"Accept the things I cannot change."

"I need to acknowledge how people and situations truly are, rather than how I want them to be."

"Life isn't always fair."
"You can't always get what you want."

REMIND YOURSELF WHAT YOU CAN AND CANNOT CONTROL

One aspect of keeping expectations realistic is knowing what is and is not within your control. In general, you can control yourself, your thoughts, your emotions, and your behavior. This relates to primary accountability, which we discussed in an earlier chapter. What you cannot control are the thoughts, emotions, and behaviors of others. If you stay focused on yourself and your responsibilities and respect your limitations, you will find yourself feeling more empowered and far less frustrated.

Examples

"I cannot control other persons, places, or situations. I can only control myself."

"The only true power I have is over myself. Let me keep my focus there."

"Keep an internal focus."

ACKNOWLEDGE THE POSITIVE ASPECTS

Despite how easy it is to reduce moments to positive or negative, it is rare that any given moment is 100% one or the other. You can romanticize a moment by talking about how wonderful it was and leaving out the negative moments. For instance, remembering how amazing that first date was, but forgetting how you got lost trying to get there and how anxious you felt. On the other hand, you can describe a moment as being nothing but bad, when it actually had its good aspects. Yes, traffic was horrible, but you listened to a fascinating podcast while you were stuck in it. Happy people don't deny the negative parts of their lives, but they consistently look for the positive.

Examples

"Count your blessings."

"Look on the bright side."

"It could have been worse."

ACKNOWLEDGE YOUR GENERAL LEVEL OF DISTRESS

Negative self-talk doesn't just come from the event at hand; it is affected by your emotional state leading up to it. If you already feel distressed, you may have more negative self-talk about a situation than if you entered it feeling relaxed. The analogy of the "last straw" or the "straw that broke the camel's back" acknowledges that even a small thing is sometimes too much. If you notice a lot of negative self-talk about a situation, it may have less to do with the situation and more to do with your general level of distress. Realizing that can help you turn your attention inward to your distress and keep you from getting caught up in the external situation. Any time you (or others) think you are overreacting to a situation, that's probably the case. We will talk much more about this in Chapter 16: Becoming Aware of Your Emotions.

Examples

"I'm having a really strong reaction to this. What else is going on with me?"

"I'm clearly in a hurting space right now and I don't think it's just about this."

"I can see that I am hurting. Let me have lovingkindness for this hurt."

"I have a very low level of tolerance and patience right now."

BE AWARE OF WHAT YOU'RE FEEDING YOUR MIND

Negative self-talk is not just fed by you, but also by external sources. A possibly Native American story about two wolves battling for a person's soul illustrates this. The evil wolf is full of anger, regret, greed, and self-pity; the good wolf is full of joy, peace, love, and humility. Which one is the strongest and will win? The one you feed.

If one wolf is negative self-talk and the other is positive, their food is what you fill your mind with: the movies, music, and podcasts you consume, the books and blogs you read, the friends whose company and counsel you seek. Are they feeding your negative self-talk or your positive self-talk? You may want to do an inventory of the people you talk with and the media you consume and consider whether each one is a source of encouragement, consistent with the values above, or a source of discouragement that reinforces the thinking you are trying to leave behind.

Examples

"Is this the kind of person I want to be?"

"Is this how I want others to think of me?"

ADOPTING BELIEFS THAT ARE RESPECTFUL OF OTHERS

If you think of self-talk as the part of a plant that is visible above ground, beliefs are the roots that feed it. If you don't change your core beliefs, your self-talk is likely to drift back to where it was before. On the other hand, if you change your core beliefs, your self-talk will follow. Below are some of the essential beliefs that help people choose to not be abusive and controlling and that leave them feeling empowered and effective in the world.

THERE ARE MANY RIGHT ANSWERS

It is important to remember that most of the time, there is more than one way to solve a problem or do a task. Your way may be right for you, but it may not be right for someone else. Most of the time your answer is based on assumptions that work for you but may not for someone else. For example, what is the best route to drive somewhere? It depends on whether you want to get there in the fastest way, the shortest way, the easiest way . . . depending on what matters most, the answer might be different. People may have preferences and priorities that are important to them but not necessarily to you. The point is to do your best to respect the different ways others do things. If you ask them to do something differently, focus on *why* you would like them to do it differently. Their way is not wrong or bad— just different.

ASSUME YOUR PARTNER IS YOUR ALLY

Another core belief is a working presumption that any close relationship is inherently a collaborative one. While this is not always the case, it is true the vast majority of the time. From this perspective, any hurtful or problematic behavior your partner exhibits is incidental and unintentional. The other person's primary goal was not to hurt you or be combative. If you need to address the behavior, do so as if you are speaking to a teammate, not a foe.

If relationships are like dancing, you will occasionally step on each other's toes or bump into each other. This is inevitable when you're dancing so close, but it's accidental, not intentional. If your foot hurts, you may need to speak up, but you don't need to treat it like a personal attack.

Besides, if you truly think your dance partner is trying to hurt you, why would you want to dance with them in the first place?

It is important that you treat your partner with goodwill, that you give them the benefit of the doubt. Assume they are innocent until there is clear proof of guilt. The belief that the other is your ally will be proven true most of the time. In those rare situations where it's not, there will be increasingly clear indications that will remove any doubt. But until that evidence is compelling, presume they are trying to work with you.

While you are changing your thinking, you may literally need to keep a mantra going in your head: "They're on my side. They're on my side"— especially when you are feeling escalated or having a difficult interaction. Gradually, over time, with practice, such thoughts can become more automatic and natural.

DON'T TAKE THINGS PERSONALLY

Part of egotism is forgetting that other people have their own lives and priorities. It can be easy to jump to the conclusion that if someone else is unhappy or struggling or not behaving how you would like them to, they are intentionally doing it to you, but that is usually not the case. There are many reasons someone you care about may be acting or feeling a certain way, and often it has little to do with you. Be careful not to presume that they are intentionally trying to hurt you, defy you, or cross you; that is rarely their intent. Instead, remind yourself that although their behavior may have affected you, it is rarely the case that they did it on purpose to affect you.

Say your partner was abrupt with you on the phone. Although you may not have appreciated their tone, do not assume they were doing that on purpose toward you. Perhaps they were in a hurry to get somewhere or they were distracted by something. Say your child doesn't respond to you as readily or obediently as you would like. Do not presume they are intentionally trying to be uncooperative. The vast majority of the time, children are not thinking, "How can I piss my parent off and defy them?" Instead, they are excited about something or distracted by something or troubled in some way or a hundred other things.

DENYING YOURSELF PERMISSION TO BE ABUSIVE

Abusive and controlling behaviors are very tempting to choose because they often result in quicker, easier, and at least temporarily effective solutions. People who are not abusive and controlling may be tempted, but they simply do not consider abuse and control as an option. They keep looking for alternatives. You need to do the same.

If you actively look for them, you can find nonabusive and noncontrolling options for dealing with nearly every situation. They sometimes require more time and thinking to identify, and they may be more difficult to carry out, but they let you do what is right, rather than what is easy. It's easy to say you had no choice, but that's almost never true.

The times when you will have to handle a situation by being abusive and controlling are really quite rare. They only arise when you truly need to defend yourself or keep someone (usually a child) safe and there truly is not another viable option. Even then, it's important that you use the bare minimum to keep yourself or the other person safe. Revenge, retaliation, honor, and justice are not justifications for abuse and control.

If you think you might be in such a situation, run it by your group or other people you trust to see if they can identify realistic nonabusive and noncontrolling options. Most of the time they can, and so can you, if you are willing to look for them.

ADULTS CAN MAKE THEIR OWN CHOICES—INCLUDING ONES YOU DISAGREE WITH

Another easy time to justify abuse and control is when it's for the person's own good or when you see that if you don't control them, they will suffer. But one of the basic human rights is the right to make your own mistakes and learn things through direct experience—even if it's the hard way. Many controlling behaviors are used in the name of love and care, but if the other person has not given consent (or if you are not confident they would give consent if asked), it's not okay.

You are welcome to share your concerns if the other person is open to hearing them. You are welcome to share suggestions if they are open to hearing them. But ultimately, they get to decide for themselves. Even seemingly wrong or bad decisions can have an upside. This is how people learn the hard way—through the direct experience of the consequences of their decisions.

Say your partner loaned money to a family member or friend who never paid it back. Even if you could have prevented the situation by being controlling, perhaps they needed the experience to learn the wisdom behind "Never lend more than you're willing to give away." You can seek to influence another person's choices, but if you actively seek to make them behave a certain way, without their consent, you are being controlling. It doesn't matter whether you think they are mistaken or wrong.

WHAT WOULD SOMEONE WHO IS NONABUSIVE DO?

Sometimes it can help to imagine what someone else who is choosing to be nonabusive would do. If you are in an abuse-intervention group or have been in the past, you can channel the wisdom and support of your peers. Ask yourself how your group or close friends would advise you to act in a certain situation. What might they say to you? Some people have found this particularly helpful as they were breaking out of their old patterns and embracing the new ways of thinking they learned in the group.

ABUSE AND CONTROL ARE ALWAYS VIOLATIONS OF PERSONAL FREEDOM

All the justifications and excuses and reasons for being abusive and controlling aside, it is ultimately hurtful when you deprive someone of their freedom and the liberty to make their own choices. You need to be strong and unwavering in your commitment to avoiding abusive and controlling behaviors. You need to do whatever you can to identify viable alternatives.

"BUT WHAT IF THE OTHER PERSON IS BEING ABUSIVE? ISN'T IT OKAY THEN?"

It can be particularly tempting to be abusive and controlling when the other person is behaving in an abusive or controlling way. But even then, you can choose not to be abusive. Do your best to take the high road and respond in an assertive, nonaggressive way. As they say, two wrongs don't make a right.

CHAPTER 16

BECOMING AWARE OF YOUR EMOTIONS

Many abusive people are not particularly emotionally aware. They struggle to name many emotions beyond general states such as "fine," "okay," and ones related to anger. They're more focused on what's going on externally than the emotions they're experiencing, and often think that if they are outwardly calm, they're not feeling anything. An important aspect of improving your self-awareness is improving your awareness of your emotional states.

No two people are exactly alike. But how do you figure out who you are and how you are different from others? Logic works well for understanding people in general. Logically you know that if someone doesn't eat for a day they'll feel hungry, and if they go into forty-five degree water they'll feel cold. But logic doesn't tell you that one person might want to go all day without eating and another definitely won't. One person would never go into water that cold, but another might even enjoy it. This is where emotions come into play.

EMOTIONS ARE A FORM OF PERSONAL LOGIC

Your emotions are a form of *personal* logic that help you figure out what's right for *you*. With so many possibilities out there—what to do for a living, who you should spend time with, how you should live your life—your emotional reactions help you figure out the right personal choices.

Because different people experience the same situations very differently, being emotionally aware is a vital part of being self-aware. If you think of your life as a path you are walking, emotional awareness is like GPS. The more you ignore your emotions, the more likely you are to drift from your path and what is right and best for you. You can use your emotional responses to better understand yourself and what the right decisions are for you.

ALL EMOTIONS ARE IMPORTANT

There are no "bad" or "negative" emotions—they all have value and need to be considered. A better distinction is between those that are comfortable and those that are uncomfortable. You tend to pursue things that produce enjoyable or comfortable emotions (happiness, contentment, love, joy) and avoid things that produce uncomfortable or unpleasant emotions (sadness, anxiety, loneliness). Comfortable emotions pull you toward things and uncomfortable emotions push you away, but they're all important information that helps you figure out how to live your life.

EMOTIONS ARE ALWAYS JUSTIFIED

Even when a certain emotional response doesn't make sense or seem appropriate, there's always a good reason for it. The fact that you don't understand it means you haven't fully examined it yet. That should be a prompt to engage in further self-reflection and discussion to figure out what's going on.

Say you go to a friend's party that you've been looking forward to for weeks, but you leave it feeling sad and disappointed. At first, you can't explain why—a bunch of friends were there, there was lots of talking, joking, and good food and drink. You should have had a great time. So why did you feel so bad afterward? You might be tempted to say you *did* have a good time and to dismiss your feelings, but that would keep you from gaining an important insight. As you give it more thought, you might realize that although many friends were there, several of your favorites weren't, and you missed seeing them. Further, while you knew a lot of people there, you didn't feel particularly connected with them and ended up keeping to yourself more than engaging with others. Finally, there was one particularly uncomfortable moment when you tried to join a conversation and folks clearly were not interested in including you. After that, you kept to yourself and left early, feeling sad and lonely. Reflecting on the situation now, you realize that the rejection hurt more than you thought. You thought you felt connected to everyone in this social circle, but you're actually only close to a few people in it, none of whom were there. In the wake of all this, you can shift your thinking from "I feel connected to everyone in this social circle" to "I feel close to four people in this social circle." You only came to that important awareness because you sat with your unexpected emotional reaction. As a result, going forward you can focus more on those particular friends rather than the larger group.

Your emotional responses always come from some truth within you. In the example above, it's "I mainly feel connected to these four people in this social circle, not everyone in this social circle." Once you recognize and understand where your emotions are coming from, they will always make sense. If those friends aren't at a social gathering, you won't have as much fun. But until you understand what your emotions are trying to tell you about yourself, they may not make sense, particularly when they run contrary to expectations. ("I was at a great party with lots of people I know—I should have had a blast!")

WHAT MATTERS MOST IS NOT WHAT HAPPENS, BUT HOW YOU FEEL ABOUT WHAT HAPPENS

Because everyone is different, the same event can have very different meanings for different people, and a purely factual report will not make those meanings clear. How you feel about the things that happen to you matters more than what actually happens to you. Emotions provide personal context. An event has no subjective meaning until you learn how someone experienced it emotionally. This is why it's so important to be honest about how you actually feel—regardless of what you "should" feel. Going back to the example of the party, although you left the party feeling sad and disappointed, other people left feeling happy and energized. One couple met for the first time and left feeling like it was the best party ever. These different emotional reactions to the same event highlight how different people can be.

Say somebody tells you it rained. That might be a factually accurate statement, but it tells you nothing about how the person was affected by the rain—what it meant to them. They might have been happy about it because their garden really needed it, or frustrated because it interfered with their outdoor plans, or sad because it meant they didn't get to see the sun.

This is true even for events that you might expect would generate an obvious or common reaction. If a friend tells you their father died, it might seem obvious how they're feeling—probably very sad and heartbroken. But that might be wrong. They might actually feel relief if the father had been suffering with a painful terminal illness. They might feel indifferent if they hadn't seen their father in decades and they learned of his death a year after the fact. They might feel devastated if they were extremely close to their father and the death was sudden and unexpected. Without emotional context, you don't know what a situation means to someone.

The same is true for others who are trying to understand you. If you give them objective facts and details, you tell them about the world, but not about *you* in the world. It is vital that you talk about your emotional experiences of events so people (including you) can understand what those things mean to you.

EMOTIONS HELP YOU MAKE THE RIGHT CHOICES

Everyone is subjected to a lot of expectations, big and small, for how they should live their lives. Expectations about what you should do for a living, what you should be doing right now in this moment, what you should be eating, how you should spend your time, and on and on and on. Those expectations come from your family and friends, society in general, and most of all, yourself.

Although there's nothing wrong with having expectations, doing what you are "supposed to"—rather than what you truly want—can cause problems. "Shoulds" and "supposed tos" are often well-intentioned and seemingly reasonable, but they may be based on inaccurate information, a misunderstanding, a poor understanding of you, or an assumption that you're just like someone else. Whatever the reasons, some of the expectations you have about yourself are probably not right or reasonable for you.

If you think of yourself as a ship on the ocean, expectations are the wind and currents: sometimes you go with the flow, sometimes you go against it. Your emotions are the GPS that shows you the way. If you invariably follow everyone's expectations for you, ignoring the map your emotions provide, you're going to get lost. You'll feel dissatisfied, unhappy, and discontented, perhaps without knowing why. You'll end up going where the wind and currents take you, which is often not where you actually want to go. In order to resist the wind and the currents and to get where you want to go, you need a map and a sense of direction. That is the role your emotions play: to show you what is right for you, not simply where everyone else thinks you should go.

That does not mean the opinions and expectations of others are irrelevant. They can be very helpful—they may have knowledge, wisdom, perspective, or understanding that you don't. But you need to examine how *you* feel before you automatically follow someone's suggestion. Then you'll see if it's right for you.

For example, say a friend who is heavily into fitness recommends that you start taking a certain nutritional supplement. You've never heard of it before, but you trust your friend and consider them your fitness guru. Should you take it? If you're not emotionally connected with yourself, you might, but it's not clear whether that would be the right decision for you. The key is to first check in with yourself and see how you feel about it. Maybe you feel enthusiastic and excited about trying out a mystery supplement—if you trust and respect your friend and are a big believer in nutritional supplements. Maybe you feel wary, and hesitant to take anyone's word without doing your own research. Maybe you have an immediate fear and concern about putting substances into your body, and wouldn't even consider following your friend's recommendation because it runs contrary to how you want to live. It's irrelevant whether the nutritional supplement actually works or not. What matters is that your decision is made with integrity—that it's true to your values. Your emotions make that clearer.

EMOTIONS ARE A UNIVERSAL LANGUAGE

No matter what kind of work you do, no matter where in the world you live, you've experienced stress, success, pride, and frustration. The details of everyone's lives vary, but their emotional experiences are quite similar everywhere in the world. This is why the more someone talks about their emotional experiences the easier it is to relate to them, even if you don't know much about their life.

Others may speak a different language or have a very different cultural background from you, but the core human emotions—love, hate, stress, sadness, and so on—are universal. Behaviors can be quite different from culture to culture, but emotional facial expressions have been found to be basically the same around the world. For example, there are three common facial expressions of anger: glaring eyes, furrowed brow, and either lips pursed or teeth bared. Behavioral expressions of anger, on the other hand, vary widely across (and even within) cultures. Some people raise their voices in anger and others talk quietly. Some people get ruder when they are angry, others become more polite.

EMOTIONS ARE OFTEN EXPRESSED METAPHORICALLY

People often use images and embellishment to convey emotions. For example, someone might say, "I felt like I was about six inches tall" to describe how intimidated they felt. Someone who has just met the love of his life might say "The moment I saw her she became the only person in the room." She was not literally the only person in the room, but the metaphor describes how focused he was on her and how strong his attraction was.

This is why good art, which is all about metaphor, is emotionally evocative. Whether it's music, painting, books, or movies, it stirs up strong emotions of excitement, joy, fear, love, and sadness—while mediocre art leaves you unmoved.

A common mistake people can make, especially if they are not particularly emotionally aware, is taking an emotional metaphor literally. For example, if you ask your partner how their day was and they say they feel like quitting their job, they aren't saying they actually plan to quit their job, but rather that they feel overwhelmed and frustrated. The responses to a question like "How was work?" could range from "I want to keep this job forever" to "I am never going back to that awful place again." None of the responses are necessarily literally true, but they're attempts to convey intense and complex feelings about the situation. Maybe it wasn't just a "Work sucked" day, but an "I'm going to kill my boss with a stapler" kind of day.

When someone, particularly someone close to you, seems to be making an inaccurate statement, it may be because they are speaking metaphorically. They are not trying to state the actual facts of the situation, but instead are trying to tell you how they feel about the situation. A common cause of arguments is one partner taking an emotional statement literally and debating its accuracy. Be careful not to mistake emotional metaphors for literal or factual statements.

Consider a situation in which your partner declares that you never help around the house. You might be tempted to correct them by pointing out that you actually helped three different times in the past week, but you'd be completely missing the point. They were not making a factual statement, but a metaphorical one: it *feels* like you never help around the house. Maybe they feel like this because of all the other things they have to do, or because all your contributions were on a single day, or because they're overwhelmed in general. Move past the "facts" to seek to understand the feelings—which are often more important, anyway.

EMOTIONS CONTINUALLY SHIFT AND CHANGE

Although you may think you have a single predominant feeling each day (*"I was depressed today"*) or even a single emotion in the moment (*"I'm sad"*), in truth you typically experience multiple, even conflicting, emotions at the same time. Those emotions are continually shifting and ebbing and flowing throughout the day. Answering truthfully how you felt in any given day would be like trying to say what color a photograph is. No photo contains a single color; even black-and-white photos have many shades of grey.

As you climb into your car to drive to work you may feel some happiness and excitement about a project you're working on, some dread and anxiety over a meeting with your boss's boss, and some satisfaction that traffic seems pretty light. A few minutes later, you might feel moved and touched to recall how sweetly your child hugged you twice last night because they "love you so much." That might be immediately followed by feeling startled as a car changes lanes right in front of you. If someone asks you how you are feeling and you want to answer honestly (versus politely simply saying "fine" or "good"), what do you say? Most people would mention an emotion or two that they are feeling most strongly and seem most relevant (*"I'm excited about the project, but a bit worried about the meeting with the big boss"*), although there are a number of other emotions bubbling under the surface as well.

UNDERSTANDING YOUR EMOTIONS

Whether you're aware of them or not, and whether you're consciously thinking about them or not, you are continually having emotions. Ignoring them does not stop them, and when you stop being aware of them you lose access to valuable information that can help you understand yourself, manage yourself, and make good choices. A whole book could be easily written on understanding and managing emotions, but for now we'll just offer a few suggestions. Some of the information on self-awareness and self-management that is presented in later chapters can definitely be used with emotions as well.

INCREASING YOUR VOCABULARY

Have you noticed that most specialized activities have terminology unique to them? Whether it's a profession (health care, auto repair, IT), field of study (science, mathematics, religion), or hobby (woodworking, skiing) there are often a number of specialized terms and phrases to facilitate clear and precise communication. Without those specialized terms it would be much harder to understand things. If "snow" is the only word you have for snow, then all snow tends to look the same (or at least your descriptions of it will seem that way). On the other hand, skiers have multiple terms for snow, including "powder" and "slush," which help them understand ski conditions and plan accordingly. The Inuit people have even more words for snow because their lives and livelihoods depend on the many different types. Imagine trying to work on a construction site where every tool was simply called "tool" or every wrench was called "wrench."

The same is true for understanding your emotions. If you have a limited vocabulary to draw from when you think about and talk about emotions, you are less likely to fully understand them and be able to help others understand them. Having a larger vocabulary allows for better communication and understanding. Feeling "bad" is not very descriptive or helpful because it can describe a wide variety of unpleasant emotional experiences including anxiety, sadness, depression, and guilt. More specific words allow for a better understanding and a more appropriate response.

Do your best to avoid using the words in the following categories to describe your emotions:

Words that are commonly used but don't say much: *bad, good, fine, okay*

Words that describe physical states instead of emotions: *tired, worn out, exhausted*

Words that place blame or assume intent: disrespected, demeaned, put down, disregarded

The words in this last category are problematic because they imply that someone made you feel a certain way by behaving that way toward you. One way of checking if an emotion involves blame is to see if it still makes sense if you put it after "you." If it does, it is usually a blaming word.

Appendix D contains a long list of emotion words that you are welcome to make use of to better understand and express what you are feeling.

PRACTICING WISE MIND

Following your emotions is different from being impulsive or reactive. When you think of someone being "emotional" or making an "emotional decision," you may think of someone impulsively following their heart without any consideration of the consequences or longer-term implications. Emotional decisions are often spontaneous, which can invite problems. Examples include marrying someone you recently met or taking a trip without preparing for it.

Rational decisions typically involve gathering facts and using them to reach conclusions, like Star Trek Vulcans do. The problem with relying solely on logic is that it doesn't take into consideration your personal preferences. It may be logical to forgo the slice of cheesecake because it has so many calories in it, but if you absolutely love cheesecake, you may be depriving yourself of something you would truly savor, even if it does have a lot of calories.

It is more effective to engage in a thoughtful, reflective process and be informed by your emotions—but not driven by them. In the moment, you may feel strong love for a new romantic partner and think "I should marry them," but that doesn't mean you should take your emotional response literally. Instead, you should seek to practice Wise Mind.

Wise Mind is a Buddhist concept used in dialectical behavior therapy that can be represented visually by two overlapping circles.

Reasonable Mind involves logic and problem-solving. It is objective, detached, and impersonal. If you use only your reasonable mind, you might make good generic decisions ("*I will not eat the cheesecake because it is not very healthy and has tons of calories*"), but you won't take into account your unique preferences. This is what happens when you are not very emotionally aware or connected. It comes from a purely rational space and doesn't consider your distinct and individual wants and needs.

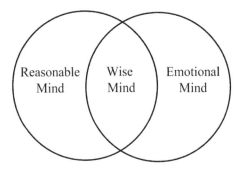

Emotional Mind involves your emotions. It is a personal take on whatever is going on and includes your individual wants and needs. If you use only your emotional mind to make a decision, you may meet your need in the moment, but it will be without consideration for the impact or longer-term consequences. ("*I'm going to eat a large slice of cheesecake because I LOVE cheesecake.*") This leads to impulsive or reactive decisions that can be quite problematic. It comes from a purely emotional space and doesn't consider practicalities.

Wise Mind blends emotion and reason. It acknowledges your emotions and finds realistic and reasonable ways to honor them. Wise Mind identifies reasonable choices and considers how you feel about them, leading you to decisions that are right for you and workable in the real world. (*"I will eat a small slice of cheesecake."*)

THERE ARE OFTEN OTHER EMOTIONS BEHIND YOUR ANGER

Like every other emotion, anger has value. It alerts you when your boundaries are being crossed and motivates you to stand up for your rights. It is a strong feeling of displeasure in response to a perceived wrong that manifests in an urge to fight back. Appropriate anger can lead to social justice and reform that challenges and corrects societal wrongs.

However, anger is one of the more problematic emotions. As the writer Ursula K. Le Guin stated, "anger continued on past its usefulness becomes unjust, then dangerous . . . It fuels not positive activism but regression, obsession, vengeance, self-righteousness. Corrosive, it feeds off itself, destroying its host in the process."

Many professionals agree that anger (and similar feelings like frustration, indignation, annoyance) is often, but not always, a secondary emotion. There are often unexpressed core emotions behind the anger. Anger is often the result of another uncomfortable emotion plus blame, particularly in people who are prone to being abusive. Say your teenager arrives home an hour after curfew. You could feel anxious that something might have happened to them—or you could get mad at them for making you feel anxious. Say your partner tells a funny but embarrassing story about you at a social gathering. You could feel embarrassed—or get angry at your partner for embarrassing you. In other words, when you have an uncomfortable feeling and you believe someone else caused it, you become angry at that person for making you feel that way. This diverts your attention away from the uncomfortable feeling and toward the person you blame for causing it.

There are a few problems with this kind of anger. First, it shifts the focus from you and how you are feeling to the other person and their behavior. The new external focus moves you away from accountability.

Second, it covers up more core feelings. Instead of becoming aware of your anxiety or embarrassment, you can overlook how you really feel. Finally, anger tends to push people away and limit the amount of compassion they feel for you.

Anger tends to keep people at a distance, but the feelings behind it tend to draw people in and elicit compassion. If your teenager sees that you're genuinely worried because they were late, they might feel guilty. But if all they see is your anger, they might just feel defensive or afraid. If your partner learns their words embarrassed you, they're likely to be apologetic and to be more careful than if they just see anger, which might intimidate them and leave them feeling anxious and uneasy.

USING YOUR EMOTIONAL BAROMETER

The **emotional barometer** is a concept from Dan Wile's book *After the Honeymoon: How Conflict Can Improve Your Relationship*. It's a great tool for helping you recognize signs of significant emotional distress. Wile taught readers to use the emotional barometer in response to the ongoing annoying habits of their partner, but we've broadened its application to *any* ongoing annoyances in your life.

This is the way it works. Everyone has ongoing irritations or annoyances in their life that persist despite their best efforts. Family members leave wet towels on the floor, dirty dishes on the counter, the cap off the toothpaste; traffic is terrible, a neighbor's dog barks all night. You can end up getting into big arguments over these small issues where you end up frustrated and feeling like nothing has been resolved. The simple solution is to accept these things as being beyond your control. They are aspects of the imperfections of your partner, your living space, and life in general.

On the other hand, ongoing annoyances can be valuable tools that facilitate emotional self-awareness. Although they occur regularly, chances are your reactions to them vary. Sometimes they don't bother you at all, sometimes they annoy you, and sometimes they really get under your skin. But the annoyances themselves are remarkably consistent—what changes is your underlying emotional state. When you have less distress and more tolerance, they tend to be less annoying. When you have more emotional distress, you tend to be less tolerant, and the annoyances are more intense.

Because of this variability, you can actually use the annoyances as an emotional barometer—a gauge of how you're doing emotionally in general. Your emotional distress could be a wide variety of emotions, including stress, overwhelm, sadness, and discouragement. Whatever they are, they leave you feeling heavier, more burdened.

The idea is to use your level of reactivity as an alert that you're experiencing significant underlying emotional distress. When you find yourself really bothered, that's your prompt to become more self-reflective and figure out what is going on. The more intolerant you feel, the more likely it is that other things are going on that you are not managing well. The ongoing annoyance illuminates your general intensity level, but it doesn't cause it. Once you can identify what you're actually feeling, you can willfully address that—instead of the irritability that's on the surface.

For example, say one of the things that bugs you about your partner is their tendency to leave their wet towel on the bathroom floor. You've shared your concern, they've acknowledged it, but it's gone on for years. One day you walk into the bathroom and slip on their wet towel. You grab the towel off the floor and realize that you are really upset. Thoughts like "WHY do they keep doing this? One of these days I *am* going to slip on their stupid towel and break my neck!" The old way of dealing with that would be to go and confront them, and when they don't respond correctly (which is almost certain since you're already so mad) berate them for how thoughtless they are, how little they care about you, etc. A huge argument might follow that would ultimately lead nowhere.

Instead of going down that road, try this alternative. Back up to the moment that you have a significant emotional spike—when you slip on the towel. In that moment, realize "Whoa! I am REALLY upset right now. I haven't been this angry about this in a long time—what is going on?" Instead of immediately acting on your high intensity, you use your reactivity to become introspective. What else is going on? Why is the towel on the floor so bothersome *this* morning? You might even ask for your partner's assistance in sorting out what you're actually so upset about, because it's clearly not just about the towel. You can think of the towel as the check-engine indicator on your dashboard. When it lights up, the problem isn't the indicator, it's whatever triggered it from under the hood.

Despite all of our individual differences, appropriate levels of emotional intensity are strikingly consistent among people. Anytime you think someone is overreacting—having a more intense emotional reaction than they should—they probably are, whether it's the other person or you. That should be the prompt to investigate what else might be going on. If you think their intensity should be about a three on a ten-point scale but it's closer to a seven, you might ask where the other four points are coming from. Once the underlying issues and emotions are identified, the reaction will make perfect sense—it will add up. It wasn't just about the trigger.

PROCESSING EMOTIONS WITH WORDS

It is common for people who are abusive to struggle with talking about their emotions. This may be rooted in a belief that talking about emotions does little to help and in fact makes them more intense. However, scientific evidence indicates that using words to process emotions actually makes them much more manageable.

For over a century, therapists and others have believed that talking about emotions and emotional events can help people manage their feelings. There is now scientific evidence that supports this and offers an explanation. The original study exposed college students to an emotionally evocative event and then divided them into three groups. The first group was instructed to reflect on the emotional event without writing or talking about it. The second group was instructed to write about the event but not talk to others about it. The third group was instructed to talk with others about the emotional event, but not to write about it. During brain scans days later, the students were asked to recall the emotional event. The two groups that had written or talked about the event showed increased activity in the rational part of their brain (the prefrontal cortex) and decreased activity in the emotional part of their brain (the amygdala). The group that had only thought about the emotional event displayed the opposite pattern: decreased activity in the rational brain and increased activity in the emotional brain. The researchers saw this as evidence that using words to talk about emotions—whether written or spoken—engages the rational part of the brain and helps us manage distress. It's not important whether someone else is listening, just whether words are being used.

Much of the thinking you do is nonverbal. When you are lost in thought and someone asks you what you are thinking, you struggle to find the words because you weren't thinking in words at all! A key part of making emotions manageable is engaging your higher reasoning by putting them into words. The process of translating emotions into words appears to serve as a bridge between the emotional and rational parts of your brain so they can work together. If you don't find words to express your emotions, you're likely to feel more reactive and more overwhelmed by them. If you talk or write about them, you are actually able to engage more of your adult mind and make more thoughtful and appropriate decisions.

This chapter has explored ways to become more skilled at emotional awareness. Physical awareness, or awareness of your body, takes emotional awareness to another level. This is the focus of the next chapter.

CHAPTER 17

BECOMING AWARE OF YOUR BODY

In the last chapter we talked about the importance of being emotionally self-aware, and in the chapter before that, awareness of your thoughts and beliefs. Yet another aspect of knowing yourself well is awareness of your body and your general physical states.

The first step toward understanding how emotions affect your body is knowing that each emotion you experience varies in intensity like a light on a dimmer switch—not an on/off switch—depending on what you think and do. It's not enough to say you're having certain emotions. You need to talk about how intense they are. Typically, the stronger you feel it, the more significant it is. One indication of your emotional intensity is how much you feel it in your body.

UNDERSTANDING HOW ADRENALINE AFFECTS YOUR EMOTIONS

For most mammals, an emotional response means they need to respond physically. If it's afraid because it sees a predator, it needs to flee. If it's excited because it sees food, it needs to pursue. If it's angry because its territory is being invaded, it needs to defend. If it's aroused because it sees a potential mate, it will want to pursue or be pursued. In each case, adrenaline is released into the body to facilitate a physical response.

Adrenaline, also known as epinephrine, prepares the body to respond behaviorally—to run, attack, defend, mate, etc.—in a number of ways. Energy levels spike, putting the body into an alert, restless state. Heart rate and blood pressure rise to carry oxygen and energy to muscles faster.

Breath gets quick and shallow to move oxygen into the body and blood faster. Mental clarity increases. Blood is diverted from the digestive tract to the extremities, prioritizing mobility over digestion.

Some people think adrenaline is only released by fear or anger, but it's actually triggered by a wide variety of emotions, and it does the same thing for all of them. That pounding of your heart could be caused by fear, excitement, anger, or desire, to name just a few. It's easy to mistake one emotion for another or flip from one to another.

Adrenaline levels directly translate into physical sensations in your body. The higher the emotional intensity, the higher the level of adrenaline, and the more physical responses. Let's compare common physical experiences of low-, medium-, and high-intensity anger.

Low intensity: feel warm, a little more alert, face tense, slight increase in energy

Medium intensity: feel hot, flushed, more focused, faster thoughts, tight chest, energized, increased heart rate, shallower breath, butterflies in stomach

High intensity: *sweaty, restless, thoughts racing, tunnel vision/hyperfocus, whole body tightens up, physical agitation, heart pounding, rapid and shallow breath, knots in stomach*

You can see how the physical sensations intensify as well—from a little warm to getting sweaty; a little more energized to unable to sit still. These physical experiences are true for pretty much everyone, regardless of cultural background. When adrenaline is released into the body, human beings respond in the exact same way.

Even with low-intensity emotion, you can feel physical changes. They may be more subtle and less extreme, but they're there. You just need to be tuned-in enough to notice that your body feels different when you're having a mild emotional reaction than when you're completely relaxed. Because some sensations arise in response to a wide variety of emotions, and some only to certain ones, you can't necessarily tell which emotion caused the sensation. Even so, you can get a sense of how intense your emotions are if you pay attention to how strong the sensation is.

While the same physical sensations can arise whether you are angry, excited, fearful, or something else, people who are prone to being abusive are quick to interpret all of them as anger. If you're not emotionally aware and connected, it's easy to misinterpret anxiety, sadness, or embarrassment as anger.

Many people assume that just as you're hardwired to respond to adrenaline with emotions and sensations, you're also hardwired to act certain ways. That, however, is not the case. If you think of your body and its physical sensations as hardware, your behaviors and thoughts are software. Your software is the programming you get from the cultures you're exposed to throughout your life. For example, in the US people tend to get less polite when they get angry. In Japan, on the other hand, people tend to get more polite when they get angry. Even within the US, many people raise their voice as they get angrier, but others get very quiet when confronted with the same intense emotion. None of that is hardware; it is a product of culture and learning. It's how you've been programmed to behave.

Aggressive behavior is not caused by adrenaline or high intensity. While it is true that higher levels of adrenaline increase energy and physical agitation and the desire to get active, that doesn't have to result in *aggressive* action. There are plenty of ways of expressing even high-intensity anger without becoming abusive.

PAYING ATTENTION TO YOUR PHYSICAL NEEDS
Part of being aware of your body is noticing your needs to eat, sleep, and rest. There are times when it's appropriate to temporarily ignore them, like when you're in the middle of an important task or conversation that you cannot easily interrupt. However, routinely and regularly ignoring your physical needs causes all sorts of problems. You may be able to get away with it for a while, but you are not invulnerable; you are not a robot. Your body needs ongoing care. If you don't take care of it, it will wear down faster and not work as well.

Just as negative mindsets and uncomfortable emotions can increase the temptation to be abusive and controlling, so can uncomfortable physical states. People prone to being abusive tend to be less aware of their physical needs and tend to ignore them when they come up. Hunger, fatigue, physical discomfort, sickness, and injury all contribute to internal distress, which then increases the temptation to be abusive and controlling. Part of being accountable is being aware of your body so you can manage and care for it. The better you take care of your body on an ongoing basis, the less internal distress you will experience. The less internal distress you experience, the less there is to take out on anyone else. By being kind and caring to your own body, you make it that much easier to be kind and caring toward others.

The first part of managing your body is to become aware of it and connect with it. Noticing your basic physical needs—to eat, sleep, rest, use the bathroom, heal, and to be sexual—is like looking at the dashboard of your car to see whether it needs gas, oil, service, or to cool down. Ignoring what you see there doesn't make problems go away. It just means you'll have to address them when they become bigger problems down the road.

There's nothing wrong with allowing a certain level of physical discomfort as long as you acknowledge it. You don't have to immediately make it go away. Feeling hungry doesn't mean you need to eat immediately, but it does mean you should eat something sooner rather than later. The longer you ignore it, the more likely your body will suffer. Quickly meeting your basic physical needs allows you to be proactive rather than reactive. Better to fuel up your car when it's low than to drive it until it needs a tow.

Listed below are some of the most basic physical needs and the problems that arise when they are ignored.

HUNGER

The calories in food are the basic fuel of the body. When your body runs low on calories, you may become irritable and agitated. Your thinking can be compromised. This can lead to bad and reactive choices, including becoming abusive and controlling.

There are many different healthy ways to fuel your body. You have choices about what you eat, how you eat, when you eat, how much you eat, and how frequently you eat. Extensive research shows how eating affects your health, mood, and ability to heal and recover from disease. Healthy eating trends change all the time, but there is widespread agreement that diet and eating patterns have a significant impact on your physical and mental health. We encourage you to sort out for yourself what a healthy diet and eating pattern look like for you. Once you decide that, do your best to keep to it. What is important is that you notice when you feel hungry and are thoughtful about how you refuel.

SLEEP

One of the primary ways a body restores itself is through sleep. A large outpouring of research in recent years indicates that the benefits of high-quality sleep go well beyond simply feeling well-rested. Weight, mood, memory, the immune system, and various other internal systems are also significantly affected.

While the optimum amount of sleep varies from person to person, research indicates that most people need at least seven hours of high-quality (deep, uninterrupted) sleep a night. External and internal factors including noise, being woken up by others, and sleep apnea contribute to poor-quality sleep. In general, good-quality sleep will leave you feeling well-rested and restored. Addressing sleep problems and bad sleep habits could vastly improve your life.

Be careful about using artificial sleep aids such as sleeping pills, alcohol, or other drugs to help you sleep. They may help you fall asleep, but they are likely to interfere with the quality of your sleep sooner or later.

FATIGUE

Although people sometimes equate fatigue with the need to sleep, there is a difference between feeling sleepy and having a fatigued body. In addition to sleep, your body needs moments of rest when it is free from physical and mental exertion. Denying yourself rest can damage your body and lead to underperformance, irritability, poor judgment, reactivity, and impulsivity. Your body is not an unbreakable machine, and except for certain ongoing activities like breathing, it can't do much of anything without occasional breaks during waking hours.

Resting can be as simple as sitting, slowing your breath, or reducing your physical or mental activity. Many types of self-care incorporate some amount of rest, including recreational activities and spiritual practices like prayer or meditation. We will elaborate on this in the chapter on self-care.

PAIN

One way people disconnect from their body is by avoiding physical discomfort, including everyday aches and pains. Physical discomfort can have many causes, but it is often the body's way of letting you know something is wrong. It can be caused by something as minor as being in one position for too long and addressed by simply readjusting how you sit. On the other hand, it can indicate a serious issue that requires medical attention.

People who disconnect from their bodies are often slow to seek medical care. This is no different from failing to fix your car when it's not running correctly, as if it would simply get better on its own. Ironically, many people who are disconnected from their bodies have no problem taking the car to a mechanic or doing the work themselves. Ignoring physical discomfort, especially when the cause of it is unknown, can worsen medical conditions, cause chronic pain, and contribute to bad moods, intolerance, and impatience with others.

There are two kinds of medical care: preventive and reactive. Preventive medical care typically includes a routine physical examination by a doctor (every few years for healthy young people; up to annually as you age) to make sure everything works the way it should—even if you don't have any discomfort. Reactive medical care responds to new or ongoing discomfort, changes in the way your body functions, and issues that are of concern to you or someone who loves you.

Choosing not to address your medical needs can shorten your life. Research has shown that men who are in long-term romantic relationships tend to live longer, in part because their partners get them to a doctor more often. Regardless of your gender or whether you are partnered, it's important that you acknowledge that every body occasionally needs repair or intervention to function optimally. Taking care of your medical needs will allow you to live a longer, healthier life and make you less inclined to be abusive and controlling when you don't feel well.

SEXUAL DESIRE

One physical need that is often overlooked and not discussed is sexual desire, probably because sexuality is a very personal topic. Most cultures have a lot of shame about sexuality and encourage silence around it, but like other needs, ignoring your sexual needs doesn't make them go away.

All people are sexual creatures with bodies that experience sexual arousal and pleasure, but the role sex plays varies tremendously from person to person and from time to time over a person's lifetime. It is hugely important for some people and virtually irrelevant to others. One common misconception is that a person's sex drive, which is determined by a combination of physical, psychological, and environmental factors, naturally reduces with age, but this is not necessarily the case. There are many older adults with very active and rich sex lives—sometimes more so than when they were younger.

Failing to meet your sexual needs can have negative consequences for physical health, but usually the consequences are primarily psychological and emotional. Unlike sleep or food or medical care, you do not need sex for survival, but a healthy, sexually connected life can lead to a happier life. Neglecting your sexual needs and desires can lead to varying levels of discontent and unhappiness that can make it more tempting to be abusive and controlling.

Some people who are otherwise disconnected from their bodies still experience and pursue satisfaction of sexual desire, but the ways they meet those needs can be unhealthy and even damaging to themselves as well as others.

It is a mistake to expect that it's your romantic partner's responsibility to meet your sexual needs. Blaming them for not satisfying you is not fair. YOU are responsible for addressing and meeting your sexual needs, not your partner. While you can certainly ask for their support and assistance in helping you to meet your sexual needs, it's neither their responsibility nor their fault if your needs are not met. We will talk about sexual self-care in a later chapter on self-care in general.

OTHER NEEDS
There are some bodily needs that people are less likely to neglect, including the need to urinate, defecate, and hydrate. As with any other physical need, neglecting these can lead to problems.

PRACTICING MINDFULNESS

One way to increase your self-awareness, including awareness of your body, is to practice mindfulness. Mindfulness has become more popular in the US in recent years, but it has been practiced in eastern countries for thousands of years. Practicing mindfulness means doing your best to be fully connected to the present moment by experiencing it through your five senses without thoughts, analysis, or judgment.

It is very easy not to be in the present moment. You might be reflecting on some past moment, analyzing a situation, or recalling a memory. You might be thinking ahead to some future moment, figuring out what to do or imagining what it will be like. You might be lost in your thoughts about the present, putting together a to-do list or reviewing your schedule. You may also be lost in an imagined moment that does not actually exist, daydreaming or fantasizing about other places, lives, circumstances. All of these thoughts take you out of the present moment, the moment that is happening right now.

Mindfulness is resisting the temptation to get lost in your head and choosing to be present in the current moment. What can you see around you right now? Right now, what can you hear? Right now, what can you smell? Right now, what can you feel? Right now, what can you taste? As soon as you start to think about what you're doing, you shift out of the present moment and into your head. When that happens, the idea is to gently stop thinking and turn your attention back to your senses.

Practicing mindfulness helps many people calm and relax. This is probably partly because it keeps them from getting caught up in their thoughts, which can lead them to feel anxious, agitated, or depressed about the past or future. Mindfulness helps you stop worrying by making you realize that the only thing that truly exists is the present moment.

In bringing you into the present moment where you are more fully connected to your five senses, you may feel more alive and connected. Life shifts from being imagined to being real. You are not imagining being in a boring meeting for the next two hours—instead, you are alive in a room with fluorescent lights, the sounds of people breathing, the discomfort of your butt on a hard plastic chair, etc. Life becomes more real and vivid.

Being mindful may actually lead to increased discomfort. You may feel more keenly how uncomfortable your chair is, how tight your chest is, or how shallow your breath is. You may notice how tense and tight your body is and how anxious you feel. You may notice that the thoughts that keep popping into your head are about how much you hate this meeting, how bored you are, and how trapped you feel. But connecting with the real discomfort you feel in the moment can help you make better, more informed choices going forward, the same way connecting with uncomfortable emotions can.

A vital aspect of mindfulness is to be as present in the moment as possible—*without judgment*. You, like most people, are continually evaluating things as good or bad, positive or negative. All of that involves thinking and analysis. Mindfulness involves letting go of the thinking and analysis to just be. When you're practicing mindfulness, you still have thoughts, but you try to avoid attaching to them. Instead, you watch them passing by. That discomfort in your butt is neither good nor bad, it just is. The squirrel you can see through the window just is. You may have reactions to certain things, and you can observe your reactions, but those are not the things; those are simply your reactions to the things. Mindfulness allows you to separate your ego from the moment. It can be a huge relief to let go of all the judgment and analysis you are continually engaged in, even if just for a few moments.

Practicing mindfulness helps you become more aware of your body and how you truly feel, as opposed to how you're telling yourself or expecting to feel. It helps you get more present with other people in the room instead of getting lost in your thoughts. It's a great way to get out of your head and into your body in the moment. Your thoughts can take you all kinds of different places, including places you don't want to go; mindfulness is a great way to avoid getting stuck there.

Since it has become popular in the US, a number of misconceptions about mindfulness have appeared. Some people think it means calming and relaxing yourself. While it may increase a sense of calm, that's not the goal (and not always the outcome). Some people presume that it's the same as meditation, but it is not. Many meditation practices involve focusing on something to clear the mind, but mindfulness is almost the opposite—it involves being aware of everything that is present in any given moment. Some people think mindfulness is something you do for a set period of time, the way you would meditate, but the goal is to seek to be mindful in every moment.

Countless books, classes, websites, blogs, podcasts, and apps can help you practice mindfulness, but here are a few tips to get you started.

Do a scan of your body and environment using your five senses, and say, either aloud or in your head, "Right now I notice . . ."

"Right now I notice that my shoes are feeling tight on my feet. Right now I notice that I am feeling a little self-conscious. Right now I notice that my face is feeling slightly cool. Right now I notice that I can hear the ticking clock over my head."

An even simpler practice is to simply notice your breathing without necessarily trying to slow it down or change it. Notice how your breath is going into your body. Notice how your body feels as the breath goes in. Notice how the breath exits your body and notice how your body feels as that happens.

There are many other ways to practice mindfulness. We encourage you to research and practice on your own. As with any skill, the more you practice, the better you'll get at it and the more likely it is to become an enduring habit.

Mindfulness helps you become more aware of your thoughts, emotions, and body. It helps you clear and calm your mind. It helps you become more aware of, connected to, and present in the moment, for better or worse. It is an invaluable skill and tool for becoming nonabusive and noncontrolling. Awareness of your body is an important step, but that alone is not enough. It's vital that you be able to soothe yourself when you are distressed. That is what we will talk about in the next chapter.

CHAPTER 18

LEARNING TO SELF-SOOTHE

Self-soothing is settling yourself in the moment when you are distressed. It's not concealing your distress from the outside world, but truly calming yourself from within. Many people who are abusive struggle to do it. For people who like to think of themselves as strong, independent, and tough, the idea can evoke images of a helpless child who needs to be taken care of, but even the strongest animals need rest. Gas-powered cars need coolant. Electric cars need to recharge. Part of remaining strong is being able to settle when you need to.

Unlike most mammals, humans experience emotional distress in response to their thoughts. Even when nothing is actually happening, people can get incredibly agitated! For most mammals, adrenaline increases when something happens to activate emotions, then decreases when the event resolves. They get and eat the food and they settle; they escape from the danger and they settle; they chase off the invader and they settle. Once the problem is gone, they settle. Unfortunately, people are not that simple. Your emotions and adrenaline are triggered not only by what happens in the moment, but also by your thoughts and memories.

A simple way to explore the power your thoughts have on your body is to pay attention to the physical sensations you can detect right now. How warm are you feeling? Notice how physically tense you are feeling. Do you have tightness in any particular area of your body? How about your energy level—any restlessness or agitation? Now spend a moment or two thinking about something that is either stressful in your life right now or has been in the past. How about a task that you've been avoiding? Think about making yourself do it. Imagine what might make it hard for you and why you don't like doing it. Spend a couple minutes just thinking about that unpleasant activity.

Now notice how you feel physically. You will probably notice some changes in your body. You might feel warmer. You might have more tension in different parts of your body, especially where you tend to carry tension; maybe your jaw, your shoulders, your hands. You might also feel a little more restless and agitated. That change in your physiological stress level is simply a response to your thoughts. Those thoughts triggered the release of adrenaline, which triggered those changes in your body.

Until you change your thinking, your thoughts can trigger emotional reactions that trigger a release of adrenaline. If your distress is water in a bathtub, calming your body pulls the plug. But if your thoughts are still pouring from the tap, the tub won't drain.

Adrenaline is important for animals, but not so much for people. Humans usually don't need to prepare for a physical response. Self-soothing reduces the amount of adrenaline that is released into your bloodstream, making it easier to use your intellect and words. Physical agitation can be quite distracting when you are trying to think something through.

Emotional arousal can also interfere with your ability to access memories, especially of recently learned things. Research has shown that when highly emotionally aroused, people most easily recall the things they know best. Professional basketball players practice free-throws until they're automatic so even when they are highly emotionally aroused, they can be sure to make their shot.

High emotional arousal can also interfere with your ability to sleep, making it feel like you drank a cup of coffee before trying to go to bed. It can make it hard to concentrate. It can lead to immature thinking that relies more on your emotional brain than your prefrontal cortex, the source of advanced reasoning. It can even make it harder to eat and digest food.

UNDERSTANDING THE RELATIONSHIP BETWEEN CHRONIC STRESS AND
ANGER

When high emotional arousal persists over extended periods of time, it becomes chronic stress. Chronic stress refers to how stressed a person is over time by ongoing stressful events—and by their *thinking* about ongoing stressful events. Research has found that people's subjective stress (how stressful they think their life is) is a better predictor of physiological arousal than their objective stress (how many stressful events are actually going on).

Chronic anger is a physiological state that is very similar to chronic stress. Chronic stress involves continually worrying about things; chronic anger involves continually being angry, irritable, grumpy, or resentful about things. Both chronic stress and chronic anger are primarily created and sustained by your thoughts. Both lead to the ongoing, nearly continuous release of adrenaline into your body.

A large body of research has found that chronic stress and chronic anger can shorten your lifespan and even kill you. They literally wear the body down over time. The immune and cardiovascular systems are particularly affected, raising the risk of high blood pressure, heart attack, heart disease, stroke, and infectious diseases. Lowering your stress and anger levels can significantly improve your physical health and extend your life.

If you want to get back to a calmer physical state, you need to start by adjusting your thinking about the stressful event and lower your adrenaline level. Many self-soothing techniques do these at the same time. We will briefly mention a few here and then examine the concept of self-compassion.

PRACTICING CONSCIOUS BREATHING

There are many ways to do conscious breathing, but they all involve tuning into your breath to slow it, deepen it, and make it more regular. One way is to inhale for four counts, hold for eight counts, and exhale for seven counts. Controlling your breath triggers the relaxation response in your body, which helps to stop the release of adrenaline and return the body to a calm, resting state. There are many apps, websites, and podcasts that teach how to slow, deepen, and make your breath more regular.

This is one technique you can use virtually anywhere—while standing, while driving, during meetings—to help yourself physically calm:

First, start by turning your attention toward your breath. Notice how you are breathing in the present moment. Whenever you are ready, slowly and deeply inhale to a mental count of four, expanding your lower abdomen. This means your stomach should move out. Hold the breath for a count of eight. Then slowly exhale to a count of seven. Repeat several times, doing your best to keep your focus and mind on your breath. If other thoughts come into your head, gently turn your attention back to your breath.

PRACTICING PROGRESSIVE RELAXATION

Progressive relaxation is mentally working your way around your body and relaxing each set of muscles. You could simply notice tension and release it, or you could actually tense each area so that you can feel it and then relax it, allowing all the tension to flow out of it. You can work around your body in any direction; the most common is to start at your feet and work your way up. Turn your attention to a specific body area, notice any tension there, then consciously relax it, which may include gently moving or bending it. Do that for a few moments and then move on to the next area. This technique can take ten minutes or longer, depending on how long you focus on each area and how many areas you focus on. Some people use progressive relaxation to help them fall asleep.

PRACTICING MEDITATION

Meditation describes a wide variety of practices that achieve some level of clearing the mind of extraneous and distracting thoughts. In fact, all of our examples of self-soothing could be described as meditative.

Examples of meditation include focusing on a single word such as "om" with your eyes closed, saying a single phrase over and over again either in your head or out loud, and focusing all your attention on a single visual point or a process such as your breath. Ritualized prayer qualifies when you repeat a specific phrase over and over, such as Salah or the rosary. The idea is to stay focused on the process and keep your mind clear of other thoughts. When other thoughts start to intrude (about what you need to do later, something from the past, or something you need to figure out), notice them, gently let them go, and turn your attention back to the focus point.

DOING GUIDED VISUALIZATION

Guided visualization is a form of daydreaming in which you imagine yourself someplace else, perhaps relaxing on the beach, walking in the forest, or having fun at Disneyland as you relax your body and breath. If you'd like, you can listen to calming music or nature sounds while you run a comforting movie in your head.

USING POSITIVE AFFIRMATIONS

Thinking or speaking positive affirmations can keep you calm by replacing your negative self-talk with encouraging and optimistic statements. AA and other twelve-step programs make regular use of these. By changing your thinking, you can help your body to calm. This was covered extensively in the chapter on self-talk.

PRACTICING MINDFULNESS

We talked at length about mindfulness in the chapter on awareness of body. Practicing mindfulness is primarily about becoming more self-aware, but it often has the added benefit of helping you self-soothe. As you become more present in the moment, your thoughts about other things fade, which can help you to calm.

Note that the self-soothing exercises above are not mindfulness exercises. They are different from mindfulness in that they seek to willfully change how you feel and what you do rather than simply call your mind to something.

PRACTICING SELF-COMPASSION

Practicing self-compassion is practicing self-awareness and mindfulness from a compassionate stance. It is not simply noticing how you feel, but doing so from a place of lovingkindness. This shifts it away from self-awareness and into self-soothing.

Both self-awareness and mindfulness involve a certain level of detachment. They are intended to be neutral, objective, like you are observing an event without any real emotion or care. For example, you might notice that your eyes are burning a bit, your breathing is a little shallow, your shoulders are slumped.

Self-compassion takes this further and considers how you are affected emotionally and what a loving response would be. It acknowledges that you are not just a thing or a body having experiences, but a person who is affected by those experiences and who is deserving of love and care.

When you practice self-compassion, you do not simply observe what you think and feel, you consider what you want and need. You would notice your lack of engagement and the fatigue in your body, then interpret those feelings in the context of your experiences. You might think something like, "Boy, I sure am worn out. It's been a long day. I really worked hard today and I don't know that I'm up to doing much more. I should just call it a day and take care of myself. I can do more work tomorrow."

Self-compassion is active nurturing. If someone who loves and nurtures you were to notice what you're experiencing right now, what would they say to you? What would they do for you? Self-compassion builds on your observations and guides you to figure out how to take care of yourself.

Self-compassion also acknowledges that you are not alone in your suffering. When you feel miserable, it's easy to think you're the only one, that no one has felt as bad as you do. It's easy to feel isolated and alone, especially when you see how well other people seem to be doing. It can make you feel like you should just push through whatever you are feeling. But it's vital to remind yourself that whatever you are going through, others have gone through it too, and there are other people who are going through the same kind of suffering as you. Your suffering is part of what it means to be a human being, and other human beings experience it, too. Acknowledging your common humanity can reduce your sense of isolation and serve as a reminder that your suffering will pass, just as it has for others. Others have been where you are and have made it through. Self-compassion has the effect of validating your suffering instead of letting you become self-critical or dismissive.

You are imperfect. You make mistakes. You have weaknesses. Yet for all that, you are still lovable. Acknowledge and manage your imperfections. Remember that no one else is perfect, either, and just as they are still lovable, so are you.

Self-compassion is an antidote to shame. Shame is rooted in the belief that love is conditional—that you only deserve love and care if you act certain ways. But self-compassion is rooted in unconditional love—that everyone, including you, needs and deserves love and nurturance, regardless of who you are or what you have done.

We encourage you to read Kristin Neff's book, *Self-Compassion: The Proven Power of Being Kind to Yourself* to learn more about this. You might also want to check out her website, www.self-compassion.org, where you can take a free online quiz to determine how self-compassionate you are.

STEPPING AWAY FROM DISTRESS

You can temporarily step away from distress by shelving it, or more thoroughly step away from it by practicing acceptance.

Shelving your distress is temporarily turning away from it by "putting it on the shelf." This means to consciously and intentionally remove your focus from certain thoughts and feelings until you can deal with them. This is not the same as denial, because you fully intend to turn your attention back to the distress at a later, better time.

Shelving distress is often necessary simply because other things need immediate attention and distress does not. You can do what you have to in the moment without getting distracted by thoughts and feelings that are not urgent. People often shelve their distress while they're at work, in a meeting, attending to children, driving, watching a movie, going to a show, or spending time with others. Another good time to shelve distress is when it's time to sleep. If you don't, the emotional agitation might keep you awake.

To shelve your distress, simply divert your attention to the immediate task at hand—paying attention in the meeting, following the directions in the recipe, or losing yourself in the performance. If the distressful thoughts or feelings start to come up, gently redirect your attention to what the present moment requires of you. Make sure you return to it when you can—a few minutes, a few hours, or a few days later, tops.

Shelving distress indefinitely is problematic. You can only put so many things on the shelf before it comes tumbling down. It's not a permanent solution, but it is a practical one. The more enduring solution is acceptance.

PRACTICING ACCEPTANCE

Acceptance involves changing the way you respond internally to something you're unable to change externally. The first line of the Serenity Prayer, "God grant me the serenity to accept the things I cannot change," tells you to find a way to make peace with things you can't do anything about. This is important advice. Many things are beyond your control: the weather, traffic, tasks taking longer than expected. The key is not to try to control them, but rather to learn how to work with them as they are.

Acceptance modifies your expectations and works with things as they actually are. For example, you might have hoped it would be sunny and warm at the beach, and maybe the weather forecast said it would be, but it's cloudy and cool and looks like rain. Accepting the weather would mean embracing the fact that it's cloudy, cool, and possibly rainy. The sooner you can embrace that reality, the sooner you can move forward in a way that is congruent with that reality, and the more likely you are to feel much less distressed.

The Buddhist practice of radical acceptance, which has been incorporated into dialectical behavioral theory and popularized by Tara Brach's book *Radical Acceptance*, involves acknowledging reality as it is, whether you like it or not. Refusing to accept reality doesn't change it—it just makes you miserable. Insisting on having a picnic in the pouring rain because it was supposed to be sunny will not keep you from getting wet. Refusing to accept that traffic is worse than expected will not get you there any quicker, it will just make you more frustrated. Radical acceptance means you don't have to like what's happening, but you do have to acknowledge that it's happening.

A related Buddhist concept is the difference between pain and suffering. Pain, in various forms, both physical and emotional, is inevitable. It is part of the experience of life. Suffering, on the other hand, is not inevitable. Suffering happens when you refuse to accept life's pain, and instead try to fight or resist it. Suffering is holding on to how you wanted something to be or projecting how you want it to be in the future rather than acknowledging it as it actually is. Suffering doesn't see the impermanent nature of pain, which, like everything else, will pass. Pain is inevitable; suffering is optional. Pain is the distress you feel in the present moment; suffering is the distress you feel when you want the present moment to be different.

If your partner unexpectedly died, you would probably experience significant distress. You would likely feel sadness, grief, and loneliness, among other emotions. You might think about the future you will no longer have together, and the things you will miss about your partner. Part of that is pain—the pain of the loss. Part of that, though, is suffering: refusing to accept the reality that your partner has died. You might continue to hold on to the future you'd envisioned together. You might think your grief would be endless, that you could never be the same, that life would never be the same. You might even feel like you couldn't go on without your partner. All of that would be suffering—holding on to how you want things to be rather than accepting how they truly are. Practicing acceptance in this situation would mean acknowledging that your partner has passed and finding ways to move forward while grieving. It would mean focusing on what you can do in the present moment and what the present moment has to offer rather than getting lost in thoughts of what might have been, what could have been.

For a less dramatic example, imagine you're at the beach. The clouds have not broken as promised, and in fact, the wind is picking up and it's getting even colder and cloudier. You suffer because you are thinking "it *should* be sunny out, it was *supposed* to be sunny out." You are thinking about the things you wanted and expected to do—lay out on the sand in the sun, get warm and then cool off in the water—that you can't really do now. Pain, on the other hand, is what you are actually experiencing in the moment. You might feel a little chilly, and sad about having to keep your jacket on.

There is nothing wrong with hopes, expectations, dreams, and goals. Even when external events get in the way, there may still be things you can do. The Serenity Prayer mentions the "wisdom to know the difference" between what you can change and what you cannot.

For example, if your goal and desire is to spend Saturday evening connecting physically with your romantic partner, but they come down with a cold and go to bed early, you may feel sad and disappointed and perhaps a little lonely. The evening did not work as you had hoped and planned, but you can still find a way to make it through as best as you can, accepting that it will be spent alone, with your partner sick in bed. You can then move forward with the night as it is, rather than getting stuck on how it isn't. Radical acceptance in this situation would mean letting go of wanting to spend intimate time with your partner and embracing the reality of, for example, watching a movie on your own.

Variations of this concept are counting your blessings (that you have a home and friends and money to dine out or stream movies) or looking on the bright side (you'll have a chance to watch that movie you've been wanting to stream) or thinking "it could be worse" (. . . you could have gotten sick) or "at least . . ." (at least you have friends). The problem with those approaches, though, is that they don't require you to acknowledge and accept the reality of your distress. Instead, they jump ahead to how you can get yourself to feel less distressed.

***

All of the above are some basic ways of managing your distress in the moment. In the next chapter, we will explore ways you can better manage yourself over time to reduce the amount of distress you feel in the first place.

CHAPTER 19

LEARNING TO TAKE CARE OF YOURSELF

Distress does not *cause* abusive and controlling behavior, but it can tempt you to give yourself permission to behave badly. Therefore, part of committing to being nonabusive is to take good care of yourself. Being accountable is not just taking responsibility for your abuse, but also for your well-being. Taking care of yourself is essentially managing yourself well, and the first step toward that is being clear about your wants and needs.

UNDERSTANDING THE DIFFERENCE BETWEEN NEEDS AND WANTS
Needs are things that are core for your survival, like food, sleep, and physical safety. Wants are things that you would like to have, but don't need to survive: an ice cream cone, a soft bed, seeing a particular movie. As you identify your wants and needs, keep several things in mind.

First, know what your wants and needs are. Self-awareness and emotional awareness should help with that.

Second, be careful not to confuse a want with a need. There are many things that you may want that you actually do not need. As a general guideline, needs tend to be general and wants tend to be specific ways of meeting specific needs. There are typically many ways to meet a need, but you might have a very specific want. When you mistake wants for needs, you put yourself at risk of becoming rigid and controlling. When you mistake needs for wants, you might make inappropriate compromises.

In general, you should prioritize your needs over your wants. You might want to watch another episode of your favorite show, but you shouldn't overlook your need for sleep. You can make the occasional exception, but needs should usually take precedence.

Likewise, you should generally be more flexible about getting your wants met and firmer about getting your needs met. Kids learn as they grow up that they may need to eat, but they don't need a certain kind of food. As the Rolling Stones said, "You can't always get what you want . . . but you can get what you need."

It's also important to differentiate wants from needs in your partner and children, and to prioritize their needs over your wants. When it comes to meeting their wants, there's room to negotiate.

PRACTICING SELF-CARE

When people hear the term "self-care," they typically think of activities that maintain or improve their physical health: eating right, exercising, and getting enough sleep. These are all important parts of health maintenance, but physical health is only part of self-care. Another common way of thinking of about self-care is doing something for fun, like going to a movie, getting a mocha, or spending the evening reading a good book. These are all examples of recreation, which is also part of self-care, but again, only part.

We define self-care as putting energy and effort into maintaining a balanced life. Your life is multifaceted—there are a variety of areas that need your attention and from which you can draw support. Good self-care gives energy and attention to a number of them. You can think of it as a pie chart. With good self-care, the slices of pie are all about the same size. With poor self-care, a couple slices (maybe work and family) are very large and the rest are just slivers.

Self-care comprises the beams that support the roof of your metaphorical house. With good self-care, you have many roofbeams, if one beam weakens, the others can carry the weight. With poor self-care, you only have a few beams, and they each have to bear a heavier load. If one were to weaken, those few beams might struggle to bear the extra weight and the whole structure might collapse. The goal is to have as many beams—as many *strong* beams—as possible supporting your roof. Good self-care puts a number of beams in place and regularly strengthens those that are already there.

Many people don't realize how many facets of their life need maintenance and provide support. Listed below are the areas of self-care that are common to every adult on the planet, regardless of cultural background.

VOCATIONAL

Vocational self-care refers in part to how you earn income: your job or jobs. It also refers to your professional goals, including volunteer work and post-retirement work that may not generate income.

How satisfied are you with your job? What are your professional goals? To what extent do you feel fulfilled by your position? Some people live to work, and others work to live. Which one describes you?

People with poor vocational self-care are often professionally dissatisfied or unhappily unemployed. They feel little enthusiasm for what they do for a living and often have to drag themselves to work. People with good vocational self-care are often doing work that is fulfilling, enjoyable, and consistent with their values. If their current work is less than fulfilling, they are doing it because it is moving them toward other goals, like waiting tables to support a fledgling acting career or working to put themselves through school.

FINANCIAL

Financial self-care refers to managing the money in your life: your income and what you're doing with it. This includes your budget—your income and expenses—regardless of whether you're actually tracking it. How much money is coming in and going out? What are your financial goals? Do you have enough money to take care of yourself? To what extent are you saving and spending in ways that work for you? How are you striving to meet your current and future financial needs?

People can have very different positive relationships with money. Maximizing savings is a good financial plan for some and a bad one for others. Many people prioritize doing fulfilling work and living a particular lifestyle over making as much money as possible. For example, an attorney might be happier working in legal aid than they would if they made twice as much working in commercial law. Finances can facilitate personal goals, but more money does not necessarily mean more happiness.

People with poor financial self-care are often unable to meet their financial needs and goals. They spend more than they make or do not allocate their money in ways that are consistent with their values. People with good financial self-care align their budget with their income, don't spend more than they make, and manage their money in ways that honor their core values and needs.

EDUCATIONAL

Education is more than going to school. It includes any activity that increases your knowledge, like reading books, learning online, traveling, having new experiences, watching documentaries, getting an apprenticeship, being mentored, and attending trainings. You might pursue a hobby like gardening or woodworking. You might study the history of your state. You might learn a particular skill or how to do a particular task.

In general, how are you increasing your knowledge base in ways that feel right to you? Are there things you would like to learn more about? Is there anything you're curious about? Bad educational self-care means you are doing little to increase your knowledge, particularly in ways that are important to you. For example, if you don't learn how to manage your type 2 diabetes, or don't learn new skills that help you advance professionally, you will experience negative consequences. You might love cooking, but rarely make time to learn new recipes. Good educational self-care means regularly increasing your knowledge in areas that are important to you, including ways to better meet your needs.

LEGAL

When you hear the word "legal," you might think of being convicted of a crime or being on probation. More broadly, though, it covers your relationship with all of society's rules, not just criminal laws. It includes conflicts with neighbors, traffic violations, tax problems, and certification and licensing, as well as the rules in your apartment building or at work. To what extent are you living your life in a manner that doesn't cause legal difficulties? Poor legal self-care means you are struggling to comply with the law or are dealing with the consequences of breaking it. It could also indicate ongoing struggles between how you wish to live and the rules you are subject to. Good legal self-care means you're currently free from legal issues and can live true to yourself without running afoul of any laws or rules.

DOMESTIC

Domestic self-care refers to maintenance of your living space. It includes housecleaning, paperwork, laundry, and yard care. People vary widely in terms of how well-organized they prefer their space to be. What is important is not that a living space looks a certain way, but that you feel comfortable and satisfied there. When you share a space with a loved one, one person may do more of the domestic work, but it is actually both of your responsibility.

With poor domestic self-care, you are not maintaining your living space in a way that works for you, and you feel significant frustration and dissatisfaction about it. With good domestic self-care, you are content with the present state of your living space and how you are maintaining it, however that may be.

HEALTH MAINTENANCE

Health maintenance refers to maintaining a healthy body through diet, exercise, and sleep. Exercise and sleep have been found to have a wide range of benefits and are especially important to your overall self-care, not just your physical self-care. We will elaborate on these benefits below.

The main goal of exercise is typically to improve physical health and promote weight loss, but exercise has many other benefits. It's a sleep aid, since a physically fatigued body sleeps better. It's a mood enhancer that releases endorphins. It's a stress-reducer that metabolizes the adrenaline produced by stress. And it can help make other emotions such as grief and anger more manageable. Regular exercise can also help with your energy level.

The importance of sleep has gained increased attention in the past couple of decades. A growing body of research has found that the quantity and quality of sleep has far greater impact and ramifications than previously thought.

Sleep deprivation, especially over an extended period of time, is problematic. On average, most people need seven or eight hours of sleep each night, although the optimum amount varies a great deal from person to person as well as over time. Some people function well on six hours of sleep or less. Others need nine hours or more to feel at their best. Young children need the most, and older adults can comfortably get by on less than when they were younger. Contrary to popular opinion, you can't make up for lost sleep by sleeping in on other days, nor can you store up sleep by sleeping more ahead of anticipated times of sleep deprivation. The goal should be to have as few sleep-deprived days as possible, especially in a row. The more consecutive days you go without enough sleep, the more problems will arise, especially if you do this on a long-term basis.

Quality of sleep refers to how deeply you are able to sleep as well as how disrupted your sleep is. While both quality and quantity matter, recent research has shown that quality trumps quantity: nine hours of poor-quality sleep is more problematic than six hours of high-quality sleep. Research has found that high-quality sleep can improve mood, encourage healthy weight loss, improve memory and learning, and enhance healing.

A number of things can compromise your sleep quality, including environmental factors like noise, light, and people coming and going. Events that require you to repeatedly awaken such as a crying baby, a child needing attention, the need to urinate, or a phone or pager going off can be disruptive. Diet, caffeine, alcohol, and certain medications can make you sleep less soundly. Sleep apnea, in which the airway is temporarily blocked and the sleeper must briefly awaken to start breathing again, is common in people who are overweight or heavy snorers. Not keeping a regular bedtime and not having a comfortable sleeping space can contribute to disrupted sleep. Finally, your thoughts can negatively impact the quality of your sleep—especially worrying and ruminating about things when you'd like to be sleeping.

With poor health maintenance, you don't eat, sleep, or exercise as you'd like to and in the ways that are most helpful and restorative to you. With good health maintenance, you are regularly able to eat in ways you feel good about, do the amount and type of exercise you find most beneficial, and get sleep of enough length and quality that you feel rested and restored. If you have limited time for self-care in general, your best investment would be in regular exercise and high-quality sleep. All self-care has value, but the benefits of these are especially broad and deep.

MEDICAL

Whereas physical self-care keeps your body healthy, medical self-care deals with physical problems, including illness, injuries, and dental care, as well as aches and pains. At times, this area of self-care requires little or no attention, and at others it is a primary focus.

With poor medical self-care, you ignore or are slow to address physical ailments and issues, which can make them worse and lead to complications. Poor medical self-care can result from not complying with medical directives that you believe would be good for your health and physical well-being. This could include not reliably taking medications, not scheduling medical appointments, and not following medical advice. Good medical self-care involves regularly monitoring your physical well-being, noting when you may be developing a medical or dental issue, and addressing concerns promptly. It includes complying with medical directives unless you believe they are unnecessary or unhelpful, and getting a second opinion to help you make the decision.

PSYCHOLOGICAL

Whereas medical self-care addresses issues with your body, psychological self-care addresses issues with your mind, including depression or anxiety. It involves struggles related to abuse, control, or neglect you experienced when you were younger. It might require you to improve your ability to be emotionally aware, connected, and expressive with yourself or others. One way to address these concerns is by meeting with a therapist or counselor. Others are to talk in a deeper, more vulnerable way with friends or family, read self-improvement books, listen to podcasts, and engage in self-reflection through journaling.

With poor psychological self-care, you actively avoid psychological problems, even when doing so makes your life harder. With good psychological self-care, you regularly check in with yourself, identify concerns, and actively address and resolve them.

ROMANTIC

Romantic self-care involves your primary romantic relationship, if you have one, and your goals for one if you don't. If you are polyamorous, this might include multiple romantic relationships. If you are not presently in a romantic relationship, this may not be an area of concern right now.

Romantic self-care involves more than going on dates, giving gifts, or writing love notes. It refers to your level of satisfaction with your romantic partner—and vice versa. It also refers to the ongoing energy and effort you invest in your relationship. All relationships, including romantic ones, are living things that require ongoing care and maintenance. When neglected, they tend to weaken and become less satisfying. Because of their central status in most people's lives, romantic relationships typically require the most ongoing care and maintenance. This includes sharing and listening to the latest developments, challenges, and successes in each other's lives, discussing and working through issues between the two of you, and negotiating mutually satisfying solutions. We will give all this much more attention in Chapters 23–25.

If you are presently in a romantic relationship, poor romantic self-care is characterized by limited quality interactions, limited communication, limited attention to the relationship, and taking the relationship, and your partner, for granted. Any abusive behavior you engage in will, of course, further and significantly damage the relationship, which will not immediately recover even after the abuse stops.

If you are not currently in a romantic relationship but want to be, poor romantic self-care is characterized by failing to search for and make such a connection, unless you are intentionally choosing not to date for now.

Good romantic self-care is characterized by regularly investing time and energy into your relationship through communication, play, and attention, or by actively dating and seeking out potential romantic connection. It includes identifying and resolving conflicts and concerns while strengthening the bond and connection you have.

SEXUAL

When evaluating this area, many people primarily focus on whether they are having sex with someone else, how often they are having sex, and whether the sex is good, which they often define as resulting in orgasm.

However, sexuality covers much more than specific sexual relationships or the particular sexual behavior in a relationship. It refers more broadly to your sense of sexuality.

Your sexuality exists regardless of whether you're sexually active with someone else (if you are polyamorous, with more than one other person). It encompasses the role sexuality plays in your life, including your sexual fantasies, dreams, and goals—as well as being sexual with yourself, including masturbation. It takes into consideration how well you honor yourself sexually according to your values.

Sex can fulfill a variety of needs beyond explicitly sexual needs and cravings. It can be a form of play and recreation with another person or with yourself. It is a way of connecting closely to someone else. It might be a spiritual practice that connects you with your higher power. You may use it at times as a form of stress relief. It can be a way to give and receive nurturance to another person and to yourself. Sex can meet more than one of these needs at a time, and it may meet different needs at different times.

Sexual health is not defined by frequency of intercourse or intensity of orgasm, so it's important not to define good sex solely by those measures. You can have high levels of sexual satisfaction without intercourse or orgasms. Sexual behavior includes a much wider variety of things than you may think. It includes your thoughts, fantasies, and goals, as well as your behaviors, and it's not limited to interactions with genitals. It can include touch of almost any part of the body, and kissing. It can include looks and words. You can be in a sexual space without being naked. You can be sexual appropriately in public with a look, a word, or a single caress. A sexual encounter can be as brief as a few seconds or can last for hours. It, of course, always requires the uncoerced informed consent of the other person.

Poor sexual self-care typically involves a lack of sexual connection with yourself and the role you want sex to play in your life. It can also reflect a poor sexual connection with your sexual partner, but be careful not to hold them responsible for your sexual well-being. It typically means that your sexual behavior is not particularly in line with your sexual values and goals. Good sexual self-care typically involves being sexually self-aware and connected, including with the role you want sex to play in your life, and honoring your sexuality by making space for sexual connection on a regular basis (whatever that means to you). If you are in a relationship, it means appropriately advocating for your sexual wants while respecting your partner's wants, needs, and boundaries.

FAMILY

Family self-care refers to the quality and nature of your relationships and interactions with family members, including extended family and people you consider family: your children, parents, siblings, aunts, uncles, cousins, nieces, nephews, extended family, and people who are like family to you. How satisfied are you with the frequency, content, and quality of your family relationships? How well are you maintaining them? Are you interacting with them in the ways you want to? Your family members obviously play a role in this, but the focus here is on your choices.

In some cases, you might choose not to have any contact at all, or to limit contact to certain situations or types of interactions. You can't pick the family you're born into (or the one your partner was born into!), so part of the challenge is sorting out how close you want to be with the one you have. People also sometimes "adopt" others to be a surrogate parent or offspring. All of these are aspects of family self-care.

With poor family self-care, you feel dissatisfied with how you're managing your family relationships. You may not be spending enough time with certain family members or not spending time with them in the ways you wish. On the other hand, it may mean you're spending more time than you want to with them or interacting in ways that you do not want to. Good family self-care means you're comfortable with the level and quality of contact you have with your family members, and you feel satisfied with the frequency and nature of your contact with them. It may also mean you have people in your life that you're not actually related to who fulfill your needs for family.

SOCIAL

Social self-care refers to your interactions with people you are not related to or romantically involved with, and includes friends, coworkers, and neighbors. You may interact with these people in a variety of ways, including networking, sharing information, borrowing things, providing physical assistance, and doing things for fun.

People vary greatly in terms of how many friends they need and how much time they want to spend with other people, but everyone can benefit from at least occasionally interacting with people outside of their family. It's obviously good to have friends, but it's of particular importance to have a few close friends—people you trust, confide in, and talk with about anything, including personal struggles and issues. Having close friends is the third of the three core aspects of self-care that have a wide range of benefits. Research has found that people who have a few close friends live longer, healthier, happier lives and rebound more quickly from physical and psychological problems than people who do not.

Poor social self-care in this area means having no close friends (other than your romantic partner), rarely having contact with them (less than monthly), and/or having a very limited network of social supports in general. While people vary in how many friends they want and need, with poor social self-care you are generally dissatisfied with your social network. Good social self-care means having two or three good friends you talk with at least monthly, at least a few others you occasionally connect with, and interactions with others who provide you with companionship, support, and information. It means that you are quite satisfied and well sustained by the friends that you have.

SOLITUDE

Solitude refers not just to time spent alone, but specifically to time spent checking in with and being fully present with yourself. Your relationship with yourself is probably the only lifelong relationship you'll have, and it might be the most important one you'll have. As in any other relationship, a good relationship with yourself means spending time communicating, connecting, checking in, and reflecting on how you are doing and how things could be improved. Ask yourself questions like "How am I doing? What am I feeling? How have things been going for me lately? What am I wanting or needing?"

You can check in with yourself mentally, silently, or in a journal. You can do it while you do chores, take a walk, drive, or do any number of things, as long as you are fully present with yourself. Spending time alone with yourself requires not being distracted by your phone, the internet, or anything else. Social media has significantly eaten into opportunities for being alone, so you have to intentionally make space to be present with yourself.

People vary greatly in terms of how much solitude they want and need, but everyone benefits from occasionally touching base with themselves. Poor self-care in this area would mean rarely or never spending time alone in reflection or checking in with yourself. It often looks like filling in your alone time with reading, the internet, games, or being on your phone. It means you have limited self-awareness, and little understanding of how you are doing and what you want or need. Good self-care in this area means making regular time to check in with yourself emotionally, reflect on recent experiences and future plans, and seek out insight and personal understanding. It means you are well-connected with yourself and have good self-awareness, including of how you are doing and what you want and need.

RECREATION

Anything you do for fun falls into the category of recreation and hobbies. How do you play? What do you do for relaxation? How do you unwind? Examples include going to cultural events like movies, concerts, and festivals; dining out; doing hobbies like woodworking or gardening; playing games; and watching or playing sports. These activities may overlap into other self-care areas.

Poor recreational self-care would be failing to make time for fun or forcing yourself to do "fun" things you don't actually enjoy. Good recreational self-care is making time to pursue a variety of fun activities, however you define them.

CREATIVITY

When people think of being creative or artistic, they often think of painting, playing music, and writing, but this area includes any form of self-expression. Not everyone considers themselves artistic, but everyone is creative. Besides the more conventional arts such as music, theater, writing, and art, other examples of self-expression include gardening, interior decorating, woodworking, and cooking (for fun).

Creativity provides you with an opportunity to connect more deeply with yourself and express what you care about and what matters to you. It can be a way of bringing your thoughts and emotions into the world. This is one domain where you are fully in control. It's more important for some people than others, but everyone can benefit from tapping into a creative outlet of some kind.

Poor creative self-care means that you rarely make time to express yourself through creative outlets you enjoy, or not having a creative outlet and not trying to find one. Good creative self-care would be identifying your favorite ways to express yourself creatively, regularly making time and space for them, and feeling satisfied with the time you spend doing them.

COMMUNITY SERVICE

Although people with experience in the criminal justice system might think of community service in terms of picking up litter or cleaning up graffiti as a condition of probation, here it is defined more broadly. Community service is doing things for people you don't know personally or know well. It acknowledges the reality that no matter how isolated you feel, you are part of the larger community of humanity and enjoy benefits from the efforts of people you have never met. As they say, we all drink from wells dug by others and sit in the shade of trees we didn't plant.

Doing community service is kind and altruistic, a way of giving back and paying it forward. You could volunteer for charity work in a food bank or soup kitchen, coach a sports team, organize a community project, or help a neighbor you do not know very well. Anything you do voluntarily in the service of people you don't know qualifies. The benefits to you can include an elevated mood, a greater sense of connection with others, and a stronger sense of spirituality.

With poor self-care in this area, you are not volunteering your time or helping people you don't know—or you might be helping others in a way that gives you little satisfaction. Good self-care in this area means that you are regularly doing community service work that you find fulfilling and gratifying.

SPIRITUALITY

When people think of spiritual practices, they often think of organized religious activities like going to church or reading a holy book like the Bible or the Quran. While those qualify, a spiritual practice does not have to involve an organized religious practice. Spirituality refers to your connection with something greater than yourself. It pursues—if not answers—existential questions about why you are here and what everything means. In twelve-step programs, it is referred to as your higher power.

Everyone needs a sense of spirituality, even atheists, but yours doesn't have to involve a formal religious practice. Not everyone can relate to the Judeo-Christian concept of God or get interested in attending a religious service. There are many less conventional spiritual practices. One is to spend time outdoors, where nature is your higher power. Another is to pursue mindfulness, and simply seek to be as present in the moment as you can be through your five senses. Another is to sustain a belief that science and scientific principles will ultimately provide explanations for everything in the universe. Still another is nurturing your faith in the greater good of humanity.

A solid spiritual practice is particularly important during difficult times in your life. When things are at their worst, when you are the most depleted and under-resourced, a strong sense of spirituality can make a huge difference. With poor spiritual self-care, you are unaware of your spirituality, not connecting with it, or not actively practicing it. Good spiritual self-care involves regularly connecting with and practicing your spirituality and having a deep sense of connection with your higher power, however that is defined.

***

Every area of self-care that we've covered in this chapter is relevant for every adult, anywhere in the world. Some are vital for everyone, and others may be less important for some. Areas that are of vital importance for everyone include professional, financial, legal, domestic, physical, medical, family, social, recreation, and solitude. Neglecting any of these areas can lead to significant problems over time. Areas that are less vital and may not compromise the quality of life for some people are educational, psychological, romantic, sexual, creativity, community service, and spirituality. Some of these areas may carry little importance for some people, who can be quite happy and well-adjusted without putting much energy into them. But each of these areas can be an important and vital resource for dealing with life and its challenges.

The thought of putting energy into so many different parts of your life can feel overwhelming, but you don't have to do it all at once. The key is to distribute your attention and energy among a variety of areas over time. In the old vaudeville acts where they spun plates on the tops of sticks, they didn't have to continually spin each plate. Once they gave one a good spin, they could leave it for a while and come back before it slowed down so much the plate on top would fall. If you give each area of your self-care a good spin every now and then, you can move on to other things. Checking in with a good friend every few weeks may be enough to sustain a satisfying friendship, but if you only talk once or twice a year, it might fall apart. You don't need to do your hobby every day or every week, but if months go by, it isn't feeding you the way it could. Ask yourself which areas need the most attention right now, then prioritize those; you can adjust again later.

Good self-care is not immediately gained or lost. It takes time to build it up and wear it down. Actively practicing it is like riding a bike: you can coast, but eventually you'll come to a stop. The better your self-care, the longer you can neglect it, but like riding a bike, it can take a little pedaling to get back to full speed.

Practicing good self-care is part of recovery, which we will discuss in detail in Chapter 26: Learning to Sustain Your Positive Changes. It prepares you for managing difficult times and gives you more resources to draw on. If your self-care is poor, you're more vulnerable to feeling stressed and overwhelmed. You won't have as many resources to manage the challenges of life. The longer you live like that, the more likely you are to act out or handle things poorly.

If your life isn't balanced on a strong foundation of good self-care, you'll be less aware of your emotions and more likely to go into denial, which can easily lead to relapse. Good self-care grounds you and helps you be more self-aware and honest with yourself. It makes you more likely to deal appropriately with emotional distress instead of acting it out by becoming abusive and controlling. Good self-care is a cornerstone of staying nonabusive and noncontrolling.

We have developed a Self-Care Plan to help you evaluate and prioritize the various areas of self-care. This is something you may revisit periodically, say on an annual basis, as your priorities shift. A copy of the Self-Care Plan is in Appendix E. Self-care looks at how you manage yourself on an ongoing basis. It's the view from 10,000 feet above ground. In the next chapter, we move to ground level and shift the focus from your general self-care to how you are managing yourself in any one moment. To do this, we'll introduce a tool we call the Journal that will help you do just that.

CHAPTER 20

THE JOURNAL: A TOOL FOR UNDERSTANDING AND CHANGING YOUR BEHAVIOR

In this chapter we want to introduce you to the Journal, a tool that can help you significantly increase your level of self-awareness in a variety of domains. Journaling can help you focus on yourself and understand how you respond to situations in your day-to-day life. It can also help you shift from an external focus, which drives abusive behavior, to an internal focus, which will help you more effectively manage your life.

When you think of journaling, you might think of writing your personal thoughts, feelings, and reflections in a diary. What we call journaling is similar to that, but it looks at specific moments in your life through the lens of this program. We have developed a two-page questionnaire that can guide you through any situation and help you focus on the aspects that are relevant to becoming nonabusive and noncontrolling. It draws on a number of concepts from earlier chapters and a few that will be discussed later.

You can complete the Journal for pretty much any situation you are dealing with—in your relationship, as a parent, with other people, even when you are alone. You can also complete it for old situations, even ones from many years ago, if you remember them clearly enough. For each situation, do your best to answer each question. The questions are designed to help you become more aware of yourself and others and to identify ways to self-soothe, self-manage, and self-advocate thoughtfully.

You can certainly learn from your successes by completing the Journal for situations where you handled yourself well, but most of your journals should be for times when you struggled to behave well. Everyone makes mistakes at times and doesn't handle themselves as well as they could, but the goal is to learn from them. People who deny that they make mistakes or behave imperfectly are fooling themselves and are more likely to stay stuck in their problematic behaviors. Mistakes and bad behavior are great learning opportunities that can help you become a better partner to yourself as well as to others.

You also don't need to focus solely on situations where you felt angry. In fact, if you are doing a good job of identifying the emotions behind your anger, most of your journals should be on those.

We ask people in our groups to complete at least fifty of these journals before finishing the program. This helps them get a solid sense of themselves and the world around them and how to effectively manage the many challenges in life—little as well as big—without becoming abusive or controlling. Doing this work is not just about changing the way you behave, or even the way you think, but the way you live. It is a lifestyle change. It changes the way you see the world. This doesn't happen easily or overnight. Completing the journals helps you practice and remember a variety of core skills and concepts and increases the likelihood that the changes you're making will endure.

At first glance, with nearly two dozen questions spread over two pages, the Journal may be overwhelming, but the more you complete, the easier it gets. Even people with very limited schooling who cannot write very well are able to fill these journals out just fine, using fewer words and incomplete sentences. You are welcome to skip over sections you don't understand or know how to answer at first. Start with the questions you *can* answer. Over time, the others will become clearer.

If you are not part of a group that uses journals and reads aloud from them every week you are at a bit of a disadvantage. When people are unsure how to complete a section early on, they leave it blank and get input on how they could have completed it from the group. They also get to listen to other people share their journals and answer the various questions, which can make it all much clearer. All the journals are handed in to the group facilitator, who gives them back with written notes. Feedback can be enormously helpful, not only in how to complete the Journal, but in how to behave differently and think about and do things differently going forward. All of that is lost when you're not in a group. Even so, many people report that simply answering the Journal questions is very helpful for focusing, identifying problem areas, gaining insight, and sorting out what they can do differently next time.

We encourage you to make copies of the Journal in the appendix and complete some on your own. Each question is explained below; please refer to the appendix for brief explanations and examples of completed journals. We will note which chapter discusses each of these items in greater detail so you can refer back to that information.

***

1. EVENT/SITUATION

This is a brief description of the situation. It's tempting to provide a lot of detail, but the focus should be on how you dealt with the situation, not the situation itself. The more you focus on the situation, the less you're focusing on what you thought, felt, and did. As we explained in the chapter on accountability, a key aspect of staying nonabusive and noncontrolling is to maintain an internal focus. Describing the situation indicates an external focus; describing yourself indicates an internal focus.

2. SIGNS OF PHYSICAL INTENSITY

These are your internal experiences, which other people would typically be unaware of. In an intense situation your physical sensations will probably reflect a surge of adrenaline, but even with lower intensity you'll be able to detect slight changes in your body, especially as you become more self-aware. Pay attention to changes in body temperature, muscle tension, breathing, energy, and alertness. You can also refer to the list of physical symptoms at the end of Appendix D: Emotions for ideas of what you might be experiencing in your body. *Chapter 17: Becoming Aware of Your Body; Appendix D: Emotions.*

3. SIGNS OF BEHAVIORAL INTENSITY

These are the observable behaviors that indicate how intensely you are feeling your emotions. They include what you say, what you do, your facial expressions, and your body language. Even at low intensity, others will be able to detect changes in your behavior that convey your emotional state. Taking note of these signs helps you become more aware of your emotional intensity and how you come across to others. *Chapter 17: Becoming Aware of Your Body.*

4. EMOTIONS

People usually have multiple emotions in any given situation. Be careful to list only emotional words (refer to the list in the appendix) and to leave out negative self-talk, blaming statements, judgments, and physical states. Most emotional words are single, individual words, so if you're putting down phrases like "this is a waste of time" or "you don't care about me," they are probably not emotions. Try to avoid listing angry emotions; instead, identify the emotions behind them; anger is often another emotion plus blame. Identifying emotions helps you become more aware of your core feelings. *Chapter 16: Becoming Aware of Your Emotions; Appendix D: Emotions.*

5. HIGHEST INTENSITY DURING THE SITUATION (1–10)

The stronger your emotions, the higher the number. Make sure to use the entire range of the 10-point scale. When your feelings are very intense, rate yourself a 10. If you barely felt anything at all, rate yourself a 1. A low score reflects that you were only a little emotional in the situation. A medium score reflects a moderate amount of emotional intensity. A high score reflects feeling quite intense.

This rating helps you see that you experience different levels of intensity in different situations. It helps you gain clarity on just how strongly you were feeling and whether you overreacted. This is another aspect of self-awareness. *Chapter 17: Becoming Aware of Your Body.*

6. Intensity at the Beginning (1–10)

This rating increases your awareness of how much intensity you brought into the situation. People sometimes mistakenly assume that all of their emotional intensity is a response to the situation, and that they always enter a situation in a neutral, unemotional space. This is not necessarily the case. It's especially important to be aware of this factor when you've overreacted. *Chapter 17: Becoming Aware of Your Body.*

7. How Much of My Intensity Was Due to This Specific Situation?

Did the intensity of your emotional reaction fit the situation? Did you overreact? It's easy to blame your emotional intensity on the triggering situation if you don't realize how intense you already felt. This is especially common when people overreact and/or are abusive. Journaling this factor lets you focus on where your underlying emotional intensity is coming from, rather than just on the present situation. We talked about this in the section on emotional barometers in *Chapter 16: Becoming Aware of Your Emotions.*

8. Negative Self-Talk

List here the thoughts that escalated your intensity and were not necessarily accurate. You can think of this as the devil on your shoulder. Include negative assumptions, negative attributions, unrealistic expectations, and other inflammatory thoughts. People sometimes write "none" in this section, but that's rarely accurate. Most people have some sort of negative self-talk in nearly every situation they are in—they just don't necessarily take it seriously. They might pull it out like a weed, using positive self-talk to challenge it or chase it away. *Chapter 5: Abusive Thoughts and Beliefs; Chapter 15: Becoming Aware of Your Thoughts.*

9. Abusive/Controlling Behaviors

List any ways you were abusive or controlling during the situation. Be specific. If you don't think you were, you can skip ahead to question 16. Writing journals on situations in which you were not abusive or controlling can help you identify what you did well, but most of your journals should be on situations in which you were. People who rarely complete journals on situations where they behaved badly are usually in denial, and therefore limited in how much they can truly grow or change. *Chapter 1: Abusive Behaviors; Chapter 2: Controlling Behaviors; Chapter 3: Sexual Abuse; Chapter 4: Financial Abuse.*

10. WHAT DID I WANT TO MAKE THE OTHER PERSON DO, FEEL, OR THINK?

Abusive and controlling behavior is typically either intended to make another person behave differently or is a negative reaction to what someone else is doing, feeling, or thinking. It is rare that someone gets abusive or controlling when someone is acting exactly as they want them to. This question sharpens your understanding of what you disapproved of and how you tried to change it.

11. BELIEFS THAT JUSTIFIED MY ABUSIVE/CONTROLLING BEHAVIORS

This is one of the questions that people struggle to answer correctly. They often incorrectly put negative self-talk here, but as we explained in Chapter 5: Abusive Thoughts and Beliefs, beliefs are not the same as self-talk. Whereas negative self-talk is specific to the current situation, beliefs are more fundamental and general ways you see and think about the world. List here the beliefs that made your behavior seem okay.

Changing your beliefs is a critical and foundational aspect of becoming nonabusive and noncontrolling. The first step in changing them is identifying them. *Chapter 5: Abusive Thoughts and Beliefs.*

12. HOW DID MY ABUSE/CONTROL AFFECT THE OTHER PERSON?

Put yourself in the other person's shoes and imagine how the ways you behaved might have negatively affected them. This is empathy. You may not know for certain how they experienced your abuse and control, but you can make a reasonable guess. Considering how they suffered can deter you from acting that way in the future. It can also help you be more accountable and to make repair. If no one was present, leave this question blank. *Chapter 11: Understanding the Impact of Abuse on Your Partner.*

13. HOW DID MY ABUSE/CONTROL AFFECT OTHERS?

Think about how people who were not the target of your abuse and control but were present may have been negatively affected. This is most obviously children who may have seen or heard the abuse, but includes neighbors, passersby, and anyone who was negatively affected by the aftermath, such as friends of the victim. *Chapter 12: Understanding the Impact of Abuse on Children.*

14. WHAT ROLE DID MY PAST ABUSE/CONTROL OF THAT PERSON PLAY?

Part of what makes abusive and controlling behavior so damaging is that it happens over and over again. Because of this pattern, new incidents of abuse can be more damaging. It's like hitting someone in a place they are already bruised. If your target was someone you'd previously abused, consider how that prior history may have contributed to their suffering in this situation. *Chapter 11: Understanding the Impact of Abuse on Your Partner.*

15. WHAT DID I GAIN FROM MY BEHAVIOR?

Being abusive and controlling often does get you things. That's one reason you do it. Identifying what you gained from this situation allows you to figure out better ways to get what you want and need.

16. WHAT DID I LOSE FROM MY BEHAVIOR?

There are costs to being abusive and controlling. Identifying your losses, whether they happened in the moment or afterwards, can provide further incentive not to be abusive and controlling in the future. Oftentimes, the benefits to you from being abusive and controlling are immediate and the negative consequences are delayed. This helps you realize what you lose by behaving in abusive and controlling ways.

17. WHAT DID I WANT IN THIS SITUATION?

Abuse and control are tools to meet your wants and needs. Gaining clarity about what you truly wanted or needed can help you identify more effective ways of getting it. *Chapter 19: Learning to Take Care of Yourself.*

18. WHAT DID OTHER PEOPLE WANT?

It's important to think about what others wanted, too. You may not know for sure, but you can speculate. Be as thoughtful about them as you were about yourself in the previous question. *Chapter 21: Learning to Regard Others.*

19. POSITIVE SELF-TALK

Think of this as the angel on your shoulder. If you can't identify any positive self-talk that you had during the situation, you can write what you *could* have said to yourself. The goal is to shift your thinking in a more productive and constructive direction by identifying helpful thoughts that keep you from becoming escalated and reactive. *Chapter 15: Becoming Aware of Your Thoughts.*

20. NONABUSIVE/NONCONTROLLING BELIEFS

This is another question that people typically struggle to answer. The core beliefs that help you choose to be nonabusive are more general than positive self-talk, and usually not specific to this one situation. Your beliefs are often in the back of your head; you may not consciously consider them in the situation. If you're not aware of having had any nonabusive/noncontrolling beliefs at the time, come up with some to write in here. Figure out rebuttals to your responses to "Beliefs that justified my abusive/controlling behaviors." *Chapter 15: Becoming Aware of Your Thoughts.*

21. HOW DID I APPROPRIATELY MEET MY NEEDS?

List here ways you met your needs without being abusive or controlling. If you did helpful things, like being assertive of otherwise taking care of yourself, list them here. If you don't think you did anything to meet your needs, note that. *Chapter18: Learning to Self-Soothe; Chapter 19: Learning to Take Care of Yourself; Chapter 23: Learning to Communicate Effectively; Chapter 24: Practicing Conflict-Resolution Skills.*

22. HOW DID I CONSIDER THE NEEDS OF OTHERS?

What specific things did you do to address others' wants and needs? Write that down here. If you didn't really consider anyone else's needs or take steps to address them, note that. *Chapter 21: Learning to Regard Others.*

23. MY EXPERIENCE OF THE SITUATION

This helps you sharpen your perspective of the situation by boiling it down to a few key points: how you felt ("I feel"), in which situation ("when"), what you wanted and needed in that situation ("I would like"), and what you did or will do about it ("I will"). This is also a guideline for sharing the key aspects of your experience with others. You are free to use different words than those listed. The important thing is to communicate with others about your emotions, your wants and needs, and how you want to address them, including how you might need help doing so.

I FEEL _____ WHEN _____.

I feel: Put one or more emotions here. Remember that emotions are typically single words, not phrases. Refer to the list of emotions in Appendix D for ideas.

   when: Briefly describe the specific behavior or situation. Try to be as concrete and specific as possible. Avoid general statements or negative attributions.

I WOULD LIKE _____ AND I WILL _____.

I would like: Briefly identify what you wanted or needed in that situation.

   and I will: Identify what you can do to address your wants or needs. This highlights primary accountability—that ultimately you, and no one else, are responsible for your well-being.

WHAT (IF ANYTHING) I WOULD LIKE TO DO DIFFERENTLY NEXT TIME

List here what you could do better next time. If you were abusive or controlling, what could you have done instead? Even if you weren't, do you wish you had done something else?

***

If you are serious about making real changes and want to do everything you can to achieve them, completing journals on distressing situations is a vital part of the process. Over the years, we have heard repeatedly from group members about how important the journals were for understanding what they were doing—both right and wrong—and how to apply the program concepts to their lives to make lasting changes. Repetition plays a big role, so you need to repeatedly complete journals on situations you are struggling with. In our program, group members need to complete at least fifty journals to complete the program. This level of practice increases the chances that they'll shift their behavior.

In the past several chapters we have focused on helping you become more aware of yourself—your head, heart, and body—and take better care of yourself. Starting with the next chapter, we shift the focus from awareness of yourself to awareness of others, which is vital for healthy relationships.

PART FOUR:

IMPROVING YOUR RELATIONSHIPS

CHAPTER 21
LEARNING TO REGARD OTHERS

Being self-aware, able to soothe yourself, and able to manage and care for yourself are all important aspects of staying nonabusive and noncontrolling. They will lower your internal distress, which makes you much less likely to take it out on others. But that isn't enough. Neglect also needs to be addressed.

It is common for people who are abusive to neglect their relationships. Relationship neglect involves being tuned out from the people you care about, failing to take their wants and needs into consideration, not acknowledging how they are different from you, and not being open to their influence.

There's a difference between taking care of yourself and being selfish. Being selfish is taking care of yourself at the expense of others. Unselfish self-care is taking care of yourself while being considerate of others. When you keep other people in mind as you make decisions and consider how they're affected by your choices, you are being what we call **relational**. In this chapter we will identify basic ways to be relational. Before we do that, though, we want to briefly address codependency, which is sometimes confused with being relational.

A NOTE ABOUT CODEPENDENCE
Codependence is a term that originated in the substance abuse field. It describes a condition in which somebody is overly focused on taking care of someone else as a means of avoiding addressing their own issues. The partners of some alcoholics did not appear to want them to get sober;

managing their partner's addiction gave them a sense of purpose and direction. If their partner got sober, they lost that sense of purpose and struggled to address their own issues. So the alcoholic was dependent on the alcohol, and the partner was codependent on the alcoholic being an alcoholic.

While codependency is a real issue, it is easy to mislabel a variety of healthy behaviors as codependent. For example, it is appropriate for parents to prioritize the needs of their juvenile children over themselves, and it common for partners who are being abused to try to pacify and accommodate their partner to reduce the amount of abuse and control inflicted on themselves and their children. This is sometimes mischaracterized as codependency, but it's actually a healthy way to seek safety in the moment. Typically, when the danger of abuse and control stops (either because the relationship ends or the abusive partner stops their behavior for good) those pacifying behaviors fall away.

Being relational is very different from being codependent. While both involve focusing on and taking care of someone else, people who are relational do it while still thinking about and taking care of themselves. Codependent people focus on the other to avoid thinking about and taking care of themselves. If being selfish is practicing self-care without thinking about others, being codependent is being relational without thinking about yourself.

Practicing being relational

Being relational is the ongoing practice of thinking not only of yourself, but of the people you care about most, like your romantic partner and your children. It involves not only checking in with yourself, but checking in with them about their feelings, wants, and needs.

Ironically, some people who struggle to be relational have close relationships with objects: a beloved pair of shoes, a fishing rod, a firearm, a tool—but most commonly a car. If your car is important to you, imagine what would happen if you used it for driving but otherwise ignored it. You never wash it or clean it or check the oil or look under the hood. You never notice when it starts making funny sounds or doesn't run as well. You don't bother to consider when it might need an oil change or notice the tires are getting bare and need to be replaced or rotated. It would be cluttered, dirty, prone to breakdowns, and unlikely to last long. For some people, the idea of neglecting a car is unthinkable! Yet they spend more time caring for their cars than for the people in their lives. It's important to take care of your relationships at least as well as you care for your belongings. You need to devote time, energy, and attention to them, and treat them like they're important to you.

When you pay attention to the ways the people close to you are different from you, you will understand that they are not an extension of you. They are each their own distinct person, and you need to remember that they have minds of their own and distinct thoughts, personalities, wants, and needs. You can be certain that they'll be like you in some ways and different from you in others. It is much easier, of course, when people share your wants and needs. If they like to keep the air-conditioning icy cool like you do, or are hungry when you are, or like the same movies you do, it's easy to acknowledge them simply by pursuing your own wants and needs. It's trickier when they're different from you. If they like to keep the house warm when you like it cool, do you think of them when you set the thermostat? If they're hungry but you're not yet, do you think about eating sooner? If they like different kinds of movies, do you offer suggestions you think they'll like as well?

Listed below are some concrete ways to practice being relational. Our goal is to help you take care of yourself while being thoughtful of others. There are a number of ways to do this, but like anything, it will take time, practice, and repetition to make these changes more enduring and automatic.

CONSIDER OTHERS AS YOU CONSIDER YOURSELF

In the last few chapters, we've advised you to routinely notice how you feel, think, and behave, and to take care of yourself regularly in a variety of ways. Now, we ask you to take that further. Whenever you are with someone else, for each moment you take to check in with and focus on yourself, also take a moment to focus on the other people.

For example, say that after running errands with your family you notice that you're feeling tired. How do you think the others are feeling? You might ask them if they are tired, too. Or say you're outlining your plans and hopes for the weekend. Take a moment to ask the people close to you for their plans, too.

Thinking of others whenever you think of yourself serves several purposes. Most obviously, it can make you less selfish. Second, it helps you be kinder and more considerate. It's hard to take care of or even acknowledge others if you don't think about them. Third, it is a repeated reminder of humility—that you matter, but not any more than anyone else does.

This is sometimes called getting perspective. To what extent do you seek to see the world through the eyes of your loved ones? To what extent do you consider how they might experience the world differently than you? Several of the questions in the Journal address this: How did my abuse or control affect the other person? What did other people want? How did I consider the needs of others? The more you practice thinking along these lines, the easier and more automatic it becomes.

PRACTICE THE PLATINUM RULE

You've probably heard of the Golden Rule, which appears in virtually every religious practice known, but you may not have heard of the Platinum Rule. The Golden Rule is "Do unto others as you would have them do unto you," or "Treat other people the way you want to be treated." It's a good guideline for interacting with strangers because it prioritizes universal needs and pro-social values. It emphasizes our common humanity and is the epitome of common sense. If you're trying to figure out how to behave with someone, considering how you would like to be treated in that situation and acting accordingly is not a bad way to go. You may not always be exactly right, but if you don't know much about them, it's a fine place to start.

The problem with the Golden Rule is that it doesn't acknowledge the ways people are different from each other. As a result, practicing the Golden Rule can be problematic. It's not realistic to know how strangers or near strangers are different from you, but you can certainly learn that about your partner and children. In fact, not seeing how they're different from you can be hurtful and invalidating.

For example, say you love surprise parties. If you want to throw your partner a party, then using the Golden Rule, you should make it a surprise party! That works fine if your partner feels the same way. On the other hand, if they don't—say they prefer small, intimate celebrations—your surprise party could go over really poorly.

Another example might be how you like to be taken care of when you don't feel well. If you like to be left alone when you're sick but your partner likes to be checked on regularly, practicing the Golden Rule would feel like neglect to them. And if they practice the Golden Rule with you when you're sick, you'd probably feel imposed upon and bothered.

This is where the Platinum Rule comes in. While the Golden Rule directs you to treat other people the way you want to be treated, the Platinum Rule directs you to treat other people the way *they* want to be treated. Don't love people the way you want to be loved, love people the way *they* want to be loved. The Platinum Rule reminds you to consider not just what you might want, but also whether the other person might want something different.

Applying the Platinum Rule requires you to take the time and make the effort to consider how the other person might actually want to be treated in a particular situation. It means putting yourself in their shoes, not your own. You have to know them—or get to know them. You may have to ask them questions and then really listen to them and think about them. You'll need to acknowledge, respect, and honor the ways they are different from you.

A second aspect of the Platinum Rule is that you can't expect people to automatically know what is right for you. You need to tell them and educate them. They may be able to figure some of it out on their own, but there may be aspects of you that they don't see or understand very well. When that's the case, it's up to you to fill them in. Do not expect them to read your mind. Likewise, because no one is perfect, at times they may forget how you are different from them or what is most important to you and you may need to patiently remind them.

In his book *The Five Love Languages*, Gary Chapman outlines what amounts to a master plan for the Platinum Rule. He makes the important point that people want to be loved in different ways, then identifies five different ways that people express and understand love: through words of affirmation, quality time, gifts, acts of service, and physical touch. (We would add a sixth, shared experiences, to that list.) For some people, loving words mean a ton, but others don't care much about them. Some people love to be physically nurtured while others can hardly stand it. Chapman emphasizes that you need to figure out your partner's love language as well as your own and keep in mind that they're not necessarily the same. You should then seek to express your love toward your partner in *their* love language.

PRACTICING HUMILITY

Humility acknowledges the limitations of your power. It remembers your smallness in the world, that you are but one of billions. It realizes that you matter, but that you matter no more than anyone else. It acknowledges that although you are the center of your world, you are not the center of anyone else's—including your partner and your children—even if you'd like to think otherwise. Most of all it lets you see yourself as equal to everyone else: neither more nor less. Humility helps you avoid egotism, practice acceptance and grace, and be humble.

STAYING OUT OF EGOTISM

As discussed in Chapter 13: Moving from Disconnection to Connection, egotism is a state of low-grade self-absorption in which people struggle to consider those around them. Humility reminds you of your connection to the people around you and helps you realize that most of your power is over yourself. You have very little legitimate power over other people, places, or situations. Ironically, acknowledging what you are powerless over (which is most things) can help you connect with your true power, which is over yourself. You can't control much of what happens, but you can control how you deal with it. This empowers you to be more effective in the world.

PRACTICING ACCEPTANCE

Accepting the things you cannot change lets you avoid wasting time or energy on them so you can focus on changing yourself. Humility and acceptance reinforce each other. The more you practice one, the easier it is to practice the other. Refusing to accept things you cannot change simply leads to greater frustration and suffering.

PRACTICING GRACE

Practicing grace means treating others with goodwill, generosity, kindness, and consideration even if they aren't treating you that way. It allows others to be imperfect and make mistakes without making them suffer for it, just as utility and insurance companies often allow late payments during a grace period instead of cutting off vital services immediately. Other companies might be within their rights to rigidly refuse late payments, but they are not being gracious. The more you realize that others matter as much as you do, the easier it is to behave in a gracious manner.

BEING HUMBLE

Being humble means seeing yourself as no more important than anyone else. You can still take pride in what you do and see the value in yourself, but in a way that doesn't set you above anyone else. No matter how much money you make or how well known you are, everyone still poops and pees, everyone needs to eat and sleep, everyone will die. You have value and importance, but no more than anyone else.

Humility is not just something you have, it is something you practice. You can practice it multiple times a day when you are reminded of your powerlessness. No matter how much you wish you could part the traffic and drive through, you can't. You need to accept your powerlessness to get where you're going any faster. When things don't go as planned—someone doesn't return your call, you stub your toe, you get caught in the rain—humility is accepting that you don't have control over those things and you can't always anticipate them, either. But you *can* control how you deal with things you can't control.

RESPECTING OTHERS' PRIORITIES AND PERSPECTIVES

One aspect of egotism is believing that the way you see the world is the only way to see it, and that there's a right and a wrong way to do things. From this mindset, perspectives and priorities that are different from yours can look like threats that you need to neutralize. If you believe you know the best route to the store and someone drives a different way, egotism insists on pointing out why your way is better.

Your way may be right for you, but it may not be right for someone else. It's important to remember that your perspective is not necessarily the only one. There are many ways of doing things, many right answers, many legitimate approaches. When people do things differently from you, they are not wrong—they're just different. When you are able to see differences as alternatives instead of challenges, you can learn to coexist with them.

There's no right way to load a dishwasher, clean a garage, manage money, or drive a car. You might load the silverware with the handles down so they get cleaner; your partner might put them with the handles up so they're easier to grab. You might believe it's important to have a lot in savings; your partner might believe extra money is to be enjoyed now. You might like driving fast to get there quicker; your partner might like driving slow because it's safer. In each case, there's no clear right or wrong. Each simply has a different, equally legitimate, priority. You do not have to embrace—or even agree with—that priority, but you do need to acknowledge that it's as legitimate as your own. Once you can do that, you can engage in a true discussion. You might negotiate a consensus or even find a win-win. We will talk further about negotiation and how to resolve problematic differences in Chapter 24: Practicing Conflict-Resolution Skills.

PERSPECTIVE IS EVERYTHING (THE BUSINESS-CARD METAPHOR)

Imagine that someone is facing you and holds up a business card and asks you if it has printing on it. You can clearly see a name, address, and phone number, so you answer yes. But they say no, it's completely blank. You're confused. You insist that you can clearly see printed words and numbers. They insist it's blank. You might wonder if they're messing with you. Maybe they're delusional. It is clear as day to you that the business card is not blank.

Have you figured out what's actually happening yet? The card has printing on one side and is blank on the other. Each of you are both right and wrong: right in affirming your own perspective, and wrong in failing to consider the other's. Even when someone contradicts you, you could both be right, and having very different experiences.

The business-card metaphor can help explain people's very different feelings about having a firearm in the house. The two most common reasons people own firearms are for recreational hunting and for security. People who keep or carry weapons for security can feel safer just knowing they could defend themselves if they had to. That knowledge alone provides comfort and an increased sense of safety.

However, your partner or children may feel very differently. Because of your history of being abusive, controlling, and angry, having a firearm in the home could make them feel *less* safe. They might fear that you'd use it against them—even if you've never even thought about doing so. It doesn't matter what you actually think; their fear can persist because of your history. The same firearms that help you feel safer in your home may make your family feel less safe.

If you truly care about your partner and children's experience, ask them to tell you honestly how they feel about the firearms in the house. If they express any level of fear or concern, you should give serious consideration to removing the weapons from the home out of consideration for your family. After all, shouldn't they be able to feel safe, too?

In a later chapter we will talk about how to sort out differences in perception and opinion by being informational. When someone sees things differently than you, it is far more effective to seek to understand their perspective than to insist on asserting your own. When you thought the business card had printing on both sides and the other person thought it was blank on both sides, you each lacked the other's perspective and literally didn't have the full picture. Only by communicating your perspectives to each other could you get a full picture. You can apply this to almost any situation.

EVEN LOGIC IS BASED ON PRESUMPTIONS

When it comes to subjective things, like whether a movie is good or who sings the best song, there can be many perspectives—many right answers, if you will. But when it comes to objective things—to facts and logic—there often truly is only one right answer. Someone can think 1+1 equals 3 or 5 or 20, but they would be objectively wrong. Everyone knows that 1+1=2.

But some people would argue that 1+1=1 is true most of the time, and that only sometimes is it true that 1+1=2. And every now and then, it can equal 3—though rarely more.

Would you have any idea what they were talking about? Are they bad at math, crazy, or just messing with you?

If you ask what they're talking about, they might clarify that they're describing human conception. Most of the time, two people conceive a single baby, so 1+1=1. Sometimes, people have twins or even triplets, so in those situations 1+1=2 or 3, but most of the time, in that context, 1+1=1 is often right.

The assumption here was that everyone would think about math. The mistake was presuming that your perspective was everyone else's perspective. You presumed that you were talking about math—they weren't. They presumed you were talking about conception, and you were not. Even when you're trying to operate with logic and reason, you are making assumptions that may not be true for everyone involved. If the other person doesn't share your assumptions and priorities, you are much less likely to reach agreement.

Here's another example. Say you're complaining about the "crazy" way your partner drives to their mother's house, which is just a few miles away. You drive there directly, down the main road, but your partner takes a series of zigzagging side streets. Your approach clearly makes the most sense; everyone knows the shortest distance between two points is a straight line. Your partner's way makes no sense! When asked if you have ever asked your partner why they drive that way, your reply is, "Of course! I have repeatedly asked 'Why do you drive that way?!'"

The problem is, that's not a real question. It's a rhetorical one; more of an accusation, really. So, instead, you go back, ask a genuine question, and actually listen to your partner's response. Here are three possible reasons your partner might have for their "crazy" driving—and there could be many more.

Response #1

You and your partner are going to their mother's house for Sunday brunch. Your partner suggests taking separate cars because they have errands to run afterward. You leave at the same time; you take the main road and your partner takes the side roads. You figure you'll get there first, but when you arrive, your partner has already parked and gone inside!

"How did you get here so fast? Did you go like eighty miles an hour?" you say when you get inside.

"No," they reply, "I drove the speed limit. It's just that the main road has a bunch of stoplights and that one intersection takes a while to get through. I took the side streets to avoid the stoplights. Your way may be more direct, but mine is actually faster."

"Oh," you reply, chagrined. It had never occurred to you that the most direct way was not also the fastest way.

Response #2

Your partner asks you how long it takes you to drive to their mother's house.

You say, "Fifteen or twenty minutes, depending on traffic."

Your partner replies, "For me, it could take two or three hours if I drive that way."

"What?" you reply. "I said drive, not walk! What are you talking about?"

"Let me explain," your partner replies. "You know I'm a recovering alcoholic with almost nine months sobriety right now. My favorite places to grab a drink are all on that main road you drive down. If I drive down that road, especially to go see my mother, I am at real risk of pulling over and having a drink or three at one or more of those places. That isn't an issue for you, but it is for me. So I drive the way I do to avoid temptation. You think the way I drive is crazy, but the way you drive would be far more risky for me. I'm actually being sensible driving the way I do."

You are humbled. You've never struggled with addiction, so you never considered the temptation of driving by favorite bars.

Response #3

"Your goal is to get to my mother's house as quick as possible, but my goal is to get there as calm as possible," your partner explains. "Driving your way gets me there too fast. I need the extra time driving through the neighborhoods to stay calm as I prepare myself mentally. It's kind of like a mini time-out."

It had not occurred to you that your partner might have a different priority than you.

***

Even with "logic" and "reason" you make assumptions and presumptions that are perfectly legitimate for you, but not for someone else. It can be easy to dismiss a perspective by deeming it wrong, illogical, or irrational. If someone has another perspective, it's important to be curious about it, seek to truly understand it, and take it seriously, even if you don't share it.

INTENTION VS. PERCEPTION

Another common but mistaken assumption is that when you interact with another person, they experience you just as you intended them to. That, of course, is not always the case. Everyone is occasionally off in what they do—you know what they say about good intentions. When such misunderstandings or misperceptions are brought up, it can be easy to put all the responsibility on the other person and insist that your intentions define the reality of the situation; regardless of how they experienced you, your intentions are what matter. That is not the case, though. The other person's experience of you is just as legitimate as your intentions, even if it wasn't what you intended.

For example, if you give your partner a gift you think they will love, then see that they're only so-so about it because it's not the right brand, it can be easy to focus on the fact that you tried. You might think, "Well, it's the thought that counts" or "Why do they have to be so picky?" But the fact is, your gift wasn't really what your partner wanted. You had good intentions, but ultimately didn't buy the right gift.

Say your partner is struggling with depression and you share your concern with their parents, hoping they'll call and cheer them up. You expect your partner to appreciate your thoughtfulness, but they get angry at you for involving their parents, who are not particularly supportive. You had good, loving intentions, but the fact is that you didn't make the right choice.

Even with the best intentions, you will inevitably be hurtful toward your partner from time to time. What is key is whether you can acknowledge how your behavior affects them, regardless of what your intentions were. The real transgression is not when you unwittingly hurt them, but when you deny or dismiss the fact that they were hurt by your actions. Even unintentional hurt needs to be acknowledged and owned. Can you acknowledge the difference between what you intended and what the other person actually experienced?

The other half of this equation is remembering not to presume you know someone's intentions, either. If your partner or child hurts you, it doesn't mean they intended to. On the contrary, hurt is usually unintentional.

For example, say you're cooking a nice meal and your partner shows up an hour late. It can be tempting to assume that this reflects disrespect, lack of care, and selfishness—in other words, that their hurtful tardiness was intentional. But if you remain open to the possibility that they didn't intend to hurt your feelings, and that they may have simply lost track of time or run an errand that took longer than expected, it could soften your response.

It is common for people with a history of abuse and control to assume their children and partners engage in hurtful and disrespectful behaviors on purpose. They say people are trying to "push their buttons" by doing things they "know" are aggravating or inappropriate, presumably to "get a reaction" or to "get back" at them. In truth, it is rare for people to willfully and intentionally piss others off. They usually have other reasons for doing whatever they're doing. Or they do those things *in spite of* the fact that it pisses you off—not because of it. Talking about "getting your buttons pushed" is often negative self-talk: a distorted and inaccurate interpretation of what's really going on. It mistakenly presumes the other was trying to upset you, which is rarely actually the case.

This is the difference between behaving hurtfully and abusively. Both cause suffering, but abusive behavior is willful and intentional, whereas hurtful behavior is unwitting. It is important to acknowledge that even when hurtful behavior is unintentional, it is still hurtful. You can still say "ouch" and express how and why something hurt you. Just remember that most of the time it wasn't done with the intent to hurt you. Yes, they stepped on your toe, but it was not on purpose.

Remember that intention and impact don't always match up, and one doesn't always define the other. Just because you didn't intend to be hurtful, that doesn't mean you were not. Just because someone else was hurtful does not mean that they intended to be.

CHALLENGING YOUR EGOTISTICAL ASSUMPTIONS

It can be easy to fall into your own little bubble, caught up in how everything relates to you, only thinking of yourself and your struggles. That's workable if you live alone and are not in an intimate relationship. But only being aware of yourself is problematic if you live with others and/or are in an intimate relationship. Below are some mantras that can help you catch and challenge your egotism and increase your ability to tune into others and be relational.

IT IS NOT ALWAYS ABOUT YOU.

Just because you are negatively affected by something someone does, it doesn't mean they were thinking of you when they did it. The impact on you is often incidental. It is rarely intentional. They have their own agenda and their own priorities, which sometimes result in things you don't like, but be careful not to take it personally. It rarely is.

YOU ARE NOT THE ONLY ONE IN THE ROOM.

Your wants and needs are not the only ones that matter. There are people around you who may have different perspectives, priorities, wants, and needs that are equally important. Make sure to take them into consideration as well.

THE WORLD DOES NOT REVOLVE AROUND YOU AND YOUR NEEDS.

Your wants and needs matter, but so do those of others. It is unrealistic, unreasonable, and unfair to always expect everyone around you to prioritize you. At times, the differing wants and needs of others should get to be the priority.

IF YOU WANT THINGS A CERTAIN, EXACT WAY, THEN LIVE ALONE.

If you are going to share space with others, you need to expect that they will do things that don't always please you. The only way you can have your living space exactly as you wish is to live alone. As soon as you add someone else to the picture, their wants and needs and perspectives and opinions matter as well.

BEING MINDFUL OF YOUR POWER AND PRIVILEGE

Privilege refers to the special rights and benefits you get from being a member of a socially dominant group. Dominance is defined by political and economic power; in other words, which group members tend to occupy the dominant political positions in the US and which group members make the most money. You get these benefits whether you want them or not—it's not like you can refuse them. Typically, people with privilege don't realize they have it, but people without it are very aware of the lack. In the US, the dominant groups are males (vs. females, gender queer, or trans), adults—especially adults who can vote (vs. children or older adults), whites (vs. people of color), wealthy (vs. working-class), and heterosexual (vs. LGBTQ), to name a few. Perhaps the most obvious example of privilege in the US is the fact that all of our presidents have (so far) been male, most have been middle-aged, all but one has been white, most have been upper-class, and as far as we know, all have been heterosexual.

Privilege tends to be compounded: each privileged group you belong to adds more power and benefits. For example, two adults might have adult privilege (their issues are taken more seriously because they can vote), but the one who also happens to be a white man gets much more privilege and power than the one who happens to be a woman of color. Being part of an underprivileged group (like working-class) does not remove the privilege you get from being part of other dominant groups (like white, male, and adult).

Most people belong to both privileged and unprivileged groups, but it is important to be as mindful as you can of the privilege that you have and as careful as you can not to take advantage of it. This means being conscientious about how people in the unprivileged groups may struggle in ways that you do not.

ACKNOWLEDGING, INCLUDING, AND CONSULTING WITH YOUR PARTNER
Make sure to solicit your partner's input about decisions that are important to them and to give it equal weight and consideration to your own. As you make decisions about yourself, consider how they will affect your partner and children.

If a camera were to follow you around, it should be obvious when you are in a room with people you care about vs. when you are in a room alone. There should be greetings and welcomes. You should show interest in and respond to the others. As you consider what you need, you should also consider what they might want and need. You should take into account how your decisions will affect them.

Give others your full attention when they share things that are important to them. Do your best to respond with curiosity, interest, reactions, and most of all, emotional acknowledgment.

If you are a parent, you may think being a good parent depends primarily on how you treat your children, but how you treat the other parent is just as important. This is often overlooked and undervalued, but if you take note of how children are verbally abusive to each other, it is often by putting down the other child's parents—especially the parent they are closer to. "Your momma" alone is a put-down, without anything after it. As fathers have gotten more involved in parenting and same-sex couples have children as well, kids have increasingly put down fathers or both parents to hurt each other. The point is that saying bad things about a child's parents hurts the child.

If you are no longer with your children's other parent, it can be easy to have negative feelings toward them. The romantic relationship was clearly unworkable, but no matter how you feel about your ex as a former romantic partner and person, it is vital for your children's well-being that you consistently treat them respectfully. A substantial body of research indicates that what is hardest on children is not their parents divorcing or breaking up, but their parents not getting along. Research has found that children who have either two parents who are happily together or two parents that are happily apart do pretty well. Children whose parents are together but get along poorly and children whose parents are separated and get along poorly suffer significantly across a variety of domains, including mental health and academic achievement.

Part of treating the other parent with respect is fulfilling your financial obligations to them by paying spousal support or child support. Not only do they benefit from that financial support, but so do the children. It's also doing your best to collaborate with them on meeting the children's needs and wants. This requires a certain amount of flexibility around scheduling and a willingness to respond to what the children need in the moment, even if it does not exactly follow the parenting plan. You should be sure to share with the other parent any relevant information about the children that they may not know, including things that happen while the children are with you and things you learn about them.

It is vital that you not talk negatively or disrespectfully about the other parent in front of the children. This requires being aware of when they may be within earshot while you're talking with other people. Obviously, this also means behaving well toward the other parent, especially when the children are present—and preferably even when they are not. You may have all kinds of complaints about the other parent, some of which may be legitimate, but it is important not to expose the children to them. All that does is put them in the middle, where they feel pulled apart by your parental tug-of-war.

This just scratches the surface of this topic. To learn more about all this, especially if you are no longer with the other parent, consider seeking out resources on coparenting with an ex. One resource for fathers who have been abusive (although much of the information is relevant to abusive mothers as well) is *Caring Dads* by Katreena Scott, Tim Kelly, Claire Crooks, and Karen Francis.

***

Part of being relational with those closest to you is understanding how your abuse and control have negatively affected them, and doing what you can to repair the damage you caused. We have already covered common ways people who have been abused suffer in Chapter 11: Understanding the Impact of Your Abuse on Your Partner, and in Chapter 12: Understanding the Impact of Abuse on Children. In the next chapter, we will talk about ways that you can repair the damage you have caused to your loved ones.

CHAPTER 22

LEARNING TO MAKE THINGS RIGHT

The first step in building a better, more solid and loving relationship with your partner is to stop your abuse and patterns of control. The second step is to repair the damage your abuse and control have caused. We discussed earlier how to limit the negative impact of new abusive behavior with accountable acknowledgment, apologies, and repair, but that doesn't address your broader history with your partner. The damage caused by multiple acts of abuse and control over an extended period of time cannot be undone with a single apology or a few acts of repair. This chapter talks about how to facilitate a deeper healing process through amends.

The concept of making amends is widely known because of twelve-step programs, but we have seen many people struggle to understand what it truly looks like. It's more than just an apology and more than just behaving appropriately.

Here's an example that should make it more clear. Imagine you're in your home when you hear a crash. You look out your window and see that a car has just sideswiped your parked car. You run outside to get a better look at the car that did it, and maybe get its license plate number. As you walk outside, the car pulls over and the driver gets out.

"Is that your car?" the driver asks.

"It sure is!" you reply, pretty upset.

"I am so, so sorry," the driver says. "This is completely my fault. I take full responsibility for what happened."

You nod in agreement, glad to hear the apology and the accountability.

"I wasn't paying attention, trying to fiddle with the stereo and the car drifted," they go on. "I want you to know that as of this very moment, I am making a firm commitment to never get distracted like that again so that I never hit another car. That's definitely not okay!"

"Sounds good," you reply.

"Furthermore, I'm going to take a driver's education class to further my skills. I want to make sure I have all the skills I need to assure that nothing like this happens again," they say.

They apologize again, shake your hand, walk back to their car, and drive off.

What is missing from this picture?

Paying for the damage to your car! And if they really want to make things right, they should pay for the rental car you'll need while your car is being repaired, plus the lost wages you'll incur getting all this taken care of. Stopping the behavior, making apologies, taking accountability, and learning how to behave differently are all important parts of the process, but they don't undo the damage. That is amends work: taking care of the damage that has already been done.

Making amends is different from doing immediate repair; it goes beyond acknowledging and apologizing for what happened and seeks deeper healing for the person who was hurt. Amends can be made for a single, specific act of abuse, but it's usually intended to heal the damage from an ongoing pattern of abuse. It is a form of restitution and reparation whose primary goal is to benefit the other. You might benefit from the amends, as well, perhaps by feeling better about yourself, but that is not what's important.

Amends are typically made later in your change process, after most of your abusive behavior has stopped. After all, you don't try to rebuild a house while it's still on fire. You need to put out the fires before you start to rebuild. Repair can be done immediately after you have been abusive, but deeper healing must wait until your patterns of abuse have stopped. Another reason to hold off on amends is that early on, they can become yet another form of abuse and control: to pressure your partner to "get over" the abuse or put it behind them while they're still trying to recover from it.

Making amends always involves behaviors that go above and beyond what is expected of a respectful person. Behaving well, respectfully, and collaboratively does not qualify as making amends. You are expected to behave that way. In other words, anything kind and considerate that you are doing now that you weren't doing before is an improvement, but it doesn't qualify as amends. You need to do more than that—you need to go above and beyond what a respectful person would do. If one of your patterns of abuse was not doing your fair share of the housework, starting to do your fair share of the housework would be a significant improvement, but it would not qualify as making amends because you should have been doing it all along. That is not above and beyond. Doing the majority of the housework for an extended period of time would shift that correction into the realm of amends because it is above and beyond.

Here is another analogy to clarify why amends need to go above and beyond. Say that you fall into a pattern of spending more than you have for a few months, which results in a rising credit card balance that you cannot pay off every month. After a few months of this, you change your spending habits and stop spending more than you have. Although you have corrected your spending pattern, your balance at the end of the first month is still more than you can pay off. The change you made means you're not incurring more debt, but it doesn't magically make your old debt go away. Until the old debt is gone, you'll need to pay more than you spend.

Positive changes are most welcome. It's vital that you behave respectfully in the present, but doing so doesn't magically undo the damage caused by your old behaviors. Making amends does not mean behaving well, but behaving *better* than well. It does not mean doing your fair share, it means doing *more* than your fair share for a time. The longer you behaved abusively, the longer it will take to make up for it.

One way to evaluate whether a positive behavior qualifies as making amends is to ask yourself: "Should I be doing this anyway?" If the answer is yes, then you're not going above and beyond, you're demonstrating normal, respectful behavior.

Here is an example of amends that went above and beyond. One way an abusive partner had been controlling was to always choose the movies they and their partner watched together. This meant the partner watched a number of movies they didn't want to see, and didn't get to watch some of the movies they wanted to. The first change the abusive partner made was to stop their abuse and control over time, which led to many positive changes in the relationship—including deciding with their partner what they both wanted to do. This meant that for the first time, their partner had as much say as they did about which movies they watched together. To make amends, the abusive partner agreed to watch any movie their partner chose, without question or complaint, for a period of time. That allowed the partner to watch a wide variety of movies with them that they had always wanted them to see together. Some were movies the abusive partner would not normally have watched or liked, but they felt appropriately obligated to do so to make up for all the movies they had made their partner watch over time.

Amends are only made to someone who wants them. If someone does not want you to make amends to them, then do not try. Their needs are the only priority, so use the Platinum Rule here: set things right the way they want you to, not the way you want to. When you're thinking about making amends, it's a good idea to run your plan by the other person to make sure it's something they would welcome and find healing. We have seen attempts at making amends that turned out to be hurtful or damaging because the person wanted to surprise someone or didn't adequately consult with them ahead of time.

It is a good idea to present your amends as such, and not just as you being nice or kind. Make it clear that you are acknowledging the unnecessary pain, suffering, and damage you put someone through. That acknowledgment alone can be quite powerful and make your amends even more effective. For example, a man was going through a divorce while attending our program. He made serious and significant changes to his behavior, even though it was too late to save his marriage. Many months after he had stopped his patterns of abuse, he learned that his ex-wife was planning to move. Knowing that his abusive behavior had led to the end of the marriage and to her economic struggles, he offered to help her move. They were no longer close, and she didn't expect—or even ask—him to help, but it meant a lot to her. It was even more powerful when he acknowledged that it was the least he could do, since she wouldn't have been in that position in the first place if he hadn't treated her so poorly for so many years.

TYPES OF AMENDS

There are two types of amends: direct and indirect. Direct amends are made to the people who have suffered from your abusive and controlling behavior. Indirect amends are meant to help people who have suffered from someone else's abuse and control. Indirect amends are necessary because it is sometimes impossible or impractical to make amends to everyone you have been abusive toward. They may not want to be in touch with you; you may be unable to locate them; and you may not even be aware of everyone you have hurt, like strangers or casual acquaintances who witnessed your behaviors. If everyone who has been abusive and controlling made both direct and indirect amends, just about everyone who has been abused would experience some kind of facilitated healing and recovery. Indirect amends are often easier than direct amends, so it's vital that you prioritize direct amends. Listed below are examples of each.

EXAMPLES OF DIRECT AMENDS

LISTENING WITH A THICKENED SKIN

This is a fairly standard amend: listening fully and openly to someone's account of your abuse, even if they get quite emotional. It is normal and reasonable to listen to someone's feelings and struggles. What makes this go above and beyond is a willingness to listen even if it gets intense and takes a long time. In normal circumstances, you might be inclined to shorten the conversation or ask the person to calm down, but when you're making amends, you thicken your skin and take the heat. This can feel like being in the "hot seat" in group, where you are confronted by other members. Despite your unease and discomfort, you must do your very best to stay present: with the conversation and in listening mode. The only reason to limit it is if the other person becomes abusive or you are getting so fatigued or saturated that you are unable to listen well any longer. This amend should be made early on when you are able to truly listen and acknowledge the other person's experience without becoming reactive or defensive.

OFFERING PREEMPTIVE REASSURANCE

Once you've established a pattern of abuse, your family might experience even technically nonabusive behavior as abusive. This can happen when your emotional intensity increases, when things do not go your way, and when situations arise in which you historically became abusive.

To make amends here, be mindful of these situations. When they arise, acknowledge that you're in a situation where people might be concerned that you'll become abusive (maybe you are tired, frustrated, and in heavy traffic, which normally gets you very worked up) and explicitly reassure your family that you are handling it and will not become abusive. This presumes that you are actually managing yourself well internally and are confident you can follow through on your commitment.

People don't usually need to provide this kind of reassurance, so doing this goes above and beyond. Over time, if you consistently handle yourself well, your family will trust you more and there will be less need to do this. But for now, it will help allay their fears and anxiety. We call this **preemptive reassurance**; it is reassurance offered before you become abusive when you know you won't become that way in that situation.

FACILITATING PROFESSIONAL ASSISTANCE

This involves actively helping the people you have abused get professional help. They might meet with an individual therapist, join a survivors support group, get health care, or access other services (body work, education) that help their healing and recovery. One way to support them is to pay for those services with your own money—not with shared family money. You could do everything possible to either provide or pay for childcare during those times, again with your own money. You might provide transportation and anything else they need to consistently and reliably access help.

REPLACING DAMAGED ITEMS OR EXPERIENCES

If you damaged something you can replace, replace it. If you ruined an experience you can recreate, recreate it.

For example: An abusive parent ruined their child's seventh birthday party by acting out. They made it up to their child by giving them another seventh birthday celebration nine months later; it went very well. In another example, an abusive partner with a history of acting out on family vacations used their own personal savings to pay for a second family vacation on which they behaved well.

WRITING LETTERS OF ACCOUNTABILITY

Another common and widely supported amends is to write letters to the people who have been affected by your abuse.

These letters should draw on material that you will generate while working on your Accountability Statement, which we explain in the last chapter of the book. The Accountability Statement exercise is purely for you; it can help solidify your resolve and reduce your shame about past bad behavior. After you do the exercise, though, you can use the material in letters to specific people. In those letters you should acknowledge your abuse and control, how you suspect they suffered from it, and the excuses you made for it. Take full responsibility for what you have done. Share how you feel about it now, and how you have changed the way you think and behave so you won't do it in the future. You should only give a Letter of Accountability to people who have made it clear that they would definitely like one. Receiving one can be retraumatizing for some people, especially if they are no longer in contact with you.

Letters of accountability will be explained in more detail in Chapter 27: Sustaining Your Changes.

OFFERING ENHANCED APOLOGIES

Regular apologies don't qualify as making amends; they're expected of you, and are a given part of doing quick repair. However, a more elaborate or enhanced apology might qualify.

For example, someone verbally abused their partner in front of the partner's coworkers. After getting the partner's okay, they showed up at the partner's workplace and apologized to them in front of their coworkers, taking full responsibility. The public apology was much more effective than a private one would have been; it made it clear who was truly responsible for the incident.

An example of an enhanced apology comes from someone in our group. They had spoken very negatively and critically about their partner to their friends, which is fairly common. With their partner's permission, they sent a written acknowledgment to their circle of friends of how they had misrepresented and falsely vilified their partner over the years. They took full responsibility for their abusive and controlling behavior with them, which was a major contributor to their partner's seemingly irrational behavior.

Another extended apology was made by a person in our group who became verbally abusive when a cashier at a fast-food restaurant got their order wrong. The person stormed off, starting the mile-long walk home. As they arrived home twenty minutes later, they had settled enough to admit to themselves that they had behaved abusively toward the cashier. They turned around and walked back to the restaurant, found the worker, and made a full, accountable apology to them. They could easily have never returned, but the extra effort gave their apology extra weight and significance, which was not lost on the cashier. It affirmed the cashier's right to be treated with respect, even by angry customers.

There are many different ways to repair the damage caused by your past abuse. Take some time to give real thought and consideration to how you can make amends. It is absolutely okay—and often necessary—to talk directly with the victim of your abuse about what you can and need to do to make things right. The first step, of course, should be never doing the behavior again, but that alone cannot make things right.

EXAMPLES OF INDIRECT AMENDS

DONATING TO DOMESTIC VIOLENCE SERVICES
One of the most direct ways of helping those who have been abused is to support the services that work with them, many of which are nonprofits. Your support could be financial, via donations of cash or needed items. You might be able to volunteer, although it is important to consider how they would feel having an abusive partner volunteering for them. Any donations you make should come out of your own money unless your partner fully supports it.

SHARING YOUR STORY

Some abusive partners have been willing to share their story through the media or at events, talking honestly and accountably about their abusive past. This is a way to dispel myths and stereotypes about abusive partners, and can encourage others who are struggling with abusive behavior to get help. These public testimonials can be validating for abused partners whose experiences are finally being confirmed. This should only be done after first consulting with and getting the full support of the abused partner. Some would not want this done because it would out them as a survivor of abuse, which they may not want others to know.

REACHING OUT TO ABUSIVE AND ABUSED PARTNERS

Reaching out to people who are struggling with either side of this issue has to be done carefully, because any intervention can increase the risk and severity of the abuse. However, as someone who has struggled with the issue and made real changes, you are in a unique position. Abusive partners sometimes seek services after someone who has been in a program reaches out to them, shares information, and encourages them to get help.

INDIRECT AMENDS MUST BE FOCUSED ON DOMESTIC VIOLENCE

There are many things you can do that are good turns but are not making amends. Examples include donating to nonprofits that aren't involved in domestic violence, helping a homeless person, volunteering at a community center, sponsoring someone at AA, and countless other acts of kindness. Indirect amends have to be related to domestic violence.

UNDERSTANDING YOUR ABUSED PARTNER'S RECOVERY PROCESS

As you begin to make positive changes and interact with your partner, you may find some of their behaviors and reactions unexpected, confusing, or troubling. This is part of the healing process. It's a little different for everyone, but there are some common factors.

First, know that it is common to underestimate your partner's hurt and how long it will take to recover. While some abused partners may never fully recover from being abused and controlled, many can, if they're not subjected to it anymore. This healing and recovery process is typically measured in months and years. The first and most important step in supporting your partner's recovery process is to remain nonabusive and noncontrolling. If you don't, it is highly unlikely that your relationship can even begin to heal.

Below we examine the most frequent questions abusive partners have about their partners' responses and how to support and understand their recovery process.

"I'VE STOPPED BEING ABUSIVE, BUT MY PARTNER DOESN'T SEEM TO BE ABLE TO GET OVER IT. HOW MUCH LONGER IS THIS GOING TO GO ON?"

The recovery process does not end when the abuse and control stop. It's just beginning.

This is one of the first true tests of your changed behavior. Can you remain nonabusive and noncontrolling when things are not going your way? Some people assume that as soon as they stop being abusive and apologize for their past behavior, their partner will be ready to move on. But depending on how extensive the abuse was and how long it went on, it may take months or years for your partner to truly recover, if they ever can. Your partner's reaction to your most recent abuse is the tip of the iceberg; they have feelings that date back to when the abuse first started. In the meantime, they may display anxiety, mistrust, emotional distance, sexual disinterest, and other symptoms of their trauma. While this may be frustrating for you, it is a natural consequence of the abuse and control that your partner has suffered through. The recovery process cannot be accelerated, only honored and respected.

What you can do to help

Have patience. Respect and support their recovery process. Listen to their feelings and concerns without being defensive. Acknowledge them without justifying, rationalizing, or explaining your behaviors.

"MY PARTNER IS ACTING REALLY DIFFERENTLY THESE DAYS. THEY SEEM TO BE CHANGING INTO SOMEONE I HARDLY KNOW. WHAT'S GOING ON?"

One of the primary goals of recovery is for your abused partner to reclaim their sense of self. As the target of abusive and controlling behavior, your partner's actions and thoughts were often determined (or at least strongly influenced) by you. They gave in to you when they didn't want to, to satisfy you and avoid being the target of further abuse and control. As a result, many abused partners lose some of their sense of self—their awareness of what they want, what their own interests and desires are, and what they know. Perhaps the most important aspect of their recovery is to recover that. This may include trying out new activities, new behaviors, and new styles of interaction, or going back to old ones that you previously blocked. It also means being able to express these differences without fear of reprisal from you. It should be expected that they will not act exactly like they used to, but will gradually evolve into their own distinct person.

What you can do to help

Respect their space and process. Support their right to explore who they really are. Resist the temptation to interfere with their process of self-exploration by telling them what to do or what is "right." Remember that they are distinct from you and will have different feelings, interests, and needs than you at times. Do not take their changes personally.

"EVER SINCE I BECAME NONABUSIVE, MY PARTNER IS PUSHING MY BUTTONS. THEY'RE DOING THINGS THEY KNOW I DON'T LIKE. ARE THEY TRYING TO MAKE ME LOSE MY TEMPER?"

Part of honoring themselves involves doing the things they have always wanted to but haven't out of fear of reprisal. It may seem like they are trying to push your buttons, but this is rarely the case. They are simply trying to be the person they have always wanted to be.

As the abuse stops, they may return to behaviors they always valued but that you disapproved of. It is only natural for them to explore "unacceptable" behaviors that have always been important to them. It is not about provoking you, but being true to themselves.

What you can do to help

Respect those differences and their right to have their own feelings, opinions, and interests, including ones you do not share or approve of. You don't have to like those things, but you do need to respect their right to them. Learn to tolerate your discomfort. Make it clear, through your behavior, that there will be no reprisal. Be especially alert to slipping back into old patterns of control when your stress level is high. If the changes are truly unacceptable to you, pursue respectful conversation and negotiation.

"NOW THAT I AM LESS ANGRY, THEY SEEM ANGRIER. I'VE NEVER SEEN THEM SO UPSET, BUT I AM TREATING THEM BETTER THAN I EVER HAVE. WHAT'S GOING ON?"

Abused partners' anger tends to increase as they break through their denial and it becomes safer to express their feelings. They are often unaware of the seriousness and impact of the abuse, in part because of your denial about it. As you become more honest and accountable, they may honestly consider the full implications of your behavior for the first time.

Also, many partners do not feel safe sharing how they really feel while the abuse was going on. They tend to stuff their feelings and keep them private, so you may have little idea of how they suffered. As you make changes that they believe are permanent and genuine, they may begin to feel safe enough to feel and express those long-repressed feelings. Chief among these may be anger, but any feelings that were previously unacceptable may also surface. Until they express those feelings, your relationship cannot truly prosper, so their more honest expression of their feelings can be seen as a positive sign.

What you can do to help

Listen to and validate their feelings without becoming defensive. If they become abusive, set boundaries between abusive behavior and language and nonabusive expressions of anger. Take time-outs, if needed, to avoid overreacting or trying to control their feelings. Listening to their intense emotions with a thickened skin can be considered amends work.

"MY PARTNER CONTINUALLY BRINGS UP THE PAST THESE DAYS. IT SEEMS LIKE THEY NEED TO RECALL AND CONFRONT ME ON EVERY TIME I'VE BEEN OUT OF LINE IN OUR ENTIRE RELATIONSHIP. THEY KEEP BRINGING UP CERTAIN SITUATIONS OVER AND OVER AGAIN. WHEN WILL THEY GET OVER IT AND LET THE PAST BE THE PAST?"

Abused partners may need to talk—repeatedly—about situations they previously kept to themselves because they were afraid of your reactions. As they start to feel genuinely safe, they may finally be able to talk about things they have wanted to talk about for a long time. Until they work through those "old" feelings, it will be hard for them to truly let go of the past.

They need you to validate their experiences of abusive situations that you dismissed in the past. They may need to revisit memories multiple times until they feel like you truly understand and acknowledge their experiences. They may also have to bring up the same event multiple times if it is repeatedly triggered by things happening in the present. Although the event may be in the past, the injury is still in the present.

What you can do to help

Thicken your skin so you can listen to feelings and issues that may be difficult to hear. Listen without being defensive. Focus on their experience, not your justification. Acknowledge their feelings. Ask questions so you can better understand their experience. Remember your own experiences as a victim of abuse in other relationships, particularly as a child. Ask them what else you can do to help them work through it.

"MY PARTNER HAS BEEN GIVING ME MIXED MESSAGES. ONE DAY THEY LOVE ME, THE NEXT THEY HATE ME. THE NEXT DAY THEY TALK ABOUT HOW MUCH BETTER THINGS ARE, TWO DAYS LATER THEY'RE TALKING ABOUT DIVORCE. I FEEL LIKE AN EMOTIONAL YO-YO. WHY CAN'T THEY MAKE UP THEIR MIND?"

Abused partners give mixed messages because they have mixed feelings. This may feel like manipulation or even abuse, but it reflects the very real ambivalence they are feeling. They may feel more loving and hopeful when they recall the good things: your sense of humor, how romantic you can be, your ability to solve difficult problems. On the other hand, they may feel angry and pessimistic when they recall the abusive and controlling behavior you have demonstrated. Their mixed feelings can also reflect fluctuations in their hopes that you can make real changes. Their hopes may rise when they see you catch yourself before becoming abusive, but fall when you have a setback or slip-up. Finally, your partner's mixed messages may be a response to the mixed messages you're giving them: being distant and aloof at some points, but warmer and more loving at others.

It may be months or longer before they can sort out their feelings and decide whether to remain in the relationship. Even then, they may change their mind as new developments or information come to light. You are unlikely to change your behavior and thinking immediately. Sorting out whether to stay is a difficult and complicated decision for many partners.

What you can do to help
Be patient. Realize how difficult and complex the situation is. Give them the space they need. Do not take it personally. Focus on your own self-care so you are not so emotionally dependent upon your partner. Work your own program of staying nonabusive and noncontrolling.

"IT'S BEEN MONTHS SINCE I WAS ABUSIVE, YET THEY ACT AS IF NOTHING HAS CHANGED. WHEN WILL THEY ACKNOWLEDGE THE WAYS I'VE CHANGED FOR THE BETTER?"
There is a delay between the moment a person stops being abusive and the moment their partner trusts that they've changed. One reason is that there have probably been periods that were relatively free of abuse in the past. From your partner's perspective, this could just be another "break." Even during times when there was no overt abuse, your controlling behaviors may have been present. Your partner may be hesitant to believe that any true changes have taken place.

Another reason for the delay could be that you have broken your promises to change in the past. They may be taking a "wait and see" approach before they're convinced, and any abusive or controlling incidents at this point will reinforce their skepticism. It may be months before they begin to believe the changes are real and permanent.

Some abused partners will not be confident that you have truly changed until all external pressures like probation and separation have been removed. If you remain nonabusive and noncontrolling after that, they may finally begin to believe that your changes are genuine and will last.

What you can do to help

Be patient. Look to yourself and your support system for acknowledgment and reinforcement of your positive changes rather than to your partner. Remember that your actions speak louder than words. Remember it takes time to rebuild the trust that you have lost.

"EVEN WHEN I'M NOT BEING ABUSIVE WHEN I'M ANGRY, THEY REACT LIKE I AM. ISN'T IT OKAY FOR ME TO SHOW ANGER APPROPRIATELY?"

Partners who have been abused are very tuned-in to the progression of abusive behavior, particularly the early warning signs, which were often nonabusive indications of escalating anger—a firmness in the voice, a more intense look. Even now, those behaviors may trigger memories of past trauma and a realistic fear of impending abuse, so do your best to not exhibit them. Keep in mind the Bully Effect that we described in Chapter 11: Understanding the Impact of Abuse on Your Partner.

What you can do to help

Try to share the primary feelings—anxiety, hurt—behind your anger. Talk with your partner about ways you can show your anger that don't feel threatening to them. When you are becoming escalated, preemptively reassure them that you will not become abusive and that you are not angry with them. Accept that there may not be much latitude for you to express anger because of your history of abuse.

"NOW THAT I'M NONABUSIVE I REALIZE THAT WE NEED TO SHARE THINGS EVENLY IN THE RELATIONSHIP. SO HALF THE TIME WE SHOULD FOCUS ON ME AND HALF THE TIME WE SHOULD FOCUS ON THEM, RIGHT?"

Early in the recovery process, the abused partner needs and deserves more than half the time, attention, and focus. Whether you knew it or not, you and your behavior received the majority of the attention and focus while you were being abusive and controlling. Even when you were not around, your family may have been thinking about your abusive actions. Their thoughts, feelings, and needs were ignored, neglected, or diminished. Therefore, a fair division of time early in recovery is not fifty-fifty. Your family deserves more of the time and energy as compensation and to process and recover from your abusive behavior. None of that time and energy should count toward their "half." That debt is yours to pay with increased energy and attention.

What you can do to help

Be ready to put your family first throughout their recovery process. Rely on yourself and your support network, not your partner. This is part of making amends to make things truly right again. Do not expect your partner to fully step into giving you the same amount of energy and attention until they are through most of their recovery process.

"I'M WORKING HARD, USING THE TOOLS I'VE LEARNED TO STAY NONABUSIVE, BUT THEY'RE NOT USING THE TOOLS THEMSELVES. SHOULDN'T THEY BE LEARNING AND USING THE SAME SKILLS I AM LEARNING?"

The things you are learning in this book and learning in your group (if you are attending one) are for you and you alone.

It is not unusual for you to want to share the tools, concepts, and definitions you are learning with others. This can be especially tempting when your partner behaves imperfectly, but no one else in your family is reading this book or attending a group. This is not their program—it's yours. It's not realistic to expect that if one person is taking a class, everyone in the family should study for it. Accusing your partner of not working the program or requiring that they use the tools is controlling. Your partner may have their own issues to work on, but it's their responsibility to get help, not yours to tell them what to do.

What you can do to help

Stay focused on yourself and work your program. Answer your partner's questions about your program and the skills you are using without telling them to use them. Support them in seeking counseling or a support group if they so choose.

"I HAVEN'T BEEN ABUSIVE FOR MONTHS, BUT THEY SAY LITTLE HAS CHANGED. WHAT GIVES?"

For many abused partners, the relationship feels the same until the underlying beliefs have shifted and the more subtle, smaller abusive and controlling behaviors have stopped. The key goal is to change the underlying beliefs that drive your controlling and abusive behaviors.

It is not unusual for people to replace verbal and physical abuse with more subtle behaviors that aren't as extreme but can still be very oppressive. Your changed behavior will not feel believable to your partner until your beliefs change. Only then can the relationship start to feel healthier and safer.

Making profound changes to your beliefs and behaviors is a very challenging step that may require months or even years of work. You did not get this way overnight, and you're not going to be able to change overnight.

Even once you have made that shift, your partner may be hesitant to trust it or believe it. There may be a significant period of time where they are waiting for the other shoe to drop. Only after you have behaved differently for an extended period of time may they come to trust or believe it.

What you can do to help

Become aware of your subtle forms of abuse and control as well as the beliefs that support them. Listen to and accept your partner's experience of your behavior. Conscientiously work at becoming noncontrolling. Shift your underlying beliefs. Check in with your partner to find out what their experience of you is.

Although your partner's early responses can be challenging, they are likely to settle and shift over time. Be patient and remember that if you stay consistently respectful, there is a good chance they can heal, recover, and ultimately come to trust the better partner you have become.

***

Another key aspect of being relational is learning how to work effectively with your partner. Two core skills are key here: communication and conflict resolution. We will focus on each of these in the next two chapters.

CHAPTER 23

LEARNING TO COMMUNICATE EFFECTIVELY

You are continually interacting with other people. While others may think similarly to you, at times their thoughts, perspectives, priorities, feelings, and experiences will be quite different from your own. Because you are not telepathic, you do not automatically know what they are thinking, especially when they are having different thoughts, feelings, wants, or needs than you. Likewise, they may not know what is going on with you unless you talk with them.

Communication is the means of understanding what is going on with someone else and letting others know what's going on with you. It uses words, gestures, and facial expressions to convey to others what you think, feel, need, or want. It also involves listening—not only with your ears, but with your eyes and heart—to what other people think, feel, need, or want. The essence of good communication involves listening. If you understand what is going on with the other person, you will be much more able to express yourself in a way they can understand.

The goal of effective communication is to work with people in a cooperative, collaborative manner. Don't approach it like a formal debate where the goal is to win the argument by proving the other person wrong. Instead, approach it as a dialogue in which the goal is mutual understanding and support.

Although you communicate with many different people—coworkers, neighbors, friends, strangers—your immediate family is probably the most challenging and the most important. Because those relationships are so important and you spend a lot of time together, it is vital to do your best with them.

Outlined below are a number of practical communication skills and tools that can help you understand other people better and help them better understand you. Keep in mind that these are for you—don't get too focused on your partner's communication shortcomings. No one is perfect. Lead by example, not with criticism.

TECHNIQUES FOR EFFECTIVE COMMUNICATION

USING "I" MESSAGES

You are the expert when it comes to what you think, feel, want, and need. Using "I" messages like "I feel," "I think," and "In my opinion" keeps your focus on yourself. The more you focus on the other person by making "you" statements, the more likely you are to get it wrong, to make them defensive, and to get distracted from the important part of your communication: yourself. Remember that "I" statements reflect an internal focus (which is what you are striving for) whereas "you" statements reflect an external focus.

"You" statement: "You were thoughtless and inconsiderate to show up so late."

"I" statement: "I feel disappointed when you show up half an hour later than I was expecting."

FOCUSING ON HOW YOU FEEL

The most important information you can share about yourself is your emotional experience. What matters most is not what happens to you, but how you feel about what happens to you. The same event can affect different people quite differently, and until you talk about your emotions, others will not necessarily know what is going on inside you, even if they know about the event. While your tone of voice can convey how you feel, using words can make it much clearer.

When you talk about emotions, use feeling words rather than thoughts, opinions, or beliefs. Most emotions are described with a single word, but thoughts tend to require multiple words. A test for whether you're talking about an emotion or a thought is to change "feel" to "think" and see if it still makes grammatical sense. If it does, it's probably a thought, not an emotion. For example, "I feel that's a bad idea" still makes sense as "I think that's a bad idea," so it's actually a thought. On the other hand, "I feel sad and hurt" does not make sense as "I think sad and hurt"; those are emotions, not thoughts.

Thought: "I wish you would have let me know sooner that you were going out with friends tonight."

Feeling: "I feel hurt, sad, and disappointed when I think we get to spend an evening together without the children around only to learn a couple hours before that you are going out with friends instead."

Be careful not to use blaming words ("judged," "dismissed," "controlled") instead of emotions. They may seem like emotions, but they are actually accusations. A good way to tell them apart is to substitute "you [emotion] me" for "I feel." If it still makes sense, it might be a blaming word.

Blaming: "I felt disrespected and rejected when you spent so much time at the cookout with your family rather than with me."

Feeling: "I felt sad, disappointed, and hurt when you spent so much time at the cookout with your family rather than with me."

BEING SPECIFIC

Being specific leaves less room for misinterpretation and misunderstanding. If you need to make a general statement, provide specific examples.

General: "Today was very frustrating."

Specific: "I was frustrated today at how poorly the kids listened."

MAKING COMPLAINTS, NOT CRITICISMS

This draws on John Gottman's research into what differentiates successful romantic relationships from unsuccessful ones. Criticisms are general, evaluative statements about another person: "lazy," "completely unsupportive," "uncaring." They are not particularly informative or helpful, and they are common in unhappy relationships. It is hard to respond to—or even fully understand—criticisms because they are so general.

Complaints, on the other hand, identify specific behaviors so they can be discussed and addressed: "left dirty dishes on the table," "did not come with me to the hospital," "did not ask me about my day."

Criticism: "You sat around all day and didn't lift a finger."

Complaint: "I wish you would have helped me manage the kids more today, especially since the baby had a fever."

FOCUSING ON THE BEHAVIOR, NOT THE PERSON

We generally have issues with behaviors, not with people. If you focus on the specific behavior, the person who does it is less likely to get defensive and more likely to listen to you. Try to separate the issue from the person. Think of it as looking at the issue side by side rather than focusing on the person nose-to-nose. It is much easier to look at the behavior together.

Person: "You were so disrespectful."

Behavior: "Swearing at me was so disrespectful."

BEING TACTFUL BUT DIRECT

While at times it may be best to ease into a sensitive issue, sooner or later you will need to clearly state what you are trying to convey. Being indirect and hoping the other person will eventually catch on can lead to confusion and misunderstanding. Maybe they will understand what you are suggesting, but maybe they won't.

Indirect: "I did get kind of wet, and that wind was blowing kind of hard, but you know, it's good to get that fresh air, and I didn't really have to wait too long."

Direct: "Next time I would like to meet inside in case the weather is bad."

CHOOSING YOUR WORDS CAREFULLY

The more important and emotional the topic, the more important it is that you think before speaking. Sometimes there's a fine line between inviting a negative, defensive reaction and inviting someone to consider your point. Avoid words that are hurtful or judgmental. Try to keep your language as neutral as possible. If you are giving someone critical feedback, make it clear that although you have a concern, you still care about them as a person. Research has found that people in successful relationships listen better when they are eased into difficult conversations. John Gottman calls this a "softened start-up."

Thoughtless: "You're acting like your mother again."

Thoughtful: "In general, I've been feeling really good about how this weekend has been going, but there is one concern that I would like to share with you about how many critical statements you made about me."

PUTTING IT AS SIMPLY AS POSSIBLE

If you wish to make a point, make it as clear and simple as possible. The more you make the point in the midst of a much longer speech and conversation, the greater the risk it will be overlooked or not understood. If you are trying to make a point, get to it as quickly as you can.

Rambling: "I was busy going through papers on the desk and also trying to balance the checkbook. I was trying to get it done before dinner and I knew that afterward we had to go shopping. As I was going through the papers and looking for the checkbook, I found an unopened bill from a couple weeks ago. So I think we need to find a new place to put bills when they arrive in the mail"

Simple: "I found an unopened bill from two weeks ago in the middle of a pile of papers. I think we need to find a special place to put bills."

AVOIDING NEGATIVE LANGUAGE

Words like "always," "never," and other absolutes indicate overstatements. If you must use them, make it clear that you are stating a feeling, not a fact—how it feels to you, not what actually happened.

Likewise, watch out for making assumptions. The more you focus on concrete information, the more likely you will be understood. Phrases like "in my opinion," "in my experience," "from my perspective," or "it feels like" make it easier for other people to hear you.

Negative: "You are never on time."

Accurate: "I noticed that you seem to run about ten or fifteen minutes late about half the time, which is stressful for me."

DISCUSSING ONE ISSUE AT A TIME

Try to bring up one thing at a time. When you've identified the issue, stay focused until it has been resolved. Try to avoid bringing up other issues, even if they are equally important. Repeatedly changing the subject can distract you from the original issue and delay a resolution.

Multiple issues: "I need your input on who can babysit. You know the kids have been a handful lately. Have you seen the state of John's room? It really needs to be cleaned. We also need to figure out when to have that talk with the kids."

Single issue: "I have a few concerns about the kids. First, what thoughts do you have about who we could get to babysit them Saturday afternoon?"

IDENTIFYING WHAT YOU WANT FROM THE CONVERSATION

Different conversations have different goals. Do you mainly want the other to listen to you? Do you want suggestions? To make a specific change? To negotiate a solution? Because there are many different ways a person can respond to what you share, there's a risk that they won't respond how you hoped they would. You might need your feelings acknowledged, but they might jump to problem-solving. You might want to negotiate an agreement, but they think you simply need to be validated. If you're clear about what you want going in, letting the other know how you would like them to respond will increase the chances of getting what you want.

Unclear goals: "So what do you think?"

"What's your response?"

Clear goals: "What I most need from you right now is to just let me talk for a while about what is going on with me. I don't need any advice or solutions, just understanding."

"I'm hoping we can figure out a solution here that works for both of us."

COMMUNICATING IN A TIMELY WAY

Communication about emotions, issues, and concerns should be a regular, ongoing process, not something saved for special occasions. Repeatedly putting off conversations leaves your concern or issue unaddressed and makes it less likely that anything will change. As explained in Chapter 16: Becoming Aware of Your Emotions, verbally processing emotions can make them more manageable, but if you put it off too long, it's less effective. As things come up for you, try to talk about them as soon as you can, rather than saving them up. The more important it is and the more intense you feel, the sooner you should talk about it—except as mentioned below.

Delayed: "I can't believe how much you interrupted me in front of my parents last Thanksgiving."

Timely: "It really bothered me how much you interrupted me last night while I was trying to talk about work with my parents."

FINDING AN APPROPRIATE TIME FOR IMPORTANT CONVERSATIONS
The more important the conversation, the more important it is to schedule it for an appropriate time. Make sure to allow enough time, privacy, and energy for a conversation with few or no distractions. If you feel too intense, wait until you are more emotionally grounded.

Inappropriate time: "I don't care if it's almost midnight and you're tired. We're talking about this now!"

Appropriate time: "I really want to talk about this, but I know it's late and you're tired. When would be a better time to have this conversation?"

STAYING CALM
Although there is nothing wrong with becoming emotional as you speak, getting too escalated can interfere with what you are trying to say. A high amount of physical agitation, even if you are staying nonabusive, is likely to make it harder for the other person to focus on what you are saying. If you are struggling to manage yourself or the other appears to be getting distressed by your intensity, consider taking a time-out.

Too intense: "I don't care if I'm talking too loudly, this is important. Do you understand me?!"

Appropriate intensity: "While this is very upsetting to me, I promise not to lose my cool."

CHECKING FOR UNDERSTANDING
Don't assume the other person understands what you've said or how you feel about what you said. If you're not sure, ask them to summarize what you have been saying, then clarify as needed.

No check for understanding: "*So that about covers it. What's up with you?*"

Check for understanding: "*Does that make sense? What do you think about what I've been saying?*"

FINDING ANOTHER WAY TO SAY IT

If someone doesn't understand what you are saying, it can be tempting to simply repeat yourself. But if they still don't understand, try to make your point a different way. Sometimes stating something a little differently leads to much better understanding.

Repeating yourself: "*How many times do I have to say it? Move the car!*"

Clarifying: "*Could you please move the car all the way out of the driveway and onto the street?*"

USING YOUR EYES, VOICE, AND BODY

The way you carry yourself conveys at least as much as your spoken words. The more important your message, the more important this is. Strive to make regular eye contact; looking away conveys that what you are saying is not important. Use a firm, clear tone; an overly quiet or loud voice can distract from what you are saying. Try to speak with people at eye level; stand if they are standing, sit if they are sitting, kneel to speak with a child.

Ineffective body language: *Speaking softly, looking at the floor.*

Effective body language: *Speaking in a clear voice and making eye contact.*

AVOIDING COMPARISONS

It can be tempting to make your point by comparing the person you are talking with to someone else, but that can leave them feeling like they don't measure up. Do your best to make your points by focusing on the specific concerns you have with them. It doesn't really matter how they compare with someone else. The point is that you have a concern about them.

Making a comparison: "*Your sister does a much better job of keeping her room clean than you do.*"

Focusing on the person: "*Your room needs to be cleaned better than this.*"

STAYING WITH THE CONVERSATION UNTIL IT IS RESOLVED, IF POSSIBLE

Unresolved issues can leave both people feeling unsettled and lead to further conflict later. Do your best to stay with the conversation at least until you have each been able to fully express yourselves. Resolution of a difficult conversation often leaves both people feeling much better. Try not to leave off in the middle of it, if possible. If things cannot be resolved in a single conversation, make it clear that you are willing to continue the conversation at a later time.

Leaving prematurely: "I completely disagree, but I need to go do some work in the yard."

Staying with the conversation: "I want to share my concerns and hear what you think, so I'll get to the yard later. But I definitely need to be done by two o'clock."

BEING WILLING TO TAKE BREAKS

Sometimes resolution cannot be found in a single conversation. Some difficult conversations may require two, three, or more sessions . It may take longer than you have right now. One or both of you may be getting tired, hungry, distracted, or too intense. Other things may require your attention. You might feel a bit stuck. Rather than sticking with a conversation when you are not up to it, you can agree to pause it until another time. Stepping away for a few hours or a day or more can lead to new perspectives and ideas that lead to agreement—but it is vital that you follow up.

Sticking with it: "We are not leaving this house until we resolve this."

Taking a break: "It doesn't feel like we're getting anywhere with this right now. How about we just have dinner, watch a movie, and revisit this tomorrow afternoon."

TECHNIQUES FOR BETTER UNDERSTANDING

Good communication is not just about what you say, but about how you listen. Listening well is key to understanding other people, and it helps other people understand you, too. When you can speak about yourself in someone else's language, they will understand you better. Stephen Covey makes this point in his bestselling book *Seven Habits of Highly Effective*

People when he writes "seek first to understand, then to be understood."
Listed below are specific tools to help you to best understand others.

FINDING OUT HOW THEY WANT YOU TO LISTEN

At different times, people need you to listen in different ways. They may
want you to validate their feelings, offer solutions, receive criticism about
yourself, negotiate an agreement, or offer general support. Each of these
can look quite different, so it is important to ask what they're looking for
and to respond accordingly.

GIVING THEM YOUR FULL ATTENTION

It can be tempting to multitask while someone is speaking. You may be
able to get away with doing a chore or task that doesn't require much
concentration if the conversation is light. However, the more important
the conversation is to the other person, the more important it is that you
give them your full attention. This means not multitasking, turning toward
them so you can see their face, and not getting distracted by your own
internal thoughts (or your phone). The more fully you give the other
person your attention, the more likely you are to understand what they are
trying to convey.

BEING CURIOUS AND ACTIVELY ENGAGED

Another temptation is to passively listen without being fully engaged. If
you're not thinking hard enough about what they are saying that you can
ask questions or offer thoughts, you're not really trying to understand
them. Ask questions, seek clarity, and be genuinely curious about what
they have to say.

BEING OPEN AND NONJUDGMENTAL

It can be easy to jump to conclusions when someone is talking, to make
assumptions about what they are saying. Be careful to check with them to
make sure you're on track. Let them speak their mind instead of mentally
cutting them off—or even worse, actually cutting them off. Stay open to
what they are trying to convey, even if you don't agree with or believe it.

LOOKING FOR THE COMMON THEME

Sometimes it seems like people are bringing up a laundry list of issues, jumping from one topic to the next. But if you listen closely, you can usually find a common theme, which is the real point. Be careful not to miss the forest for the trees. If the other person seems to be talking about a variety of different issues (individual trees), look for what they have in common (the forest).

LISTENING ACTIVELY

Active listening is listening to what the person says, then summarizing or reflecting back what you heard to make sure you understood it. If you don't have it right, the other person can clarify what they were trying to say.

Active listening is fine when you are not in an argument, but it is much more difficult when you disagree or feel strongly about the topic. In those cases, focused listening can be more effective. We will review that in the next chapter on disagreements and conflict.

TAKING THE OTHER PERSON'S PERSPECTIVE

When you listen well, you try to see the world through the other person's eyes. Part of that is remembering that they may see the world differently than you. They may have different priorities, different needs, and a different emotional experience than you. Your goal as the listener is to make sense of how the world looks from their perspective, not yours.

USING EMPATHY

What matters most is not what happens to someone, but how they feel about what happens to them. The best way to understand someone is often to approach them with empathy—to listen for and acknowledge their emotional experience of the situation. This means focusing on how they felt or might have felt in that situation, as well as how they feel about it now. Keep in mind that when people speak emotionally, they often use metaphors: "The whole world is against me," "No one understands me." Be careful not to take those metaphors literally. They are not factual, objective statements; they are emotional, personal, subjective statements intended to describe the person's emotional experience.

NOT OFFERING UNSOLICITED ADVICE

One common mistake, especially if the other person is in distress, is to offer solutions or fixes. Although that is sometimes helpful, it's often not what the speaker wants or needs, and it can shut down the other person's emotions. The thinking is that if you fix the problem, they (and you) will feel better, but this is often driven by *your* discomfort with their emotions. In that case your goal becomes stopping their emotional expression as quickly as possible instead of allowing them space to process their feelings. As explained at the end of Chapter 16: Becoming Aware of Your Emotions, scientific research clearly indicates that using language, either spoken or written, to process emotional events engages more of the prefrontal cortex, which is the source of higher reasoning in the brain. Interrupting a person when they are talking about their feelings can prevent their brain from integrating the event and fully processing their emotions so that they can better manage them.

OFFERING EMPATHY OR SOLUTIONS WHEN YOU'RE CRITICIZED

It can be very difficult to listen to someone when they seem unhappy with you. If they are talking about you, it probably involves their feelings about you or their concerns about your behavior. Either way, if they're talking about things you've said or done, it's vital to sort out whether they are hoping for empathy or solutions. If they say they want both, it's best to offer one at a time, starting with empathy.

To listen empathically to someone's concerns means focusing on their emotional experience of you and how they have been emotionally affected by you. If they talk about you and your behaviors, it is vital that you focus on them and their emotional experience of your behaviors. The conversation is really only about them and how they felt—not about you and what you did.

To problem-solve their concerns about you, focus solely on yourself and your behavior. Which of your behaviors concern them? What do they want you to change? How can you address their concerns? One way to avoid taking this personally is to imagine that you and the other are standing side by side, looking at a behavior of concern and trying to figure out a solution together. Think of it as a performance review with a supervisor, where you figure out areas for improvement together.

Improving your listening and speaking skills can significantly improve your working relationship with the other person. Even so, there will be times when the two of you will have significant disagreements and conflicts, and good communication alone may not be enough. The next chapter presents additional skills and tools for working your way through conflicts.

CHAPTER 24

PRACTICING CONFLICT-RESOLUTION SKILLS

One particularly challenging aspect of communication is navigating disagreements and conflicts. Many people view disagreements and conflicts as a bad thing, a sign that things are going poorly in the relationship. Furthermore, many think that conflict just leads to greater unhappiness. For these reasons, some people seek to avoid conflicts whenever possible. It can be easy to fear that you'll have to choose between getting what you want and being in the relationship—that you can't have both. But people are different from each other in many different ways, and conflict is inevitable. The goal is not to avoid conflict, but to successfully navigate it so both people can feel better afterwards. One of the signs of successful romantic relationships is the ability to work through conflict together.

Conflict typically emerges when two people in a relationship have different priorities, experiences, solutions, wants, or needs. Some conflicts are based on real differences and others are caused by misperceptions, misunderstandings, and miscommunications. The challenge is to work through them. While good communication can certainly help, it may not be enough.

This chapter presents ways to work through your differences with your partner. Our focus is mainly on conflict in your romantic relationship, but all of these skills can be used in any relationship, including with your child, coworker, friend, and family member.

CONFLICT CAN BE A PATH TO INTIMACY

People often think arguments are painful and to be avoided. They imagine each one leading to a negative experience—hurt feelings, resentment, greater distance, even the end of the relationship. Even when arguments go well, they are often uncomfortable, so many people avoid them altogether in an attempt to keep the peace.

When arguments are seen as debates or battles, people sometimes give in just to end the conversation, but conflict doesn't have to be like that. When arguments are approached as discussions intended to increase understanding and collaboration, they become positive events that bring people closer. Constructive conflict might still be uncomfortable and challenging, but it leads to greater intimacy and understanding. It provides an opportunity to know each other better and be better partners. Healthy conflict should be actively pursued as a vehicle for getting to know each other better and improving the quality of the relationship. Avoiding conflict, on the other hand, ultimately increases the distance between people. Avoiding conflict means avoiding intimacy and closeness. Over time it can lead couples to being superficial, artificial, and ingenuine with each other. Below are two examples of how healthy conflict can lead to greater closeness and connection.

SCENARIO 1: GETTING A GIFT YOU DON'T REALLY LIKE

Your friend surprises you with an early birthday gift. You have known each other for years, but this is the first time they've ever done this. They want to show their appreciation of you and your friendship with a gift, which turns out to be a hat. Unfortunately, you never wear hats. Have they ever seen you wear a hat? It's just not your style. What do you do?

One way out is to avoid the conflict altogether. You thank them, tell them you appreciate the gift, and that you're touched by their kindness. They say they knew a hat was a bit of a risk, but they were quite enamored with it and thought you'd like it. You agree and thank them again. All goes well—no hurt feelings, no problems, and you leave the hat to die a slow death in your closet.

A year and many visits later, you and your friend get together and they have another birthday gift for you. Guess what it is? Another hat! They say that since you enjoyed last year's gift so much, they thought they'd get you another one. You fake enthusiasm and appreciation again and add another unwanted hat to your closet.

Alternatively, you could engage in the conflict. Going back to the first gift they gave you, when you see that it is a hat, you could thank them for the gift, appreciate their kindness, and indicate that they really didn't have to give you a gift—but if they do, a hat wouldn't be the thing. You don't wear hats, never have and never will. If they ever were to get you something else, a better gift would be socks, which you love and can never get enough of. Your friend is apologetic and feels bad about the gift—oh no! Hurt feelings! You let them know you are still touched by it and want to keep it since it has special meaning because it was given to you by this dear friend. There is some brief awkwardness, but things move along quickly and all is well. You take the hat to your closet as a reminder of a friend who cares for you, but perhaps does not know you as well as you thought.

A year goes by and your friend has another birthday gift for you. This time it's a pair of socks! Not only is it a gift you will actually use, but you are genuinely touched that they remembered what you said last year. There is no fake enthusiasm. It is heartfelt, thanks in part to your willingness to be honest and assertive last year. The brief conflict and slightly hurt feelings let them get to know you a little better and demonstrate that they were paying attention and really do care. It brings you closer than ever and deepens your connection. This is how conflict, while perhaps uncomfortable in the short run, can create greater closeness and connection.

SCENARIO 2: GIVING FEEDBACK TO YOUR SEXUAL PARTNER

There are many times that some conflict is inevitable and feedback would be very helpful. One is when you are with a new sexual partner. Sex with a new partner can be fun, exciting, memorable, and erotic, yet it's inevitable that you will both do things the other doesn't want. Because everyone has distinct preferences about how they want to be touched and treated, you're not going to be a completely perfect sexual fit with anyone. How do you address your differences?

If you want to avoid conflict, you could act like you enjoy everything your partner does, offering nothing but praise and appreciation, affirming that they are a great lover. While this might be true in many ways, the things you don't like are unlikely to change if you don't speak up about them. You could also avoid asking them for feedback about your own performance so you won't have to hear what they didn't like. But this means they have to pretend everything you do is exactly right for them, even though some of it is not. Choosing this path means there are no hurt feelings and you can each feel good about your performance, but your sexual connection will not deepen and grow. After the infatuation wears off, the sex might actually get worse, since neither of you is satisfied, even in areas that might be fairly easy to change or adjust.

Alternatively, you could give your partner gentle feedback. That inevitably means pointing out things that didn't go over so well, or asking for things they didn't do. This could lead to some hurt feelings and temporary discomfort as you both acknowledge that they are not a perfect lover, but it will allow them to become a better lover to you. Likewise, if they have feedback for you, your feelings might be a little hurt, but if you integrate it you will become a better lover to them. There is a little awkwardness, a little hurt ego, a little discomfort, but it all leads to greater sexual connection and closeness.

This is why sexual intimacy in a healthy relationship typically gets better over time. While the initial excitement may be gone, in its place is a more nuanced and unique sexual connection that is a better fit for each of you. This only happens if you are willing to give and receive constructive feedback and engage in healthy conflict rather than avoiding it.

THE THREE COMPONENTS OF CONFLICT RESOLUTION

Successfully working through conflict involves three key components. The first is **making yourself known and advocating for yourself**; in other words, communicating who you are and making clear what you want and need. The second is **getting to know the other person and understanding what they want and need**. Finally, it means **working together to reach**

agreements that treat everyone with equal respect, consideration, and importance.

The previous chapter explored ways to express yourself and better understand other people. This chapter explores how to advocate for yourself and reach mutually satisfying agreements.

THE THREE TYPES OF ADVOCACY

There are three basic ways to advocate for yourself: **aggressively (or passive-aggressively)**, **passively**, and **assertively**. Let's look at them in more detail.

Aggressive advocacy seeks satisfaction of your wants and needs at the expense of other people. It means winning while the other loses. It means not giving fair consideration or weight to what the other person wants. It can be described as selfish.

People who are aggressive use abusive and controlling behaviors. They operate from a one-up position and a Power Over mindset. They view conflict as a means of getting what they want at any cost. They seek to win arguments and prove the other person wrong.

When they have more power than the other person, aggressive people tend to push others into a passive position. Others quickly learn that trying to advocate for themselves with an aggressive person, particularly one in a position of power, often works out poorly. They become passive simply to avoid an unpleasant battle rife with abuse and control, even if they usually consider themselves fairly assertive.

Passive advocacy is at the opposite end of the spectrum. It prioritizes the wants and needs of others over your own. It loses so the other person can win, and gives in so the other can get their way. It does not give fair consideration or weight to your wants or needs.

People who are passive seldom advocate for themselves. When they do, it tends to be indirect, in ways that may not be clear to other people. They operate from a one-down position in a Power Over mindset. They feel resentful and victimized because they feel helpless and powerless. They tend to be terrified of conflict and avoid it at all costs.

Some professionals identify a separate category for **passive-aggressive advocacy**. This is aggressive as well, but in an indirect way that makes it easy to deny. It presents itself as agreeable and pleasant but is actually quite combative. Those who believe this is a separate category believe that some people who are passive never become aggressive. We consider passive-aggressive advocacy another form of aggression.

You might think that if you're not being aggressive, you're being passive, but that's not true. The healthy alternative is to be assertive.

Assertive advocacy seeks satisfaction of your wants and needs while remaining considerate of others. It operates from a position of Personal Power and works from a collaborative stance. It views conflict as a productive encounter that can lead to resolution and win-win solutions.

While some people shift back and forth between these approaches, most people are primarily aligned with one. We believe that being assertive is the healthiest and most effective approach for everyone. We encourage you to do your best to live in an assertive, nonaggressive space. The rest of this chapter offers tools to that effect.

CLIMBING THE STAIRCASE OF ASSERTIVENESS

Sometimes people will immediately respond to your requests, and sometimes they won't. There are a variety of explanations when they don't: perhaps they didn't fully understand your request, didn't take it seriously, or aren't able to fulfill it. You may need to be persistent. If you persist, you might get want you want. Being persistent, though, becomes controlling when you refuse to accept a person's response (or nonresponse). Part of being assertive is acknowledging that although you have the right to advocate for what you want and need, the other person is not obligated to meet your wants or needs. It means respecting their response, even if you don't agree with it.

Assertiveness is not just a single moment of expressing what you want. It is an ongoing process that might include multiple requests and steps. These steps build upon each other fairly predictably, and it's important to do them in order. Skipping over steps—especially multiple steps—can lead to abusive and disrespectful behavior.

Think of them as a staircase of assertiveness. Start with the lowest step and work your way up one at a time. Use the least amount of assertiveness necessary. Before each step, ask yourself a series of questions. Does what you want seem fair to both people? What does the other person want? What do you want? Can this person do what you are asking? How important is this to you? Is this the right time?

Weigh the pros and cons of taking the next step. You will rarely need to go beyond the second or third step. If you get there, consider whether your request is workable and reasonable.

STEP 1: MAKING YOUR REQUEST

Use polite words and a gentle voice. Be direct and keep your request as simple and brief as you can.

"Could you please not leave your dirty clothes on the floor?"

STEP 2: EXPLAINING AND REPEATING YOUR REQUEST

Explain the circumstances and the reason for your request. Share how you feel about it. Use "I prefer" statements.

"When you leave your clothes on the floor by the bed, I have to step over them or trip over them. I don't feel like I should have to pick up after you that way. It leaves me feeling frustrated and annoyed."

STEP 3: MODIFYING THE REQUEST

Restate your objective. Seek to understand why the other person is unwilling to budge. Ask about their wants and needs. Look for a win-win solution (discussed later in this chapter).

"I notice that you're still leaving dirty clothes on the floor by the bed. I'm wondering why they keep ending up there and what can be done about it. Can you help me understand why you haven't been able to change that? Is there anything I can do to help make that happen?"

STEP 4: REASSERT YOUR REQUEST MORE FIRMLY

Use a firmer, more expressive voice. Explain why this is important to you. Demonstrate compassion and understanding while maintaining what you want and need.

"You continuing to leave your dirty clothes on the floor by my side of the bed is really frustrating for me and I am starting to get resentful. I understand that it doesn't seem like a big deal to you, but it matters to me.

I really need you to be more mindful of this and respect the boundary I am trying to set here."

STEP 5: GIVE WARNINGS

Talk about what you intend to do if your request is not honored. Talk about what you will do if it is honored. Only give warnings you would actually follow through on.

"I would rather be in bed with you, but if this continues, I'm going to start sleeping in the other room until it gets taken care of."

STEP 6: CONSULT OTHERS

Ask others for advice about what can be done. Go to a higher authority who might be able to intervene on your behalf. Identify other options. If you come to realize that the behavior is part of a larger pattern, you may decide to insist on couples counseling to address the larger issue.

LEARNING TO SET GOOD BOUNDARIES

Boundaries mark the line between you and other people, and differentiate what is yours from what is everyone else's. They come in many forms. They can be physical—how much physical contact you are comfortable with, or an actual fence or wall. They can be informational—how much information you are willing to share about yourself. They can be financial—how much money you are willing to spend or lend.

Boundaries can vary in their flexibility depending on your preferences. Some boundaries are quite firm (who you are willing to have sex with) and some are flexible (how late you are willing to stay up). This usually correlates to the level of trust and closeness you feel toward the other person, but you will have limits even with the people to whom you are closest.

Boundaries can change over time. They tend to relax as you get closer to someone and get firmer the less you trust them. They can also change as you gain experience. After a bad experience loaning money to a friend, they may get firmer. As you process your feelings about your past, they may relax, making you more willing to share personal information.

You have different boundaries for different people. For example, you'll share things with a friend that you would not with a stranger. Only you can define your boundaries. Other people can help you figure out where they are, but only you know where, when, and how to set them.

Not all boundary violations are the same. For example, touching someone on the shoulder when they do not want to be touched there is a violation, but touching someone on the groin when they do not want to be touched there is much more serious.

There are four basic steps in setting boundaries with others.

STEP 1: IDENTIFYING YOUR BOUNDARY

The first step is knowing where your boundary is. You cannot inform others if you don't know yourself. There are three different ways of figuring out your boundaries: through direct experience (the hard way), by learning from the experience of others (the easy way), and by imagining yourself in a particular situation (also an easier way).

A common way to find your boundaries is to examine past experiences—good and bad. If you shared personal information in the past that led someone to make a quick judgment about you, you may be more careful about sharing information now. You set a boundary based on direct experience—you learned things the hard way.

Setting boundaries based on the wisdom of others or by imagining the outcome is learning things the easy way. For example, the common wisdom about loaning a friend money is to never loan more than you'd be willing to give them. If you adopt that rule for yourself, you can avoid the experience of not being paid back more than you are willing to give away.

Another way to find your boundary is to imagine the situation and see how it makes you feel. For example, if someone asks to stay with you for several weeks, imagining what that would be like could help you figure out whether you are willing to allow it.

STEP 2: MARKING YOUR BOUNDARY

Once you know where your boundary is, you need to mark it so it's recognizable to you and others. This is like putting up a fence along a property line. Some boundaries don't need to be marked because they are understood. For example, you don't need to let people know that you don't want them breaking into your house, stealing your money, or using your toothbrush. But other boundaries vary from person to person: what personal information they will share, what they are willing to do, and how close they want to sit to someone, for example. In each of those cases, it is often necessary to communicate your limit so others can respect it.

The simplest way to inform people of your boundary is to tell them in person or in writing. If you don't, they may inadvertently cross it, thinking you're okay with it. Only when you make it clear what is and is not acceptable to you can you be confident that people know your boundaries.

STEP 3: LETTING PEOPLE KNOW WHEN THEY CROSS YOUR BOUNDARY

If a person crosses your boundary it's up to you to let them know, or they might keep crossing it. When someone walks into your yard, you can ask them to leave. A verbal mention is enough for most people; they were either unaware they were trespassing or didn't think it was a big deal.

The first time someone crosses a boundary—unless it's one that anyone would be aware of—it's best to presume it was done unwittingly. Simply letting them know that you don't want them to cross that boundary should be enough for them to stop. For example, if someone brings up a topic you find disturbing and you let them know you don't want to talk about it, they very well may not bring it up again. But if they do after you've made your boundary clear, they're probably doing it intentionally, and you will need to enforce your boundaries more strenuously.

STEP 4: ENFORCING YOUR BOUNDARY

This step is only necessary when someone is intentionally violating your boundaries or ignoring your requests to stop. If someone keeps trespassing on your yard, you might call the police to have the person escorted off the property or arrested. Examples of enforcing your boundaries include stopping conversations, physically leaving, or changing the nature of your relationship with the person. You might refuse to engage with them in that way again or set more restrictive conditions for future contact. At the extreme, you might call the police.

LEARNING TO RESPECT OTHER PEOPLE'S BOUNDARIES

Abusive behavior is intrinsically a boundary violation. Part of being nonabusive means respecting the boundaries of others as long as their boundary doesn't encroach on yours. There are several important guidelines for respecting the boundaries of others.

STEP 1: TRYING TO ANTICIPATE THE OTHER PERSON'S BOUNDARIES

If you are solely focused on yourself, you might not even consider that someone's boundaries are not the same as yours. You might assume that if you are okay with something, they will be, too. It is important to think about what the other person might want and need. Don't assume they share your boundaries. Consider how their boundaries might be different from yours. This is a key aspect of being relational.

STEP 2: BEING CLEAR ABOUT THE OTHER PERSON'S BOUNDARIES

You may be able to figure it out, but if you're not clear what someone's boundary is, ask them. Seek to remind yourself what the other person's boundaries are.

STEP 3: NOT CROSSING OTHER PEOPLE'S BOUNDARIES

It's easy to respect someone's boundaries when theirs are the same as yours. It is more challenging when theirs are different. You may be tempted to talk them out of their boundary or to minimize the difference between yours and theirs, but it is vital that you take theirs seriously. For example, you may have no problem staying out past midnight on a weekend, but if they want to be home by ten, they have the right to be home by ten.

STEP 4: GETTING PERMISSION TO CROSS SOMEONE'S BOUNDARIES

If, for some reason, you need to cross a person's boundaries, get permission. If your ball goes into a neighbor's yard, you need to ask them if you can go retrieve it. If you need to get something out of your partner's wallet, you need to ask first, unless they've made it clear before that they are fine with that.

LEARNING TO NAVIGATE CONFLICTING BOUNDARIES

What if your boundaries conflict with the other person's? This could be called a border dispute. There are times when your boundaries, which are right for you, collide with someone else's boundaries, which are right for them. When this happens you may need to negotiate a solution.

USING FOCUSED LISTENING FOR HIGH-INTENSITY CONFLICTS

For discussions that are not particularly emotionally charged, the usual methods of communication work fine. One person shares a thought, then the other; the conversation goes back and forth like a game of catch. This works well for making a grocery list or coordinating schedules, but it isn't as effective when you are each set on getting what you want and emotions are getting intense. When this happens, you're both probably primarily focused on making points about yourselves, your views, your wants, and your needs. You're probably not really listening to each other very well, except to make your own cases. You are listening in order to reply, not to understand.

It's hard to switch back and forth between expressing yourself and understanding the other when the conversation gets intense and the stakes feel high. It's likely you'll end up just trying to get the other person to understand you. Understanding the other person takes a back seat to being understood, and if they're doing the same thing, the two of you can get quite stuck. One way to resolve this is to shift into something we have named **focused listening**.

Focused listening means that the two of you agree to focus on just the concerns of one person at a time. Rather than jumping back and forth from one person to the other like you would in a normal conversation, you will take more extended turns. Once one person has fully expressed themselves, shift the focus to the other person. Because there is extended focus by agreement, each person only has one role at a time: either to speak or to listen.

Take all the time you need, whether it's a few minutes or over an hour. When the speaker feels fully understood and acknowledged, flip roles. You may not need equal times as speaker and listener, but you're making a commitment to give each of you a full turn as the speaker, however long that takes. It is vital that each person gets a full turn as the speaker. You may need to do this more than once, but you should not take a significant break until each person has had a turn in each role.

The more challenging role in focused listening is to be the listener, whose single goal is to try to understand the other person's concerns. Any opinions, needs, feelings, or wants that the listener has are temporarily shelved. You can write those thoughts down so you won't forget them, but don't bring them up while you're in the listening role. Instead, you should ask open questions, seek to fully understand where the other is coming from, and reflect back, paraphrase, or summarize what you think they're getting at. The goal is to completely understand where the other person is coming from. Remember that you can understand someone without having to agree with them or go along with them. You can understand why someone might want to drive at high speeds without agreeing that you think they should.

If you can't agree who should speak first, we suggest going with the person whose feelings are most intense. The person who is not feeling as reactive should be the first listener.

LISTENING FOR INFORMATION INSTEAD OF LISTENING WITH AN AGENDA

When someone has a different perspective than you, it can be tempting to argue with them about how your perspective is correct or superior. The problem with this is that you're not listening to understand; you're **listening with an agenda**. This is a concept that was originally developed by a colleague, Dave Wight, who described it as "listening intentionally." To listen with an agenda means being focused on making your point and winning the argument. There is no real interest in understanding the other person's perspective except to dismiss it and prove it wrong. Listening with an agenda is characterized by rhetorical, leading, and yes-no questions—all of which are intended to make your point. It is argumentative and consistent with a Power Over worldview.

Professionals who are supposed to listen with an agenda include debaters and courtroom attorneys. Debaters are not trying to understand the other person, but to win the argument. Attorneys are not trying to figure out whether someone is actually innocent or guilty, but to convince others that they are innocent or guilty. Neither really cares about the other point of view, except to disprove it.

The problem with listening with an agenda is that it keeps you from truly understanding where the other person is coming from and why. It mistakenly presumes that there is a simple and single way to view an issue or event. It prevents you from developing full comprehension of the issue in all its complexity. It puts distance between you and the other person rather than pulling you closer together.

The parable of the blind men and the elephant illustrates this well. As the story goes, each blind man grabs a different part of an elephant and presumes they know everything they need to know about this object. One grabs the trunk and says it is a hose. Another touches the side and says no, it is a wall. Yet another grabs a leg and says no, it is a tree trunk. Because each is only focused on his own experience, he is unable to get the full picture.

The alternative to listening with an agenda is listening for information (which Dave Wight described as "informational listening"). When someone sees things differently from you, in a way that does not make sense to you, the idea is to seek additional information so you can better understand the discrepancy. This is listening with an open mind and seeking to understand the other, even if you disagree with them. It is characterized by genuine, open-ended questions. It includes follow-up and clarifying questions. The goal is to make sense of the other person's perspective without giving up yours, to reconcile the perspectives without dismissing either one. It challenges you to find out how you can both be right.

A key aspect of listening for information is a willingness to consider things that are beyond your direct experience. Remember that a business card can be blank on one side and have printing on the other. Remember that 1+1=2 if you're talking about addition, but 1+1=1 most of the time if you're talking about reproduction. Listening for information is consistent with a Personal Power worldview.

Professionals who are expected to listen for information (when they are doing their jobs well) include investigative journalists and detectives. A journalist working on a story may have an idea of what they think is going on, but they are willing to adjust as they get new information. A detective may have an idea of who committed a crime or what happened at a crime scene, but they are willing to adjust as new evidence surfaces. They have a theory, but they are willing to modify or expand it as they encounter information that appears to contradict it.

Listening for information will allow you to make much better sense of the world and the people in it. This is especially important in your closest relationships; it will bring you closer, which is presumably the goal.

LEARNING TO NEGOTIATE SOLUTIONS

This chapter has touched on ways to make yourself known and advocate for yourself, ways of being mindful, and ways to be aware of other people. The last skill, negotiation, brings together your needs and the needs of others to look for a solution that suits everyone.

The concept of looking for the win-win comes from Roger Fisher and William Ury's book, *Getting to Yes: Negotiating Agreement Without Giving In*. Its techniques have been used around the world to resolve conflicts big and small—between nations and neighbors. Its core concept has become a cornerstone of mediation practices, and it is quite simple yet profound: Most apparently unresolvable conflicts are conflicts between *solutions*, not wants and needs. The key to negotiation is shifting the focus away from a particular solution and toward identifying and addressing the underlying wants and needs of each person.

When conflicts reach an impasse, it's usually because the parties have different solutions to the issue, and each assumes the other should give in—a win-lose solution. Compromise, on the other hand, can often mean both people have to give in a little, creating a lose-lose that is fair but leaves both parties suffering.

For example, say you and your partner both want to go out for dinner, but at different places. You want to go to the Chinese restaurant and they want to go to the Mexican restaurant. If you go to the Chinese restaurant, you win and your partner loses. If you go to the Mexican restaurant, your partner wins and you lose. If you pick a third place that neither of you likes as much as your first choice, you both lose. It's a face-off: you're going nose-to-nose, you against them, and them against you. The problem is that none of these solutions meet both of your needs.

If the goal is to find a win-win—a solution that satisfies you equally—you'll need to recognize that the conflict is not between differing needs, but between differing solutions. Focus first on your underlying wants and needs, and temporarily let go of your hopes for a specific outcome.

Why do you want to go to the Chinese place? You're very hungry and you want to eat soon. Plus, you don't have a lot of money so you want to go someplace inexpensive. The Mexican place your partner prefers is slower and more expensive than the Chinese place, which is why you object to it. Why does your partner want to go to the Mexican place? When you ask, they say that if they're going out for dinner, they want to go somewhere with a nice setting and ambience. The Mexican place is nicely decorated; the Chinese place is plain and unremarkable.

Once you've identified all of your underlying wants and needs, the goal is to come up with new solutions that meet as many of them as possible. Believe it or not, with this method you can usually meet all of them. This shifts your position from nose-to-nose in a conflict to shoulder-to-shoulder—the two of you are figuring out a solution together, side by side, rather than facing off against each other.

If you're going to find a restaurant that satisfies both of your wants and needs, you'll need someplace that is quick, cheap, and has some atmosphere. Can either of you think of a solution that checks all the boxes? Your partner may propose splitting a meal at the Mexican place; the portions are large and they're not too hungry, and the chips and salsa are free and arrive right away. You can snack right away on the chips and salsa and it won't be as expensive because you will only be purchasing one entrée. Or perhaps you suggest going to the Chinese place for dinner and then the coffee shop down the street to hear some live music afterwards. That, too, checks all the boxes: you get fast and inexpensive food, and your partner gets atmosphere and ambience at the coffee shop, which is even better for them. Or perhaps one of you suggests a completely different restaurant that's a little farther away: you both like it, it's relatively inexpensive, it has nice ambience and fairly quick service.

Either of you can suggest a solution that you think might work for both of you. If someone objects, they need to indicate why. Sometimes another need is at play that hasn't been mentioned or thought of yet, and you can suggest another alternative in response to the new information. For example, when your partner suggests splitting a meal at the Mexican place, you might add that you're not really in the mood for Mexican food because you've had it recently. That adds a new want to the list: something other than Mexican food. If you're creative and flexible in your thinking, you often can come up with a win-win.

In that rare situation where it is not possible to find a win-win, you might need to agree to meet more of one person's needs in this situation, but more of the other's in a later one. That, however, should be the rare exception. Doing it too often can lead to unhappiness and resentment; it probably means you're not trying hard enough to find a win-win. If you are going to this option repeatedly, you're probably not doing the other steps as skillfully as you could be. Consider seeking outside assistance at that point, such as talking with friends for ideas or meeting with a couples counselor.

To review, here's how to negotiate a win-win solution:

1. **Identify both parties' underlying wants and needs.**
2. **Brainstorm ways to meet as many of those as possible, if not all of them.**
3. **Evaluate the proposed solution.**
4. **Propose alternatives if necessary.**
5. **In rare cases: Give priority to one person this time and agree to prioritize the other person's next time.**

***

A great book that provides a number of suggestions for engaging in constructive conflict is *Nonviolent Communication: A Language of Life* by Marshall Rosenberg. We would recommend you consider reading this book or taking a class on those concepts to learn more.

PART FIVE

LIVING IN RECOVERY

CHAPTER 25

THE QUALITIES OF HEALTHY RELATIONSHIPS

In this book we have focused a great deal on what a bad, abusive relationship looks like, but what does a good, healthy relationship look like? Most obviously, it is free of abuse and control, but that's just one aspect. There are plenty of misrepresentations of healthy relationships in songs, movies, and other media, so your idea of a perfect relationship might not be quite accurate. You might think you would always get along perfectly, know exactly what the other wants and needs, and would be perpetually happy, but those are unrealistic and unreasonable expectations.

So what is fair and reasonable to expect in a healthy relationship?

Listed below are common qualities of healthy long-term romantic relationships. You may notice that many of these qualities draw on concepts we covered in earlier chapters. We have actually been touching on the qualities of healthy relationships throughout the second half of the book, but here we compile them in a single place. These qualities are present regardless of cultural background. They may manifest differently from couple to couple, but they are all core elements of healthy relationships.

While these qualities apply to both partners, we encourage you to focus on your own behavior first. Ultimately, though, you will both need to practice these skills.

EACH PERSON IS TO BE RESPECTED AND NOT ABUSED IN ANY WAY.
A healthy relationship is free of abusive behavior. Treating each other with respect is vital. No one ever deserves to be abused, and abusive behavior is never justified.

EACH PERSON CONSISTENTLY SHARES THEIR THOUGHTS, FEELINGS, AND EXPERIENCES WITH THE OTHER OVER TIME.
Part of being in a relationship is relating to the other person by sharing what is in your head and heart. You don't have to share everything with your partner. You have the right to choose what you do and do not share with anyone, including your partner. However, while you may keep certain things to yourself, most things should be shared, especially if the other person is interested. This requires courage and vulnerability. It is part of being intimate, which we will talk about a little later in this chapter.

EACH PERSON IS CONSISTENTLY OPEN TO AND INTERESTED IN HEARING THE THOUGHTS, FEELINGS, AND EXPERIENCES OF THE OTHER OVER TIME.
Part of being in a relationship is wanting to know what is going on in your partner's head and heart. There may be certain things that you are not interested in or simply don't want to hear about, but aside from those select areas, you should generally be open to hearing what your partner is thinking and feeling. This includes intentionally turning your attention toward them and giving them an opportunity to share.

EACH PERSON TAKES RESPONSIBILITY FOR THEIR EMOTIONAL AND PHYSICAL STATE AND THEIR OWN SELF-CARE, INCLUDING ASKING FOR THE ASSISTANCE OF OTHERS.
A common misconception of healthy relationships is that each person takes care of the other. We talked earlier about primary accountability, which affirms that you are responsible for your own emotional and physical well-being—even when you are in an intimate relationship. You, not your partner, are responsible for your well-being. You can ask for help, including from your partner, but it is ultimately your job, not theirs, to take care of you. Likewise, you are not responsible for your partner's well-being. You do have some responsibility to support them in taking good care of themselves, but the responsibility is theirs.

Each person has the right to refuse any request for help, with the understanding that the refusal will have an impact. Everyone has the right to say no, and it's important that they are not punished for it. If it's not okay to say no, it's not a request—it's a directive, which is generally not okay.

You have the right to say no to any request your partner makes. Keep in mind, though, that doing so may have consequences you don't like. If your partner invites you to an event in which you have little interest and you decline, they might take a friend instead. If the event is recurring, they may continue to go with this friend, which means spending more time with them and away from the relationship. You might rethink your response in hindsight and realize that you'd rather go with them just to spend more time with them, even though you're not interested in the event itself.

EACH PERSON TAKES RESPONSIBILITY FOR THE IMPACT OF THEIR BEHAVIOR ON OTHERS.

Part of being in a relationship is being aware that everything you do affects the people around you, especially those closest to you. Your actions have positive, neutral, or negative impact, and the negative impact can be unintentional.

At the very beginning of the book, we described unintentionally abusive behavior as hurtful behavior. While it is possible to stop all of your abusive behavior, it is highly unlikely that you (or your partner) can stop all of your hurtful behavior. That is a natural part of being in close relationship with another person: at times each of you will make choices that inadvertently hurt the other. Remember that the fact that you didn't intend to be hurtful doesn't mean you weren't hurtful. Regardless of your intention, you need to acknowledge the impact of your choice on the other person and validate their experience.

For example, say that an accident on the road delays your arrival home from work by half an hour. Your partner needed you to watch the baby, and now they can't go to their meeting because it's too late. On one hand, you weren't trying to be late; you had no control over the traffic. On the other hand, you assumed traffic would flow smoothly and your partner missed their meeting because you were late. It's important that you validate their experience by acknowledging your assumption and apologizing for arriving home so late they missed their meeting.

At times, taking care of yourself might mean you end up hurting someone else. The goal is to be as considerate as you can without unduly compromising yourself. If your partner is a light sleeper and you usually have to get up before them, being considerate means getting up as quietly as you can, but even so, you may sometimes disrupt their sleep. You cannot promise to never disrupt their sleep, but you can be as careful and quiet as possibly while getting ready for your day.

EACH PERSON IS MINDFUL OF THE OTHER'S WELL-BEING AND STRIVES TO OFFER EMPATHY AND ASSISTANCE.
Although you are not responsible for your partner's well-being, to love someone means to care about them. It means wanting to know how they are doing. It means being empathic on an ongoing basis and offering what assistance you can without taking responsibility for them. After all, the opposite of love is not hate, it is indifference.

EACH PERSON'S FEELINGS, OPINIONS, AND EXPERIENCES ARE LEGITIMATE.
Healthy relationships make room for differences of opinion, feelings, and experiences. Everyone has a right to be themselves without feeling threatened. When there are differences, each partner should respect the other's basic right to disagree.

EACH PERSON GIVES SERIOUS CONSIDERATION TO THE OTHER'S PERSPECTIVE.
You don't have to agree with your partner, but you do need to consider their perspective. Dismissing their point of view without giving it real thought is a sign of contempt. People in healthy relationships invest time and energy in trying to understand where their partner is coming from, even when they disagree. Everyone deserves that consideration.

EACH PERSON SEEKS TO BE AWARE AND CONSIDERATE OF THE OTHER REGARDLESS OF WHETHER THEY ARE PRESENT.
Being mindful of your partner is something you should seek to do whether they are physically with you or not. Their thoughts, feelings, wants, and needs should matter to you even when they are not next to you. They should not be out of sight, out of mind.

You don't have to think about them every second of every day, but your thoughts should regularly and routinely turn toward them as the opportunity allows.

EACH PERSON ACCEPTS THAT MISTAKES WILL BE MADE.
No one is perfect. It is not fair or realistic to expect your partner (or yourself) to be perfect. Although each of you will do your best, you will inevitably get things wrong sometimes. You will make mistakes, big and small. In a healthy relationship there is room to make mistakes, and room to correct them and learn from them. Remember, though, that even though you both understand that mistakes are inevitable, mistakes still cause problems that need to be acknowledged.

EACH PERSON ESTABLISHES AND MAINTAINS THEIR OWN BOUNDARIES.
You are responsible for establishing and maintaining your own boundaries. It is not fair or reasonable to expect your partner to know your boundaries until you make them clear to them. When your boundaries change, you need to tell them. If they cross your boundaries, you need to let them know, and to enforce them appropriately.

EACH PERSON RESPECTS THE OTHER'S BOUNDARIES.
Part of being respectful and loving to your partner is respecting the boundaries they set. Disrespecting their boundaries is abusive and controlling. If you are struggling with a boundary your partner has set, the appropriate way to deal with it is to raise your concern and engage in constructive conflict, if needed.

ABUSE OCCURS WHEN THERE IS ONLY ONE SET OF BOUNDARIES, ENFORCED BY ABUSIVE BEHAVIOR.

Your boundaries matter, and so do your partner's. It is important to understand that what you want and need does not exclusively define the relationship—your partner's wants and needs are equally important. In a healthy relationship, both people's wants, needs, and boundaries are routinely and regularly considered. Healthy conflict involves working out solutions together when your boundaries collide.

EACH PERSON SEEKS A MUTUALLY BENEFICIAL SOLUTION TO DISAGREEMENTS.

You should always strive to find a win-win solution to any disagreement. Win-win solutions are almost always possible when couples use the negotiation techniques from the "Getting to Yes" model. This means focusing on wants and needs rather than solutions.

EACH PERSON SEEKS TO ACCEPT UNRESOLVABLE DIFFERENCES IF THEY CHOOSE TO STAY IN THE RELATIONSHIP.

As couples researcher and expert John Gottman points out, when you choose a partner, you choose a set of problems; no one is exactly how you want and need them to be. They may be able to make some changes for you without compromising who they are, but it's highly unlikely they can change everything, so it's important to weigh each behavior and decide whether it is truly unacceptable. Truly unacceptable behaviors are also known as deal-breakers. No matter what other positive qualities they have, a deal-breaker makes the relationship untenable for you. Healthy relationships end because of this kind of incompatibility. The classic divorce-related legal term is "irreconcilable differences."

On the other hand, there may a variety of behaviors that you don't care for but are willing to accept—that aren't worth ending the relationship over (at least right now). If you choose to remain in the relationship, you need to acknowledge that you are choosing to accept those behaviors. You are choosing your partner "warts and all." It is vital that you take responsibility for choosing to remain in the relationship knowing that your partner has certain undesirable qualities. If you don't, you're setting yourself up for resentment. In healthy relationships, people acknowledge that their partner has undesirable qualities, but that they love them and are choosing to be with them anyway.

All of the above are important qualities of a healthy intimate relationship. But what makes a relationship "intimate"? Sexual intimacy is a relatively superficial form of intimacy, but it's not the only form. There are also emotional and intellectual intimacy.

Intimacy refers to allowing someone to be extra close with you, beyond what you typically share with strangers or casual acquaintances. It can include physical closeness (sexual and nonsexual), intellectual closeness (sharing your inner and more personal thoughts), and emotional closeness (sharing your true feelings).

People vary a great deal in terms of how much intimacy they want and are capable of. We believe that there are many benefits to deeper intimacy, but for a variety of reasons many people choose to be less than fully intimate with others. The general goal, therefore, is not necessarily deep intimacy with your romantic partner, but rather a level of intimacy with your romantic partner that is *mutually satisfying.*

Abusive and controlling behaviors are intimacy killers. Abusive partners often report that their partners have lost interest in sex and have less sexual contact with them. It's even more likely that your partner will respond to ongoing patterns of abuse and control by sharing less of their true thoughts and feelings with you. They may push many underground to avoid further abuse and control.

Most abused partners report feeling unsafe, controlled, and unseen in their relationship. Instead, they want to feel safe (from abuse), free (from control), and cared for (rather than neglected). Intimacy plays a vital role in all of these. In the remainder of this chapter we will describe what sexual intimacy looks like as well as deeper emotional and intellectual intimacy.

PRACTICING SEXUAL INTIMACY

Some people talk about being "intimate" when they actually mean having sex; when they say they had "intimate relations" with someone, it usually means they had sex with them. Sexual connection is only one aspect of intimacy, but it deserves examination here because it gets so much attention and is rarely talked about thoughtfully.

Abusive and controlling behaviors are great libido killers, and it's common for people who have been abused and controlled to lose sexual interest in their abusive partner. That sexual desire can return if the abusive behavior stops for good, but it can take time. If your partner has displayed diminished interest in being sexual with you, keep in mind how your abusive behavior may have contributed to that. Be patient with their healing and recovery process and keep in mind that healing cannot even start until you have stopped your abusive behavior.

For many people whose sex education was received in school, the focus was on sexually transmitted diseases and infections, how babies are made, anatomy and genitalia, and forms of birth control. The next dose of sex education tends to come to adults in the form of ways to liven up your sex life with a variety of sexual positions. Unfortunately, a lot of basic information on healthy human sexuality is rarely covered. Outlined below are a few of the more common misconceptions about human sexuality and some clarifications about what healthy sexuality can look like.

WHAT CONSTITUTES SEXUAL BEHAVIOR?

When you think of sex you may think of nudity, genitals, sexual intercourse, and orgasms. While all of those are aspects of sex, sexual behavior is much more wide-ranging than that. It can include sexual words, looks, flirting, kissing, casual touch, and lots of other behaviors—many of which can be done in public, fully clothed, without risking arrest for public indecency. Basically, sexual behavior includes any sort of behavior that is intended, on some level, to be erotic. This can include normal behaviors like eating a piece of food or looking at someone with erotic intent. If you imagine doing the behavior with someone you don't feel sexually attracted to and it makes you feel uneasy, it's probably sexual.

This opens up a wide range of behaviors that can express your sexual affection, desire, and playfulness to your sexual partner, even in front of others. This is one way to help free sexual behavior from its confinement in the bedroom or even the home.

The dark side of this is that the same subtle or "innocent" behaviors are sexually abusive if you exhibit them with a nonsexual partner. When you compliment someone on their physical appearance, is it because you find them attractive? Do you give the same kind of compliment to people you are not sexually attracted to—say, people of the same sex, if you are straight? If you don't, your "innocent" compliment has a sexual or erotic quality. Unless the other person is okay with that, the compliment is inappropriate.

ALL ROADS DO NOT NEED TO LEAD TO INTERCOURSE OR ORGASM

For some people, any sort of sexual interaction with their partner seems like a signal that intercourse and orgasm will surely follow, and they are disappointed if it doesn't. As a result, their partner may be hesitant to flirt or to show or request physical affection if they aren't interested in going that far. This can severely reduce the frequency and variety of sexual connection. It's like never being able to see, smell, or taste food unless you're ready to sit down to a full meal. There's no room for snacking, tasting, or treats, just full meals.

Healthy sexual connection involves a wide range of connection, including brief exchanges that don't have to lead to full-on sexual intercourse, orgasms, or nakedness, although, of course, sometimes they might. Many partners report wanting more physical affection and connection, but feeling very limited by the expectation that any step on that path leads to full-on sex.

SEX IS ABOUT MORE THAN ORGASMS

Orgasms are great, but lots of great sexual connection doesn't involve them. The physical pleasure, playfulness, intimacy, and nurturance can be fulfilling in and of themselves. It should be as much about the journey as it is about the destination. If you expect all sexual connection to lead to orgasm, then you'll probably severely limit the sexual connection.

SEXUAL CONNECTION DOES NOT ALWAYS INVOLVE BOTH GIVING AND RECEIVING

Sexual connection is often at its most pleasurable when each person simultaneously gives and receives pleasure. However, for this to be true, they both need to be in a sexual space at the same time, and sometimes that's not the case. It's perfectly fine for both people to focus on one person's sexual enjoyment in a given moment; for the giver to get pleasure simply from giving, even if they're not in a particularly sexual space themselves.

Sometimes partners feel pressured to fake enjoyment because their partner isn't okay with them not being in a sexual space when they are engaged in sexual activity. It's important to respect the space a person is in and not require them to pretend they're feeling something they're not. It is perfectly okay to have a sexual connection when only one person is feeling desire, as long as the other person is supportive of that.

PRACTICE THE PLATINUM RULE WITH SEX

Every person is different sexually. They may even be sexually different with different sexual partners, depending on the sexual dance they do together. Part of the fun of sexual connection is figuring out together what you each find most enjoyable and pleasurable. There will certainly be areas of enjoyment that you share, but you will probably have some differences. Do your best to identify and honor them without compromising yourself. You don't have to do anything you don't want to, even if your partner wants you to. Likewise, your partner doesn't have to do anything they don't want to, even if you want them to.

DEVELOPING AND PRACTICING INTIMACY

Intimacy starts with your relationship with yourself. It challenges you to know yourself better, to know what is in your head and in your heart. There are some thoughts and feelings you know but keep to yourself, and others you're not even aware of yourself. Sharing the ones you know and exploring the ones you haven't even been able to name is all part of becoming more intimate. Intimacy with yourself is challenging. It requires you to see yourself as you truly are: struggles, imperfections, and all. It is the opposite of denial. It involves turning toward yourself. This can lead to increased discomfort as you sit with your actual emotions and the realities of your life. This is what drives many people into addiction—they don't have it in them to sit with the painful realities of their lives, which are often (but not always) related to trauma and woundedness that they experienced when they were younger.

Intimacy in relationship means knowing someone for who they truly are and getting behind their walls, facades, and public masks. It means letting someone see *you* for who you truly are, behind your walls, facades, and public masks. This includes the specifics of your personal history as well as your habits, likes, dislikes, and preferences. But the core of intimacy is knowing and sharing what you think and feel at any given moment. It is knowing and sharing what is in your head and in your heart from moment to moment as well as what stays in your head and heart as the moments pass. Ultimately, intimacy is more about sharing how you think and feel about your life than what about what actually happens in your life.

Intimacy in relationship can be terrifying because it requires you to be vulnerable. It can make it easier for others to hurt you—on accident as well as on purpose. It increases the possibility and depth of rejection. If someone sees you for who you truly are and does not love you or care for you, that hurts much more deeply. Better to put out a fake you—if they reject that, then it won't hurt so much.

Traditional masculinity—as defined by the qualities in the "Act Like a Man" box—is all about protecting yourself from being hurt and mistreated (regardless of your gender), and most of all from being intimate. It creates emotional armor to keep others from hurting you. The better someone knows you, the more they can hurt you, so you hide behind emotional disconnection and stoicism. The more you lean on and depend on someone, the more they can hurt you, so you fool yourself into thinking you don't need anyone but yourself. You deny you have needs so you won't have to depend on others, or even on yourself. As Paul Simon wrote, "I am a rock, I am an island . . . because a rock feels no pain and an island never cries." Actively seeking true intimacy goes against everything in the "Act Like a Man" box, but the more you avoid intimacy and connection, the more you avoid true love and nurturance.

One severe consequence of avoiding intimacy with others is avoiding intimacy with yourself, too. It requires you to live a shallower, less right, and less fulfilling life. It's like trying to navigate the world with a sparsely detailed map—you'll make more wrong turns and spend more time lost and confused and in the wrong places.

Intimacy allows for more connection, support, and love. It allows you to better know yourself, who you are, what matters to you, and what you want and need. It can deepen your connection with yourself, which allows you to know yourself better, which allows you to be more clearly seen by another person. The better you know yourself, the better you can help others to see you and know you as you truly are. The more clearly they see you, the more deeply they can love you and care for you as you truly are.

Intimacy also deepens the connection you feel with another person. As they get more vulnerable, you can better know and understand what is truly in their head and their heart. It allows you to better know the landscape of their lives—their peaks and valleys, the dark and light spaces, the rocky terrain, beautiful forests, and dark caves. The better you know the other, the better you can understand them and love the true them, rather than some imposter. You can nurture them and care for them that much better, as they truly want and need you to. Intimacy allows for much better practice of the Platinum Rule—loving them as they truly want to be loved—while they can love you as you truly want to be loved.

One of the challenges of pursuing intimacy is that it can trigger unresolved trauma in either or both of you. Those emotional wounds can be from previous romantic relationships, although the deepest and most enduring ones are from childhood experiences. Closeness can enflame old traumas, just as regular activity can inflame old injuries. This is a primary reason people avoid getting too emotionally close: it will hurt too much.

If you have the courage to lean in to those emotional responses and own them, you will be able to experience deeper healing. On the other side of the pain you can be happier and truly free of old hurt and trauma. It can be tempting to blame the other person for causing that pain, but they're not causing it—just triggering it. It is akin to unwittingly touching someone on a tender spot on their body. Your touch may be gentle, but it can still cause pain. Part of becoming intimate is learning about your own and the other's emotional tender spots and how to be gentle with them while helping them to be gentle with you.

Practicing intimacy requires courage, honesty, trust, compassion, and persistence. It means having the courage to look into your own head and heart and admit what you see there. It means having the courage to share that with another, knowing that it might lead them to hurt you more deeply than they could otherwise, even on accident, let alone on purpose. It requires you to be honest about your true history, your true wants and needs, and what you are truly thinking and feeling. You need to be honest with yourself and with those you choose to let in. It requires you to trust that you can handle knowing your true wants, needs, thoughts, and feelings. It means trusting that those you choose to share it with will not judge you and will treat you with respect and see what you have shared as sacred. It requires ongoing compassion, both for the other and for yourself. You need to actively practice loving kindness toward the other and toward yourself, particularly as more tender spots are revealed. Finally, it requires you to persist in this process, moment to moment, day after day, as you experience new things, have new wants and needs, and continue to evolve and change. It needs to be a regular, ongoing practice that continues until the moment you die.

Many of the tools for practicing intimacy were described in earlier chapters. They allow you to become aware of your thoughts, emotions, body, wants, and needs. They allow you to express them to the people you wish to be close with. They empower you to advocate for yourself. They teach you to listen well and deeply to others when they express not just what happened to them, but what they think, what they feel, and what they want and need. They encourage you to be relational and actively turn toward the other to better know and understand them. They explain what it means to live by the Platinum Rule.

Disconnection drives abuse and control: disconnection from self, other, and relationship. Connection is the antidote to abuse and control: connection with self, other, and relationship. Intimacy is a natural consequence and the next step toward connecting with self, other, and relationship. It is a huge deterrent to abuse and control. The greater the connection with self, other, and relationship, the greater the level of intimacy, and the less likely you are to be abusive and controlling.

CHAPTER 26

LEARNING TO SUSTAIN
YOUR POSITIVE CHANGES

Being nonabusive and noncontrolling is a lifelong commitment and a daily practice. If you do not approach it as such, you are at significant risk of drifting back into bad behaviors and bad patterns. This chapter talks about relapse and the relapse process; the next chapter talks about how to sustain the progress you've made.

There are two phases early on when abusive and controlling behavior can significantly but temporarily decline: the honeymoon phase and white-knuckling. They each describe superficial changes that are quite different from the comprehensive changes that lead to a sustained reduction of abusive and controlling behavior.

During the honeymoon phase things are going well, and it's easy to stop your abusive and controlling behaviors. This sometimes happens on vacation, when you don't have to deal with day-to-day demands and you can just have fun. It might be when your partner is in a great mood and behaving just the way you want them to. There are plenty of times when a temporary stop in abusive behavior is due to outside events, rather than real internal change. As soon as the outside events shift—the vacation ends, your partner does something you don't like—your abusive behavior returns. A leaky roof doesn't leak when it's sunny outside, but as soon as the next rainstorm comes along, the problem is evident again.

White-knuckling, a term from the substance abuse field, is using sheer willpower to stop a behavior. It refers to holding on so tightly that your knuckles turn white. This is a fine short-term solution to stopping abusive behavior early on, but it only works for so long. It's like holding your breath: at some point, you have to breathe again.

WORKING YOUR PROGRAM

Patterns of abuse and control are rooted in belief systems that support them. If you believe you have to be abusive and controlling in order to take care of yourself, you will give yourself permission to do so. If you want to stop being abusive and controlling, you need to change how you see the world, how you live in the world, how you take care of yourself, how you meet your wants and needs. You need to develop a new *lifestyle*.

Many recovering alcoholics and addicts understand sobriety in a similar way. Sobriety is not just about abstaining from alcohol and other drugs; it is about developing a sober lifestyle. People who have stopped using but continue to struggle mightily are sometimes described as "dry drunks." This is why someone who is successfully practicing sobriety does not describe themselves as "recovered," but as "recovering." Sobriety is a lifestyle that needs to be maintained daily for the rest of one's life. This is true for people who have patterns of abuse and control as well. You are not addicted to abuse or control, but you have developed a lifestyle that supported it to the point that you feel you have little choice. You need to exchange that lifestyle for one that has no need or desire for abuse or control.

Just reading a book or going to a program will not fix this problem. Taking what you learn and seeking to practice it from now on will. You might leave the program, but the program won't leave you. Your changes must be permanent. It's no longer the agency's or book's program—it's *your* program. Your program that you'll need to work on an ongoing daily basis.

"Working your program" describes the sum total of everything you do to live your life free of abuse and control. It includes what you learn from this book and what you learn from your group, if you attend one. But it goes beyond that. It includes things you learned years ago and continue to do to this day because they are helpful. It might include specific spiritual practices, self-care activities, or longtime traditions that are helpful and important to you. It might include things you have learned in therapy, a substance abuse program, or a twelve-step group. It might include things you learned from books or other research. It might include things you figured out on your own. The point is that your "program" is not just what you've learned from a single source, but the wisdom and insight you've accumulated over time from many different sources. If something helps you to stay nonabusive and noncontrolling, or supports a lifestyle that's in line with that, it's part of your program.

PRACTICING RECOVERY

The concepts of recovery and relapse originated in the substance abuse field but over the decades they have been applied to other areas of lifestyle change as well. We believe they are quite relevant to abuse and control. We use the word "recovery" in the sense of developing a nonabusive and noncontrolling lifestyle. You may also be in recovery from substance abuse or other issues; that is relevant to this work, but recovery from your abusive and controlling lifestyle is distinct and independent from that. Recovery in one area does not automatically lead to recovery in other areas, although it can certainly help.

Recovery is a process that typically takes months, sometimes years, to achieve. Note that it is not a process with an end point. You are never "recovered," but always "in recovery," at best. Being in recovery does not mean your work is done, or even that you're ready to leave a program if you're in one. It means you're living a different lifestyle and having significant success in stopping and reducing your abusive and controlling behavior. It means the core ways that you think and see the world have shifted. You may have more work to do and may still struggle, but at least part of the time you are handling yourself well, better than you have before. If you're still with your partner, they can usually see pretty clearly when you make this shift. They may not trust it at first, which is understandable, but they can attest to the changes they've experienced and that continue to be true.

Early recovery typically emerges once your denial has fallen away and you have made a true internal commitment to being nonabusive and noncontrolling. It involves a significant and sustained reduction in your abusive and controlling behaviors. It reflects new ways of thinking and behaving, most notably shifting from an external to an internal focus, from Power Over to Personal Power. It typically indicates greater self-awareness, better self-soothing and self-management, and better accountability all around. Until you can check all of these boxes, you are not yet in recovery, but you may be headed in that direction. It takes most abusive people a number of months, sometimes more than a year, to reach early recovery. The variables are your level of denial, your motivation to behave differently, and your willingness to put in the time, effort, and energy to change. The length of your path to recovery is not determined by any one thought or behavior, or any particular day, but by a variety of behaviors that you exhibit over the course of weeks and months.

Working your program well—being in recovery—means being an ally to yourself. You have an internal focus. You are self-aware. You are connected with your body, your heart (emotions), and your head (thoughts). You are aware of your wants and needs. You are actively soothing yourself and managing yourself as well as being compassionate with yourself. Your self-care is solid and balanced. You are an ally to others and keep them in your awareness; you are mindful and relational with them. You view the people you are close to as allies and accept their imperfections. You work collaboratively with your partner and children, and trust them even when they behave in ways you do not like.

Recovery means you are working your program well. It means that you are living life differently—living your life better than you used to. You are dealing with life on life's terms.

PAYING ATTENTION TO SIGNS OF RELAPSE

When people hear the word *relapse*, they often assume it means falling back into old behavior—"he relapsed on alcohol"—but that's typically the *final* step in the relapse process. This is important, because it means that if a person realizes they're in relapse early on, they can catch themselves before they return to the old behavior. This is one reason people are able to maintain many years of sobriety: by noticing when they're headed in the wrong direction and catching themselves before they actually return to drinking or using.

The final step in this relapse process would not be engaging in a single instance of abusive behavior, but falling back into a *pattern* of behaviors and the thoughts and beliefs that support them. Just as being in recovery is not just abstaining from a behavior, but rather sustaining a changed lifestyle, being in relapse is about falling away from that changed lifestyle. The further you fall from it, the deeper you are in relapse.

Working your program poorly, or relapsing, means not being a good ally to yourself. You have an external focus. You are not as self-aware. You are not as connected with your body, your heart (emotions), and your head (thoughts). As a result, you are not soothing yourself the way you need to. You are not managing yourself as well. You are acting out and externalizing more. Your self-care is not as good. You have less compassion for yourself. You are not being as good an ally to others. You are less aware of the people around you and not being as relational with them as you could be. You are seeing the people who are closest to you as against you. You aren't working as well with your partner and children, and are instead pulling away from them and being quicker to respond in combative ways.

UNDERSTANDING THE DIFFERENCE BETWEEN RECOVERY AND RELAPSE

When you are in recovery, you live life proactively. When you are in relapse, you live life reactively. Recovery prevents fires; relapse puts out fires. Recovery feels like being in sync, being in a groove; relapse feels out of sync, out of rhythm. Recovery is like skiing down a mountain with a good rhythm, anticipating challenges twenty feet ahead; relapse is like noticing obstacles five feet in front of you and trying not to fall. You might make it down the mountain without falling, but the process won't be elegant or fun. Relapse is not about skiing; it is about not falling.

You cannot fall into relapse until you have been in recovery. If you do not have a solid program of being nonabusive and noncontrolling, then you do not have anything to fall away from. Relapse is a part of life that nearly everyone who is in recovery occasionally experiences. Everyone has times in their lives when either their choices (like working a lot of overtime) or circumstances (a family crisis) result in a less aware and more reactive state. The concern is not that you will fall into relapse, it is that you will *stay* in relapse and not realize it. Unmanaged relapse can lead back to old patterns of abuse and control. The realistic goal is to catch yourself when you are falling and take steps to prevent yourself from going deeper—or staying there.

Relapse does not happen overnight; it takes weeks, even months, not minutes or hours. The more solid your recovery, the more time and opportunity you will have to catch yourself before things really get bad. If you're flying a plane 10,000 feet off the ground, a sudden drop of 100 feet is no big deal, but if you're only 50 feet off the ground, you'll crash.

Another way to think of recovery and relapse is as a graph. The horizontal line is 0; from 1 to 10 is recovery; from -1 to -10 is relapse. The more solid your recovery, the higher you are and the longer it takes to fall into relapse; the worse your relapse, the lower you are. Only when you hit -10 have you fully resumed your patterns of abuse and control. You can actually chart where you are over time. The fall into relapse starts when you turn away from yourself and become less aware of your body, head, and heart. Your climb back into recovery starts when you turn toward yourself and become more aware of your body, head, and heart.

LEARNING TO RECOGNIZE THE STAGES OF RELAPSE

The following information is based on the work of Terrence Gorski and others, who have described the relapse process in people with addiction issues.

STAGE 1: DENIAL

Relapse starts with turning away from yourself, which looks like being oblivious to how you are feeling. This is known as denial. You may be willfully in denial to avoid dealing with certain issues or feelings, or inadvertently in denial because you've been too busy to check in with yourself. Either way, denial marks the beginning of reduced self-awareness and reduced connection with yourself.

Mike attended a men's abuse-intervention group for over a year before moving out of town to start a new job. He did great work while he was there, stopping his patterns of abuse and control, likely saving his marriage. Three years later, he has a new baby, his first, shortly after getting a promotion at work. Between the demands of being an involved new father and his new responsibilities at work, he has far less time to be present with his emotions and thoughts.

STAGE 2: CHANGES IN BEHAVIOR

People start to act differently when they are in relapse. They start doing things they normally don't or stop doing things they normally do. This may be because they are avoiding their feelings or because of outside events.

Mike's promotion gave him new and different responsibilities, and as a new dad he is busy helping care for his son, which is new to him. He used to love to cook healthy gourmet meals, but now often eats on the fly. He has much less time to himself for taking walks alone through the neighboring woods, which was his time for reflecting on himself and his life.

STAGE 3: LOSS OF ROUTINE

Part of being solidly in recovery is having a variety of healthy, effective routines and habits. These might include an exercise routine; domestic routines for cooking, cleaning, paying bills, and checking the mail; and social routines that guide when and where you get together with friends. When some of these routines are disrupted by external demands or avoidance behaviors, self-care is increasingly compromised.

Mike used to make it to the gym several times a week and play basketball at least once a week. He stopped playing basketball when his son was born and now he's lucky to work out twice a week, if at all. One source of fun was tinkering on an old Ford Mustang, but he hasn't touched it in months. He used to track his expenses regularly, but he hasn't even balanced his checkbook in months.

STAGE 4: REDUCED SOCIAL CONNECTION

High-quality friendships are a very important resource that can make a huge difference in quality of life. Talking with good friends helps you connect more honestly with yourself and can give you perspective. In relapse you tend to have less contact with friends, and the contact you do have may not be as honest; you may not be exactly forthcoming about what's really going on in your life. You might intentionally withhold information in order to avoid certain feelings or unintentionally withhold it because you lack self-awareness in general. Either way, this limited connection can lead you to drift further away from yourself and your program.

Mike has rarely socialized since the birth of his son. If he's not at work, he wants to be with his son and support his wife, who struggled with postpartum depression. The rare moments he spends with friends are focused on his son's development; he rarely shares anything else, including the growing pressure he feels as a manager, husband, and father.

STAGE 5: LOSS OF JUDGMENT

Given all the other disruptions, it's not surprising that you might start to make poorer choices. You are less self-aware, have less assistance from friends and less time to be thoughtful. This can lead to poorer judgment, which just contributes to the growing chaos.

Mike's wife shares her concerns that he has been increasingly irritable and reactive. She encourages him to take things a little easier and consider reaching out to friends for support. In the wake of that, Mike's colleagues invite him out. Although these were not the friends she was thinking of—she meant those he has known for years, not newer coworkers he hardly knows— he accepts the invitation and joins them for a night of raucous drinking. He awakens the next morning badly hungover and needing to get to his car, which he left at the bar because he was too drunk to drive home. His limited sleep and hangover limit his productivity at work that day, so he has to put in extra hours over the weekend and be less available for his wife and child.

STAGE 6: FEELING OUT OF CONTROL

As relapse progresses, you tend to feel increasingly out of control of your life. The loss of routine, poor self-care, increased isolation, and low self-awareness all lead to the feeling that life is increasingly unmanageable. Poorer choices reduce your sense of power and make it feel like everything is caving in. You probably feel increasingly reactive and desperate. Life feels highly unmanageable.

Under heavy strain at work and at home, Mike is cutting nearly everything else out of his life. He no longer takes the time to prepare even basic meals, instead eating fast food on the go and leaving his wife to fend for herself. After his drunken night out, there has been increasing distance between Mike and his wife and it is becoming the norm to not talk with each other at all. He has had several nearly abusive outbursts with her and was barely able to catch himself before unloosing a verbal tirade at her. He is less efficient at work, which his boss has noticed. He feels utterly alone in the world and ineffective as a father, husband, and employee.

STAGE 7: OPTION REDUCTION

This is the final and most dangerous step of the relapse process. With life feeling increasingly unmanageable and the usual resources, skills, and perspectives not being utilized, it very much feels like the walls are closing in. It can feel like there is no escape and no viable solution. Life can feel utterly overwhelming. This is where the "fuck its" or "to hell with its" show up, where you make decisions without caring about the consequences. If it continues, it leads to tunnel vision, where it seems like you have only three ways to move forward: commit suicide, "go crazy," or return to your old bad behavior.

Option 1: Suicide

You may have thoughts of wishing you were dead or wishing that all the pain would just go away. It is important not to take these thoughts literally or to act on them. It is common for people who are feeling hopelessly depressed or desperate to wish they were dead. Just because you are wishing you were dead or having thoughts of ending your life does not mean that you truly want that. Those feelings are more about wanting to get away from the distress than wanting to end your life.

These feelings will pass. Whatever you do, do not take steps to actually kill yourself. If you are not able to manage these thoughts and feelings on your own, seek professional assistance immediately. If you have a therapist or attend a group, let them know immediately. Talk with people you trust about how you are feeling. If you do not know what else to do, go to the emergency room or call a mental health crisis hotline. The National Suicide Prevention Lifeline is available around the clock at 1-800-273-8255.

There are many people who can help you navigate these dark thoughts so that you end up feeling a little better. Remember that no matter how bad you may feel, the feelings will pass, just not as quickly as you would like.

Option 2: "Go crazy"

A second way to get away from all this is to have what they used to call a "nervous breakdown": either a flare-up of existing mental health issues or the development of new ones. Whereas option #1 is externally leaving the world, option #2 is internally leaving the world. If you are having significant mental health issues, alert your therapist or group leader. If you are not currently meeting with a mental health professional, consider setting up an appointment with one ASAP. You can also reach out to trusted friends and family for support. Self-compassion can also help. Typically, as with suicidal thinking, you will start to feel better as you manage your distress. This will pass, although not as quickly as you would like.

Option 3: Return to the old bad behavior

For an alcoholic or addict, this would mean drinking or using again on an ongoing basis. For people who have been abusive, it means returning to patterns of abuse and control. Of the three options, most people who have been abusive choose this one: to fall back into old bad habits and patterns as if nothing had changed.

At his wits' end, Mike realizes something has to give. Losing his job is not an option, so he decides to prioritize that over everything else, which he was guilty of in the past, before he made significant changes and attended an abuse-intervention program. He starts to inappropriately assert his authority around the house, becoming verbally abusive toward his wife. He vents his distress on her, accusing her of being unappreciative of him, taking advantage of him, and never being satisfied with what he does for her. He neglects his son and treats his wife with disdain.

He feels a bit of relief when he stops pushing himself to be an involved father or husband, but the appreciation he gets from his boss provides only brief comfort. He feels sullen, resentful, and irritable most of the time.

***

The relapse process can be progressive, with one step leading to the next leading to the next. However, it's far more common that most or all of the stages are triggered around the same time by external events, like working overtime for a long time, having a baby, or dealing with an extended family crisis or a serious long-term health issue. Whatever the cause, the result is the same: significantly less time and energy to check in with yourself, disrupted routines, and less social support, which make you feel more disorganized, overwhelmed, and powerless, with little time to make thoughtful choices or decisions.

STOPPING YOURSELF FROM FALLING FURTHER INTO RELAPSE
The good news is that you can interrupt the relapse process at any point by simply turning toward your feelings and getting honest with yourself. That may happen easily and naturally if the outside events contributing to your relapse shift—if you stop working overtime or you get a week off. If the external factors are ongoing, you may have to put in more effort, which could increase your emotional distress—but that's the only way to willfully interrupt the cycle and start making different, healthier choices. When you realize you are in relapse, you need to figure out an action plan to get out of relapse. The deeper you get, the more urgent this becomes.

When Mike's wife expressed concerns about the changes in his behavior during the loss of judgment stage, he took her seriously. It was a wake-up call that showed him he was pretty far along in relapse, and he was able to see it and name it—both to himself and his wife. He'd promised himself years earlier when he left the group that if he ever found himself deep in relapse, he would call either the group facilitator or a group member. He called the group facilitator. This is how the conversation went:

"I'm calling because I think I'm in relapse. I haven't been abusive yet or particularly controlling with my wife, but I'm definitely getting more

irritable and reactive. She commented on that the other day and I realized that I needed to do something. So that's why I'm calling you."

"So how long do you think you have been in relapse for?" his former group facilitator asked.

"Well, initially I thought it had only been for a few weeks, just through the holidays," (he was calling in mid-January), "but as I've thought about it more I think it actually probably started back early in the fall, so for about four or five months."

"Well, good that you decided to call. I'm sure we can sort this out. Relapse can often get triggered by significant changes in a person's life. How have things been going?"

"Well, obviously my wife and I are still together and getting along pretty well overall. No abusive episodes or anything like that. We even have a son now!"

"Really? How old is he?"

There was a pause and you could almost hear the light bulb going on in Mike's head. "Five months. Damn! Why couldn't I make that connection?" he replied with chagrin and playful frustration.

"Well, these things are usually clearer in hindsight. Any other significant developments?"

"I'm still at the same job that I left Portland for, although I did get a pretty significant promotion."

"Yeah? When?"

Another, briefer, pause, and an even more chagrined response. "Six months ago. Damn! How could I have not seen this?"

Although Mike was a bit embarrassed over not having made the connections between his promotion, his son's birth, and his relapse, simply naming it was already providing relief and perspective. He had already set up an appointment with a therapist to get some more support. He talked for a few more minutes sketching out other things he could do to pull himself out of relapse, including checking in more frequently with his wife, taking a little more time for himself (which she had encouraged all along, but he'd felt guilty doing), and talking with his boss about modifying his workload.

As a result, he settled back down, his mood and demeanor improved, and his wife was pleased and relieved that she had the kinder husband back that she had so enjoyed in recent years.

BEING AWARE OF SITUATIONS THAT CAN LEAD TO RELAPSE

To manage relapse, you need to know when you're in it. One way to look out for it is to monitor what's happening in your life. Certain circumstances increase the risk significantly by making self-care difficult for an extended period of time or knocking your life out of balance. Here are some of the most common:

A family crisis that persists throughout multiple weeks

An extended illness that persists throughout many weeks or months

An extended period of time with multiple new demands on your time and energy

Loss of a loved one, a job, or a romantic relationship

Moving to a new home or doing a major remodel of your home

The birth of a child

The extended holiday season

Working significant overtime hours over the course of many weeks

If you are in one of the situations above, it doesn't mean you're in relapse, but it does mean you are at risk. The more time and energy your circumstances take away from areas of self-care, the greater your risk of relapse. Another key factor is how long the situation lasts. It typically takes weeks to fall into relapse, so even a fairly major disruption will not push someone solidly in recovery into relapse unless it continues for a number of weeks. In the example above, Mike had two major changes (the birth of a first child and an increase in work responsibilities) that pushed him into relapse months later.

There may be certain times of year when you are more at risk of relapse. Your job may be more demanding during a particular season, for instance, and your family may demand more of your time and energy at certain points. The end of the year can be particularly disruptive because of the concentration of national holidays and seasonal events. If you know such a time is approaching, you can prepare yourself so your time in relapse is as brief as possible.

KNOWING YOUR RELAPSE WARNING SIGNS

Besides looking for outside events that can push you into relapse, you can also look for changes in your feelings, thoughts, and behaviors that indicate the same. As you become less self-aware, less connected, more reactive, and more overwhelmed, certain behaviors often appear or disappear. By keeping an eye out for them, you can catch yourself when you start to drift into relapse. A list of these behaviors is included in Appendix G in the back of the book; take a few minutes to review it, knowing that it is incomplete—there are many other indications of relapse. This list is just intended to be a start. Circle the warning signs you have seen in yourself in the past, and add any that are not listed.

People sometimes confuse relapse warning signs with the signs of physical and behavioral intensity that are noted in the Journal. There is often some overlap, but the signs of intensity typically happen in the moment of a situation and are only briefly present. Signs of relapse tend to reoccur for weeks or months and be ongoing.

The behaviors on this list are not necessarily indications of relapse for everyone. Their presence alone does not mean you're in relapse. Ask yourself which ones are indications of *your* relapse.

Finally, these warning signs do not *cause* relapse; they are *symptoms* of relapse. Making specific behaviors go away does not mean you are getting yourself out of relapse. If you take a decongestant when you have a cold, you might temporarily cure the congestion, but your cold is still there.

MAKING A LIST OF YOUR RELAPSE WARNING SIGNS

Think about times when you realized, in hindsight that you were probably in relapse. There may have been a lot of chaos and disorganization in your life; you may have been extremely busy for an extended period of time; you may have been dealing with some of the life events listed earlier. With those times in mind, look over the list of possible signs of relapse in Appendix G and mark any that were present. Add any that are not listed. The behaviors you mark don't have to appear *only* when you're in relapse, but they should routinely appear *mainly* when you are in relapse. The specific behaviors will vary from person to person, as will the number of behaviors.

Review the list you have come up with. Do any of the behaviors appear when you're not in relapse? For most people, the answer is yes. How many of those behaviors could show up in a given week if you were not in relapse? That number varies from person to person; some people might see two or three behaviors, while others could see five, six, or more without being in relapse. Write that number—how many behaviors you could display even without being in relapse—at the bottom of the list. That is your cutoff score. If you check off fewer than that on your personal list in a given week, you're probably not in relapse. If you check off more than that number in a week, there's a good chance you are in relapse.

The last thing to do is review your personal list of warning signs and ask yourself which ones, if any, *only* show up when you're in relapse. These are the behaviors that *never* show up at other times. Put a star by those. Those are your critical items. If you check off any of those items in a given week, even just one, then you are probably in relapse.

You now have your own list of relapse warning signs. We encourage you to review it regularly, at least every couple of weeks or every month. The idea is to see how many of the behaviors you've exhibited in the past week. If it's more than your cutoff score, or any of the starred items, you are probably in relapse. That should prompt you to take steps to acknowledge that you're in relapse and figure out what you need to do to manage it and get yourself out of it.

GETTING OUT OF RELAPSE

FIGURING OUT HOW YOU GOT THERE

Once you realize you are in relapse, you need to gather some information. First, what got you into relapse in the first place? Check the list above for situations that often lead to relapse. Consider other contributing factors. Next, ask yourself how long you have been in relapse. A week? A month? Longer? Finally, think about how much longer the contributing factors are likely to continue. What can be done to bring them to a close?

With that information at hand, you can start to develop a plan for getting out of relapse. If the contributing factors will come to an end in the next week or two, you may be able to ride it out, knowing that you'll be able to set things right afterward. If that's the case, willfully get back with your program and get back what you were doing that was helpful.

On the other hand, if the contributing factors are likely to continue for a while, you need to figure out a way to manage your life differently. The suggestions below address that situation.

BEING EXTRA VIGILANT

You know that you are at greater risk for acting out and making poorer choices, so be extra careful. Mind your reactivity and your self-talk. Be careful not to project or externalize your emotions. You are likely to feel more distressed inside, so be careful not to take it out on the people around you. Other people may seem more annoying right now, but remember the concept of the emotional barometer: they are not causing your distress, they are just triggering it and maybe slightly adding to it, like the straw that broke the camel's back.

WHITE-KNUCKLING IT

You may be more tempted to be abusive and controlling while you are in relapse, but you can refuse to give yourself permission. Simply resist that temptation. You might need to be extra careful to keep your mouth shut and to really think before speaking, given that you are in a more reactive space.

PRIORITIZING KEY AREAS OF SELF-CARE

When you have limited time and energy, it's important to prioritize critical areas of self-care. You probably don't have time, space, and energy to do your full range of self-care activities, but you can focus on the ones that mean the most and have the most positive impact. These vary from person to person, but exercise, spiritual practices, solitude, and recreation often rank high. Make sure to take care of the most important areas first, since you will probably not be able to get to everything.

STAYING CONNECTED TO OTHERS

You will likely be struggling during this time, so it is especially important to reach out more to those you are closest to and who presumably know that you have a history of being abusive and controlling. If you are in or have been in an abuse-intervention group, this is an especially appropriate time to contact peers or facilitators, who understand what is at stake and can actively support you in staying true to your changes rather than drifting into old bad behaviors.

CHANGING YOUR CIRCUMSTANCES

Finally, remember that no one can sustain positive behavior and work their program indefinitely while being in relapse. Inevitably, they will drift back into old bad behaviors to cope and make it through. If the circumstances causing your relapse are not going to be changing any time soon, it is vital you take active steps to change them. That might include changing jobs or work responsibilities, setting firm boundaries with others, or otherwise disengaging from situations that are likely to remain unmanageable.

KEEPING A RELAPSE JOURNAL

Unfortunately, people are not always able to catch themselves until they fully relapse and revert to old bad behaviors. When that happens, all you can do is try to pull out of it as quickly as possible, keeping the abusive and controlling patterns to a minimum. Such struggles provide learning opportunities: you can learn from your mistakes so you do not repeat them. In that vein, a Relapse Journal is included in Appendix H. It is a questionnaire to fill out after a deep relapse that can help you prevent it from happening again. Listed below are the questions with brief explanations. "The incident" refers to the peak moment of bad behavior, but there are often a few moments that stand out. It's often right after these moments that people realize something needs to change and that they are in deep relapse.

BEFORE THE INCIDENT

1. **How long do you think you were in relapse before the actual incident?**
   People have often been in relapse longer than they realized. With the clarity of hindsight, when do you think you first slipped into relapse? Becoming more familiar with what happened in those early days can help you catch it next time.

2. **What were the warning signs that you were in relapse?**
    Review the list of relapse warning signs to identify which ones were present while you were in relapse. Were there any that you had not previously considered? This may lead you to revise your personal list.

3. **What was your self-talk like during your relapse?**
    Which recurring thoughts did you have when you were in relapse? Which beliefs contributed to it? For example, "Nobody cares," "Everyone's against me," "I'm being taken for granted," "There's never any time for me." If you can identify certain thoughts or beliefs that enabled your relapse, you'll be able to identify positive self-talk and pro-social beliefs that can challenge them next time.

4. **What was going on in your life just before and/or during your relapse? Consider any circumstances that affected your work, primary relationship, family, finances, and health.**
    If you know which events and circumstances triggered your slide into relapse, you can figure out how to get out of it and avoid it in the future.

5. **Was anything else affecting your mindset just before and/or during your relapse?**
    Sometimes people are more vulnerable to relapse when something triggers a particular state of mind. Examples include an anniversary of a loss or other significant event; current events that you find particularly troubling; and negative influences such as spending time with certain friends or consuming inflammatory media (music, movies, talk shows).

6. **Which emotions were the most intense during your relapse?**
    Because relapse starts when you turn away from uncomfortable emotions, it's important to know which emotions you might have been trying to ignore. The usual suspects are those that devolve into anger, but try to identify the emotions behind the anger: overwhelm, sadness, depression, discouragement, or loneliness, to name a few.

7. **Who did you talk with while you were in relapse? Did anyone express concerns about how you were doing?**
    Social support can play an important role in stopping relapse. If you can identify what sort of social support you had (and utilized) during your relapse, you can sort out whether this is an area you need to shore

up—either by expanding your circle of support or better utilizing it in the future.

8. **Were you aware you were in relapse before the incident? If no, why not? If yes, what should you have done?**

   The sooner you realize you are in relapse, the sooner you can take steps to manage it and get out of it.

DURING THE INCIDENT

9. **Which signs of physical and behavioral intensity appeared immediately before the incident?**

   These signs are used in your regular Journal entries; they are different from your relapse warning signs. Noting their presence can help you catch yourself before you act out again.

10. **Briefly describe the incident.**

    This is like the Event section of your regular Journal. Describe the moment in which you were actually being abusive and controlling. If there were multiple moments, summarize them here. Describing the actual incident can help you learn from it. We recommend that you complete a regular Journal on this situation as well.

11. **Which thoughts justified your behavior during the incident?**

    How did you give yourself permission to behave badly? Write out your negative self-talk and the beliefs that justified your abuse and control. Consider identifying positive self-talk and nonabusive and noncontrolling beliefs that could challenge these thoughts in the future.

AFTER THE INCIDENT

12. **How did you feel immediately after the incident?**

    Right after an incident, people often start to realize that they are doing much worse than they thought. They often feel regret, embarrassment, guilt, and shame. It's important not to forget how bad you felt about what you did. That memory can motivate you to do things differently next time.

13. **What did you do immediately after the incident?**

    This clarifies which steps, if any, you took away from relapse. If you were not able to shift out of relapse, writing this down can help you see why.

14. **How did the incident impact everyone involved?**

While you're in relapse, it can be difficult to comprehend what happened and how it affected others. It is important to seek clarity about the damage your behavior caused so you can avoid doing it again and make appropriate repair.

15. **What did you do to stop the incident?**

Identifying the concrete steps you took to disengage can remind you of what you can do next time, hopefully even sooner.

16. **Are you still in relapse now? If so, how will you get out? If not, how can you tell?**

Depending on when you fill out this Relapse Journal, you may still be in relapse. If you are, what can you do to move toward recovery? If you aren't, how do you know? What has changed?

GOING FORWARD

17. **What have you done to prevent another incident?**

Write down specific actions you have taken to make sure nothing else will happen.

18. **What do you still need to do to prevent another incident?**

Write down what else, if anything, needs to be done to really put this relapse behind you.

19. **What is your plan for the next time your relapse warning signs appear?**

Write down a concrete action plan for the next time you realize you're sliding into relapse. This is also covered in your Continuing Accountability Plan, which we discuss in the next chapter. It might include updating your existing Continuing Accountability Plan.

20. **What have you learned from this relapse?**

Write down any other takeaways or lessons learned from this episode.

***

The next chapter, the final one of the book, teaches you how to sustain your program.

CHAPTER 27

SUSTAINING YOUR CHANGES

This last chapter explains how to sustain your progress over time and alerts you to some pitfalls you may encounter going forward. It's wise to start by reflecting on where you were, how far you have come, and what you are doing differently now. We encourage you to start by doing an Accountability Statement.

WRITING AN ACCOUNTABILITY STATEMENT

Although you may want to completely forget all of your abusive and controlling behavior and the damage it has caused, it is vital that you remember it. After all, those who forget the past are doomed to repeat it. The more you avoid and deny your past, the greater your risk of falling back into old behaviors. It is also easy to think that what you did was not as extensive or as bad or as damaging as it actually was. The more you dismiss or diminish it, the greater your risk of giving yourself permission to do it again.

This is also an issue with people who have had problems with substance abuse. They tend to forget and minimize how serious their substance use was and the problems it caused in their lives. Forgetting allows them to sustain their denial and continue their use. This is why Alcoholics Anonymous developed the Fourth Step, which is used by many twelve-step programs now: a searching and fearless moral inventory of yourself.

To help you sustain your progress and understand how far you've come, we developed the Accountability Statement. It's based on similar exercises that are used in other programs for abusive partners all over the country, and is like a Fourth Step, but more extensive. It guides you through a full accounting of your abusive and controlling behaviors as an adult toward anyone, including your romantic partners and any children with whom you had contact. It helps you take an unblinking look at how those individuals have or may have suffered as a result. It is an accounting of all of the ways you justified and gave yourself permission to be abusive and controlling in the past.

When you have acknowledged all of that, you then need to take full responsibility for your thoughts and behaviors and the damage they have caused others. You need to fully acknowledge how you feel about this now and how your thinking, beliefs, and behavior have changed so that you will not return to your old ways, to the best of your ability. Finally, you need to acknowledge how you have already made amends and how you plan to continue to do so going forward.

All this is covered in eight sections that are explained in detail below. You can think of this assignment as a bit like a final exam. As you will see, it covers much of what we have written about and applies it to your own life. We will identify which chapters relate to each section below.

For this assignment we ask that you include any abusive or controlling behavior you have exhibited to anyone as an adult, starting at the age of eighteen. If you are under twenty-one, focus on the last three years. If you are doing this exercise in a group, it should be a verbal presentation, not a written one. You can write up exactly what you want to say, but most people simply write notes and talk them through in the group.

Section 1. Write a Full Description of Your Violence

List any and all abusive behaviors you have engaged in with anyone. Make sure to consider every category of abuse: physical, verbal, psychological, property, financial, sexual, and collateral. Give approximate frequencies (twice a week, daily, three times a year, etc.) and then do the math to figure out the actual numbers. In your estimates, err on the side of slight underestimation—list the minimum frequency. For example, if you estimate that for the past ten years of your twelve-year relationship you put your partner down at least two or three times a week, that frequency would be converted to 1000x (2x/week—low estimate—x 50 weeks x 10 years = 1000). Be specific and explicit about the abuse. Do not offer explanations or elaborations. Most people organize this section by each specific past victim; others organize it by specific behavior; still others organize it chronologically. Consider reviewing the following chapters for help with this section: Chapter 1: Abusive Behaviors; Chapter 3: Sexual Abuse; Chapter 4: Financial Abuse.

SECTION 2. WRITE A FULL DESCRIPTION OF YOUR CONTROLLING BEHAVIORS

List all the types of controlling behaviors you have exhibited. Give one specific example of each type of controlling behavior. First try to do this on your own, seeing how many different ones you can think of. After that, refer to the list of controlling behaviors in Appendix A to see if you've missed any. You do not need to give frequencies. Since most abusive behavior is also controlling, you do not need to list anything here that you listed in the first section. Consider reviewing Chapter 2: Controlling Behaviors as you complete this section.

SECTION 3. WRITE ABOUT HOW YOUR MY ABUSE AND CONTROL AFFECTED OTHERS

This section requires speculation; you cannot know for sure all the ways your abuse affected others, but you can put yourself in their shoes. List each victim and consider the impact of your abuse on each one, both at the time and over time. Consider their emotional reactions as well as other ways they may have suffered or may continue to suffer. Make sure to include any consequences to them that you have observed and the consequences they've told you about.

For many people, this is the most difficult section to complete; it typically requires the most work. A first attempt often needs to be expanded and elaborated. For example, many simply list the emotional experience of the victims (sad, afraid, depressed) without talking about additional consequences (loss of sleep, concentration problems, withdrawal from friends). Consider reviewing Chapter 11: Understand the Impact of Abuse on Your Partner and Chapter 12: Understand the Impact of Abuse on Children for help completing this section. This is an especially important section on which to get constructive input—but not from those you were abusive toward.

SECTION 4. IDENTIFY THE OLD BELIEFS THAT JUSTIFIED YOUR ABUSE AND CONTROL

Which views, opinions, and beliefs led you to give yourself permission to be abusive and controlling in the past? If you'd been asked immediately after you engaged in abusive or controlling behavior why you did it, what would have been your honest response? What were your justifications at the time? Which general beliefs did you hold that allowed you to be abusive? Consider reviewing Chapter 5: Abusive Thoughts and Beliefs and Chapter 7: Denial for help completing this section.

SECTION 5. TAKE FULL RESPONSIBILITY FOR YOUR ABUSIVE AND CONTROLLING BEHAVIOR

This is not a question, but rather a statement with which you presumably agree. This statement should be the beginning of a paragraph about what "full responsibility" means to you. It should be a direct but general rebuttal of all of the excuses and justifications identified in the previous section. This is usually the shortest section, often only a paragraph or two in length. Consider reviewing Chapter 10: Becoming Accountable for help completing this section.

SECTION 6. WRITE HOW YOU FEEL ABOUT IT NOW AND HOW YOUR BELIEFS HAVE CHANGED

This is actually two questions. For the first, list your feelings and reactions in the present to what you listed in the first four sections. You might refer to Appendix D: Emotions for help with this section. Consider your emotional reactions as you wrote the first three sections and include them here. For the second question, generate a set of new beliefs that you have in the present. For each old belief listed in section four, you should list at least one new belief here. Consider reviewing Chapter 15: Becoming Aware of Your Thoughts for help with this section.

SECTION 7. IDENTIFY WHAT YOU ARE WILLING TO DO DIFFERENTLY

This should be a list of all the ways you are working your own program of being nonabusive and noncontrolling. What specific things are you doing day to day, week to week, and month to month to make sure you remain nonabusive and noncontrolling? This can include positive and helpful things you've done all along (regular exercise, meditation), things you learned from this book or attending a program (changing your self-talk, taking time-outs), and things you learned elsewhere, from other programs (AA), professionals (an individual therapist, a sponsor), and books. Consider reviewing these chapters for help with this section: Chapter 14: Learning to Stop Your Abuse in the Moment; Chapter 16: Becoming Aware of Your Emotions; Chapter 18: Learning to Self-Soothe; Chapter 19: Learning to Take Care of Yourself; Chapter 21: Learning to Regard Others, Chapter 23: Learning to Communicate Effectively; Chapter 24: Practicing Conflict-Resolution Skills; and Chapter 26: Learning to Sustain Your Positive Changes.

SECTION 8. WRITE DOWN YOUR PLAN FOR MAKING AMENDS

List the ways you have repaired or plan to repair the damage caused by your abuse and control. Remember that amends need to be for the benefit of others and go above and beyond what is expected of an average, respectful person. List only the things you seriously intend to do. Consider reviewing Chapter 22: Learning to Make Things Right for help with this section.

***

You can start working on your Accountability Statement at any time, but as we mentioned earlier, it's a bit like a final exam. In order to complete it well, in an honest, genuine manner, you need to have accomplished the following:

- attained a full understanding of what constitutes abusive and controlling behavior
- moved through your denial about your past abuse and control and taken full responsibility for your actions

- acknowledged and become willing to fully examine how your behavior may have affected others
- come to understand all the old thoughts and beliefs that led you to give yourself permission to be abusive and controlling
- made significant changes to the way you think and behave

This is typically not all true until you have been in a program for many months, sometimes even years.

If you plan to share your Accountability Statement in your group, you should share it late in your stay, but it's important not to wait until the very end. We recommend that you attend the group at least twice more after you share it. This will make it clear to you that the other group members don't think any differently or more negatively about you in the wake of your sharing. Many abusive partners feel at least some shame over what they have done, and that shame has contributed to their silence and denial. It's important that you don't just share this entire thing and dash. Give yourself a chance to see how the group continues to treat you with respect even afterward. Experiencing respectful treatment from your peers even after the statement is shared is a powerful step toward banishing shame.

Finally, do not involve your victim(s) in this exercise, either in helping you work on it or by sharing it with them. Although they might remember certain abusive episodes better or speak compellingly about their suffering, the purpose of this exercise is for you to remember and discern, *on your own*, without the input—at this time—of any of the people you have been abusive to. You can get their input later when you write them letters of accountability (discussed in Chapter 22: Learning to Make Things Right and below). This is a searching and fearless moral inventory for *yourself*. After you complete it and receive constructive input on how to improve it, you can turn it into individual letters of accountability for specific people.

WRITING LETTERS OF ACCOUNTABILITY

Letters of accountability are written to specific people to whom you have been abusive and controlling or who were significantly exposed to your abusive behavior, including your children. These letters should follow the same basic structure of the Accountability Statement: acknowledge your past abuse and control, how you suspect they suffered from that behavior, and the excuses you made for that behavior. In the letter you take full responsibility for the acts of abuse and control you have engaged in, share how you feel about it now, and explain how you have changed your ways of thinking and behaving so that you will not engage in any further abuse in the future.

Letters of accountability should have the same sections in the same order as the Accountability Statement, but they are specifically for one person and should be written using paragraphs, not lists of behaviors and answers to questions. Abused partners who are given such "letters" that are little more than lists are often very hurt and disturbed by the detached and unemotional presentation. Take the information from each section and turn it into sentences and paragraphs written to that specific person in a relational manner.

The Accountability Statement might be shared verbally in a group, but letters of accountability should be written out so they can be read by the recipient in private. If you struggle with writing things out that way, you might record your words and share them with the recipient so they can listen to it in private. This allows them to review what you have written or recorded more than once if they wish.

We recommend that you have someone else read your letters before you share them with the recipients. This can help make sure you've written them in a sensitive, thoughtful, relational manner. If you attend an abuse-intervention group or program, you might ask people in the group.

The most obvious and important person to write such a letter to is your partner if you were abusive to them and you are still together. You might also write letters to ex-partners if they indicate that they would like you to. If you have children who were exposed to your abusive behavior, they deserve letters, too, written at an appropriate age level with age-appropriate detail, one for each child. For a letter to a juvenile child, you should talk with the other parent first and run the letter by them before sharing it with your child. You might also write letters of accountability to other people to whom you were regularly abusive, such as other family members, friends, and coworkers.

Before writing a Letter of Accountability, make very certain that the other person wants one. Current partners almost always do. Ex-partners may or may not, depending on whether they still have contact with you and to what extent they have put the relationship and related abuse behind them. Children may or may not, depending on their personality, interpersonal style, and the quality of their relationship with you. The older and more severely abused the child was by your behavior, the more important it is to consider writing them a letter. Younger children who are not yet teens usually don't have a strong opinion about it; it's best to get input from the other parent. Other family members, friends, and coworkers will vary a great deal about whether they want or need such a letter. In general, the ones who might most want one are those who were exposed to significant patterns of your abuse and control and were significantly negatively affected by it over time.

When you have a letter ready, you need to consider how they might want to receive it. Some may want it left for them or mailed to them so they can read it alone when they feel ready. Others might want to read it in your presence. Still others might want you to read it to them in person at a time of their choosing. Do your best to accommodate their wishes.

Most current partners will want to talk about the letter after they have read it. It's important that you are ready and willing to have a thorough discussion; make sure to allow enough time, energy, and openness for it. They may want to talk about acts of abuse and control you left out, ways they have suffered that were not mentioned, feelings the letter stirred up (including anger, sadness, and grief), old memories triggered by the letter, and numerous other reactions and thoughts they might have. Keep the focus firmly on them during this conversation, staying as open and unreactive as you possibly can. Do not get defensive. While some partners will be happy, appreciative, and grateful for the letter and the changes you've made, others may initially be quite upset. Be prepared for your partner to have some strong emotional reactions, do some intense sharing, and ask you some challenging questions. Some partners may be quite happy and ready to move forward after the letter is shared, but others may be quite upset and need to process. It's possible that their distress will last for some time and require multiple conversations. If that's the case, do your best to be as available and responsive as you can be.

LEARNING HOW TO STAY OUT OF TROUBLE

Once you've developed a new way of living free of abuse and control, it is vital that you sustain it over time. One aspect, which we've already discussed, is managing relapse. Another aspect is watching out for pitfalls that could lead you astray. Extensive research has been done over decades into the factors that increase the risk of falling into old behaviors. Listed below are the most prevalent.

WATCHING YOUR BELIEFS

Not surprisingly, people who believe it's okay or justifiable to engage in bad behavior are more likely to do so. Which beliefs did you have that gave you permission to be abusive and controlling? Do you still have any of them? What new beliefs do you have that don't make it okay to be abusive and controlling?

BEING CAREFUL WHO YOU SPEND TIME WITH

Research has consistently found that people are strongly influenced by the people they spend time with. This includes friends, family, coworkers, neighbors—anyone you have some sort of contact with. If you hang out with people whose beliefs support abuse and control, you are more likely to follow suit. They might believe your partner is to blame for your problems, or that you had good excuses for your bad behavior. They might embrace and support the negative beliefs listed in the fourth section of your Accountability Statement. These folks are problematic even if you never actually see them behaving in abusive or controlling ways. They often support your negative self-talk and your pro-abuse beliefs, which can strengthen them within you.

On the other hand, if you primarily hang out with people who have nonabusive and noncontrolling beliefs, it will be easier for you to behave well. They might see your partner as being on your side and refuse to assume their behavior is a personal attack on you. They might give your partner the benefit of the doubt and refuse to make excuses for your past abuse and control. These people tend to support your positive self-talk and pro-social beliefs, which can strengthen them within you.

Each of these groups has an impact, so the best social circle involves few to no people with abusive and controlling beliefs and lots of people with the opposite. A so-so situation involves both groups or none. The worst situation involves mainly people with pro-abusive beliefs and few who do not.

It is not just the influence of people that you need to be mindful of, but also of the media you consume. Be careful what you fill your mind with while reading, listening, and watching. Social media, music, movies, and books that encourage and support pro-abuse beliefs or justify abuse and control can have a negative influence on you. Likewise, content that encourages you to think in more pro-social and nonabusive ways will have a positive influence.

ABSTAINING FROM SUBSTANCE ABUSE

Substance abuse is a huge contributor to people not working their programs well and who fall back into other bad behaviors. It can also interfere with your ability to learn how to be successful. Keeping addictions in check through sobriety and healthy ways of living is vital.

KEEPING YOURSELF BUSY

The more time you have on your hands, the more time you have to get into trouble. A regular schedule helps you focus on what you want rather than drifting into unproductive ways of thinking. If you find yourself with extra time, take advantage of it by doing the things you normally don't have time for. There might be friends you haven't reached out to for a while, personal projects you've put on the shelf, or interests you've wanted to pursue but never seem to have the time for. This is also a good time to complete or update a Self-Care Plan to figure out which areas of your life most need attention.

PURSUING FULFILLING WORK AND PLAY

The more engaged you are with your life, the more aspects of your life you feel excited, happy, and passionate about, the more motivated you'll be to stay out of trouble. Research has found that the less someone has to lose, the more likely they are to get into trouble. The less fulfilled people feel, the easier it is to mistreat others and blame them for their distress. Having fulfilling work, extracurricular activities you love, and people you feel a strong connection and commitment to (your partner, children, and friends) are all incentives to stay out of trouble.

DOING YOUR BEST TO MANAGE YOUR STRESS

Research has shown that people who handle stress poorly and don't take good care of themselves are likely to end up in trouble. Likewise, people who are prone to relapse struggle to take good care of themselves.

TAKING ADVANTAGE OF YOUR RESOURCES AND OPPORTUNITIES

Individuals who are prone to falling back into old bad habits and behaviors are less likely to take advantage of the resources that are available to them to sustain their new ways of living, including support from friends and opportunities for fulfilling work. Part of being accountable is taking responsibility for your own well-being and doing whatever you can to take good care of yourself.

BEING REALISTIC AND STAYING HUMBLE

Life is tough and the world will not always cooperate with you. Mistakes get made, opportunities don't work out. People who expect things to go just right or exactly their way or who are not able to adjust tend to get less of what they want and be more frustrated with the results. This mindset can lead to feelings of defeat that make it easier to fall back into old, bad patterns. When things don't go the way you want them to, do your best to practice humility and be flexible. People who are able to do that tend to be more successful down the road.

WATCHING OUT FOR THE "FUCK ITS" AND "I DON'T CARES"

These are indications that you are in deep relapse. When things start to go poorly, when you start to become more reactive than proactive (which is inevitable at some point), it's important not to get defeated. No matter how bad things get, giving up or giving in will only make it worse. On the other hand, doing your best to get back to your program will help you pull out of your spiral if you can hang in there. The storm will pass—guaranteed. Just hang on until it does.

CREATING A CONTINUING ACCOUNTABILITY PLAN

The last tool we have to offer you is a worksheet for creating a Continuing Accountability Plan. This will help you identify the most important things you'll need to keep in mind after you complete this book and leave your group.

Now that you are presumably accountable for your behavior and well-being, how can you stay that way? If you are in a program, we encourage you to complete this plan and share it with your group just before you leave so they can offer constructive input on how to improve it or point out things that are missing.

It is important to write out your Continuing Accountability Plan so you can refer to it in the future. You might think of it as a letter to your future self, for when you're struggling to remember specific important things that helped you change and could get you on the right path again.

Listed below are the ten questions that make up the Continuing Accountability Plan as well as brief explanations of each. The worksheet is included in an Appendix I.

**

1. **How do you plan to stay accountable? How will you continue to evaluate and monitor yourself?**
   List the things you will do from day to day to make sure you don't drift away from the changes you have made. What are the concrete ways you plan to stay self-aware?
2. **How did you avoid accountability and keep your abusive and controlling behavior a secret in the past?**
   List the things you did in the past or might do in the future to avoid addressing problems. (Ex.: abuse substances, isolate yourself, work too much)
   What are your typical pathways into denial and avoidance? (Ex.: not making time to check in with yourself on recent events, blaming others for your struggles)
3. **Which thoughts and behaviors indicate that you might be headed toward a relapse into controlling and abusive behavior?**

List the items from your Relapse Warning Signs list. Note that these are different from the signs of physical and behavioral intensity used in Journals.

4. **When you notice those thoughts and behaviors, what actions will you take?** List the specific things you will do to get out of relapse when you realize you are in it. (Ex.: check in with yourself, reach out to friends, review this document)

5. **What are the slippery situations that tend to lead to abusive and controlling behavior?**

   List the specific situations in which you have been most strongly tempted to be abusive and controlling. Examples might include certain subjects (financial disagreements, parenting disagreements) or circumstances (dealing with certain family members, when you have been drinking) that you have responded to in the past with abusive and controlling behavior. These are your personally high-risk situations that need special attention and consideration.

6. **What steps will you take to avoid being abusive and controlling in those slippery situations?**

   Make situation-specific steps plans for how to deal with each situation listed above without becoming abusive and controlling. Think about each one separately.

7. **What needs were you trying to meet by using abuse and control?**

   Abuse and control are typically a means to an end. What were you trying to accomplish? (Ex.: feel good about yourself, feel nurtured, feel empowered)

   What did you need? (Ex.: solitude, financial security)

8. **What do you do now to meet those needs?**

   List specific ways you presently meet each need listed above in nonabusive and noncontrolling ways.

9. **Who is in your support network?**

   List the names of specific friends or family members you can talk openly with, share your relapse warning signs with, receive support from, and hear concerns about your recovery from. These are people you feel close to, trust, and who know you well—including how you are in the present. They are people you're in regular contact with who would be honest with you if they were concerned about you. Ideally, you should list several people here. If no one fits that description, then indicate as much. If that's the case, this is an area to focus on in the future: developing close connections.

10. **What are some of the ways you continue to be controlling?**

List some of the areas of your life that still need work if you're going to remain nonabusive and noncontrolling. As much progress as you may have made, there is always more that can be done. List the main ways that you're still being controlling. Identify what you need to improve in order to be successful. List the additional personal goals you have.

MOVING FORWARD

You may have only taken a few days or weeks to read this book, but it outlines a process of discovery and change that typically takes people months and even years to achieve. This means that although you have come to the end of this book, you are probably nowhere near the end of your work and change process. These, then, are some parting words for you as you continue on your journey to being nonabusive and noncontrolling.

First, this work takes courage. It takes courage to admit to having engaged in bad behaviors that have caused harm to people you love. It takes courage to acknowledge that this behavior is abusive and controlling. It takes courage to look at the suffering you have caused some of the people you love the most in your life. It takes courage to push yourself to change the ways you have thought, felt, and behaved for much of your life. It takes courage to do this against the social pressures that especially support male-identified people to embrace power and control.

Second, this is difficult work. It is difficult to change your beliefs, to change your habits, to change the way you live in the world from day to day. It is difficult to do this with limited support and understanding from others, except, perhaps, from your partner or children.

Third, this is ongoing work. It is not something that you fix once and then you're good. It is a lifestyle that needs to be lived and practiced day in and day out, year after year after year. This is a way of living you need to recommit to on a daily basis.

There may be moments when the work seems like it is too much, that it will never be enough, that it will never be done. There will be moments when you make mistakes, when you do or say the wrong thing, or perhaps even fall back into a pattern of abusive and controlling behavior. In those moments, do not despair and do not give up! These need only be setbacks, brief lapses, rather than a return to old patterns of bad behavior. In those moments when you fall, you need only pick yourself back up and keep moving forward. Use those moments of struggle to learn how to do this work even better. Gradually, over time, and with practice and persistence, the work does get easier, more automatic, and becomes the new normal. Do not let these moments of struggle get you down or lead you to give up—this work is too vital and too important for you and for the people you love.

While this book has outlined much of what needs to be done to stop your abuse and control, reading a book alone will not necessarily lead to real, sustained change. It's important to actively and regularly practice these skills in real life. Just as reading a textbook on medicine does not make someone a doctor and reading a book on car engines does not make someone a mechanic, reading this book will not make you nonabusive and noncontrolling. You must actually do these things, actively change your thoughts, beliefs, and behaviors. You must apply these things to your day-to-day life. You must practice these ways of thinking and behaving over and over again until they become habitual and enduring. It is practice, immersion, and repetition with guidance that helps someone learn a skilled trade, and this is no different.

WHERE TO GO FROM HERE

If you are already in a program, great! We hope this book helps you make even better use of what the program is teaching you. If you are not in a program, we strongly encourage you to get involved in one. Although it is possible for someone to make these changes on their own, with just this book for support and guidance, most people need more intensive involvement.

In particular, we strongly encourage you to get involved in a specialized group, an abuse-intervention group, that deals with these issues. We have found that individual therapy is not nearly as effective in helping people do this work as a specialized group is, even if the therapist is knowledgeable about these issues (which itself is quite rare—unfortunately, most therapists have little to no understanding of these issues or how to appropriately address them). Reading this book alone does not begin to compare to the power and impact of being involved in such a group. This book is intended to be a supplement to group work, not a replacement for it.

The benefits of a group are extensive. It provides a place to examine, address, and discuss these issues in a routine way on a weekly basis. Having that time commitment will ensure that you keep this material in mind and in practice. You can bring up specific personal challenges and get input on how to deal with them. You can ask questions that help you understand the material covered here and how it applies to real people's lives. You can hear from others who are also doing this work and learn from their struggles and successes. You can get ongoing support from people who are doing this same work without feeling judged or ashamed.

Contacting a program and joining a group also take courage. Most people who seek out such services are quite anxious and worried when they start out, whether they admit it or not. You may fear being judged, being labeled, being shamed, or somewhat ironically, being treated in abusive and demeaning ways. For people who are not court-involved, being in a room with court-involved people can be unsettling and uncomfortable, especially if they have different cultural backgrounds. But most people find that after joining a group and seeing what it's actually like, their fears are allayed. They find that however different other group members may seem from them, their struggles are the same. People attending twelve-step meetings for the first time often have the same experience: however diverse the group may be, the core issues and struggles are the same.

Perhaps the biggest reason to do this work and practice it beyond reading this book is in the name of love. Your abuse and control have hurt and caused damage and suffering to the people you love the most—your partner and your children. It is possible that you have even justified some of your abuse and control as being done in the name of love, although, in truth, it is not loving at all. Becoming nonabusive and noncontrolling is about becoming more truly loving and nurturing—of your partner, of yourself, and of others. Everyone alive deserves to be loved and to love. Do not deny yourself or the people you love this opportunity to experience you in a different, better, more loving way. You have the power to change. Find the courage, energy, time, and commitment to do so. Everyone you know will benefit from your efforts.

APPENDIX A

12 REASONS COUPLES COUNSELING IS NOT RECOMMENDED WHEN DOMESTIC VIOLENCE IS PRESENT

Domestic violence is "a pattern of coercive behavior used by one person to control and subordinate another in an intimate relationship. These behaviors may include physical, sexual, psychological, and economic abuse."
—*Oregon Domestic Violence Council*

1. Focusing on the relationship assumes that each person contributes to the abusive and controlling behavior, when in truth the abusive partner is fully and solely responsible for their abusive and controlling behavior.
2. Focusing on issues other than the abusive and controlling behavior allows that behavior to continue.
3. Danger to the abused partner may increase due to the therapist's involvement in the relationship. Because the abusive partner's goal is to maintain control of the relationship, any interference on the therapist's part may lead to an increase in their abusive and controlling behavior. The therapist may unwittingly elicit information or initiate interventions that escalate abuse and control.
4. The abused partner may be blamed. When abusive and controlling behavior is identified, the abused partner may be asked "What was your part in this?" Alternatively, the abusive partner may use the therapist's comments and observations to justify their abusive and controlling behavior (e.g., "Remember they said how your refusal to answer my questions only makes things worse"). Many abused partners already tend to blame themselves; the therapist may unwittingly encourage this.

5. Out of fear of further abuse, the abused partner may not be honest about the abuse and control or other issues in the couples' session, giving the false impression that things are better than they really are.

6. On the other hand, the abused partner may have a false sense of security and safety in the couples' session. This may lead to disclosure of information that would normally be withheld, believing that the therapist will keep them safe. Once they have left the safety of the counseling room, the abusive partner may then retaliate with more abuse and control.

7. In couples counseling, if the therapist focuses extensively on the abuse and control, the abusive partner may feel targeted, shamed, scapegoated, and to blame for every problem in the relationship. In an abuse-intervention group, while they are held accountable for their abuse, they are not blamed for every problem in the relationship. Couples counseling may discourage the level of disclosure that is possible in a group.

8. Before other issues in the relationship can be effectively addressed, the abusive and controlling behavior must end. Abusive and controlling behavior tends to distract attention away from other issues like a smoke screen. This is akin to couples counseling where one or both parties are active alcoholics; until they are sober, such interventions have little effectiveness. Similarly, until the abuse has stopped, other interventions have limited effectiveness.

9. Couples counseling colludes with the abusive partner's denial. It allows them to continue to blame the abused partner and/or the relationship for their abusive and controlling behavior. They can then take advantage of the couples' sessions to further their agenda of control and Power Over.

10. There is often no competent assessment for domestic violence in couples counseling. This typically involves interviewing each person alone, privately, to encourage honest disclosure and allow for greater safety. If an assessment is done with both people present, the goals of honest disclosure and safety will be undermined.

11. A couples counselor who is focused on the relationship may be hesitant to strongly confront just one of the individuals, concerned this will be

viewed as favoritism. Such failure to directly confront abuse and control contributes to minimization and denial.

12. Couples counseling can keep an abused partner in the abusive relationship longer than they would otherwise stay in the false hope that the counseling may make things better. Some forms of couples counseling require couples to make a time commitment (e.g., 3-6 months) of not separating while in counseling, which may prolong an abusive relationship.

Summary by Chris Huffine, PsyD, of a discussion by the Tri-County Batterer Intervention Provider Network.

7/1999, rev 4/2021

APPENDIX B

CONTROLLING BEHAVIORS

Listed below are some of the behaviors that can be used to control other people. As should be apparent, many of the behaviors below are not automatically controlling, but can be controlling depending on how they are used. This is only a partial list—there are many other ways of being controlling that are not listed here.

1. Abusing the other person
2. Accessing their electronic devices
3. Acting forgetful
4. Agreeing insincerely
5. Apologizing
6. Arguing
7. Asking leading questions
8. Asking rhetorical questions
9. Backseat driving
10. Badgering
11. Being contrary
12. Being defensive
13. Being impatient
14. Being overly sensitive
15. Being overprotective
16. Being sarcastic
17. Being superficially polite or nice
18. Being willfully incompetent
19. Blackmailing
20. Blaming
21. Blowing up
22. Bringing up the past
23. Brown-nosing
24. Calling excessively
25. Changing the subject
26. Correcting them repeatedly
27. Criticizing
28. Doing their tasks
29. Dominating the conversation
30. Eavesdropping
31. Exaggerating
32. Flattering
33. Gaslighting
34. Gesturing dismissively
35. Getting the last word
36. Giving gifts
37. Giving the silent treatment
38. Giving the third degree
39. Giving unsolicited advice
40. Going off the deep end
41. Going over their head
42. Gossiping
43. Handling their belongings
44. Hanging up on them
45. Having a short fuse
46. Hiding their things

47. Humiliating them in public
48. Hurrying them
49. Ignoring
50. Ingratiating yourself
51. Interrogating
52. Interrupting
53. Intimidating
54. Invoking a higher authority
55. Invoking your experience or expertise
56. Isolating
57. Joking or kidding insincerely
58. Keeping items exclusively in your name
59. Keeping them ignorant or uneducated
60. Limiting access to shared items
61. Limiting access to finances or financial information
62. Listening selectively
63. Looking at them intensely
64. Lying
65. Making demands
66. Making dismissive sounds
67. Making faces
68. Making fun
69. Making promises you don't intend to keep
70. Making secret purchases
71. Making them feel sorry for you
72. Making unilateral decisions
73. Making wild statements
74. Managing impressions
75. Manipulating
76. Micromanaging
77. Mimicking
78. Mischaracterizing what others say
79. Misusing material from this book or your group
80. Monopolizing their time
81. Nagging
82. Negating them repeatedly
83. Not passing on messages
84. Offering unreasonable choices or alternatives
85. Ordering them around
86. Pausing extensively
87. Playing dumb
88. Playing mind games
89. Playing the expert
90. Playing the victim
91. Pretending to listen
92. Psyching them out
93. Pushing their buttons
94. Raising your voice
95. Rationalizing
96. Requiring your approval
97. Requiring your permission
98. Responding ambiguously
99. Rewarding them
100. Sabotaging their belongings
101. Scaring
102. Shaming
103. Showing up late on purpose
104. Speaking for them
105. Stalking or following them
106. Staring
107. Stonewalling
108. Taking things away
109. Taking things out of context
110. Talking down to them
111. Teasing
112. Telling them how to behave

113. Telling them what they are thinking or feeling
114. Texting them excessively
115. Threatening
116. Trivializing
117. Using children
118. Using courts or the legal system
119. Using fear
120. Using friends
121. Using guilt
122. Using illness or symptoms
123. Using inappropriate humor
124. Using intoxication
125. Using money
126. Using physical size
127. Using privilege
128. Using quid pro quo
129. Using silence
130. Walking away
131. Whining
132. Withholding belongings
133. Withholding information
134. Withholding sex or affection

APPENDIX C

POWER ORIENTATION IN RELATIONSHIPS

POWER OVER	PERSONAL POWER
"Reality 1"	"Reality 2"
Abuse and control	Mutual respect
Win-lose/One winner	Win-Win/Many winners
One right answer	Many right answers
One truth (Big-T Truth)	Many truths (Little-t truth)
Differences are seen as a threat	Differences are respected
Only some needs are met	All needs are met
Me *or* you	Me *and* you
External focus	Internal focus
Blame (outward focus)	Accountability (inward focus)
Assumption of scarcity	Assumption of abundance
Competition	Cooperation
Others are viewed as opponents	Others are viewed as allies
Competitive	Collaborative
Focus on the outcome	Focus on the process
The end justifies the means	The means is the end
"Winning isn't everything; it's the only thing."	"It doesn't matter whether you win or lose; it's how you play the game."

Based on concepts presented by Patricia Evans in *The Verbally Abusive Relationship* (1996, Adams Media Corporation)

APPENDIX D

CONTROLLED SEPARATION

Abusive behavior, in its many forms, is hurtful to relationships. Once a pattern has been established, even technically nonabusive behavior can be harmful to family members. Children who may never have been the direct target of abuse may still live in fear and apprehension about when the next outburst is going to happen. To have a good relationship and a happy, emotionally healthy family, abusive and controlling behavior must be stopped. While a commitment to being nonabusive and noncontrolling is an important step in this process, that alone will not lead to an end of all such behaviors. For people who have been abusive, such behavior is both learned and a bad habit—one that can surface without thinking or planning. Like any bad habit, it is difficult to stop all at once or with perfect success. Those early struggles, which are normal and typical even among abusive individuals who are ultimately successful in becoming nonabusive, can still cause great hardship for family members. One solution that can increase the likelihood of successful change and healing of the family is a controlled separation.

Unlike many formal separations, a controlled separation is intended to help the couple heal and reconcile. It involves temporarily separating while each person independently does what is necessary to help the relationship heal and recover. During a controlled separation, both people behave as if they are living together in a committed relationship. In other words, no dating is allowed. Finances are still managed the same way with the same expectations and responsibilities. If possible and appropriate, contact with children and friends is not restricted. The couple might still attend public events together, but may not sit together during the early stages.

A controlled separation typically starts with physical separation and little to no contact. Over time, the type, frequency, and length of contact is gradually increased until the couple is living together again—without any significant abuse or patterns of control.

GOALS OF A CONTROLLED SEPARATION

1. **To ensure that no further abuse occurs.** No matter how strong and firm a person's commitment is to being nonabusive, it is likely that they will still have some missteps and be abusive again, especially early on in the process. The only way to ensure that there is no more abuse is to have no contact. For example, if they have a frustrating day and yell at themselves while their partner is around, it may scare the partner. If they are living away from their partner, their partner will not be affected if they yell at themselves.

2. **To provide the abused partner immediate relief from the past abusive behavior.** Once a pattern of abuse has been established, the partner is often on eggshells, wondering when the abuse will happen again. Even technically nonabusive behaviors (walking into a room, clearing their throat, being slightly frustrated) can be experienced by the partner and/or children as abusive due to past experiences. The only way to get immediate relief from this is for the abusive partner to not be around at all. If they are around, even if they are not being abusive, the abused partner and/or children may still feel anxious and on edge, anticipating the next abusive behavior, even if it does not come.

3. **To give the abusive partner time to learn more of the basic skills and tools.** They can practice managing themselves appropriately so that when they do have contact, it is more likely to go well. The more they are able to prepare and practice while apart from their partner, the more likely they are to do well when their partner is around.

4. **To provide the abusive partner some relief from their partner's anger and unhappiness towards them.** It is common for abused partners to feel angry and unhappy about their partner's past abusive and controlling behavior. Those feelings may actually intensify early in their recovery process. While it is important for the abused partner to feel and express those feelings, the abusive partner may not need to be the one to hear them early on. The abusive partner may not yet have

the skills and mindset needed to listen well without reacting to that anger and hurt. Friends, family, therapists, and others can provide the validation and space the abused partner needs to process those feelings early on. Limited contact gives the abusive partner relief from having to deal with those feelings before they are ready to listen well.

5. **To have positive interactions.** It is easier to have positive interactions if they are relatively brief. It is hard for everyone to be on their best behavior 24/7, but limited interactions have a much greater chance of going well, which allows the relationship to improve. With continued success, interactions can gradually increase in frequency and length, and never beyond what the abusive partner can handle well.

6. **To establish a new, positive pattern to build on.** Every slip-up the abusive partner has, particularly early on, can feel to the abused partner like starting back at square one. An extended period with no abuse can increase goodwill and make it easier to handle the rarer slip that might still occur. Limited contact encourages the establishment of a positive pattern.

7. **To interrupt abusive behavior more easily.** When the abusive partner is not living with their partner, it is easier to stop an interaction before it escalates. It is easier to appropriately end a phone call, leave the premises, or ask their partner to leave. The quicker slips are interrupted, the less damage is incurred and the easier the repair.

8. **To allow the abusive partner a chance to learn to better take care of themselves.** Many abusive partners tend to be overly dependent upon their romantic partner, family, and work for support. They may have a limited network of good friends and make little time for themselves beyond working and spending time with their family. A controlled separation creates the opportunity for them to learn to do a better job of walking on their own two emotional feet. They have extra time on their hands while they are not with their family. They have more time to nurture friendships and pursue other long-neglected interests without taking away from their family. Abusive partners who diversify their sources of emotional support tend to be better partners and parents because they are not as heavily dependent upon their family.

9. **To give each person a chance to get perspective.** When there has been significant abusive and controlling behavior in the past, it is common for one or both people to question whether the relationship can go on. Abusive partners often fear that a controlled separation will lead to a permanent end to the relationship. However, it is very rarely the controlled separation that causes the relationship to end. Instead, that time apart allows each person space to gain further clarity on whether they can happily remain in the relationship if the abusive behavior stops. Those relationships that end anyway were usually damaged beyond repair from the abuse and/or for other reasons. On the other hand, the time apart—especially if it results in the end of most of the abuse and control—may make it even clearer to both parties that they wish to remain together. This time apart can help reinforce their conviction that they do not want to permanently break up. It can actually deepen the commitment each has to the relationship.

STRUCTURE OF A CONTROLLED SEPARATION

A controlled separation starts with little to no contact. The amount of contact is gradually increased, but not so fast that things start to go poorly. The frequency and pace of contact is solely determined by the abused partner. An early test of whether the abusive partner is serious about changing their behavior is whether they can be respectful of the limits that are set, even if they do not like them.

Discussions of high conflict and difficult issues in the relationship should be postponed as long as possible during the controlled separation. Tabling these issues until there is no longer a pattern of abuse and control increases the likelihood of them being effectively resolved. There is also a much lower chance of abuse and control occurring if these issues are not discussed until there have been significant improvements in the abusive partner's behavior.

Below is an example of a gradual increase in contact. This exact progression does not have to be followed, nor does it need to start at the very beginning. Each abused partner determines their own pace.

1. No contact at all except for emails or texts initiated by the abused partner. The abusive partner is only to respond to direct questions.
2. Texting—initiated by the abused partner

3. Limited phone contact—initiated by the abused partner
4. Emails, texting, and brief phone calls—initiated by either person
5. Dates in public settings
6. More extended phone calls
7. Brief visits in the home
8. More extended visits in the home
9. Overnights at home
10. Weekends at home
11. Moving back into the home

The level of contact should only be increased by the abused partner at a pace with which they feel comfortable. Ideally, if the rate of contact is paced correctly, there will be few to no abusive outbursts. If there is an abusive outburst, the abused partner can consider whether to decrease contact again or simply delay increasing contact until the partner can consistently handle themselves appropriately. Sustained positive interactions are a reason to increase the level of contact.

While a controlled separation can be difficult in the short run due to loneliness, financial stress, and decreased support, it can have many long-term benefits. When it goes well, it significantly reduces abusive episodes and gives the abusive partner an opportunity to consistently manage their behavior. A stretch of many months that are relatively free of abuse relieves the pressure on the relationship and can allow for a rekindling of goodwill that can lead to reconciliation. In a successful controlled separation, the abused partner experiences significant healing and a gradual return of trust, and the abusive partner experiences sustained success at being nonabusive and appropriately managing themselves. As a way to limit further damage and promote quicker healing, it is worth serious consideration.

APPENDIX E

EMOTIONS

GLAD

Accepting
Affirmed
Agreeable
Alive
Amazed
Ambitious
Amused
Appreciative
At ease
At home
Awed/in awe
Bemused
Blissful
Caring
Centered
Cheerful
Comfortable
Compassionate
Confident
Connected
Content
Courageous
Curious
Daring
Delighted
Desire
Determined
Eager
Ecstatic
Elated

Enchanted
Encouraged
Engaged
Engrossed
Enlivened
Enthralled
Enthusiastic
Equanimous
Excited
Exhilarated
Exuberant
Fascinated
Flattered
Focused
Fortunate
Fulfilled
Giddy
Glad
Grateful
Gratified
Grounded
Happy
Honored
Hopeful
Humbled
In sync
Intrigued
Invigorated
Joyful
Jubilant

Keen
Light
Lighthearted
Loving
Lucky
Merry
Mischievous
Moved
Open
Optimistic
Passionate
Peaceful
Playful
Pleased
Positive
Productive
Proud
Pumped
Rapturous
Receptive
Rejuvenated
Relieved
Renewed
Restored
Revived
Safe
Satisfied
Secure
Serene
Solid

Strong
Surprised
Thrilled
Tender
Thankful

Tickled
Touched
Tranquil
Trusting
Validated

Vibrant
Warm
Whimsical
Wistful
Wonder-struck

AFRAID

Aghast
Agitated
Agog
Alarmed
Ambivalent
Anxious
Apprehensive
Awkward
Bashful
Bewildered
Cautious
Concerned
Confused
Dread
Edgy
Fearful
Flooded
Frazzled
Freaked out
Frightened
Frozen
Guarded
Hesitant
Horrified
Inhibited

Insecure
Intimidated
Isolated
Jittery
Jumpy
Leery
Mistrustful
Nervous
On edge
Overwhelmed
Panic
Paralyzed
Paranoid
Pensive
Perplexed
Petrified
Pressured
Rattled
Reluctant
Reserved
Restless
Scared
Self-conscious
Shaken
Shocked

Shy
Spooked
Startled
Stunned
Surprised
Suspicious
Tentative
Tenuous
Tense
Terrified
Timid
Torn
Triggered
Uncertain
Uncomfortable
Uneasy
Unsafe
Unsure
Uptight
Vulnerable
Wary
Worried
Wound up

SAD

Aching
Adrift
Agony

Alienated
Alone
Anguished

Apathetic
Ashamed
Bereaved

Blah	Downcast	Lifeless
Blue	Drained	Listless
Bummed	Dreary	Lonely
Bummed out	Emotional	Longing
Burned-out	Empty	Lost
Crummy	Foolish	Meh
Crushed	Forlorn	Melancholy
Dark	Fragile	Miserable
Defeated	Gloomy	Mournful
Deflated	Grieving	Needy
Dejected	Grim	Nostalgic
Demoralized	Guilty	Overwhelmed
Depleted	Heartbroken	Pained
Depressed	Heavy	Pining
Desolate	Heavyhearted	Regretful
Despairing	Helpless	Resigned
Despondent	Hollow	Sentimental
Detached	Hopeless	Small
Devastated	Horrible	Somber
Disappointed	Humbled	Sorrowful
Disbelieving	Hurt	Stunned
Discontented	Impotent	Troubled
Discouraged	Inadequate	Unhappy
Disheartened	Incompetent	Unsatisfied
Dismal	Inconsolable	Upset
Dismayed	Indifferent	Weak
Dissatisfied	Ineffective	Wistful
Distant	Inept	Withdrawn
Distraught	Inferior	Worn down
Distressed	Insignificant	Worn out
Dour	Let down	Wounded
Down	Lethargic	Wretched

MAD

Aggravated
Angry
Animosity
Annoyed
Appalled
Apoplectic
Bitter
Cantankerous
Contemptuous
Cranky
Cross
Disappointed
Disdainful
Disgruntled
Disgusted
Dismayed
Displeased

Disturbed
Embittered
Enraged
Exasperated
Fed up
Flummoxed
Frustrated
Furious
Grumpy
Hateful
Heated
Hot
Impatient
Incensed
Indignant
Inflamed
Infuriated

Irate
Irked
Irritable
Irritated
Livid
Offended
Outraged
Pissed
Rage
Repulsed
Resentful
Ticked off
Upset
Vengeful
Vexed
Wrathful

OTHER

Absorbed
Aloof
Baffled
Bored
Captivated
Chagrined
Challenged
Certain
Complacent
Dazed
Disinterested
Disoriented
Distracted

Doubtful
Dubious
Dumbfounded
Embarrassed
Envious
Interested
Jealous
Mixed up
Mortified
Mystified
Obsessed
Out of it
Out of sync

Pessimistic
Preoccupied
Puzzled
Remorseful
Sensitive
Skeptical
Spacey
Spellbound
Stimulated
Stuck
Unsettled

PHYSICAL SYMPTOMS

LOW INTENSITY	MEDIUM INTENSITY	HIGH INTENSITY
Alertness	Alertness	Agitation
Chills	Butterflies	Blank mind
Clenched teeth	Chills	Feeling hot
Clenching muscles	Clenched teeth	Held breath
Dry mouth	Clenched muscles	Knots in stomach
Feeling loose	Feeling warm	Loss of appetite
Gasping	Flushed skin	Nausea
Headache	Headache	Not feeling well
Heaviness	Heaviness	Numbness
Increased appetite	Lightness	Racing heart
Increased energy	Lump in throat	Racing thoughts
Irregular breathing	Pressure	Seeing red
Lightness	Tension	Sense of moving in slow motion
Lump in throat	Tight chest	Shallow breathing
Reduced energy	Tight muscles	Stomach drop
Relaxed body		Sweaty palms
Release of breath		Tearfulness
Restlessness		Tingling fingers
Slow breathing		Tunnel vision
Stomach rumbling		
Tension		
Tight muscles		
Vigilance		
Yawning		

APPENDIX F

SELF-CARE PLAN

Self-care is often thought of as taking good care of your physical body through exercise, eating right, and getting enough sleep. Others think of self-care as doing something nice for yourself or having a good day. We define self-care more broadly: as putting energy and effort into maintaining a balanced life.

The more areas of your life that are well-maintained, the more resources you have to draw on. You can't attend to every facet of your life all the time, but you can strive to give energy and attention to a number of them, and shift your focus from day to day and week to week.

Better self-care means putting time, effort, and energy into many aspects of your life. Poorer self-care means more narrowly focusing your time, effort, and energy on, at most, just a few aspects of your life. When self-care is poor, the risk of relapse—returning to old, destructive behaviors—increases. Poor self-care also makes it harder to cope with stress and challenges.

Many people don't realize how many facets of their life need maintenance and provide support. Listed below are the areas of self-care that are common to every adult on the planet, regardless of cultural background. When you are finished with this worksheet, you should have a general sense of how good your self-care is as well as the areas in your life most in need of attention.

Rate your satisfaction with each area from 1 to 10.

1 = Very dissatisfied, needs extensive attention

10 = Completely satisfied, couldn't be better

Write specific, concrete actions you can take to improve your self-care in that area.

KEY AREAS OF SELF-CARE

1. Vocational
2. Financial
3. Educational
4. Legal
5. Domestic
6. Health Maintenance
7. Medical
8. Psychological
9. Romantic
10. Sexual
11. Family
12. Social
13. Solitude
14. Recreational
15. Creativity
16. Community Service
17. Spirituality
18. Resources (time, money, energy)
19. Other

1. **Vocational:** type of work, professional goals, workload, weekly hours

   Satisfaction:_____

2. **Financial:** income, expenses, debt, savings, money management, goals

   Satisfaction:_____

3. **Educational:** increasing your knowledge, pursuing your intellectual interests

   Satisfaction:_____

4. **Legal:** following laws, dealing with consequences of breaking laws, civil issues and conflicts

   Satisfaction:_____

5. **Domestic:** cleaning, laundry, organization, quality of living space

   Satisfaction:_____

6. **Health maintenance:** diet, exercise, sleep

   Satisfaction:_____

7. **Medical:** illness, injuries, dental care, following medical advice

   Satisfaction:_____

8. **Psychological:** emotional awareness, mindset, dealing with the past

   Satisfaction:_____

9. **Romantic:** connection, quality, role in your life, goals

   Satisfaction:_____

10. **Sexual:** connection, quality, quantity, role in your life, goals

    Satisfaction:_____

11. **Family:** parenting, extended family, in-laws

    Satisfaction:_____

12. **Social:** friendships, networking, being with people, quantity and quality

    Satisfaction:_____

13. **Solitude:** emotional check-ins, self-awareness, personal goal setting, quality personal time

    Satisfaction:_____

14. **Recreation:** hobbies, relaxation, having fun, frequency and variety

    Satisfaction:_____

15. **Creativity:** self-expression, making things

    Satisfaction:_____

16. **Community service:** volunteering, helping people you don't know   Satisfaction:_____

17. **Spirituality:** faith, beliefs, connection with a higher power   Satisfaction:_____

18. **General resources:** quality, quantity, sufficiency to reach your goals

                        Time: Satisfaction:_____

                     Money: Satisfaction:_____

                     Energy: Satisfaction:_____

19. **Other** areas of self-care that need attention and are not mentioned above: Satisfaction:_____

APPENDIX G

JOURNAL

Today's date: Date of event:

1. **Event/Situation:**

2. **Signs of physical intensity:**

3. **Signs of behavioral intensity:**

4. **Emotions:**

5. **My highest intensity during the situation (1–10):**

6. **My intensity at the beginning of the situation (1–10):**

7. **How much of my intensity was due to this specific situation?**

8. **Negative self-talk:**

9. **Abusive/controlling behaviors: (If none, go to #17.)**

10. What did I want to make the other person do, feel, or think?

11. What beliefs justified my abusive/controlling behaviors?

12. How did my abuse/control negatively affect the other person?

13. How did my abuse/control negatively affect others who saw or heard?

14. What role did my past abuse/control of that person play in this situation?

15. What did I gain from my behavior?

16. What did I lose from my behavior?

17. What did I want in this situation?

18. What did the other person want in this situation?

19. Positive self-talk:

20. Nonabusive/noncontrolling beliefs:

21. How did I appropriately meet my needs?

22. How did I consider the needs of the other person?

23. My experience of the situation:

    I feel:

    When:

    I would like:

    And I will:

24. What, if anything, would I like to do differently next time?

APPENDIX H

Annotated Journal

Today's date: Date of event:

1. **Event/Situation:** *Give a brief* description or summary of what happened.

2. **Signs of physical intensity:** What *internal* sensations indicated you were having a reaction? (See Chapter 17: Becoming Aware of Your Body; Appendix E: Emotions)

3. **Signs of behavioral intensity:** What *external* behaviors let others know you were having a reaction? (See Chapter 17: Becoming Aware of Your Body)

4. **Emotions:** What emotions did you experience? (See Chapter 16: Becoming Aware of Your Emotions; Appendix E: Emotions)

5. **My highest intensity during the situation (1–10):** (See Chapter 17: Becoming Aware of Your Body)

6. **My intensity at the beginning of the situation (1–10):** (See Chapter 17: Becoming Aware of Your Body)

7. **How much of my intensity was due to this specific situation?** To what extent were other issues playing a role? (See Chapter 16: Becoming Aware of Your Emotions)

8. **Negative self-talk:** What *thoughts* increased your intensity? (See Chapter 5: Abusive Thoughts and Beliefs; Chapter 15: Becoming Aware of Your Thoughts)

9. **Abusive/controlling behaviors: (If none, go to #17.)** What *specific* things did you say or do that were abusive or controlling? (See Chapter 1: Abusive Behavior; Chapter 2: Controlling Behaviors; Chapter 3: Sexual Abuse; Chapter 4: Financial Abuse; Appendix B: Controlling Behaviors)

10. **What did I want to make the other person do, feel, or think?** What was the *goal* of your behavior? How did you want the person to behave differently?

11. **What beliefs justified my abusive/controlling behaviors?** How did you give yourself *permission* to be abusive and controlling? What was your justification for being abusive and controlling? (See Chapter 5: Abusive Thoughts and Beliefs)

12. **How did my abuse/control negatively affect the other person?** What negative impact did your abusive and controlling behavior have on the other? Make your best guess. (See Chapter 11: Understanding the Impact of Abuse on Your Partner)

13. **How did my abuse/control negatively affect others who saw or heard?** How do you think your behavior negatively affected anyone else who was present? Make your best guess. (See Chapter 12: Understanding the Impact of Abuse on Children)

14. **What role did my past abuse/control of that person play in this situation?** If you were abusive or controlling with this person in the past, how might those earlier experiences have contributed to their experience of this situation? (See Chapter 11: Understanding the Impact of Abuse on Your Partner)

15. **What did I gain from my behavior?** How did you benefit from being abusive and controlling?

16. **What did I lose from my behavior?** How were you negatively affected by being abusive and controlling?

17. **What did I want in this situation?** What were your goals, wants, and needs in the situation? (See Chapter 19: Learning to Take Care of Yourself)

18. **What did the other person want in this situation?** What were the other person's goals, wants, and needs in this situation? While you may not be certain, put yourself in their shoes. Think of it from their perspective. (See Chapter 21: Learning to Regard Others)

19. **Positive self-talk:** What did you think to keep yourself calmer? What *might* you have thought to keep yourself calmer? (See Chapter 15: Becoming Aware of Your Thoughts)

20. **Nonabusive/noncontrolling beliefs:** What general beliefs do you have about the world that can help you respond without becoming abusive and controlling? (See Chapter 15: Becoming Aware of Your Thoughts)

21. **How did I appropriately meet my needs?** What did you do to take care of yourself? If you didn't, note that. (See Chapter 18: Learning to Self-Soothe; Chapter 19: Learning to Take Care of Yourself; Chapter 23: Learning to Communicate Effectively; Chapter 24: Learning Conflict-Resolution Skills)

22. **How did I consider the needs of the other person?** What did you do to take into consideration the other person? If you didn't, note that. (See Chapter 21: Learning to Regard Others)

23. **My experience of the situation:** This sketches out the key things to keep in mind about the situation.

    I feel: Put one or more emotions here about how you felt about the situation. (See Chapter16: Becoming Aware of Your Emotions; Appendix E: Emotions)

    When: Briefly describe the specific situation.

    I would like: Write what you want and need.

    And I will: State what you intend to do to get what you want.

24. **What, if anything, would I like to do differently next time?** How could you have handled yourself better? What is your plan for how you want to behave differently going forward?

APPENDIX I

RELAPSE WARNING SIGNS

Every person in recovery has a unique combination of behaviors and states of mind that indicate a slide toward or into relapse. One or more of the signs listed below may not be cause for concern, but a number of them together provide a warning—and certain behaviors almost always signal relapse. Circle the relapse warning signs on the list below that apply to you. Put a star by any that are only present when you are in relapse. Then note how many of those behaviors would need to be present at one time for you to know that you were in relapse.

Aggression
Alcohol use
Anxiety
Avoiding
problems
Being
argumentative
Being critical of
yourself
Being easily
agitated
Being easily
frustrated
Bingeing on
entertainment
Blaming
Boredom
Change in appetite
Change in attitude

Change in routine
Change in sleep
habits
Clumsiness
Complacency
Confusion
Decreased
communication
Decreased
compassion/
empathy
Decreased
confidence
Decreased
intensity
Decreased self-
care
Decreased sexual
desire

Denial
Depression
Dishonesty
Distractedness
Doubting your
ability to stay
nonabusive
Exhaustion
Fatigue
Feeling helpless
Feeling hopeless
Feeling irritable
Feeling like "I
don't care"
Feeling out of
control
Feeling sorry for
yourself
Feeling trapped

Focusing on others
Forgetfulness
Impaired job performance
Impatience
Impulsivity
Inappropriate joking
Inappropriate laughter
Increased intensity
Increased negative self-talk
Increased stress
Insisting "Everything's fine"
Isolating
Justifying
Lack of interest
Loneliness

Loss (death, finances, relationships)
Making excuses
Minimizing
Mood swings
Not saying "no"
Not working the program (fewer time-outs, journals, etc.)
Numbing out
Overconfidence
Overinvolvement
Passivity
Physical illness
Poor decision-making
Preoccupation
Problems concentrating
Procrastination

Reappearance of old behaviors
Self-pity
Selfishness
Skipping commitments
Spending time with unsupportive friends
Stuffing emotions
Swearing in traffic
Talking negatively about others
Tardiness
Unreasonable expectations
Violent fantasies
Withholding information
Working too much

List any other behaviors that are relapse warning signs for you:

How many warning signs need to be present for you to know you're in relapse?

APPENDIX J

RELAPSE JOURNAL

Today's date: Date of relapse incident:

Relapse refers not only to a return to old destructive behavior (e.g., a pattern of abuse and control), but also to a process that precedes the actual behavior by days, weeks, or even months. Relapse begins with denial/ avoidance of feelings and, without intervention, ends with a return to patterns of abuse and control. You have been given this journal to fill out because not only were you in relapse, but you were unable to intervene prior to returning to a pattern of abuse and control. In this journal, "incident" refers to the actual abusive behavior that you did. "Relapse" refers to the longer process that preceded the incident. Occasionally falling into relapse is inevitable for most people and a part of life, but actual patterns of abuse and control can be avoided if you catch yourself in time. This relapse journal is intended to help you learn from your recent experience with relapse so that another incident can be prevented. Please consider each question carefully and answer as completely, but concisely, as possible.

BEFORE THE INCIDENT

How long do you think you were in relapse before the actual incident?

What were the warning signs that you were in relapse?

472

What was your self-talk like during your relapse?

What was going on in your life just before and/or during your relapse? Consider any circumstances that affected your work, primary relationship, family, finances, and health.

Were any other noteworthy events or issues affecting your mindset just before and/or during your relapse?

Which emotions were the most intense during your relapse?

Who did you talk with while you were in relapse? Did anyone express concerns about how you were doing?

Were you aware you were in relapse before the incident? If no, why not? If yes, what should you have done?

DURING THE INCIDENT

Which signs of physical and behavioral intensity appeared immediately before the incident?

Briefly describe the incident.

Which thoughts justified your behavior during the incident?

AFTER THE INCIDENT

How did you feel immediately after the incident?

What did you do immediately after the incident?

How did the incident impact everyone involved?

What did you do to stop the incident?

Are you still in relapse now? If so, how will you get out? If not, how can you tell?

GOING FORWARD

What have you done to prevent another incident?

What do you still need to do to prevent another incident?

What is your plan for the next time your relapse warning signs appear?

What have you learned from this relapse?

APPENDIX K

CONTINUING ACCOUNTABILITY PLAN

WHAT IS CONTINUING ACCOUNTABILITY?

- Continuing to develop new behaviors and beliefs that support being nonabusive and noncontrolling after you finish reading this book/stop attending a group
- Sustaining the positive changes you have made
- Awareness that your new beliefs and behaviors can give way to old ones that could lead to a return of abuse and control
- Monitoring yourself for the relapse warning signs that indicate you are headed back into an abusive and controlling lifestyle
- Implementing your Continuing Accountability Plan before you actually become abusive and controlling again
- Regularly reviewing and revising your Continuing Accountability Plan

YOUR CONTINUING ACCOUNTABILITY PLAN

Staying nonabusive and noncontrolling requires continued commitment after you finish reading this book/leave your group. Please record your answers to the questions below on a separate piece of paper.

1. How do you plan to stay accountable? How will you continue to evaluate and monitor yourself?
2. How did you avoid accountability and keep your abusive and controlling behavior a secret in the past?
3. What are the thoughts and behaviors that indicate that you might be headed towards a return to controlling and abusive behavior? Refer to Appendix G: Relapse Warning Signs.
4. When you notice those thoughts and behaviors, what actions will you take?

5. What are the slippery situations in which you are most likely to be abusive and controlling?

6. What steps will you take to reduce the chance of being abusive and controlling while in those slippery situations?

7. What needs were you most commonly trying to meet by using abuse and control?

8. What do you do now to meet those needs?

9. Who can you openly talk with and receive support from? Who can you share your warning signs with? Who can you trust to express concerns about your recovery?

10. What are some of the ways you continue to be controlling? What are some of the aspects of your life that still need to be worked on so you can stay nonabusive and noncontrolling once you finish this book/leave your group?

ACKNOWLEDGMENTS

This book is the culmination of more than thirty years of learning, and I want to acknowledge the people who have influenced me and whose DNA is in this content.

First, there are the elders—those who were active in this field when I first started out. Each of the following people contributed to my learning over the years, and most have trained me in person: David Adams, Sarah Buel, Susan Cayouette, Don Chapin, Patricia Evans, Ted German, Ed Gondolf, John Gottman, Paul Kivel, Alyce LaViolette, Fernando Mederos, Michael Paymar, and Ellen Pence.

Next are my contemporaries who stepped into this work around the same time I did. I have had the chance to engage in discussion, cross-train, and in some cases develop friendships with the following people: Sara Elinoff Acker, Juan Carlos Arean, Jeffrie Cape, Bea Cote, David Garvin, Bob Geffner, Chris Hall, Dorthy Stucky Halley, Steve Halley, Kevin Hamberger, James Henderson, Jackson Katz, Lisa Larance, Eric Mankowski, Scott Miller, Kerry Moles, Lisa Nitsch, Terrence Real, Melissa Scaia, Nicole Westmarland, David Wexler, and Oliver Williams.

I have spent my whole career in Portland, Oregon, and have learned a ton from many lively discussions with these folks in particular, although there are dozens more: Vivien Bliss, Dean Camarda, Jeanne Goetz, Diana Groener, Bob Johnson, Matt Johnston, Paul Lee, David Leventer, Eric Mankowski, Guruseva Mason, Dennis McClure, Joe Mitchell, Roberto Olivero, Jacquie Pancoast, Glenn Rose, Curt St. Denis, Steve Stewart, Debbie Tomasovic, Chris Wilson, and Stacey Womack.

Two people who have been instrumental over the years in helping me to develop and run Allies in Change: James Lund and my current "office husband," Trey Nance. I consider myself so fortunate to have had these men co-run the agency with me. Trey in particular has as deep a commitment to this work as I do, and I am thankful to have him at my professional side on a daily basis. I also want to acknowledge the staff of Allies in Change, an ever-evolving group of people who are actively teaching this material to abusive partners on a weekly basis as well as offering constructive input on how the curriculum can be further improved. Finally, thanks to my editor, Meghan Pinson, who has been the midwife for this book.

On the personal front, I'd like to thank a handful of people who have been a steady support for me over the years. Eric Mankowski and Chris Wilson have been colleagues as well as friends, and they are enormously supportive in both domains. I want to acknowledge my immediate family: my son Benjamin Huffine, my stepson Kevin Rieschel, and their mother Stephanie Tomlinson. Pat O'Shea, Meg Sandow, and Tom Gevurtz have been friends for decades and allies in my own change process over the years.

I have learned so much from the thousands of abusive partners who have come to my groups and agencies over the years as well as the many abused partners I have had the honor and privilege to talk with—and especially listen to. Their experiences and perspectives contributed enormously to this book. I have to give a particular shout out to my Thursday night Relapse Prevention men's group, most of whom have attended the group for many years.

The wisdom and energy of each one of you lives within me and informs the work that I do on a daily basis. Thanks to all of you for the ways you have educated, influenced, and supported me over the years.

ABOUT THE AUTHOR

Dr. Chris Huffine is a licensed psychologist in Portland, Oregon. He has worked with abusive partners in the field of intimate partner violence for nearly thirty years, helping thousands of abusive partners and hundreds of abused partners learn how to change their lives for the better. In 2004, after twelve years at Men's Resource Center and Women's Counseling Center in Portland, he founded Allies in Change, a 501(c)(3) nonprofit organization. Allies in Change offers over two dozen weekly abuse-intervention groups that serve approximately 300 abusive men, women, and nonbinary people. Of particular note is the fact that a quarter of the group attendees at Allies in Change participate voluntarily. Dr. Huffine provides training to groups and individuals nationwide.

Made in United States
Orlando, FL
22 May 2023

33365849R00271